In Search of
Identity

An Autobiography

Anwar el-Sadat

FONTANA/COLLINS

First published in Great Britain by William
Collins 1978 by arrangement with Harper &
Row Publishers, Inc., New York

Portions of this work originally appeared in
Time magazine

Made and printed in Great Britain by William
Collins Sons & Co Ltd, Glasgow

Set in Linotype Baskerville

For the love of peace

Contents

Prologue

I, Anwar el-Sadat, a peasant born and brought up on the banks of the Nile – where man first witnessed the dawn of time – present this book to readers everywhere.

This is the story of my life, which is at the same time the story of Egypt since 1918 – for so destiny has decreed. The events of my life have coincided with those which Egypt has lived during that period. I therefore tell my story in full, not merely as the President of Egypt, but as an Egyptian whose life has been intimately bound up with that of Egypt.

It is, I believe, like every man's life, a journey in search of identity. Each step I have taken over the years has been for the good of Egypt, and has been designed to serve the cause of right, liberty, and peace.

This is the image I have had of myself since childhood. Now, as the landscape of my life unfolds before my eyes, can I claim that this image, which is in effect that of Egypt, has been realized – even recognized?

I leave this to the reader to find out for himself.

I

From Mit Abul-Kum
to the Aliens' Jail

I

'The treacle has arrived,' shouts the local crier through the alleys and squares of our village. My grandmother rushes outside, dragging me along beside her, towards the canal where a ship loaded with treacle has just arrived from nearby Kafr Zirqan. The road is not long, but every step fills me with joy and pride. Men stand up as we pass to greet Grandmother. Though illiterate, she is a haven for everyone; she solves their problems and cures their sick with ancient Arab concoctions of medicinal herbs unrivalled in our village or any of the neighbouring ones.

We buy a big jar of treacle and return home. I trot along behind her – a small, dark boy, barefooted and wearing a long Arab dress over a white calico shirt – my eyes fixed on the treasured jar of treacle.

How delicious it was mixed with curdled milk! It made me so happy – nothing could make me happier. Everything in the village, in fact, made me ineffably happy: going out to get carrots, not from the greengrocer's but from the land itself; slipping an onion in to roast in our oven (while the family baked bread), then taking it out at sundown to eat; our boyish games in the village by moonlight, and the nightly entertainments that took place on a rustic open stage in the heart of the land, with nature all around us and the bare sky above. And sunrise – when I went out with scores of boys and men, young and old, taking our cattle and beasts of burden to the

11

fields; when farmers went to work in a land of unlimited richness extending, as it seemed, into infinity.

Everything made me happy in Mit Abul-Kum, my quiet village in the depths of the Nile Delta, even the cold water in the winter when we had to leave at dawn for the special canal that filled to overflowing for no more than two weeks, our 'statutory' irrigation period, during which all land in the village had to be watered. It was obviously necessary to do it quickly and collectively. We worked together on one person's land for a whole day, then moved to another's using any *tunbur* (Archimedean screw) that was available, regardless of who owned it. The main thing was to ensure that at the end of the 'statutory' period all the land in the village was irrigated.

That kind of collective work – with and for other men, with no profit or any kind of individual reward in prospect – made me feel that I belonged not merely to my immediate family at home, or even to the big family of the village, but to something vaster and more significant: the land. It was that feeling that made me, on the way home at sunset, gaze at the evening scene with a rare warmth, recognizing an invisible bond of love and friendship with everything around me – the smoke rolling down the valley promising a delicious meal at the close of a village day, and a perfect calm and peace in the hearts of all.

That big, shady tree was made by God; He decreed it, and it came into being. These fresh green plants whose seeds we had ourselves sown could never have been there if God had not decreed it. This land on which I walked, the running water in the canal, indeed, everything around me was made by an overseeing God – a vast, mighty Being that watches and takes care of all, including me. Trees, seeds, and fruits were all, therefore, my fellows in existence; we all came out of the land and could never exist without it. The land is firm and tough, so all that belongs to it must be equally tough.

As these ideas floated in my young head, the echoes of

a saying of my grandmother's became almost audible: 'Nothing is as significant as your being a child of this land. Land is immortal, for it harbours the mysteries of creation.' How I loved that woman! She had a very strong personality and enjoyed a rare wisdom – a natural, innate wisdom, matured through lifelong experience. Throughout my childhood in the village she was the head of the family, as my father was away working for the army in the Sudan. She looked after us and supervised the work on the two and a half acres my father had acquired. 'The effendi's mother,' everybody in the village called her, and there is a story behind this.

Although the highest hope a villager could have was to join al-Azhar and become the sheikh of a mosque, my grandfather, who was literate (a rare accomplishment at the time) wanted my father to take a different route. He chose a secular education for him and helped him to obtain the General Certificate of Primary Education (GCPE) – an important qualification at the time, for the British occupation of Egypt was still young and all the subjects were taught in English. As my father was the first to obtain the degree in our village, whenever a reference was made to 'the effendi' and his sons, everybody knew that it was my father and his family who were meant (although many villagers have since qualified as doctors, engineers, and university professors).

My grandmother apparently wanted me to pursue the same course as my father. Initially she made me join the Koranic Teaching School in the village, where I was taught to read and write and learned the Koran by heart; then she made me join a Coptic (a Christian sect) school in Toukh, near an ancient monastery headed by the bishop of Wadi al-Natrun. The school was about half a mile away from the village. I did not stay there for long but I still remember Monsieur Mena very clearly, the Christian teacher who taught us all our subjects and was both loved and feared by us all. I can still recall the huge school bell ringing in the morning to start the day's work.

My heart beat, I remember, almost in response, and I was overcome by a deep awe and respect for knowledge.

I can still see that Koranic Teaching School in my mind's eye, so clearly it feels as if I left it only yesterday. I owe a lot to the kind teacher there, the late Sheikh Abdul-Hamid, who died recently. He was the first to instil in me the love of learning and the spirit of true faith. I remember how I sat among my fellow students on the floor, holding a writing tablet and a reed pen, my only tools of learning. My Arab dress had a large, deep pocket which I used to fill up in the morning with dry cheese and bread crusts, and from which I would snatch mouthfuls during our lessons or in the intervals between them.

Increasingly eager as I was for knowledge, I could never tear myself away from the life of the village. It was a series of uninterrupted pleasures. There was something different to look forward to every day: the seed-sowing season; irrigation time; the wheat harvest and the harvest celebrations; village wedding festivities, with the delicious *Kunafah* dessert just waiting to be devoured; cotton-harvesting which always coincided with the harvest of dates. I remember how I used to pick enough cotton to fill the front part of my Arab dress, then run off to a woman who sold dates, and barter it all for the ripe, lush fruit. Every time I took the cattle to drink from the canal, worked our ox-drawn threshing machine, or joined the boys in picking the cotton crop, I felt I was doing so for the first time. My life in the village was a succession of pleasant 'discoveries' – like a waterwheel tapping a well of delightful novelties.

The feeling that everything I did or saw in the village was new never left me throughout my childhood. It was an inexhaustible source of happiness. Nothing was old, not even those bedtime stories which my grandmother and my mother told me. I listened to them every time with a fresh ear, although they actually never changed. But they were not the old traditional tales of romantic or warlike exploits, such as those of al-Shatir Hassan or Abu Zayd al-Hilali; they were close to our real life and drew on contemporary history.

One of these stories dealt with the poisoning of Mustafa Kamil – one of our political leaders – by the British, who wanted to put an end to his struggle against their occupation of Egypt. I did not know at the time who Mustafa Kamil was or that he actually died in his prime. I knew only, at that tender age, that there were forces, called 'the British', who were alien to us, and that they were evil because they poisoned people.

My grandmother also recited to me the ballad of Adham al-Sharqawi; it dealt with his heroism, his struggles, and great resourcefulness in fighting the British and the government of the day. But the ballad which affected me most deeply was probably that of Zahran, the hero of Denshway. I recall listening to my mother reciting it to me as I lay stretched out on top of our huge rustic oven, half-asleep, while my younger brothers (as well as our rabbits) had all fallen asleep. It appealed to me afresh every time I listened to it. Denshway was only three miles away and the ballad dealt with a real incident. British soldiers were shooting pigeons in Denshway, the story goes, when a stray bullet caused a wheat silo to catch fire. Farmers gathered and a British soldier fired at them and ran away; they ran after him, and in the ensuing scuffle the British soldier died. Many people were arrested and court-martialled on the spot. Scaffolds were erected before the sentences were even passed; a number of farmers were whipped, others hanged. Zahran was the hero of the battle against the British and the first to be hanged. The ballad dwells on Zahran's courage and doggedness in the battle, how he walked with head held high to the scaffold, feeling proud that he had stood up to the aggressors and killed one of them.

I listened to that ballad night after night, half-awake, half-asleep, which perhaps made the story sink into my subconscious. My imagination roamed free. I often saw Zahran and lived his heroism in dream and reverie – I wished *I* were Zahran.

Lying on top of the rustic oven in our home in the village, I realized then that something was wrong with our life. Even before I saw the British, I had learned to hate the aggressors who whipped and killed our people.

This was not all I came to learn in Mit Abul-Kum. For I learned something else that has remained with me all my life: the fact that wherever I go, wherever I happen to be, I shall always know where I really am. I can never lose my way because I know that I have living roots there, deep down in the soil of my village, in that land out of which I grew, like the trees and the plants.

The early years of my life were all spent in my village. Then, suddenly, we moved to Cairo because my father, I was told, had returned from the Sudan. How old was I? I didn't know at the time. Only later did I realize that significant events in my life coincided with events of public, even historic, significance. So, apparently, destiny has decreed.

II

I moved to Cairo in 1925, following the assassination of the British sirdar (commander of the Egyptian Army), Sir Lee Stack, in 1924. One of the sanctions which Britain imposed on Egypt in retaliation was the withdrawal of the Egyptian Army from the Sudan; the withdrawal was carried out, and my father came back home.

We lived in a small house in Kubri al-Qubbah, near Cairo. As I had to continue my education (which had begun at the Coptic school in Toukh), my father chose a privately financed school for its reasonable fees. Only when I had taken my papers to the Islamic Benevolent Society School, as it was called, did I learn the date of my birth: 25 December 1918. The new school was in Zaytun, not far from home, and I walked there and back every day, passing Al-Qubbah Palace, one of the royal palaces of

King Fuad. I remember how in the spring my friends and I lingered by the palace orchard to pick a few apricots, though in fear and trepidation; indeed, to touch anything belonging to the king could spell death. I could never have known then that I would grow up to take part, with a number of my colleagues, in changing the course of history – that I myself would one day cross that awesome wall and sit on the very chair on which King Fuad, and subsequently King Farouk, had sat.

At the Islamic Benevolent Society School I passed the initial (preparatory) stage and the first two years of primary education. I remember that I did well – the late Dr Hassan al-Sharif (who recently served as Minister of Social Insurance) and I were alternately at the top of our class. I then moved to Sultan Hussein School in Heliopolis, where I obtained the General Certificate of Primary Education (GCPE). In 1930, my elder brother Tal'at and I joined the Fuad I Secondary School. Although, in accordance with the law of the day, only one of two brothers at school was supposed to pay fees, I failed to get an exemption. My father had to pay for both of us, in instalments. The first instalment was £16, which was my father's entire salary for a month. I took the money to school and paid it myself. The second instalment was never paid. My brother took the money and ran away; he spent it all on God knows what, then came back to declare that he did not wish to continue his formal education.

Perhaps destiny decreed this, too. If my brother hadn't thrown away his education, my father would not have been able, on such a limited income, to keep us both at school. And he would most probably have stopped me from going in favour of my elder brother.

At the secondary school I came to realize for the first time what city dwellers were and what class differences meant. The sons of the Minister of War and of the Under-Secretary to the Minister of Education were fellow students, and both came to school by car, a 'comobile', as we called it in our village. Very impressive, true, but it never made me jealous or spiteful. My classmates were, naturally, better dressed than I was, but I never suffered because of this. Many of my friends came from wealthy families and lived in luxurious houses, yet I cannot recall ever wishing to possess what they had. Indeed, I always felt proud of our house and cattle in the village, of being referred to as 'the effendi's son', and, most important of all, of the land to which I belonged – tough, permanent, and immutable, just like the values of village life, which are quite unknown to many city dwellers.

One day I went out to buy a box of matches from a shop in the street where we lived in Cairo. I asked for a box of 'mutches', whereupon the customers burst out laughing. I wondered what they were laughing at. 'You must ask for *matches*, not mutches,' they explained, but I insisted on saying 'mutches'. As their derision mounted, I became more obstinate and realized that I felt stronger than them. Who did they think they were? How could they justify their derision? They believed that superiority belongs only to the rich, and to hereditary distinctions of birth, but we in the village took no notice of such things. A man of integrity was the ideal, whatever his poverty. In the village we recognize and shun whatever is genuinely disgraceful. We belong to one another, indeed we are intimately bound together by ties of fraternity, co-operation, and love. In the city, people belong to their wealth, their power, and their large, sumptuous houses – all ephemeral and truly trivial 'belongings'.

The set of values on which I was brought up in the village, and which city life so lacked, supported me at that early stage of my life. It deepened my feeling of inner superiority, a feeling which has never left me and which, I came to realize in time, is an inner power independent of all material resources. Indeed, that feeling perhaps gains strength as material resources diminish – or even when they are lacking altogether.

I lived below the poverty line throughout the period of my secondary school education. On his limited income, my father had to support thirteen sons and daughters. So, although we lived in Cairo, we had a huge rustic oven where we baked bread; to buy bread from a bakery as the Cairenes did was simply beyond our means. My allowance was 2 millimes a day, with which I bought a cup of milky tea and felt on top of the world. My fellow students bought the best kinds of chocolate and candies from the school canteen, and had many splendid suits, so that they always looked smart. I had only one old suit, which I could not change or even renovate. Yet, recalling these things now, I cannot say that they ever made me feel inferior; even at that young age I never compared my position with that of my colleagues.

I remember that on taking the examinations for the General Certificate of Secondary Education, one had to fill out a form and submit it, complete with photograph, to the school authorities. That photograph was of paramount importance to the student, insofar as the GCSE represented a turning point in his life. I asked my father to buy me a new suit, fit for such a historic occasion. My father sympathized with the request but said: 'Give me a day or two to find the necessary money.' Three days later he came to me, and said cheerfully, 'Solution found! Go to Wikalat al-Balah (a second-hand market still in Cairo). The shops there look alike, I know, but you must find the owner of this particular shop.' He gave me 150 piastres.

The shop was small, not more than five by six feet. In front was a long bench behind which the shopkeeper stood; behind him were rolls of material on shelves, and in a corner a sewing machine. I picked out the material that I wanted. The man cut it out with his scissors, then sat down at his sewing machine. An hour and a half later I received my new suit. Naturally it could not compare with what my colleagues had ready for the occasion, but it made me very happy indeed. It served the purpose, that was the main thing. It didn't matter whether it looked rough or smooth, cheap or otherwise. Besides, with that suit or without it, I was what I was, a young villager who perceived in working the land an adequate distinction over city dwellers who lived on trade.

The time I spent at school in Cairo was marked by incessant comparisons between city life and village life; and the conclusions I drew were decidedly not in favour of the city. Indeed, many things annoyed me in Cairo. There was, for instance, the odious sight of the typical British constable on his motorcycle, tearing through the city streets day and night like a madman – with a tomato-coloured complexion, bulging eyes, and an open mouth – looking like an idiot, with his huge head covered in a long crimson fez reaching down to his ears. Everybody feared him. I simply hated the sight of him, and often wondered what had brought this ugly alien to our city. If he came to our village, I thought, he wouldn't be able to take a single step; he wouldn't dare.

There was also that steamroller which, whenever I saw it, went after me. If I went faster, it went faster; if slower, it slowed down. What exactly did it want? Obviously, to crush me under its huge iron rollers. But why? We didn't even know each other. Such questions were futile, for whenever I looked behind me, there it was, coming after me again! I could reach safety only by turning quickly into a lane that was too narrow for it, then running so fast that we lost sight of one another. For all its colossal stature it could not, clearly, match my speed.

I remember the first time I went to the movies – a terrible experience. I saw a train coming from the depth of the screen towards me at a speed I never thought possible. What should I do? I shut my eyes and curled back in my seat but the rumbling of the engine still filled my ears. Why wait? I left my seat to rush up the aisle to safety. I was struck, though, by the sight of all the other people still in their seats, watching calmly as though nothing was happening (or about to happen). 'It's their business,' I thought. But when I reached the aisle, my eyes still fixed on the screen, the train had disappeared. The scene had changed and, instead of a train, a man and a woman were there, having a meal at a small café. So I went back to my seat and watched the film quietly just like everybody else.

It was all quite fascinating. So fascinating, in fact, that I booked myself a ticket for the next performance and sat down motionless to watch the remarkable train again.

I had then passed my second-year examinations and so was eligible for a place in the third. However, my 'grade' was not, I was told, impressive enough for me to proceed to the General Certificate of Proficiency (GCP) at the end of the third year. I was asked to sit for my second-year examinations again, in the hope of obtaining a higher 'grade', which might improve my chances of obtaining the GCP and thereby also improve the school results. I refused, left the school altogether, submitted my papers to Al-Ahram School (which was privately financed), and was admitted to the third year there. At the end of that year I obtained my GCP.

In the same spirit of challenge, even though I had not yet recognized it in myself at that early age, I took my papers again to my old school (Fuad I Secondary School) and was readmitted for the fourth year. But my results at the end of that year and the school's comment were a repeat of the previous experience there. So once again I submitted my papers to Al-Ahram School, where I joined the fifth year and sat the end-of-year examinations that qualified students for the General Certificate of Education. I passed in all subjects individually, but the sum total of my marks was 'unsatisfactory'.

That result was a turning point in my life. I realized that my failure was a sign. God was not satisfied with me, perhaps because of my negligence, perhaps because of my overconfidence. To maintain my inner strength, I could do nothing better than turn to the values of our village, as I had always done. So, in that mood and with that vague feeling – a combined sense of guilt and a resolve to repent – I submitted my papers to another school, the Advanced Learning School at Shubra, where I finally read for and obtained my GCE.

III

My reference to 'repentance' during my education in Cairo may have suggested that I had, even if temporarily, abandoned the village; but I never did. Every year, when the school season came to an end, I simply flew back to my village and threw myself in her arms. That was my ideal society, where I recognized myself and my entire homeland. For a very long period Egypt to me meant Mit Abul-Kum. Only when I had obtained my GCE did I grasp the generalized concept of a homeland. And that was only natural, I believe, for it was in Mit Abul-Kum that I first felt that something was missing somewhere, that something was wrong with our lives and had to be put right, as I listened to the ballad of Zahran night after night on top of the stove in our house.

Deep down in my consciousness Zahran was identified with Mustafa Kamil and Adham al-Sharqawi; they were the same kind of man, in their defiance of the barbarous British oppressors who whipped and hanged our people in Denshway. There was a photograph of someone else in our house in Cairo – Kemal Atatürk. I asked my father about him, and he said he was a great man. Indeed, Kemal Atatürk was idealized in the Islamic world; his name was familiar as a leader who wanted to liberate and rebuild his country. Apart from Atatürk, my father admired Napoleon Bonaparte and told me a lot about him. When Napoleon was in exile on St Helena, my father recounted, the British governor of the island ordered that the height of Napoleon's door be reduced so as to force him to bend down every time he went in or out. But Napoleon defeated the governor's purpose by squatting and creeping in and out in that uncomfortable position with his head held high.

This was obviously an old wives' tale, but it reflected a living concept of heroism in the Egyptian mind, particularly as that hero was a powerful enemy of the British – our enemies, the people who occupied our land and whose presence we resisted in every possible way. Hence my admiration for Saad Zaghloul. I used to go out every evening to al-Khalifah al-Mamum Street to see the man who had succeeded him in leading the party, Mustafa el-Nahas Pasha, on his way from his home in Heliopolis to the National Assembly and back. In el-Nahas and the Wafd Party I saw a symbol of the struggle of the entire Egyptian people against the British.

I cannot say that during that early period of my life my political consciousness had matured or even taken shape. I shared the patriotic feelings of all Egyptians, of course. I took part in the demonstrations, the smashing of plates and burning down of trams, and the chanting of slogans calling for the removal of Ismail Sidki Pasha and the reactivation of the 1923 Constitution – but I didn't even know what that Constitution really was.

I can say, however, that a certain feeling had struck root in me by the time I left school – a hatred for all aggressors, and a love and admiration for anyone trying to liberate his land. I remember that in 1932 Gandhi passed through Egypt on his way to Britain. Reports of his struggle, past and present, filled the Egyptian newspapers and magazines. I was struck by his character and fell in love with his image. I began to imitate him. I took off my clothes, covered myself from the waist down with an apron, made myself a spindle, and withdrew to a solitary nook on the roof of our house in Cairo. I stayed there for a few days until my father persuaded me to give it up. What I was doing would not, he argued, benefit me or Egypt; on the contrary, it would certainly have given me pneumonia, especially since it was a bitterly cold winter.

I was in our village for the summer vacation when Hitler marched forth from Munich to Berlin, to wipe out the consequences of Germany's defeat in World War I and rebuild his country. I gathered my friends and told them we ought to follow Hitler's example by marching forth from Mit Abul-Kum to Cairo. I was twelve. They laughed and went away.

These were, in the main, early signs of a natural tendency to engage in a struggle the dimensions of which were as yet obscure to me; but they represent, I believe, my individual reactions to current events. My love for Kemal Atatürk did, however, survive. I admired his military uniform and realized that he could not have mounted his revolution, or done anything, in fact, without the armed forces.

The salient events of my life coincided, as I have said, with historic events. When I obtained my GCE, el-Nahas had, in 1936, concluded the Montreux Treaty with Great Britain. In accordance with that treaty, the Egyptian Army was allowed to expand and it thus became possible for me to join the Royal Military Academy. Before 1936 the Egyptian Army was small and only members of the aristocracy were admitted to the Military Academy. But, for all its new facilities, it wasn't easy for me to join the academy – the highest hope I had.

The Royal Military Acadamy was allowed, it is true, to admit members of the middle class, even in the low-income brackets, but two items on the application form were rather restrictive. The first required the applicant to give details of his father's property and income; the second required him to name a highly placed 'reference'. And at the interview, names were called out in this order: first the applicant's name, then his father's, then his 'reference'. My father's position as a senior clerk in the civil service (Department of Health) satisfied the first requirement – at least insofar as he had a fixed income. The other was harder to fulfil, as my father did not know any of the beys or pashas of the day. He was told that the chairman of the committee which examined application forms was a Major-General Ibrahim Khayri Pasha, and that he must be approached. The question was, of course, how to approach that pasha.

Khayri was typical of the cream of the aristocracy at the time. He had given lessons in 'horsemanship', on King Fuad's orders, to the young King Farouk, and so was the king's tutor; he was Under-Secretary to the War Minister; and his wife belonged to the royal family. Ibrahim Pasha was, in a word, a very prominent social figure indeed. How could we hope to approach him when we could hardly reach a minister's secretary?

It eventually dawned on my father that he had a friend – a warrant officer who had served with him in the Sudan – who happened to be working for Khayri. It was this friend who arranged for us, I don't know how, to see the pasha. One morning my father took me to the pasha's palace in al-Qubbah Gardens, an aristocratic district of Cairo at the time.

We entered the smart house and stood in the hallway. That was the arrangement: the pasha had to pass by us on his way out, would notice our presence, and ask us what we wanted. The pasha did in fact come down a few minutes later, whereupon the warrant officer whispered a few words to him. The pasha looked at my father and said very haughtily: 'Oh, yes. You're the senior clerk of the Health Department, and that's your son who ... I see ... all right, all right!' Then he shot towards the door with my father following and mumbled something I could not distinguish; nor could my father, I believe.

It was an experience that has remained with me all my life. I don't think I shall ever forget it. It was the first time I had ever visited a pasha's house or seen a member of that class. As it happened, I met the same Ibrahim Pasha years later in my office when I was Speaker of the National Assembly. He came to see me in connection with a few problems he wanted to solve, some concerning his sons, others concerning his confiscated property, and so forth. I helped him solve them all, and then reminded him of our first meeting in his house. I added: 'Please don't imagine that I have any hard feelings on account of that first meeting; on the contrary, I'm prepared to help you at all times. I owe you a lot. You were the chairman of the admittance board and thus enabled me – as well as Gamal Abdel Nasser and the rest of the Revolutionary Command Council – to join the Military Academy. If it hadn't been for you, the revolution would not have been possible.'

Ironic. Indeed, I recall an endless succession of such ironic situations, the most telling of which is, perhaps, that the British helped me to join the Military Academy when the reason why I wanted to join in the first place was to kick them out of Egypt.

After our meeting with Major-General Khayri, we set about looking for the name of a 'reference' to put on the application form. My father resorted to the chief medical officer of the Egyptian Army under whom he had worked, an Englishman called Dr Fitzpatrick. He responded and wrote out a testimonial. He also put in a good word for me, and personally recommended me to the chief tutor at the academy, another Englishman who also sat on the admittance board. I was thus admitted to the academy, even though, my 'reference' being the least impressive (at the time such 'references' ranged from Crown Prince Muhammad Ali to highly influential pashas and beys), my name was at the bottom of the list. We were fifty-two, all told. However, when I went to pay the fees, there was a surprise in store for me.

It transpired that Hamdi Saif al-Nasr, the War Minister, was with el-Nahas in Montreux to take part in the conclusion of an agreement abrogating the 'Aliens' Privileges' Law, according to which aliens were not subject to trial by Egyptian courts. (It was in fact odd and disgusting to see foreigners committing crimes in Egypt while the Egyptian government was helpless to call them to book or arrest them; all it could do was to refer them to their embassies, which alone had the power either to try them or release them.) When he received the list of the new cadets' names in Montreux to endorse it, in accordance with the law, the War Minister cabled the academy that he wanted six places reserved for some of his relatives. The academy had to strike off the names of the last six cadets-to-be, and I was, naturally, the first to go.

A good deal of trouble ensued. As a temporary measure, I joined the Faculty of Arts, then the Faculty of Law, then the Faculty of Commerce. Meanwhile al-Nasr returned to Cairo and secured the six places for his relatives. Then the army's chief medical officer, the Englishman who was my reference, and the chief tutor at the academy, both intervened on my behalf. When I had completely lost hope, my mother asked me one morning, to my great surprise, to go immediately to my father's office and collect the fees, as I had at last been admitted to the academy. My fellow cadets had already spent twenty-six days there.

At the academy, Atatürk continued to be my ideal. I started to read books on the Turkish Revolution, and the history of Egypt, but no further back than the French expedition to Egypt. I focused throughout on the British occupation of Egypt in 1882, the deception which had led to it, and the tragic situation that we suffered as a result.

Mustafa Kamil I still loved, but I believed he had been wrong not to resort to force. I believed that the British would not leave except by force of arms. But were the British the only culprits? What about the ruling royal family – a family of non-Egyptians? What about Khedive Tewfik, who had the British Army parade in Abidin Square, in Cairo, thus legalizing the British occupation of Egypt after the defeat of the Egyptian Army, through a deception, in 1882? Wasn't the regime of the day primarily responsible for what had happened, and was happening, to us? (At Denshway, for instance, the court was composed entirely of Egyptians – judge, defence lawyers, and prosecuting attorneys alike.)

With these questions forcing themselves on my consciousness, I came to perceive, gradually but clearly, the real dimensions of the situation. I was impatient for the day when I would graduate from the Military Academy and might be able to do something. I had high hopes; I wanted to do a lot for Egypt. But I could not as yet find a means of moving from the vision to the reality.

IV

I graduated from the Royal Military Academy in February 1938. With that graduation the energy which had been pent up for years in my subconscious was released.

In childhood I had listened, as I said, to the ballad of Zahran every night. I saw Zahran in my mind's eye advance intrepidly to the scaffold. He held his head high; he was not afraid of the British who had sentenced him to death, or of death itself. For all the enemy's might, Zahran felt superior, since he possessed a most powerful and effective weapon: rejection of anything or anyone who sought to humiliate him and his people. Zahran's image was, in fact, ever present in my mind. I saw Zahran in dream and reverie, and wished I were him. I hoped my story would grow into a ballad that would live in the hearts of posterity.

Although I came to hear of and admire Mustafa Kamil, Ahmed Urabi, and Kemal Atatürk, it was Zahran who remained closest to my heart. I identified with him and hoped to act as he did. I did not want to be sentenced to death, however, but to lead a revolution to destroy the British and deliver Egypt from their rule.

Rejection has been, and will always be, the most effective weapon in our hands, children of the good land which I love more than anything else in the world. Man cannot help being a child of his own land and the heir of his predecessors. My feeling of inner strength was still there, naturally, but, as an officer in the armed forces, I now felt possessed of material strength as well. I believed that nothing but physical force could deliver Egypt alike from the British and the corrupt government of the day.

Why wait, then? We should immediately set up an organization, I thought, within the armed forces, which would carry out the revolution I had dreamed of. That was the road to deliverance. There was no alternative to it. A revolution could not emerge from a vacuum, I reasoned; we had to prepare for it by making people as fully conscious as possible of the conditions Egypt suffered at the time. I decided to start with our own position as officers in the Egyptian Army. Since the surest way to a man's heart was to deal with what concerned him personally, I focused in my conversations with my colleagues on two things which, everybody agreed, damaged the army and our life in the armed forces in general. The first was the absolute power of the British military mission; the second, our senior officers' ignorance and blind acquiescence in whatever the British commanded.

We were stationed at the time in Manqabad, a small town in Upper Egypt. Meetings took place in my room in the officers' mess. It happened to be a senior officer's room, practically a small apartment, for, when I was transferred to Manqabad, all the junior officers' rooms had been occupied. We met there every evening, drank tea, and talked. Without giving away my purpose, I worked hard during our long conversations to open my colleagues' eyes to the realities of the situation in general and the position of the British in particular.

We held long sessions, so to speak, and had interminable conversations. Night in night out, my colleagues, who mostly lacked any political education, gained in political consciousness, and the feeling that something was seriously wrong with the situation in Egypt steadily grew. I discussed our ancient history, picking out relevant incidents and situations and contrasting them with current events, current problems, current tragedies. I deliberately refrained, however, from suggesting any solutions. And it worked. My method proved equally stimulating and persuasive. My colleagues listened to me in silence, enquired about this or that, even questioned me closely on points of interest, but ultimately assimilated the subject very well indeed. As their knowledge increased, some of them raised further questions and varied their angle of approach to old issues, always with great enthusiasm and occasionally in anguish, the subject being Egypt and the deliverance of Egypt from her present predicament. My big room in the officers' mess came to be dubbed 'The National Assembly'.

Our conversations were, of course, interspersed with anecdotes, jokes, and small talk. I took part in the frivolous side just as I contributed to serious discussions. We were all very young, with no one over twenty. Besides, that method was ideally suited to my purpose; to have isolated myself or made my colleagues feel I was different could never have helped.

The only occasion on which I felt I was different was when Aziz al-Masri Pasha visited us in his capacity as Inspector General of the Egyptian Army and took us along to visit Al-Muharraq Monastery (not very far from our camp in Upper Egypt where Jesus and Mary took refuge) with a purely cultural end in view. When we entered the monastery – none of us had previously seen one – we found a priest, or rather a junior monk, living in a cell which had no windows but a small opening, barely two inches wide, and a brick *mastaba* (a built-in bench) that served as a bed. Everybody was surprised at that way of life and pitied the priest for his unusual asceticism. But I was not surprised, nor did I perceive any unusual asceticism in what I saw. I was born in a similar cell, which we referred to as a 'hall', and had similar *mastabas* in Mit Abul-Kum on which I spent the days and nights of my early childhood.

Aziz al-Masri's visit impressed me very deeply. I felt so happy that I had actually seen that legendary figure, who had had a role to play, alongside Kemal Atatürk, during the Turkish Revolution; was one of the founders of the Society for Unity and Advancement, and of the Society for the Liberation of the Arab Nation; who had behind him a long history of struggle for freedom; and who was a great advocate of the dissemination of culture. I was myself very interested in culture, particularly at that early stage in my career. Apart from the political activities in which I was immersed as soon as I graduated from the academy, I committed myself to cultural pursuits, which I felt were equally important inasmuch as they supported my political activity. That was why I tried to join the British Institute in Egypt and obtain a BA from the University of London. I was also very fond of reading. While in Cairo, I got my books from second-hand bookshops around Izbekiah Park; in the provinces I wrote to the publishers and the bookstores for booklists. Whatever I picked was sent direct to Second Lieutenant Muhammad Anwar el-Sadat, wherever I was stationed.

It was perhaps this that particularly distinguished me from my colleagues. When in Manqabad, I remember, a special army bus used to take us every Thursday afternoon to Asyut, where we spent the whole evening. My colleagues went to the movies or sought other entertainments. I sat at a café near the railway station, smoked a hookah, and happily read the books I had bought in Cairo, until my colleagues were ready to return and we all took the bus back to camp.

The circle of friends meeting in my room in the mess widened every day and the sessions expanded. I saw Gamal Abdel Nasser for the first time at one of those sessions, when his battalion moved to Manqabad. My impression was that he was a serious-minded youth, who did not share his fellows' interest in jesting; nor would he allow anyone to be frivolous with him as this, he felt, would be an affront to his dignity. Most of my colleagues therefore kept their distance and even refrained from talking to him for fear of being misunderstood. He listened to our conversations with interest but rarely opened his mouth. I immediately realized how serious he was and wanted to know him better. However, he had obviously erected an almost insuperable barrier between himself and other people. He kept to himself so conspicuously, in fact, that our relationship at the time never went beyond mutual respect, and even that was still from a distance.

The sessions went on. Our endless discussions of Egypt's problems and the situation in general continued within the narrow confines of our circle. But now I looked for wider horizons in order to carry out the plan of political action I had laid down on graduation, and these were only to be found, naturally, in Cairo. As long as I remained in the infantry, I knew, I would always be away from Cairo. That was one of the reasons I resented service in that corps; another was my impatience with the British military mission and the commander of our post in Manqabad, whom we nicknamed Sultan Abdul-Hamid on account of his tyrannical behaviour (in this way he hoped, actually, both to conceal his ignorance and to satisfy his British superiors). But what could I do?

A chance came at last. I was one of a few officers picked to take a high-level course in army signals at the Signals School of Maadi, near Cairo. That was early in 1939. Although he arrived in Manqabad six months later than we did, Abdel Nasser was going to attend the same course. But his aloofness was still a barrier.

The course took two and a half months. Then we sat a test, and attended a finishing ceremony. It was the usual procedure. I was chosen to make a speech on behalf of my colleagues. I had little hope at the time of joining the Signals Corps; it was newly established and was regarded as the most important. Naturally strings had to be pulled if you wanted to be transferred to it.

The experience of preparing my speech gave me a pleasure that was entirely new. I discovered for the first time that I could write, that I could thread together fresh concepts into a coherent text. I did not read it out but delivered it from memory. It had a definite objective and an internal unity which apparently impressed the commander of the Signals Corps, Brigadier Abul-Saad, for, shortly after my return to Manqabad, he summoned me to serve in the Signals Corps in Maadi. It was one of the happiest days of my life. This was the chance for which I had waited so long.

I began my contacts immediately and on a very large scale, covering most army corps (the majority of army officers being stationed in Cairo). Meetings took place in my apartment in my father's house at Kubri al-Qubbah, in the Officers' Club, at cafés, and in the houses of our colleagues. Contacts were initially confined to fellow officers in the same corps, mostly my coevals, but, encouraged by Hitler's successive threats to the British in 1939–41, I widened the circle gradually. Many senior and junior officers were approached and actually responded to our call, namely, that we should seize the opportunity and carry out an armed revolution against the British presence in Egypt.

In this way the first secret organization of army officers was established in 1939. The Free Officers' Organization included Abdel Munim Abdul-Rauf, who came second after me; Abdel Latif al-Baghdadi; Hassan Ibrahim; Khaled Mohieddin; the late Ahmed Saudi Hussein; Hassan Izzat; and the late Field Marshal Ahmed Ismail Ali, who attended our meetings but did not take part in political action as he was devoted to his military career.

I did not resort to secret cells to make our armed revolution achieve its purpose, as Abdel Nasser would later do when he returned from the Sudan in 1942 to take over the leadership of our organization early in 1943, following my arrest in the summer of 1942. As Hitler's power began to decline during that year, and as the British began to recover their firm grip on Egypt, Nasser had to plan for the future. I, on the other hand, saw no reason why a long-term plan should be drawn when the breathless succession of events (with their inevitable repercussions) called for immediate action. In other words, Hitler's early victories and the British setbacks offered me the chance to act immediately. As an opportunity was already available, and as it was our duty to seize it before it was too late, I saw no need to plan far ahead.

So I took steps in that direction and speeded things up. Apart from my large-scale contacts with officers and the creation of an organizational structure for the revolution, I began a series of contacts with soldiers in my Maadi unit, lecturing them on the 'battle', the world military situation, our position *vis-à-vis* the British, and the situation in Egypt, past and present. I spoke to them too about the meaning of both 'homeland' and 'patriotism', and led them at prayer.

As it happened, some of the soldiers belonged to the Muslim Brotherhood. On the Prophet's Birthday in 1940 one of them whispered to me, to my great surprise, that a man really well versed in the religion of Islam wanted to talk to the soldiers on the occasion. I was the officer on duty for the night shift. When I learned that that man was no other than Sheikh Hassan al-Banna, Supreme Guide of the Muslim Brotherhood, I welcomed him and asked him to deliver a lecture in my stead. His choice of subjects was excellent, his understanding and interpretation of religion profound, and his delivery impressive. He was indeed qualified, from all points of view, to be a religious leader. Besides, he was a true Egyptian: good-humoured, decent, and tolerant.

I had imagined, from what I had heard about the Muslim Brotherhood, that it was merely a religious society aimed at reviving the values of Islam and working for moral advancement; but now that I heard Sheikh al-Banna, I began to think differently. The man spoke of worldly as well as 'other-worldly' matters, using a style quite uncommon among religious preachers. My admiration was unbounded. I congratulated him on his lecture and talked with him for a while. He invited me to attend the weekly sermons which he delivered every Tuesday after the evening prayers, at the society's headquarters in al-Hilmiah al-Jadidah. I accepted and actually attended a few. Each time, he invited me afterwards to his private office, where we talked for some time. I was struck by the perfect organization of the Muslim Brotherhood, and by the respect, even extraordinary reverence, which the Supreme Guide commanded. Members of the society almost hallowed him. They nearly knelt down to me and kissed the ground on which I trod, just because he had invited me to sit in his office.

The Muslim Brotherhood were, undoubtedly, a power to be reckoned with. The following incident illustrates what I mean. Sheikh al-Banna once wanted to move the society's headquarters to a new house, beautiful and convenient; but the society lacked the necessary capital. A fund-raising campaign was launched and, before the day was out, the target had been met and the house bought.

The few Tuesday sermons I attended confirmed the suspicion I had felt during Sheikh al-Banna's lecture on the Prophet's Birthday that his activity had political ends, for which he worked with great subtlety. He never dealt with questions of 'government', or 'power' in general, but always focused on Islam as both a religion and a way of life, equally essential for a healthy spirit and a healthy government. That suspicion crept up, too, in conversations between my division's senior officer and me. In fact, immediately after the Prophet's Birthday lecture, that senior officer called on me in my room very late at night. 'Well?' I enquired. He explained that he had just wanted to convey his best wishes on the occasion, but soon broached the real subject of his visit. The Intelligence had learned, he said, about Sheikh al-Banna's lecture. The sheikh's movements were being watched by the state; his organization was in fact political and he wanted to recruit members of the armed forces to achieve his purposes. The senior officer did not tell me, though I later came to know it, that a cashiered officer called Mahmoud Labib worked for Sheikh al-Banna as head of the military branch of the Muslim Brotherhood and that he had actually succeeded in recruiting some officers and soldiers.

That was my earliest warning, but I continued to attend

the Tuesday sermons regularly. None the less I did not like the sight of members kissing the hand of their Supreme Guide. I naturally dislike that kind of relationship between men, insofar as we all are equal human beings (although I continued to kiss my father's hand after I took office as President). But I deliberately went to see the sheikh shortly before the end of each sermon and accompanied him to his office for our usual conversations.

He was always extremely tactful and careful. His words were consistently designed to win my heart, and his questions were exploratory. He wanted to know what my intentions were exactly. I was fully aware of what he was after. Then, during one of our meetings, I simply told him: 'Listen, Sheikh Hassan. You are obviously being too wary ... too cautious, and I dare say unnecessarily so. Frankly, I am trying to set up a military organization to overthrow the existing regime.'

Surprised, even shocked, Sheikh al-Banna just stared at me and did not know what to say. (He might have feared that I was working for the Intelligence, or as an undercover agent for another body.) Finally I broke the silence. 'It's true,' I said. 'I seek to carry out an armed revolution. And a considerable number of army officers, from all services, are already working with me.'

Only then did he begin to ask me specific questions: Which army corps are on your side? How strong are you? How many officers would you require for such a revolution? I answered him. Suddenly, I was asked to co-ordinate our activities. I said: 'I have been very frank with you. Let me tell you further that our organization does not follow or serve any particular party or body; it works for Egypt as a whole. I hope this is clear.' The man said he agreed. 'Co-operation will be sufficient,' he added.

Not long after that Sheikh al-Banna succeeded in recruiting Abdul-Rauf, who came second after me in the Free Officers' Organization, and who then began to work for the Muslim Brotherhood.

V

Aziz al-Masri's character fascinated me from the moment I first saw him in Manqabad. His hatred for the British became so well known that Sir Miles Lampson (Lord Killearn), then British ambassador, asked Premier Ali Maher to relieve him of his army post. But Ali Maher only gave him an 'indefinite vacation'.

It seemed to me that we needed to benefit by the experience and vast knowledge of a great 'fighter' like al-Masri, and so I asked Sheikh al-Banna to arrange a meeting between us. That was in 1940, when I came to know the sheikh personally. He responded immediately. He asked me to go to the surgery of Dr Ibrahim Hassan (at the time the deputy guide of the Muslim Brotherhood) in Saidah Zaynab, book myself a medical examination ticket like all the other patients, proceed to the examination room, and leave the rest to the doctor. I did so. The moment I presented my ticket, he opened the door to his office where Aziz al-Masri was waiting.

I saluted him, reminded him of our meeting in Manqabad, then went on to talk about the situation in our country, the position of the British, and so on. I shall never forget that meeting with Aziz al-Masri. He was hesitant and told me frankly that he had his doubts about me – perhaps I worked for the Intelligence or something of the sort. 'If this was so,' I said, 'I would have contacted you direct; but, you see, I came to see you on Sheikh al-Banna's recommendation. You trust him, don't you?'

He was reasonably reassured. 'But why have you come to see me?' he asked; 'what do you want me to do for you?'

'We are,' I said, 'a group of officers working to set up an organization for the purpose of driving the British out of Egypt and changing the present situation. We hope that you, being such a prominent military figure, to whom we all look up, will allow us to benefit by your long experience and to refer to you from time to time for advice and guidance.'

'My first lesson,' he said promptly, 'is to rely on yourselves; don't look for a readymade leader. You must take the initiative yourselves. Napoleon was a general, indeed, a leader, at twenty-seven – how old are you now?'

'Twenty-two,' I said.

'Fine! Just work together, shoulder to shoulder, and that'll do the trick,' he said, then went on to complain about the situation, explaining that he had contacted many others for the same sort of purpose but that they turned out to be tricksters and every attempt ended in a fiasco. I assured him that we were serious and that he would find this out for himself if he allowed us to keep in touch with him for consultation and exchange of views.

'Well,' he said, 'the first thing is, as I said, that you should rely on yourselves. The second is culture: you should cultivate your minds. But culture is not to be confused with "degrees" or certificates of formal education; it can be acquired only by reading. Read a lot in every field and in every possible direction. The third is to ensure that your organization is watertight and, as it were, foolproof, so that no strangers can infiltrate into your ranks and no intrigues may give it away. I have suffered a lot in my time from traitors and turncoats.' He turned suddenly to me and asked: 'What is the nature of your relationship with the Muslim Brotherhood?'

'Well, I told Sheikh al-Banna frankly from the start that we work for Egypt, not for any party or bloc,' I said.

'Well done,' he commented. 'This is a perfect point of departure; you've done well.'

At the end of the meeting we agreed on how and where to meet in future. His house was in the Ayn Shams district but it was watched by the British and Egyptian Intelligence. I told him that wasn't an insuperable problem, as we had police officers within our organization, and I did often call on him at home. Sometimes we met at Groppi's.

At one time he lived in a *pension* downtown called the Viennoise; I met him there too. Meanwhile I kept in touch with Sheikh al-Banna and increasingly widened the circle of the Free Officers. World events were proceeding, as it seemed, without letup in favour of our cause. Hitler's forces swept over Europe with unexpected speed, and the position of the British daily grew weaker everywhere, so that our chance of striking the blow to get rid of both the colonizing power and the political parties seemed very near at hand.

Then an order was issued transferring me to Marsa Matruh – on the Mediterranean, in the extreme north of Egypt – where I was to serve as a signals officer in an artillery brigade stationed there. In Marsa Matruh I intensified my political activity among my fellow officers.

Until that point the Egyptian Army had shared with the British the task of defending the area of the Western Desert, where the famous El Alamein battle took place, against any possible onslaughts by Axis forces, which involved Egypt in the world conflict in spite of the fact that the Axis had not declared war against us. In other words, we were fighting for Britain, in violation of the 1936 treaty which had established the sovereignty of Egypt. Furthermore our enemy was primarily, if not solely, Great Britain. Egyptian public opinion was not at all happy with that situation; indeed, the people were extremely indignant. The sheikh of al-Azhar, Muhammad Mustafa al-Maraghi, who was a very eminent figure, once made a statement during a sermon that came to be echoed by every Egyptian: 'We have nothing to do with that war'. Subsequently Premier Ali Maher proposed to Parliament a policy of 'saving Egypt from the scourge of the war.' It was immediately adopted unanimously by Parliament. As a result we received orders to vacate Marsa Matruh, which meant that the British alone would now assume the defence of all three sectors of that area, two of which had been our responsibility.

Angered by this measure, the British asked us to hand

over our weapons on withdrawal. I was livid with rage but thought it a blessing in disguise since the demand bred hostility in the hearts of our officers towards both the British and the command of the Egyptian Army that accepted it. It was a military humiliation, quite apart from the fact that we needed our weapons. I contacted all my fellow officers and we concurred on disobeying the order. We decided that we would not hand over our weapons. If the British insisted on their demand, they would have to fight for it. Informed of our decision, the army command acquiesced and fresh orders were issued so that we withdrew with our weapons intact.

It was at that time, in the summer of 1941, that I actually laid down the first plan for a revolution. It was agreed that all units withdrawing from Marsa Matruh would assemble at a definite time near Mena House Hotel, at the end of the Alexandria-Cairo motorway, regroup, and march into Cairo to topple the British and take over. The British were so weak at the time that my colleagues and I felt confident enough to embark on the adventure without fully considering the consequences. True, there was a definite plan and I had all the details ready; neither the Muslim Brotherhood nor any other organization had any part to play in it; but was this enough? What happened, however, was that I led my unit from Marsa Matruh and, in one stride, we were at al-'Ajami, just outside Alexandria, where we spent the night. I felt very happy. The next day would see me at the Mena House Hotel, with the other units. We would study the plan, make assignments, and choose a suitable time for marching into Cairo to carry out our long-dreamed-of revolution.

None of that happened. No units were near Mena House when I got there; we washed our vehicles and sat down, my soldiers and I, to wait for them. We waited in vain. They must have gone ahead, I thought, having waited too long. So I ordered my unit to proceed to our camp in Maadi.

Thus the first plan I laid down for a revolution came to grief. It might have been a blessing, for if we had tried and failed, the authorities would have been doubly vigilant, the army would have been closely watched, and the revolution of 23 July 1952 would never have taken place.

I took it like a sportsman. Rather than despair, I redoubled my contacts with all army services. Our circle widened as never before. Every day new members joined the Free Officers' Organization. Abdul-Rauf was my deputy. Meetings were held either at his house in Saidah Zaynab, at mine in Kubri al-Qubbah, or in those of Hassan Izzat and Saudi, also in Kubri al-Qubbah. At that stage I started setting up committees within the organization, one for contacts with political bodies, another for contacts with officers in various army services who belonged to our organization, and a third the function of which I cannot recall. Meanwhile I maintained my contacts with both Aziz al-Masri and the Muslim Brotherhood.

VI

One day late in 1941 I met Aziz al-Masri at Groppi's, at his request. He wanted the Free Officers' Organization to help him leave for Iraq. He had received a message from the Germans asking him to go to Iraq to help Rashid Aali al-Kilani, who had mounted a revolution against the British there. By then the British had succeeded in persuading the Egyptian government to cashier Aziz Pasha, and the Intelligence, who knew of our meetings, had warned me to keep away from him. I did not heed their warning, as I felt it was my duty to help him. At any rate all we could offer, I told him, was transport perhaps to Beirut, which was at that time under the French Vichy government, and from there he might be able to carry on.

Shortly afterwards Aziz Pasha told me that he had received another message from the Germans saying that a German aircraft would be waiting for him at 'Mount Ruzzah', on the Cairo-Fayyum motorway, on a certain day, at sunset. I was then, incidentally, able to unravel the mystery of those groups of German travellers who had so frequently lost their way in the Western Desert, as reported by the press before the war. Their trips must have been exploratory expeditions, for the Germans, it was obvious, had fully studied the topography of our desert. Otherwise, they could never have come to know of Mount Ruzzah, which is a barely recognizable dot on the map.

We bought a pickup truck suitable for desert travel. The seller had to report it, in accordance with orders in force at the time, and the Intelligence came to know of the sale. Being under suspicion, I was ordered transferred to a place called al-Garawlah, not very far from Marsa Matruh. There I pretended to be unwell and reported sick. I was admitted to a military hospital but released and given one week off, which was not long enough for me to help Aziz al-Masri escape. So I gave the flight plan to Abdul-Rauf and left for al-Garawlah. It was then that I met Dr Yusuf Rashad for the first time. Through our friendship Dr Rashad as King Farouk's private physician was to play an important part in our revolution, although he would remain unaware of this.

I don't know what happened to the pickup truck. The British must have seized it, for Abdul-Rauf and Hussein Sabri (both excellent pilots) had to seize a military aircraft, put Aziz al-Masri with his baggage on board, and take off for Beirut, which was under the rule of the Vichy government that had surrendered to the Germans. A few minutes after takeoff, however, Sabri discovered that he had run out of oil. He apparently turned off the oil pump instead of turning it on, and so had to make an emergency landing. He landed on top of a tree, in the fields near Benha. Helped by the Qalyub chief of police, all three reached Cairo where they went into hiding.

By then the aircraft 'affair' had come to light. A suit-case with the initials A.M. led the investigators to suspect Aziz al-Masri, particularly as it transpired that the aircraft was heading for Beirut. Knowing of his anti-British lean-ings, they concluded that he was on his way to Iraq to contact the Germans. My relationship with him led them to suspect me, too. I was immediately arrested in al-Garawlah and taken in custody to Cairo.

I arrived in Cairo very early in the morning. I was taken to the War Ministry headquarters, led into the office of the minister's secretary, and left there alone. I had H. C. Armstrong's well-known book on Atatürk, *The Grey-Wolf*, and was quite absorbed in it when I suddenly felt that someone was standing by and watching me closely. It was Ibrahim 'Atallah Pasha, the army Chief of Staff, surrounded by his men. I immediately stood to attention and saluted him. He turned to his men and asked: 'Is this Captain Muhammad Anwar el-Sadat?' Told that I had arrived that morning from the Western Desert, he cast a scornful look at me and went away. If he had bothered to look at the book I was reading, I thought, he might have learned a lot – or then again, it might have meant nothing at all to him!

In the evening I was summoned to see the deputy pros-ecuting attorney. I waited for my turn. The man was busy taking down statements from witnesses of the aircraft incident, as well as witnesses from the air force, of whom there were many. I waited a very long time indeed, during which I had a chance to prepare myself fully for the questioning, especially as I had read the papers and ob-tained all the relevant information. At length, around midnight, my cross-examination started. The deputy prosecuting attorney asked:

– Do you have any link with Aziz al-Masri? Did you visit him?

- Indeed I have. The Intelligence asked me to break that link but I didn't listen as I saw no crime or offence in maintaining it.
- Do you know Abdel Munim Abdul-Rauf and Hussein Sabri?
- I do. We were classmates together. We are friends.
- Did Aziz al-Masri approach you at all in connection with a trip abroad?
- My contacts with Aziz al-Masri are based on love and loyalty. I have been impressed by his character since he visited us in Manqabad.

I went on to describe that visit at length, our journey to Al-Muharraq Monastery, what we saw there, and so on, and concluded by saying: 'When Aziz Pasha was cashiered I felt I had to call on him from time to time, out of loyalty. That's all.'

The deputy prosecuting attorney then asked:

- Have you any information about an attempted trip abroad or any contacts between him and the Germans?
- How could I possess such information when I've been 340 miles away from Cairo? I actually left for al-Garawlah five days before that incident.

As he could not establish any incriminating facts against me, the deputy prosecuting attorney ordered that I should be released and returned to my post at al-Garawlah. That shows, I thought on the way back to the desert, the advantages of the rule of the law. I thought of many other things, too, while my mind fell prey to a myriad questions. What could have happened to Abdul-Rauf and Sabri? And Aziz al-Masri – what had become of him? Why did I feel so anxious about the failure of his plan to leave for Iraq? I knew the answer to the last question. Aziz al-Masri could have contributed to the success of Rashid Aali al-Kilani's revolution, which aimed at driving the British out of Iraq, and anything that weakened the British position in the Middle East was of prime importance to me. Weakening the enemy, wherever he was, created better opportunities for us to strike our blow.

VII

Towards the end of 1941 we received orders to move out of Marsa Matruh. Gamal Abdel Nasser's battalion was, I remember, quite near by, in an area called al-Hamam. (He was not there himself however, but in the Sudan, and would not return until December 1942.) In Cairo early in 1942 I attended a training course prior to promotion but I still continued my political activity in building up the Free Officers' Organization.

Rommel had arrived in Libya with the German Panzer divisions. The general feeling in Egypt was against the British and, naturally, in favour of their enemies. The British knew this. In February 1942 they asked King Farouk to request el-Nahas, as leader of the parliamentary majority, to form a new government in the hope of winning over the Egyptian public opinion. When the king said no, Lord Killearn, the British ambassador, ordered British tanks to besiege the Royal Palace in Abidin. On 4 February an ultimatum was issued to the king, either to accept the British demand or to abdicate. Under that threat, the king summoned el-Nahas and asked him to form a new government.

4 February 1942 is a date our generation cannot forget. It was on that day that Mustafa el-Nahas Pasha lost our respect. How could he agree to be imposed upon his people, literally at gunpoint, by the colonizing power? Officers assembled in Cairo and marched out to Abidin Palace to salute the king, and he came out to return their salute. We were not of course happy with King Farouk, but then he represented Egyptian sovereignty which had also been violated. The incident was humiliating alike to

Egypt, army, and people. So when we heard, a few days after the Abidin Palace siege, that Lord Killearn had issued another ultimatum to the king in connection with an incident at Cairo airport which had hurt Britain's pride, we – the Free Officers – decided to take up positions around the Royal Palace and engage the British if their tanks besieged it again. I borrowed Zakaria Mohieddin's car (he was the only one of us who had a private car) and kept driving around the palace all night watching for anything unusual. But nothing happened, and I returned the car in the morning to its owner.

The general feeling against the British mounted every day. In the summer Field Marshal Rommel destroyed the British Eighth Army and reached El Alamein, 65 miles from Alexandria. Then the Egyptians gave vent to their emotions. They demonstrated in the streets, chanting slogans like 'Advance Rommel!' as they saw in a British defeat the only way of getting their enemy out of the country. The British panicked and began to burn their official documents and papers, evacuating British subjects and supporters to the Sudan. With El Alamein falling into his hands, the way into Egypt lay wide open before Rommel. There was no doubt at all that he would continue to advance to Alexandria, and thence to Cairo; it was only, we thought, a question of time, and a very short time too. The rumour was that Egypt would be given to Italy, and that Mussolini had actually prepared a white horse which he would ride into Cairo, just as they used to do in the days of the Roman Empire.

I called a meeting with my friends in the Free Officers' Organization. Something had to be done, I said, as we couldn't let Rommel invade Egypt unresisted. It was agreed that one of us would be sent to El Alamein to tell Rommel we were honest Egyptians who had an organization within the army; that, 'like you', we were fighting against the British; that we were prepared to recruit an entire army to fight 'on your side', and to provide him with photographs showing the lines and positions of the

British forces in Egypt; and that we would take it upon ourselves not to let one British soldier leave Cairo, in return for granting Egypt complete independence so that she would not be given to Italy or fall under German domination, and so that no one whatsoever would interfere in her affairs, internal or external.

These were the terms of the treaty dictated by me and flown to El Alamein on board the aircraft piloted by Ahmed Saudi Hussèin. I was twenty-two then, and the treaty was endorsed by my colleagues (with the exception of Abdel Nasser, who was away in the Sudan). To ensure its successful implementation and to give teeth to our resistance, I went to the glass market and bought 10,000 bottles – the sort we used to make Molotov cocktails. Al-Baghdadi, Hassan Ibrahim, Ahmed Saudi Hussein, and Hassan Izzat then took aerial photographs of the British military positions. The film and the draft treaty were put into a bag and given to Saudi to fly to Rommel in Alamein.

That day Hassan Ibrahim's aircraft was scheduled to be on alert; he gave it to Saudi, who flew it as though on a regular patrol but headed for El Alamein. It was, naturally, British made, a 'Gladiator'. So, although Saudi gave a signal of friendship, the Germans shot it down and Ahmed Saudi was killed. When it came to be known that the aircraft was lost, Hassan Ibrahim was tried and his promotion delayed, but nobody detected any planning behind the incident.

At that time I was serving at the Signals Corps in al-Jabal al-Asfar near Cairo. I expected a message from either Saudi or the Germans but nothing at all came through and I began to worry. Then, one day, I received a most unexpected surprise. Hassan Izzat came to tell me that two officers in the German Army wanted to get in touch with me with a view to co-operation. I was very happy and thought it a godsend.

One of them was called Eppler. His German mother had married an Egyptian High Court judge and borne a boy by him called Hassan Gafar who was quite a decent fellow.

Eppler was, however, different from his half-brother. He had lived a long time in Egypt, spoke fluent Arabic, and even had an Arab name (Hussein Gafar), but his Egyptian stepfather drove him out of the family home. His colleague was a German signals officer called Sandy, who didn't know a word of Arabic. I asked them how they managed to enter Egypt. They said they disguised themselves as officers in the British Eighth Army, then, tracing Bedouin tracks known only to nomad desert Arabs, they reached al-Kharijah Oasis, and thence Asyut and Cairo.

In Cairo Eppler and Sandy made a habit of spending their evenings at the Kit-Kat Nightclub, improvidently living it up. As they had huge amounts of pound notes (in sterling) printed in Greece and showed off as big-time spenders, they drew everybody's attention and, eventually, a dancer reported them to the authorities. Naturally they came to be watched by the British Intelligence, as I later learned. When I met them, however, I only knew that they lived in a houseboat on the Nile near the Kit-Kat, which had been rented for them by Hikmat Fahmi, a dancer at another nightclub (the Badiah Musabni), and that they had a German transmitter which was out of order.

I accompanied them to the Nile houseboat to examine the transmitter. I found not one but two. The German one was indeed out of order, but the other was American-made and brand new. The Hallicrafter/Skychallenger was an excellent, very powerful transmitter. Eppler explained that when the German transmitter broke down, he secretly contacted the Swiss Embassy (Switzerland being the country looking after German interests in Egypt) and the official in charge of the German section, himself a German, had provided him with the new American one. I found that it was in fact much better than the German transmitter, but that both lacked switches, so I proposed to use Egyptian-made ones. They agreed. I took the transmitter back in a taxi to my home in Kubri al-Qubbah.

At home I tried it out and found it was indeed very

powerful. I was delighted. At last, I thought, we should be able to communicate with Rommel and to present our terms for co-operation, as included in the draft treaty which I now believed had never reached him. The long silence in fact worried me. We couldn't sit idly by when time was not on our side. Rommel might be in Cairo any minute now, I reckoned; if that happened without prior agreement, that is, if Rommel didn't know of our resistance to the British and the assistance our organization was willing to give in return for Egypt's independence, the British occupation of our country might be replaced by another – whether German or Italian. The only way out of that impasse was to contact Rommel directly; and here I was, at last, in possession of a means of communication, after the earlier method had obviously failed. All I had to do was to take the transmitter to my workshop in al-Jabal al-Asfar for a final test, and then begin using it.

As I had no idea at all that Eppler and his colleague Sandy were being watched, I was surprised one morning when a message was delivered to Hassan Izzat and me, from Abdel Mughni Said (who had originally introduced us to the two spies), saying that the British Intelligence had arrested Eppler and his colleague. The transmitter had to be hidden. Hassan Izzat and I took it over to one of his friends in Shubra but, unfortunately, the friend was away. The door was locked and we were told that he had left for his village. I took the transmitter back to my home in Kubri al-Qubbah, and hid it in one of the two rooms I occupied. Later that very night, 'dawn callers' arrived. They knocked on the door several times until everybody woke up.

'Captain Anwar el-Sadat lives here?'

'Yes.'

A whole company of Egyptian and British officers, and about twenty or thirty detectives, immediately deployed themselves in the garden and throughout the house. It was hard to know exactly how many there were. We had a mongrel in the garden who, apparently overwhelmed by the sight of this army of aliens, now ensconced himself in a corner beside the oven and kept barking very hard. He was perhaps protesting against that outrage, but most probably he was defending the oven in which bread was baked for the quiet and peaceful household of which he was in effect a member.

'Where is your room?' I pointed to one of the two rooms I occupied in my father's house. It was my bedroom. During the search, Saif el-Yazal, an Egyptian Intelligence officer, found I had another pistol besides my official army one. It was lying there and rather than handing it over to the authorities he simply took it and put it in his pocket. I did not know him particularly well, nor he me, but we were bound together by the firmest of all relationships – patriotism. The hearts of all Egyptians kindled to patriotism, whatever the job they did.

When they had searched the bedroom, they wanted to proceed to my study. I told them it was occupied by female members of my family and that, in accordance with our country's tradition, it had to be vacated first. They agreed. I entered the room where I had kept the transmitter and a tin of gunpowder, made locally in the village from willow wood and fertilizers. I asked my elder brother Tal'at to take them both and hide them somewhere. He did so, leaving by the back door. The transmitter he buried under a heap of firewood in the oven room. Both oven and transmitter were guarded by the good dog, whose loud incessant barking provided cover for all Tal'at's movements.

They searched the study but found only a few books. They took the books and asked me to go with them. They wanted to take me to the Aliens' Jail but I refused, for, I told them, the law stated that officers in the Egyptian Army could be detained only in the officers' mess and guarded by a fellow officer. They bowed to the rule of law, and suggested I spend the night as a 'guest' of the police in the offices of Division B in Garden City; the army command would, I was told, summon me in the morning. I agreed.

The next morning saw me in the mess of the Cavalry Corps. My colleague Hassan Izzat was there too, but at the other end of the mess. We saw each other only at breakfast time. Ahmed Riyad, commander of the Cavalry Corps at the time, allowed us to sit side by side and talk, but whispered that we should be brief since we had to be separated immediately after breakfast. He helped us just as Saif el-Yazal had helped me by slipping my 'other' pistol in his pocket. We felt we were simply Egyptians who had to combine in resisting the enemy and the government. In spite of our different posts and official duties, we did co-operate – our duty to the homeland came first and was above everything else.

For three days and nights I could eat nothing at all. I just drank water, but it didn't quench my thirst. Something inside me was burning. My mind worked day and night in search of a way out. A denial was out of the question; there was no point in denying that I had seen Eppler, for I had done so several times. The only way out was to justify, fully and convincingly, all that had happened. But how?

Working very hard on it I had, by the end of three days, mapped out a complete story in my mind, which provided all the answers and alibis and blocked all possible avenues for 'enemy' attack. I gave Hassan Izzat all the details so that our statements would not, at the cross-examination, appear contradictory. Only then could I resume my normal life; only then could I eat, drink, and sleep.

We were taken to the army headquarters where an identification parade was arranged. The two spies identified me very easily. Eppler headed for me straightaway every time, with no hesitation whatsoever. Sandy was less bold; he walked rather cautiously until he reached me, then pointed me out.

We were tried by an Examination Council preparatory to trial by the High Military Tribunal. The Council was composed of two British officers, two Egyptian officers, and a police officer – Kamal Riyad, of Division B – which was no doubt wrong. The trial opened with one of the officers asking:

- Do you know Eppler?
- No.
- Do you know Hussein Gafar?
- No.
- Do you know that man who has identified you [pointing to Eppler]?
- Why, certainly! He's Major Abraham of the British Army.

There was some confusion in the Council for a while, then the trial resumed.

- Didn't you receive a wireless transmitter from him?
- A transmitter? Of course not! This man and his fellow introduced themselves to me as officers in the British Signals Corps. As it was in the nature of my job to co-operate with that Corps, I met him several times.

Then, recalling that the best method of defence is counterattack, I turned suddenly to Eppler and asked him:

- Do you remember, Major Abraham, our meeting at the casino el-Gammal's?
- I do indeed. But I didn't tell you my name was Abraham. I told you I was German and that my name was Eppler.
- If you did I would have reported you.
- What about the Nile houseboat?

When I denied all knowledge of it, he tried to help me remember by asking:

— Have you forgotten how the dog barked when you left the houseboat carrying the transmitter?

This made me so furious that I moved forward and very deliberately stepped very hard on his toes. He sprang to his feet and shouted:

— Now why did you step on my toes?
— Me step on your toes? [I said in great surprise] What are all these false accusations about? A houseboat, a transmitter, a barking dog, and now your feet ... Exactly what do you want of me?
— It's no use denying it. I have made a full confession and you, too, must confess.

Very calmly I replied:

— Confess what? I do know you, but as a British officer.
— What about Heliopolis?

I had in fact introduced him to Aziz al-Masri in Heliopolis, but I said:

— Well, we did meet in Heliopolis.
— And who was with us in Heliopolis?

I then invented a whole story about his coming to see me at Salt's in Heliopolis, to tell me that his friend Sandy was ill. After me, Hassan Izzat was cross-examined. His statements were identical. They then summoned Sandy and we dealt with him in the same way as we had dealt with Eppler.

The case against us collapsed. Hassan Izzat and I were taken back in custody to the officers' mess.

During that summer of 1942, in July, to be precise, Churchill had paid a secret visit to Egypt, after the collapse of the British Eighth Army and the seizure of El Alamein by Rommel. He changed the commanders of the

British Army, appointing Montgomery as commander-in-chief, then went to El Alamein to raise the morale of the British troops. He also met the two German spies, Eppler and his colleague – as I came to know later – and promised to spare their lives if they confessed. That was why Eppler made a full confession.

I was still detained in the officers' mess. One day in Ramadan my father called on me, nearly an hour before sunset, looking pale, haggard, and thoroughly exhausted. My guard, who was an artillery officer, immediately went out and left us alone to talk freely. I asked my father the reason for his visit. He tried to pull himself together and said: 'Major-General Ali Muwafi, the chief of army administration, called on me today. He said: "Your son's case is hopeless. It will be better if he confesses. If he does, leniency will be exercised in passing judgement; if he doesn't, he will be executed by the firing squad at dawn."'

I realized then that all their efforts to establish a case against me had completely failed and they were trying a cheap trick as a last resort. So I said to my father: 'To be executed by the firing squad I have to be tried by a High Military Tribunal and proved guilty. This is the system in the army. If they had convicted me already, they wouldn't have resorted to you to get a confession out of me.'

He was convinced. My father, God rest his soul, used to accept my views without questioning. He regained his composure and stayed with me until sunset. We had breakfast together, and then he went out completely reassured that his son's life was in no danger at all.

I later came to know that Muwafi called on my father at his office the following day to learn the outcome of our meeting. My father said to him, 'Listen, Pasha. If my son is guilty, shoot him! But if he is innocent, you must reinstate him.' Muwafi warned him of the consequences of my stubbornness, of persisting in denying them a confession. But my father insisted: 'Do what you like; I have nothing more to say.'

Meanwhile Montgomery had made preparations to secure victory over the Germans; he was ready with massive concentrations of troops and had cut Rommel's lines of supply in the Mediterranean. The British began to cool down a bit and their attitude to our case began to change. So, one day in Ramadan, an hour before sunset, the Chief of Staff of the Cairo military zone summoned me to inform me that in accordance with a supreme royal decree I would be relieved of my duties.

I stripped off my ranks. Muhammed Ibrahim Imam, chief of the Police Political Department, approached me and said, 'You must come with me to the Cairo Governorate headquarters; certain formalities must be attended to.' I realized that they were about to arrest me. I asked, 'Where exactly are we going? I want my orderly to know so that he can bring me my breakfast.'

'To the Aliens' Jail,' he said laconically.

As we walked together, the image of Zahran rose before my eyes almost visibly all the way to the Aliens' Jail. I saw him advancing towards death with his head held high, happy at what he had done.

At last I had achieved what Zahran had done before me. Overcome by this feeling, I realized, as never before, that Zahran was *not* defeated. He was executed, but his will was not. Was I not an extension of that same will, which had possessed me from early childhood? The will to challenge, the will to triumph?

We reached the jail. As I walked up the staircase to my room, I was overwhelmed by a strange joy – the joy of acknowledging a vast inner strength which I alone recognized.

I had won, just as Zahran had won, although he was hanged and I was stripped of my rank and arrested.

2

The Struggle
for the Liberation of Egypt

I

I passed through the gates of the Aliens' Jail for the first time on 26th Ramadan, AD 1942. Commonly believed to be the 'Night of Power' mentioned in the Koran, the eve of 27th Ramadan is a religious occasion which we observe in Egypt, particularly in rural areas, by serving a duckling, a goose, or a couple of capons (according to one's means) to break the fast.

The Aliens' Jail was reserved for cases connected with the war Britain was fighting, and its governor was one Mr Hickman, a British national of Maltese extraction. I went to my cell, which was on the first floor, and shortly afterwards, my orderly brought in some food. At sunset I performed the evening prayer, then broke my fast.

Until then I had felt more or less normal; I was hardly conscious of my sense of shock. Only when I had had my meal and smoked a cigarette (smoking being allowed, exceptionally, in that jail) was the full impact of the shock brought home to me. I felt utterly lost. What was I going to do? I would be staying in prison for quite a while, I was sure, but what was I going to do with myself afterwards? What could I possibly do now that my rank had been stripped and my army career ruined?

These and a myriad other questions jostled in my head. I strode up and down my room by sheer bewilderment – from corner to corner, wall to wall – for hours on end. At length, I sat down on the floor and leaned back against the bed (just as we do in the village), perhaps because in that position I felt closer to nature, or simply because I was used to sitting on the ground in our village. The village ... suddenly, I was thinking of the village!

True, it was only a thought, but it gave me immeasurable strength. My village was there in the heart of the Nile Delta and I should, naturally, go back to it. Why worry, then, or wonder about my destiny? A man's village is his peace of mind. All villagers have peace of mind, however lowly, poor, or weak they may be, because each has a home, or rather, a sense of home, even if his actual dwelling consists only of one room, a bathroom, and a *mastaba*. Once a man's door is shut behind him, no one could enjoy more peace of mind. Such is the quintessence of the peasant's life: peace of mind and security. Through the mutual process of giving – of direct, reciprocal satisfaction – peasant and land have come to be intimately bound together; working his land, a peasant feels in no need of anything else.

Although I had not as yet recognized my real self, I was able during that decisive soul-searching in prison to perceive a trait in my character that had earlier been obscure.

I realized that to be a simple peasant was enough to make me the happiest man on earth; the feeling that I needed nothing beyond my land, even though it didn't exceed two acres, proved to be a source of strength throughout the time I spent in jail. It is still so, in effect. Whatever the time or circumstances, the feeling that I am a peasant gives me a rare self-sufficiency. Indeed, the land is always there. I can go back to it at any time; I can work it myself, with my own hands, and that would be enough – more than enough. I control my fate; my will is mine alone; I am my own master.

A thought floated in my mind like a dark cloud moving out of the sun's path to free the light. Most people seek after what they do not possess and are thus enslaved by the very things they want to acquire. They become the prisoners of their desires even though they appear to be free – even though they are not physically kept under lock and key as I was, there, in jail.

II

The Aliens' Jail was unique. Each cell was provided with a bed, blankets, a chair, and a small table. Smoking was allowed, as I have said, although the warden had to light your cigarette himself as no matches or lighters were permitted in the cells. Encouraged by this, I asked for newspapers and was supplied with newspapers *and* books. (Discrimination between 'alien' and 'native' was practised everywhere, even in prison. In Cairo Central Prison, to which I was taken after a while, I spent a whole year completely cut off from the outside world and was denied everything – newspapers, books, a bed, even a chair.)

I thought of improving my English and so asked for some books in that language. The governor, Mr Hickman, sent me collections of short stories, which I enjoyed very much. One of the books I read in the Aliens' Jail and still remember dealt with a local society, in an English rural area, which met once a week to discuss a variety of subjects: their views of their community, current events in their own or neighbouring villages, farming, harvest conditions, and so on. A record of their conversations was kept in a special minutes book, so that it provided useful material for a quarterly publication. The idea appealed to me so much that I resolved that, once out of prison, I would initiate a similar project in my village. I thought of assembling relatives and friends for periodic meetings ... How I longed for the freedom of the countryside and that sense of inner peace one gets in one's own home. How sweet to listen again to the talk of peasants – spontaneous, genuine, and simple, yet rich in profound meanings, reflecting a culture thousands of years old.

Still, the time I spent in the Aliens' Jail was not, on the

whole, too bad. I read most of the time and went out for daily walks round the prison courtyard (walking being my favourite sport). We were only allowed two 'breaks' a day, fifteen minutes each, during which to walk within the prison walls.

Many interesting things happened while I was in prison; unfortunately, I cannot recall them all. I do remember that one day I was woken by a female voice singing, 'No, Indeed, Abdul!' a famous hit of those days, only to switch suddenly to crying and screaming exactly like someone in a melodramatic movie. I was told it was Hikmat Fahmi the dancer, who was kept in the next cell, being one of the defendants in our case as the person who had let the Nile houseboat to the German spies. In fact, all those kept in the Aliens' Jail had been involved in cases brought against them by the British authorities and, when the investigation of their cases was completed, would be removed to other detention centres. I was not surprised, therefore, when one day I was taken to the governor for another round of cross-examination in the presence of Eppler, the German spy. I did not, of course, alter my statements. I was standing there, waiting, when the telephone rang and Hickman answered it. He was apparently being asked about the outcome of my re-examination for I heard him say (not suspecting that I understood English quite well), 'It's no use! He's denying everything!'

My colleague Hassan Izzat was also detained in the Aliens' Jail but we could not see each other. When the wardens learned that we were officers, they began to help us exchange messages. They also began to show more sympathy, as well as friendliness and respect, in dealing with me. They practically introduced me to most of the prison inmates: a German called Max, who had been there for eighteen months; an Italian who had already spent eight months in prison; and many others. As no one had been there for less than six months, I concluded I was going to stay for an equally long time – a grim prospect, especially as it was already winter and our clothes were not warm enough. It was all the more serious as we spent our time in the cells and were almost totally deprived of proper outdoor exercise.

But one morning I was surprised to see the jailer come in loaded up with things for me. One item in particular, apart from the food parcels my family sent me, was breathtakingly exciting – a woollen dressing gown. I unfolded it, put it down on the bed, and kept staring at it and touching it in disbelief. It was excessively splendid, just like the clothes one sees in the movies. Incredulous, though overjoyed, I called the jailer and asked whether it was really meant for me. It had been sent to Cell no. 7, definitely to me, I was assured. Well – I put it on and felt extremely happy. Even as a captain in the Egyptian Army I could not afford such a gown. How on earth had my family got it? They must have cashed my end-of-service bonus of £80, I thought. I was deeply moved, and performed the rites of ablution prior to a thanksgiving prayer. It was not so much the dressing gown itself that moved me, delightful though it was, but the gesture – the fact that someone still remembered me, that I still meant something to people, to some people at least.

III

I began to get acclimatized to life in prison, especially when I was allowed to see Hassan Izzat That in effect meant that the investigation of our case had been completed. He used to talk about his plans for the future: catching fish behind the Aswan Dam, farming projects, and so on, while I could think of nothing but to return to my land and make a fresh start.

But the 'settling down' mood which followed from acclimatization (one of God's blessings) did not last for long. One day the jailer told me to pack my things. 'Well?' I asked. 'You're to be moved,' he said. I asked repeatedly about my destination but got no answer. So I packed my things and went to the governor's room, where I was given back my shoelaces, necktie, electric razor, and £3 (which my family had kept for me at the 'reception').

'Are your things intact?' they asked. I said they were. 'Sign here, please.' I did so, whereupon I was ordered to walk up to the prison door, flanked by soldiers. A car was parked just outside, but the staircase leading down to it was covered with blankets on both sides so that I saw nothing at all on the way down. It was as though I was being kidnapped. Hassan Izzat was already in the car. Apparently I was the last to get on board, for the moment I did so a blanket was thrown over the car and off we went.

Minutes later we were at the Cairo Railway Station. We alighted on a platform for a southbound train. We were obviously going somewhere in Upper Egypt. The platform was, surprisingly, empty of all passengers. Only policemen, in great strength, were to be seen, as though we were a formidable force that could pose a threat to the security of the state and must therefore be watched closely. A small diesel-engine train waited for us. We were bundled into it. Other passengers were already on board, also detainees, two of whom, I remember, were senior army officers who had dabbled in party politics. Each one of us was guarded by a police officer sitting close beside him. The train started.

It took us to another detention centre, this time in Upper Egypt. This detention centre was only a mile and a quarter away from Almenia (about 160 miles from Cairo). The car that took us from the train there was also covered with blankets so that we were in darkness all the way. It wasn't a detention centre in the usual sense of the term but a huge, sumptuous palace, standing in isolation on the banks of al-Ibrahimiah Canal, surrounded by areas of dry land and backing on to a small village not very different from Mit Abul-Kum. I wondered what a palace like that was doing in such a place.

I came to learn that it belonged to a prominent member

of the Wafd Party – Abdel Rahman al-Maqusi – who, being in financial straits, had rented it to the government which had turned it, or was about to turn it, into a detention centre. When we arrived, army engineers were busy erecting barbed-wire fences all around the palace, although in fact the walls were so high nobody would have dreamed of climbing them.

I stayed in Maqusah – that was the name of the place – from December 1942 to late October or early November 1943. In November 1942 Montgomery had launched his famous counterattack in El Alamein against the Italians and the Germans in the desert, after cutting Rommel's supply lines (though Rommel managed to withdraw with his forces intact). It was perhaps that victory by the allies that quieted the British and made them proceed no further in punishing us.

The early days of my stay in Maqusah were indeed hard. The palace itself was luxurious: it had French mirrors, superb woodwork, stained-glass windows, and beautiful bathrooms. I had never seen their like before and was simply fascinated by them; but, in time, I got used to them and began to see the place for what it was – a prison, no more, no less. We were particularly irritated when they fixed iron bars to the windows, surely an unnecessary precaution when the entire building was surrounded with barbed-wire fences. We removed the bars and, when they fixed them again, removed them again until, one day, it was decided that the barbed wire was adequate.

Eppler's half-brother, Hassan Gafar, was also being detained in Maqusah. Although he had played no part at all in what happened, the British still detained him as a precautionary measure. I found him a decent and very nice young man. As he knew both German and English, it occurred to me to ask him to teach me German. I approached him about it and he immediately agreed. I had read somewhere that Sheikh Muhammad Abduh (one of the leaders of Egypt's modern 'revival') had discovered that the best method of learning French was to read a novel in the language with the help of someone who knew both French and Arabic – a novel being a representative slice of life, with examples of the language used in conversation, description, abstract thought, and so on.

Hassan Gafar had a copy of a novel by Edgar Wallace which had been translated into German. It was arranged that we should read it together. We actually sat down on the staircase of the palace for our daily lesson. In the beginning I read no more than four lines a day, then half a page, then a whole page, and, eventually, seven months later, I could cover a whole chapter in a day. At the end of ten months I had finished the entire novel and my command of German proved equal to that of Hassan Gafar.

When I visited Austria not long ago, I made a speech in German. Kissinger heard it, I was told, and commented to ex-President Ford that my accent was better than his, as Kissinger came from southern Germany while I spoke with a northern accent which is closer to the 'accepted' pronunciation. During the same visit the Austrian chancellor made a point of introducing me to the cardinal of Austria, an important Vatican figure. I met him and realized he spoke a number of languages, including English, French, and Arabic. He asked me in the course of our conversation about the story of my learning German. He was quite surprised to hear it – I still remember the look on his face.

Visits by members of my family were confined to once a month, train fares being too expensive for them. However, my colleagues and I often pretended to be sick and were frequently sent to hospital in Almenia. Once while I was there I went to the library, where I met Waji Khalil. He was a companion-in-struggle who, knowing I would be in Almenia at the time, arranged to see me to let me know that his fellow officers had decided to offer the sum of £10 as monthly assistance to my family in Cairo. The effect of that gesture of solidarity was indescribable – for there I was, a detainee, miles away from my colleagues and not even, strictly, one of them any longer.

The year rolled on and Ramadan came round again, but the scene had shifted from the Aliens' Jail to Maqusah. As is my practice during Ramadan, I read through the whole of the Koran three times (once every ten days). It was already 1943 and the defeats of the Axis had started. The tide had turned and the course of the entire war was in fact beginning to change, especially after the Russians had fought the magnificent battle at Stalingrad. They were helped by the bitterly cold Russian winter – that general who had defeated Napoleon and was now the main factor in crushing the Germans. Before 1943 was out, we received orders to move to another detention centre near Cairo – the well-known Zaytun Detention Centre.

IV

Two categories of Zaytun detainees could be distinguished. The first, like me, were Egyptians fighting the British presence in Egypt, or Egyptianized Syrians and Lebanese who, motivated by opposition to French colonialism (and the traditional French presence in the Levant in circumstances similar to the British presence in Egypt), offered their services to the Vichy government and the Germans. The second comprised members of parties opposed to the ruling Wafd Party, such as the Young Egypt Party and the National Bloc Party. The latter had been formed by Makram Ubayd, who broke away from the Wafd and published a *Black Book*, a booklet in fact, revealing secrets which condemned the Wafd political practices. Although el-Nahas, the Wafd leader, was in power at the time, the *Black Book* was published and widely circulated.

At Zaytun I got to know an interesting detainee, a count who came from the Baltic. He was a very nice person. Although he lived in a small room in the basement, as completely shorn of his power as any other detainee, he could never forget that he was a European count. He still gave orders and spoke with authority as though living in his own palace. He walked about haughtily with an aristocratic air he could never relinquish. He became our laughing stock and, in fact, the sole source of amusement to us.

Life was very boring at Zaytun. Time seemed to pass too slowly and we had nothing at all to do. We thought of breeding rabbits. We initially bought two or three pairs and in three months' time our rabbits had multiplied to fill up the only spacious hall in the house. We had to walk around them to get to our rooms, and it was well-nigh impossible to walk, or even take a single step, amid that army of rabbits. What were we to do with them? We discovered a unique talent in our friend, the aristocratic count. He could cook very well, and particularly rabbit. Naturally we began to profit from his hobby. For some time we lived on rabbits, breeding and eating them, until, one day, one of them fell sick. Infection swept through them and in a few days their numbers decreased practically as fast as they had multiplied. Once more the hall was empty and spacious. Our friend had no use for the pot he had filled with rabbit every morning and was in the habit of putting between the two mattresses on his bed to keep warm when we were late for dinner.

One of the people I came to know rather well in Zaytun and still remember was the Under-Secretary to the Minister of the Interior. He had incurred el-Nahas' disfavour and so was detained although he did not belong to any party. His name was Abu Shady. I saw him again after the 1952 Revolution, when his property had been placed into state custody; I don't know why or under what circumstances. It was late 1961, after the breakdown of the union with Syria. All 'state custodianship' of property was in fact party-based. The breakdown of the union with Syria gave rise to certain misgivings on Abdel Nasser's part which made the Egyptian people suspicious of the government. Some of Nasser's assistants encouraged him to think that such popular suspicions in effect constituted a counter-revolution, and hence proceeded to place people's property into 'state custody'. Ironically, the list included Abu Shady, though he did not belong to any party but was an exemplary civil servant who behaved with a sense of responsibility and took only fair and sound measures. Still, it was natural that the breakdown of the unity with Syria should make people *talk* and criticize the regime. Abu Shady was the victim of this. The same thing happened, after 1965, to the Muslim Brotherhood.

Then the authorities were led to believe that the Muslim Brotherhood were plotting to overthrow the government, that is, to mount a counter-revolution. This, however, was purely imaginary. Perhaps the rulers really believed it or they might have wanted to achieve certain objectives of their own in this way. In any case, thousands of victims fell, including Said Qutb, an eminent leader of the Brotherhood, who was executed. Accused collectively of plotting to topple the government, some members of the Brotherhood had no specific charges brought against them but were arrested all the same and many of them received harsh sentences. All were kept in jail or in detention centres until I ordered the closure of all such centres after I had purged Nasser's major power bloc in 1971. Those serving specific sentences, whether members of the Brotherhood or involved in other political cases, were all released immediately after the 1973 battle.

V

But to return to the Zaytun, I must say it had a few advantages over Maqusah. It was in Cairo, so our families could come to visit us without having to pay expensive train fares. Besides, the Zaytun was actually a house with a big garden where we could move more freely than in the cramped courtyard of Maqusah. To kill the time, Hassan Izzat and I decided to grow clover in the **garden** to feed our rabbits. But when the rabbits had gone, we grew sweet potatoes, and that was my first experience with growing potatoes.

It was a quiet life, disturbed only by the owner of a printing office in al-Hussein District who, whenever he was released from detention, printed another leaflet attacking the government and was immediately sent back to us. The reason he preferred life in detention to life outside was that the authorities decided to pay every detainee a monthly salary of £7,50 piastres. Everybody except Hassan Izzat and me received it. I had persuaded Hassan to decline it as it was an affront to our dignity to receive money from the occupation authorities. The printer, however, liked the money, especially since his board and lodging were free. He was eager to stay in detention for as long as possible in the hope of ending up with considerable capital.

One day we were perturbed to learn that a new superintendent had been appointed. He was notorious on account of his misconduct and had been repeatedly dismissed, but then again, by string-pulling, reinstated. His uncle was a Wafdi senator for the Governorate of al-Buhayrah and his family wielded great power, stemming from their origins in Libya.

I do not remember the reasons for the row I had with the new superintendent but I can recall the consequences clearly. I assembled all the detainees and, together, we brought out all the luggage and furniture we had in our rooms and set it up on the staircase leading to the first floor so that we were barricaded against any intrusion. A little later, the superintendent came up to my room and, revolver in hand, barged in, swearing and threatening. 'You're a coward,' I said, 'to threaten an unarmed man!' Whereupon he left in great anger, ordered many soldiers to guard his room, and thought it safer not to go out again.

I wanted to give the impertinent fellow a lesson, so I climbed through the windows from one room to the next until I finally reached his. When I jumped down, as if from space, right in front of him, he panicked. 'You've locked your room, haven't you, and put guards outside!' I said. 'You believe you're safe enough, don't you? But here I am . . . I could wring your neck; I could do anything I want with you! Do you realize that?' A heated conversation ensued, after which I went back to my room. Then we barricaded the staircase completely.

In 1943–4 the world political situation had decisively changed. It became quite clear that Germany was heading for defeat, which provided a good chance for us to be released. Hassan Izzat and I thought it was time to arouse public opinion in Zaytun. So we staged a mutiny and shots were fired at us from the garden – a deliberate escalation by the government which we had expected and, I dare say, wanted. In return, we decided to teach them a lesson they would never forget. But how were we to go about it?

VI

Six of us, it was agreed, would escape. A plan was laid down and executed very meticulously. The best time for escape was in the evening during the change of guard, when the place would be sufficiently noisy. The method was to make a hole in the roof, which was not difficult (it was lath and plaster work), and to use a common stepladder to get on to the rooftop. On the appointed day I climbed out first and lay face downward so that nobody could see me; then I stretched down my arm to help pull up my colleagues while Hassan stood in the middle of the room below to help them. He was the last to come out. We all crept down to the street. It was pitch dark but we distinguished the car, an Oldsmobile, which was waiting for us as arranged, and the six of us drove away.

Hassan was proud of the car. He was told it had new tyres, a rarity in wartime as no new tyres could be acquired except by special permission of the British authorities.

But we had driven barely two miles when we had a flat tyre! Hassan suggested we go to any nearby garage to get it fixed but I refused. 'You carry on and do what you want,' I said; 'you'll be the runaway detainees, as decided. Muhsin and I have something different in mind.'

Muhsin Fadil was a fine man who had spent a good many years in France. Where should we hide until the morning, when our plan could be carried out? Muhsin suggested we go to the apartment of a French lady he knew well. She had lived in Egypt with an Egyptian friend for some time and then, jilted by him, was waiting for the war to end so that she could return to France. Her apartment was downtown, in Ismailia Square. We rang the bell. She opened the door herself and gave us a warm welcome. Muhsin told her our story and she was wholeheartedly sympathetic.

She was a great lady, in fact, who represented the spirit of the French people at their best – a noble, freedom-loving people, just like the Egyptians. She was strongly opposed to our returning to the detention centre after we had carried out our plan in the morning. Her words still echo in my ears: 'How could you go back to prison, now you're free, of your own free will? I have saved two thousand pounds. It's all I have. Take it! Take it all and run away to any other country. Come on, go!' We thanked her but declined the offer. She then suggested that we should hide in her apartment and she'd pay all expenses, however long we stayed. What a remarkable lady she was! She kept urging us to take all she had – arguing that she would make a fresh start, old as she was – simply for the love of freedom. In the morning a breakfast table was laid, complete with Arabic newspapers – it was perfect. We had breakfast, thanked her, then went out and hailed a taxi to the royal Abidin Palace.

We entered the palace. At the reception desk one of the palace secretaries stood by the Royal Ceremonies Book which was open, as usual, for anyone to sign his name, whether to express thanks for 'royal kindness' or to take leave, prior to departure, etc. We headed for it directly and signed our names. We then stated that we were detainees at Zaytun; that we had come expressly to tell the king that the government should not submit to the British authorities; that it was completely unacceptable that we should be treated so badly; that the two of us would, of our own free will, return at once to the detention centre; and that four of our colleagues had escaped with us, although they would not go back but would continue their life of freedom as hostages outside prison in defiance of the government and for the restoration of everybody's freedom.

The secretary in charge of the Royal Ceremonies Book was dumbfounded. He rushed to the Master of Ceremonies, who came down and at once recognized me (he was governor of Almenia while I was at Maqusah). He said our decision was sheer lunacy and that it would simply lead from one crisis to another. I explained that we were going straight back to the detention centre and he'd just have to lump it; whereupon we went out, while he and his junior staff simply stared at us. We took a taxi and returned to the Zaytun. The gates opened wide, so we drove right in and reported back.

Nobody had found out about our escape until the following morning. The state prosecuting attorney arrived to 'investigate' our case. At the cross-examination we stated that we had done it as a protest against maltreatment, that the whole operation was designed to give a lesson to the Ministry of the Interior and the Zaytun administration. Naturally, the superintendent was transferred and our treatment improved considerably. We had a relatively quiet time until October 1944.

Mustafa el-Nahas was still in power. Since the British imposed him as premier in February 1942, the king had been waiting for a chance to remove him. Now was the time to do it, for in October 1944, the allies were assured of victory and the British had completely calmed down, their misgivings utterly dispelled. So the king removed el-

Nahas and appointed Ahmed Maher as premier. Maher had been an eminent Wafdi leader, who as the result of differences with el-Nahas had broken away and formed another party – the Saadi Party (Named after Saad Zaghloul).

As soon as Ahmed Maher came to power, those colleagues of ours who were members of the National Bloc Party were released. There was a kind of alliance between the National Bloc, the Saadists, and the Constitutional Liberals, in opposition to the Wafd. Members of the Young Egypt Party were also released. In fact, everybody was released except our group, who were detained on orders from the British authorities. How long were we going to stay in detention? It was already late 1944 and the outcome of the war had become more than obvious. Something had to be done. I initiated a hunger strike. My colleagues could not persist but as I would not give up I had to be moved to the new Qasr al-Ayni Hospital, in accordance with existing regulations.

I ended my hunger strike in hospital. Shortly afterwards Hassan Izzat (who had escaped before as one of the four) called on me. 'What are you doing here? We must find a way of getting you out!' he said. So a plan for my escape was laid down.

At lunchtime, when the hospital was swarming with people going in and out, Hassan drove up. He parked his small Austin beside the doctors' cars but didn't stop the engine, while I managed to get away from my guard as we threaded our way through the crowd. I jumped in beside Hassan and in no time we were out of the hospital grounds. A two-minute drive took us to Fumm al-Khalij, where a hideout (a very good apartment, in fact) had been prepared by Hassan.

That was in October 1944, as I have said. I continued to live as a fugitive until September 1945, when martial law was lifted and, in accordance with the law of the land, my detention came to an end. This is the advantage of the rule of law, a principle which I respect, believe in, and apply now that I am the President of Egypt.

What happened to me for a whole year – from October 1944 to September 1945 – when I lived as a 'wanted' man, a fugitive who could be arrested at any minute and taken back into detention or even to prison, is another story ...

VII

The time I spent as a fugitive was certainly eventful. As I had to earn my living and support my family (my father being too poor to help out in any way), I was forced to emerge from my hideout and work. I grew a beard and, to complete my disguise, called myself Hadji Muhammad.

I worked first as a porter, loading and unloading a truck belonging to Hassan Izzat. The driver and I worked for a private trader, Ghuwaybah, who purveyed for the British Army at Ismailia. One day, I remember, we arrived late in Ismailia and Ghuwaybah was kind enough to let us spend the night in his own office, on the floor. (I met him lately as President and we had a very charming talk.)

Ghuwaybah was almost a millionaire, a member of a class of parvenus often referred to as the 'war rich'. When Nasser issued the 'socialist' laws of 1961, Ghuwaybah put his money literally under the floorboards and went about in rags so that Nasser and his men actually believed he was destitute. His was not an isolated case; many rich people did the same in the sixties and before Nasser's time. Down their long history the Egyptian people have always found a means of deceiving oppressive rulers, especially when that ruler's orders went counter to their wishes and their interests.

Ghuwaybah entrusted me at a later stage with taking vegetables and fruit to the British camp at Tell el-Kebir in the Canal Zone. The first consignment consisted of poor-quality oranges. I was surprised at first, but later found out that the Egyptian purveyor had struck a typical bargain with the British quartermaster. Not long after, we were asked to stop all supplies to the British as they were now getting everything from the Jews in Palestine. Perhaps the latter proved better swindlers and bribers, or there might have been a different reason, unknown to me. Whatever the reason may be, my work for Ghuwaybah came to an end.

After this I worked in a town called Mazghunah, near Cairo. My job was to transport stone rubble from ships anchored in the Nile to the site of a new road being built between Cairo and Aswan. We worked nonstop from the crack of dawn till sundown, then I went to a small restaurant for a meal. After the hard work and virtual starvation of the whole day, the hot lentil soup I usually had was delicious. When I'd had my soup and felt warm and full, I went to a tin-roofed garage to spend the night.

That was in December 1944. Early in 1945 I moved to Abu Kebir in the province of Sharqiya. A new canal was being dug in the area (it was the established practice of the Department of Irrigation to have a new canal dug every year), and I joined the work force on the project. I rented rooms from a watchman – a member of a local police force doing night duty in the provinces. One night it poured with rain and, as the roof was made from the stalks of cotton plants, the rain came in and began to patter on what little furniture there was and threaten to drench me. I fetched the small tent I always carried about with me and covered myself with the canvas, which kept me dry, though the noise of the rain beating furiously against it kept me awake for a while. Finally, whether through sheer exhaustion or because of the regular rhythm of the patter, I managed to sleep – and very soundly too – until morning. The watchman was courteous enough to offer me fresh milk (sometimes skimmed or not so fresh) every morning. I drank it, unaware that I had a poor digestion and that milk in particular did not agree with me.

Once the canal was dug I was again out of work, but not for long, as work was available at Sannur, a small town in

the desert east of the Nile. I got a job as a transport con-
tractor with the Egyptian Company for Mines and
Quarries, which had the concession to develop the marble
quarry in that region. That quarry was actually in use in
the days of the Pharaohs but had been neglected for centuries until rediscovered by Muhammad Ali. Its marble
was used to build his mosque at the Cairo Citadel. It was
almost 31 miles from the Nile. Rest points were built by
Muhammad Ali on the road to it, 10 miles apart, and they
still stand.

It was ironic that 'my' marble should have been used in
building the royal 'Resthouse', ordered by King Farouk,
near the Pyramids. Every block of marble in that building was quarried and transported by me personally to the
building site!

VIII

With the end of the war, martial law was lifted. It was September 1945 when I could put an end to running and
resume my normal life. I went back to my home, after
three years of homelessness and deprivation, wore my regular clothes, and once more assumed the normal image
– plain and undisguised – that my family and friends had
known.

Out of work, I regarded a 5-millime coin as practically
hard currency. I walked from my home in Kubri al-
Qubbah to al-Atabah every day, which was more than
12 miles, simply because I could not afford the tramway
fare of 6 millimes.

I have always been a perfectionist, and that applies to
the way I dressed as well. At the time I had a jacket which
I loved (I was proud of it, actually) and which I had worn
only a few times before my detention. I decided to sell
it to a second-hand shop in town. I took it and went to the
shop, but a few yards from it I got cold feet and stopped
dead. I was terrified the shopkeeper would think I had

stolen the jacket, as it was unlikely a man in rags would be in possession of such a smart garment. I changed my mind and returned home on foot, carrying my jacket. I knew, to be sure, that the shopkeeper would ask no questions. Indeed, I was certain he would pay reasonably well for it and that, however little, his price would help me out in such terrible straits; but I simply could not have my image tarnished in the eyes of a perfect stranger, whatever the cost.

Well, what about my image in my own eyes? Did it live up to my expectations? I was a free man once again, it is true (automatically, that is, with the lifting of martial law), but did I feel like a prisoner who has just been released? Obviously not; Egypt was still shackled and the people were as far from controlling their own fate as ever. So the minute I regained my freedom, I started to form a secret organization, feeling that personal liberty could hardly be real until my entire homeland had been liberated.

A few days after I had emerged from my hideout, in September 1945, I got in touch with an old acquaintance – Omar Abu Ali, the brother of my colleague Saudi Hussein (the pilot who had been sent to Rommel and shot down). Omar introduced me to a young man called Hussein Tewfik who had been active in Maadi, shooting British soldiers. Was the shooting of a handful of British soldiers the means of liberating Egypt? Not by any means. But it was perhaps a sort of limbering up for the main task of removing the men who had supported the British – those led by Mustafa el-Nahas, head of the Wafd Party, who had lost our respect since the British had forced us to accept him, at gunpoint, as premier on 4 February 1942. Nothing is more painful for young men than to be disillusioned in a leader who was once their idol. When we were schoolboys we had gone out twice a day to have a look at el-Nahas (cheering and applauding) as he rode down to work and back. He had been a mythical hero – a peerless symbol of patriotism, self-sacrifice, and devotion.

On the Fourth of February he lost everything and we came to regard him as a traitor. His disloyalty to Egypt and her people made his removal a national duty. We therefore decided to get rid of him.

It was the established practice for el-Nahas to make a speech at the Saadi Club on the Prophet's Birthday, which, that year, fell on 6 September. Several members of our organization and I lay in wait for him as his car left Garden City and joined the stream of traffic in Qasr el-Ayni Street. The police were deployed everywhere to ensure that no riot would prevent el-Nahas from making his speech; indeed, although Ali Maher was in power and el-Nahas ousted, nobody could possibly prevent him. There were certain conventions that everyone observed at the time.

I had trained our team in the use of hand grenades. Hussein Tewfik was picked as the man to do it, and he did hurl the grenade at the right time. However, as the driver of el-Nahas' car was forced to speed up a little to avoid running into a tram in Qasr el-Ayni Street, the grenade exploded six seconds too late and missed the car alto-gether. The splinters hit a bus carrying ATS girls of the British armed forces.

The rest of us were still in position, watching the opera-tion. When the grenade missed, we withdrew quietly. We took a tram back to Ismailia Square (el-Tahrir Square to-day), which was only a few minutes' walk from the scene of the incident. We went to Café Astra, our favourite meeting place.

It was at the Astra that we decided to get rid of Amin Osman Pasha, who had held the Finance Ministry port-folio in the el-Nahas administration since 4 February 1942. This was not why we condemned Amin Osman. Indeed, his influence on the Wafd policies, or on el-Nahas himself, was negligible. But he was more than friendly with the British, supporting their presence in Egypt with unprecedented fervour.

At the time Amin Osman had formed a kind of political party which he called the 'Revival League'. Let me put on record here, incidentally, that I had joined every single political party in Egypt, either out of curiosity or in the hope that it might provide a way out of our predicament. The headquarters of the Revival League were in Adly Street, in the centre of Cairo. One of its six political principles – the second – stated that an ineluctable bond tied us to the British. In addition to this, Osman had declared that the relationship between Egypt and Great Britain was in effect a Catholic marriage, so that even if Britain chose to dissociate herself, Egypt could never do the same. That declaration was tantamount to a self-imposed death sentence.

On 6 January 1946, the sentence was carried out. Amin Osman had returned from Britain a couple of days earlier, had called on the British High Commissioner in the afternoon, and in the evening went to the League headquarters. According to plan, Tewfik was waiting for him at the door of the building. As Osman was about to take the elevator, Tewfik called out: 'Pasha! Pasha!' When he turned around to answer the caller, Tewfik fired his pistol at him. Tewfik, in calling him, applied the rule that forbade the shooting of a man in the back.

There was a blackout in Cairo at the time and Tewfik could have got away easily. As it happened, an Egyptian air force officer called Mursi who was passing by witnessed the entire incident and alerted everybody. People started to give chase and actually cornered Hussein. He had two hand grenades I had given him but asked him not to use except in an emergency and away from people. He hurled one of them behind the wall of Sanduq ad-Dayn, and the explosion did the trick. His chasers fled with no casualties at all, and he returned quietly to his home in Heliopolis.

I was sitting all the while at a nearby café. When I heard the explosion, I rushed to the scene to make sure no one was hurt. Then, reassured, I took the tram and went home to Kubri al-Qubbah.

The story of Amin Osman's assassination was all over

the morning papers. One report spoke of the desperate attempt to save his life by the British High Commissioner, who had summoned the chief surgeon of the British Army; another referred to the meeting that had taken place in the afternoon of the same day between Osman and the High Commissioner. In those days it was a very great honour for any politician to see the British High Commissioner, for it often implied nomination for the premiership. Osman had enjoyed the care and protection of the British government (and its representatives in Egypt), the people realized, but had been killed all the same. The impact of this was quite obvious as the people were shown that the British were incapable of protecting their supporters. Indeed, those who had derived strength from their association with the British were now shown to be egregiously weak.

The assassination of Amin Osman thus achieved its objective. Apart from removing a staunch supporter of colonialism, we had seriously damaged the prestige of the British authorities and managed to mar the image of effective colonialism, with unprecedented decisiveness, in the eyes of the people.

The police were immediately active. Investigations were carried out on the spot. The air force officer, Mursi, volunteered to help and gave an accurate description of the killer, which led the police to Tewfik, who had been on their list of suspects in view of his earlier activity against the British in Maadi. They called on him at his father's house while he was having his supper. Incapable of producing an alibi, he was taken into custody.

Hussein Tewfik would not talk at all on his first day in custody. The prosecuting attorney did his best to make him break his silence on the second day but, as Hussein held out, the clever attorney asked the press to hint that it was a *crime passionnel*. Knowing that Hussein was a paranoiac case, the attorney set the trap and Hussein immediately fell into it. To defend his reputation, Hussein Tewfik made a full confession, much in the same way as Eppler, the German spy, had done, if not even more impetuously.

Tewfik made his confession on 10 January. From him the police came to know about the arms dump in Jabal al-Mokattam. That was it, I thought, but still hoped that somehow Hussein had managed not to inform the police of my part in the operation.

On 11 January King Abdul Aziz of Saud arrived in Cairo on a state visit, at the invitation of King Farouk. The city, indeed, the whole country, had been preparing for it for a long time. The late King Saud was a noble and generous hero. He had proved quite hospitable during King Farouk's visit to Saudi Arabia and the latter wanted to return his hospitality. Above all, King Saud loved Egypt. The Saudi ruling family's love for Egypt is traditional, and each monarch is always careful to maintain good and close relations with Egypt. I went out, just like everybody else, to welcome the king. We assembled in Opera Square to wait for the royal motorcade. It struck me that it was heavily guarded; I thought it was in fact ridiculous, for who would ever think of hurting King Abdul Aziz? We attacked only Egypt's enemies, never her friends.

By two o'clock in the afternoon the procession was over, and I went back home immediately. There was nothing I could do but sit down and wait, in nerve-racking suspense.

I did not have to wait too long. At two o'clock in the morning there was a knock on the door and in *they* came, just as they had done in 1942, though there were no Britishers this time. It was a very cold night. I jumped out of bed and faced them. 'Have you a search warrant?' I asked. 'We have the prosecuting attorney himself,' they replied.

'I am indeed here,' said Kamel Kawish, the assistant attorney general, arrogantly, 'and I am personally in charge of the case of Amin Osman's murder.' It was he, I understood, who had set the trap for Tewfik and driven him to confession.

When every room in the house had been searched, I was taken away into custody, back to the Aliens' Jail, just like 1942.

IX

At the jail I was put into solitary confinement. I asked about Tewfik and learned that he had been put into Cell 1, a very spacious room, on the first floor. The rest of our society's members were in solitary confinement. As I had previous knowledge of the Aliens' Jail, both staff and wardens, I came to know easily what was going on. The prosecuting attorney Kamel Kawish, I was told, held night sessions with my colleagues, cross-examined them 'amicably', and even bought them dinners. He'd come to be quite friendly with them, I was assured, especially Tewfik. What next, I wondered.

Something had to be done, naturally. I contacted my colleagues through the wardens and advised them to take back all their previous statements as that was the only means of getting them off the hook. Some of them took my advice and actually went back on their confessions. Realizing that something was happening to disturb his plans and upset the case, and that I was somehow involved in it, the prosecuting attorney ordered me moved to the second floor where I would be incapable of contacting the other defendants. After that I couldn't contact anybody.

For a whole week nobody called, nobody even approached me. Then suddenly, one night, around two o'clock in the morning, the door was opened and I was whisked off to the examination room. A means of intimidation, I thought; they wouldn't have chosen that unearthly hour otherwise as it was January and very cold indeed. The cross-examination started:

- What have you got to say?
- About what?
- Hussein Tewfik has made a confession in which he states that you have been involved ...

I realized that Tewfik had made a clean breast of everything. He had omitted nothing, down to the minutest details, almost like a tape recorder. On the other hand, some of the boys had taken back their earlier confessions and so upset the case a little. So, I argued, if it could be established that the confessions were made under duress, the whole case would collapse. Turning this over in my mind, I said to the prosecuting attorney:

- Hussein Tewfik's statement is false, through and through. As for the others, I am willing to confront them, one by one, to show you that their previous statements are equally false and that is why, incidentally, some of them have already gone back on them. Besides, an important fact should be recorded in the minutes.
- What fact?
- The fact that you summoned me for cross-examination at two o'clock in the morning.
- It is mentioned.
- I know. What I mean is it should be mentioned that this is a measure of duress. You woke me up and dragged me out of bed, unnecessarily, that is, when you could have worked by day. What you did has given me a severe nervous shock.

They put down my words, then concluded the minutes in the assurance that, due to the confessions made by Tewfik and the others, their winning of the case was a foregone conclusion. Subsequently, my questioning was conducted by day.

At one of these sessions, I remember, the prosecuting attorney asked me, 'Haven't you anything more to say?'

'There's nothing for me to add,' I replied. 'All I can say is that I still insist on confronting all the defendants.'

Seeing that I was adamant, Kawish now pursued a new line, showing some uncertainty himself.

'Do you know Omar Abu Ali?' 'Do you know this man, that man,' etc. I answered that I knew them all, of course. This one was the brother of an old friend, that one I came to know on such-and-such an occasion. I still justified being acquainted with them but denied strongly that that had anything to do with the claims in their statements and, to prove it, I insisted I was ready to confront them individually. Afraid lest my persistence should mess up his case, the prosecuting attorney then ordered that I should be returned to my cell and left alone.

For a whole week I was indeed left alone. It was a week of tension. Our minds fought a difficult battle, his trying to pin the guilt on to me, mine trying to pull the case to pieces. Having thought it out thoroughly, I had come to the conclusion that Muhammad Kamil, a young cousin of Tewfik's (who is now the foreign secretary of Egypt), couldn't have made a confession. Young as he was, he should hold out, if anyone could. I tried to contact him through the warden and eventually succeeded. His response encouraged me. He was dependable and, working together, I hoped we could pull the case apart.

Meanwhile Kawish continued his socializing with Tewfik and the other defendants. He still stayed with them well into the night, still ordered meals to be brought in from restaurants in town. It was only too obvious that he was trying to win them over, so I decided to outplay him.

One evening I surprised everybody by asking to see the prison governor. The moment I saw him – before he had a chance to enquire about the reason for our meeting – I said: 'May I have a pen and paper? I would like to send a telegram to the public prosecutor.'

He ordered them, and I started to write. I said that I demanded that another prosecuting attorney be appointed, in view of the great pressure I was being subjected to. The present examining attorney wanted me, I said, to admit to having done things I couldn't possibly have done, while the prison governor and political police officers had exercised the worst form of torture against me.

The governor was astounded when he read my statement. 'What is this you have written? Who are the police officers you say have tortured you?'

'Tewfik al-Said and al-Jazzar.'

'But when? How?'

'That's my business.'

A specific incident lay behind that story I had made up. One day before I had been moved from the ground floor to the second, the warden Tewfik al-Said opened the door of my cell to let me out for the permitted fifteen-minute walk in the prison court. We had known each other from the days of my first sentence in the Aliens' Jail in 1942. We exchanged greetings, then he suddenly said: 'There's no point in denying, Anwar. Everybody has confessed. Not only confessed, but taken us along to the arms dump in Mount Muqattam; and we've actually collected your weapons. Everything has been proved and the case is as good as won; why insist on denying it?'

'So you want me to confess?' I said.

'Yes.'

'Have you any doubts at all that we killed Amin Osman? Let me tell you that we did indeed do it because he was a traitor and had to be executed.'

'Incredible! Have you forgotten all about the laws of the land?' he remonstrated.

'There is a law, no doubt,' I replied, 'but it doesn't apply to traitors; we must deal with those ourselves.'

'Anyway,' al-Said said with relief. 'I'm glad you are confessing to me. Confession will help you get off with a lighter sentence.'

I turned suddenly to face him and said vehemently, 'Listen, Tewfik. Do you really believe we killed Amin Osman? I said that simply to challenge and confront you personally. If other people were here I wouldn't have said a word about it. For a confession to be valid, it must be made in the presence of two witnesses at least. You haven't overlooked that fact, have you?'

'It doesn't matter, anyway, he answered. 'You're wasting your time. Everybody has confessed and your denial isn't really worthwhile.'

'We'll see.'

That was the conversation I had had with Tewfik al-Said. And I had kept it in mind to use later as the basis for a telegram to be sent to the public prosecutor.

The governor took the telegram and went down to see the prosecuting attorney – Kamel Kawish. The minutes book was opened and an entry made, including the text of the telegram. The telegram could not be ignored for, although the examination was still being conducted in secrecy, if my lawyers knew of a telegram sent to the public prosecutor but not recorded in the minutes book the entire case would fall through.

Kawish then sent for me. I went down to his office. He sat, flanked by the governor and both Tewfik al-Said and al-Jazzar, and immediately started another round of cross-examination:

- Did you write this telegram?
- Yes, I did.
- Why?
- Because I have been tortured.
- By whom?
- The governor, and both Tewfik al-Said and al-Jazzar.
- Are there any physical signs of this?
- No. Torture needn't leave any physical signs. They swore at me, called me bad names, slapped me on the face, and kicked me – isn't that enough? Would that leave any physical traces? Besides, they want to force me to make a confession. Al-Said in particular tried to do this more than once. To goad me on he told me you had been to Mount Muqattam and collected weapons which he claimed I had hidden there.

Kawish was obviously surprised, for that incident was still a secret and he should not have confronted me with it at such an early stage. It was then the turn of the governor, Tewfik al-Said, and al-Jazzar to be cross-examined, but they of course denied everything I had asserted.

I turned to Tewfik al-Said and said, 'Didn't you open the door of my room one day [I specified the date] at two o'clock in the morning, wake me up, drag me out of bed on a bitterly cold night, and attack me?'

'I never did such a thing!'

'Try to remember ...'

Tewfik al-Said was utterly bewildered. He simply stared at me in disbelief. 'It happened,' I said.

'Never!' he exploded. 'I saw him only during the afternoon "break" and had a conversation with him.'

'No,' I went on. 'It was two o'clock in the morning and you attacked me, called me bad names, and hit me! You threatened that if I didn't confess I would meet a terrible fate since the case had already been "settled". You said I would obviously be convicted, especially when everybody had confessed.' I knew that such a statement, if made public and properly exploited by the lawyers, would destroy the case.

The prosecuting attorney, who also realized this, then brought me face to face with all the defendants except Tewfik. Some stuck to their confessions; others, like Omar Abu Ali, did not. I had faith in him and, knowing he'd understand, I simply looked significantly at him, whereupon he took back all he had said. Kawish was furious – the case was slipping out of his hands and he knew it. He ordered me to go back to my cell.

Back in solitude I went over all that had happened. I was happy to have Omar Abu Ali on my side and to have put on record the torture claim. But I knew there was a long way to go yet.

My next move was to ask to see the governor, and he came to visit me in my cell.

'May I have a pen and paper?'

'Again?' he said initially. 'What's up?'

'That's my business,' I said. I wrote out the following telegram to the public prosecutor:

Please help me! I have a complaint against the present examining attorney. I had previously wired you for help, to save me from the torture I have been subjected to. The prosecuting attorney has taken down statements by me and my torturers, but the torture continues. I demand another prosecuting attorney to examine my case. Henceforth I am going on hunger strike in protest. I have asked the governor to search my room to make sure there's no food in it.

Kawish summoned me on the spot. A further cross-examination followed:

- You've gone on hunger strike?
- Yes.
- Why?
- Torture!
- Who's torturing you?
- You, to begin with. And al-Jazzar, Tewfik al-Said, and the governor. The last has ordered his men to break into my room at night; they attack me, call me bad names and hit me, then withdraw, only to come in again and attack me and withdraw, all night long.

The statements of all those I had accused were taken down. They denied everything, especially the governor, who emphasized that all my accusations were baseless. But I still stuck to my guns.

Seeing that the object of the exercise was to throw the case into confusion, particularly as Muhammad Kamil wouldn't confess and as Omar Abu Ali had taken back his statement, Kawish now had no option but to arrange a confrontation between me and the most adamant of the defendants (his staunchest ally), Hussein Tewfik.

At a hastily arranged meeting Hussein simply reiterated his declared position while I made up a story which gave an innocuous reason for our acquaintanceship and meetings (it was completely false). Hussein tried to deny it but I insisted it was the truth and expressed surprise at his ability to distort facts. Then Hussein, to the great dismay of the attorney, began to crack up. Kawish was immediately conscious of the grave situation. He put an end to the confrontation and, to make quite sure I stayed away from the rest of the defendants and didn't influence them in such a way as to alter the course of the case, he ordered me to be transferred forthwith to Cairo Central Prison.

3

The Liberation
of 'Self' – Cell 54

I

It was four o'clock in the afternoon when I found myself inside Cell 54. I looked around. Cairo Central Prison was completely different from the Aliens' Jail. In the first place there was no bed, no small table, no chair, and no lamp. It was completely bare – apart from a palm-fibre mat on the macadamized floor, hardly big enough for a man to sleep on, and an unbelievably dirty blanket. You simply can't imagine how filthy that thing was. In the winter water oozed from the cell walls day and night, and in the summer huge armies of bugs marched up and down. How bugs could live in that perpetually wet place I never knew, and it still puzzles me.

I lived for a whole eighteen months in that hole, unable to read or write or listen to the radio. I was denied everything, even a simple lamp.

Eventually all the defendants in our case were transferred to Cairo Central Prison, and all in solitary confinement, naturally. It was, in a way, a privilege – and a right – insofar as our case was still being examined and we couldn't very well be made to mix with hardened criminals serving sentences in the big cells, thieves, murderers, drugpushers and safecrackers (the last were, I came to know, the most respected in the eyes of criminals).

We were initially allowed a daily break of a mere fifteen minutes, for a 'solitary' walk. After the referring magistrate had examined our case, we were given two breaks a day, of forty-five minutes each — one in the morning, the other in the afternoon — during which we were allowed to see one another and talk. Our conversations dealt mostly with our ordeal in that terrible jail, particularly the incredibly dirty toilets. Apart from their unhygienic condition (which made them unfit for human use), we had to use them 'collectively', perhaps as primitive men did in the jungle, or as happens in rural areas. The analogy is unfair, however, as land is vast in the countryside, while here you had toilets designed for, say, a thousand but always crammed with three thousand.

This seriously affected our morale. Worse still, it accounted for the fact that a 'Scabies Ward' was attached to that prison, as indeed was the case in every other prison in Egypt. It was only natural, I believe, since many prisoners with extremely unhygienic backgrounds contracted the disease swiftly in the even more unhygienic conditions of the prison. Just as had happened to our rabbits in the Zaytun Detention Centre, the disease assumed epidemic proportions. In prison the distinction between man and rabbit simply vanished.

We had to put up with these conditions for a whole year. Many of my colleagues did not show the same capacity for enduring suffering as I did, thanks to the hardiness of my early life in the village and the toughness I had acquired during my service in the armed forces. It all helped, no doubt.

Some of the defendants came from big families and, through their influence and string-pulling, we were supplied (about a year later) with spoons to use at mealtimes, and glass panes were fixed to cell windows that before had been simply perpetually open holes which let in the cold in winter and the heat in summer.

At that stage, all those awaiting trial were entitled to reject prison fare and buy food from outside — from an appointed purveyor who had a shop on the opposite side of the road. For breakfast we had treacle, bread, and maybe cheese, I can't remember; I do remember clearly that I never got my midday meal from the purveyor, as breakfast alone cost me £7.50 a month and my family were often behind with payments through sheer lack of funds.

One day Sheikh al-Banna, the Supreme Guide of the Muslim Brotherhood, got in touch with Tal'at, my elder brother, to tell him that the Brotherhood had decided to pay £10 a month to my family – just as my colleagues in the army had done when I was in the Maqusah Detention Centre in Almenia. (My colleagues had discontinued that aid when I escaped, and even when I subsequently went back to prison; perhaps they forgot all about it, God forgive them!) Sheikh Hassan's offer of help was invaluable. My brother Tal'at at the time couldn't even afford to buy me a bottle of Eno's fruit salts (which cost 12 piastres). I started taking fruit salts first thing in the morning in prison, and still do so. I haven't been able to do without them for a very long time now, almost thirty years. Quite apart from this, I had to pay rent. What happened was that as we were still awaiting trial we were allowed to rent certain items of furniture – a bed, a table, and a chair – for 10 piastres a day!

It was odd, to say the least; for while the inmates of the Aliens' Jail were the lowest of the low, and the inmates of other 'public' prisons were ordinary Egyptians, the former enjoyed obvious preferential treatment. Here we paid – we had to pay – for what? A mattress stuffed with rice husks, hard and rough, and made of very tough fibre. While there we had a comfortable bed, electricity, and good food – all free of charge. It was a clear case of discrimination, even in prison – and that in our own country.

Regrettably this was true of all our prisons from Aswan to Alexandria. Oddly enough, when in October 1975 as President I took up a pickaxe to strike the first blow at the wall of Turah Prison (thereby beginning its demolition), I felt that it was the very wall of Cairo Central Prison. The bricks were sodden and easy to break. Even the outer coat of plaster was obviously wet, and, as I removed it, innumerable cockroaches came out – ugly contingents of cockroaches. I still raised my pickaxe and hit at the wall, determined and tense, as though I could demolish it all myself. I was advised to stop but said I was all right and kept on hitting! It was a memorable moment, for I was dominated by the feeling that such prisons should be removed and replaced by others fit for human beings.

I have since ordered that new prisons should be built, which would be perfectly hygienic and sanitary and, at the same time, equipped for vocational training and production, so that instead of sitting idly in a cell and being a burden to the community, a prisoner could both acquire new skills or a new trade and earn some money producing something. With savings in his pockets and products already on sale, a released prisoner would have profited himself and become a useful member of the community. We have actually started this experiment at the prison built to replace Cairo Central Prison, on the Cairo-Alexandria motorway in the Western Desert. Attached to it is a piece of newly reclaimed land, which some prisoners have turned into a vegetable farm and fruit orchard.

But to go back to my story. The prosecuting attorney – Kawish – naturally worked very hard and consistently to convict us. Before I was moved out of the Aliens' Jail, my brother Tal'at called on me to take the laundry, as usual, including my pyjamas. In the pocket of my pyjama top I had put a piece of paper with a message in English which read:

Formation A out of action all
Formation B got in touch with me

Suspecting the linen, Kawish searched the pyjamas himself and fished out the message. He photocopied it and put it back. On his way home, Tal'at felt he was being shadowed and immediately realized that something was up.

At home he took out the paper, copied the message, and returned it to the pyjama pocket. Then the pyjamas, with the slip of paper still in place, were washed and returned to me. He was still being watched when he came back, and Kawish was awaiting the outcome. He searched the pyjamas but the paper was already reduced to a pulp – gone was the hoped-for evidence. His disappointment was acute when his men told him that the message had not been conveyed to anyone. My brother had in fact conveyed it to somebody in the small hours, when he was absolutely sure no one would think of tailing him.

'Formation A' consisted entirely of civilians, while 'Formation B' included both military and civilian members. However, no members in either formation could recognize one another. Who did receive the message? Well, it was conveyed to those men whose destiny it was to carry out the 1952 Revolution.

Immediately after the laundry had come back, Kawish called on me in prison and wanted to cross-examine me. The examination consisted of an exercise in writing. He asked me to write, in English:

Formation A out of action all
Formation B got in touch with me

First I was asked to write this out in separate characters, then with the characters attached, over and over again. I filled up three pages, because he wanted to compare my writing with the photocopy of the message in his possession. If he could prove them to be identical he could produce strong evidence against me, but his efforts failed.

Having failed to get anything out of me, Kawish never showed up again. The other defendants – 'the boys', as I called them – began to be transferred to Cairo Central Prison, as already mentioned, which meant that our case was still officially being investigated. The next step, I knew, would be the so-called referring magistrate, who would either refer the case to the criminal court or judge it to lack any criminal 'element' (that it was, in effect, no case at all), and so order the release of the defendants.

The moment the case came up before the referring magistrate, all secrecy was lifted and lawyers began to look into it. They found I had already pulled it apart by my denials, by casting doubt on other defendants' evidence and, to top it all, by accusing the prosecution attorney, the prison governor, and others of having tortured me. Lawyers were delighted to handle our case and began urging the defendants to take back their confessions. 'If only you had listened to Anwar Sadat's advice,' they taunted. 'He is a man, though, but you are youngsters!' Well, at the time I was twenty-seven while the oldest among them was twenty-two and the youngest fourteen. My name was seventh on the list of twenty-seven defendants. The charges varied, of course, but they all centred on the assassination of Amin Osman. The referring magistrate ordered the release, on bail, of two defendants, while all the others (me included) remained in jail.

Playing for time, our lawyers persistently applied for our release, on grounds of an originally invalid writ of *habeas corpus*, but to no avail. The only new development in 1946 was the decision to refer our case to a named criminal court. But our lawyers, whenever the case was brought up before the judge, still demanded more time to study the vast material and variety of evidence involved, and so secured one adjournment after another. They simply played for time, and, naturally, they succeeded – for, in time, the case was transferred to another court and its countenance decidedly changed. That was only to be expected, since our lawyers were the best in Egypt. In those days a famous lawyer received fees to the tune of £5000 or even £10,000 (something like $30,000) for defending a single case.

I should mention here that during the first twenty years of the revolution, when the rule of law was 'suspended', there was a marked change in lawyers' fortunes. The legal business practically came to a standstill and many lawyers actually went bankrupt or were on the verge of bankruptcy. Today things are back to normal. As I restored the rule of law, lawyers today are in great demand to fight social injustices. The demand for lawyers has risen even higher with the adoption of our open-door policy as foreign businessmen need legal representation in Egypt. The legal business has thus regained its earlier vitality in every respect.

II

Two places in this world make it impossible for a man to escape from himself: a battlefield and a prison cell. In Cell 54 I could only be my own companion, day and night, and it was only natural that I should come to know that 'self' of mine. I had never had such a chance before, preoccupied as I had been with work in the army and with politics, and hurried along by the constant stream of daily life.

Now in the complete solitude of Cell 54, when I had no links at all with the outside world – not even newspapers or a radio – the only way in which I could break my loneliness was, paradoxically, to seek the companionship of that inner entity I call 'self'. It was not easy. A barrier seemed to stand between us. There were areas of suffering which kept that 'self' in the dark, shadows which troubled my mind and accentuated the difficulty of self-confrontation. One of these was my first marriage.

I had married one of my relatives, in the conventional manner common in the countryside. An early marriage is a necessity in the village: it is a part of, if not the crowning of, the process of growing up. It was, in short, inevitable.

When I joined the Royal Military Academy, the contradictions inherent in that marriage emerged. I began to discover that my wife and I had nothing in common. It had been a simple, rural arranged marriage, out of tune with everything that I came to know or like, indeed, with my life itself. I worried over that but could do nothing whatsoever about it. I could not leave my wife. In fact, I never thought of it, governed as I was by certain values I could never violate.

I remember once, as a cadet, I visited a family of distant relations near Cairo. They were not much richer than my in-laws but, because they lived in the metropolis, their social milieu was vastly different. One of their daughters was getting a French education at the Lycée. A thought crossed my mind – she would make a different kind of wife. But I found the idea immediately revolting: I rose in rebellion against myself, angry and disgraced. Should I, just because I had joined the Military Academy, abandon my wife? Where was my sense of loyalty? My values? I felt ashamed.

I wasn't adequately satisfied, however, to let the matter rest. I needed full conviction and so began to deal, rather philosophically, with the entire question of marriage. What, to begin with, did I want marriage for? I was destined, I knew, to engage in public life, even as an army officer (the Royal Military Academy was only a means of realizing that lifelong dream of mine). And public life meant mixing with all kinds and 'levels' of people. Could a wife – any wife – have a role to play in such a hectic and turbulent life? A wife's place should be in the home, to look after me and my family. Besides, by nature and up-bringing, I never was fond of socializing. To this day I can't dance. When I was in the United States in 1976 and the great singer Pearl Bailey suggested I dance with her, I told her I couldn't – because, simply, I don't know how.

Such a line of 'argument' as I consciously pursued was futile. But deep down I was dissatisfied with my position. I often gave expression to these thoughts and my utter bewilderment in a little diary, which I had kept but which the political police seized after my detention.

Now, inside Cell 54, when time seemed to be at a stand-still, the problem was pressing to an unprecedented degree – even harassing. I looked at it from every angle and often defended my wife's viewpoint with more zeal than I defended my own. Over and over again I asked myself, why should *she* suffer in the process? Would it be right to leave her, when she has waited for me all these years, just because of a disparity in outlook – or so-called incompatibility? Whatever the terms she might use in connection with such desertion, and whatever becomes of my image in her eyes, I thought, would be only natural and duly deserved.

Still I often wondered what I could do, and whether I really could help it. God knows I wasn't turning against her personally – I simply had to do something about the situation before it was too late. I was so preoccupied with this, so absorbed in my soul-searching, that I was aware of the veins in my temples throbbing madly when I went to bed at night and again when I woke up in the morning.

My suffering continued for a year and a half. Then one day I felt my mind had already been made up. If I really wanted to carry out my plans for the future, my present dilemma had to be resolved one way or the other. I was thoroughly convinced that my very being depended on that particular situation.

First, I stopped my wife from visiting me in prison altogether (about nine months before my release). She imagined that I was acting on the advice of my elder brother Tal'at, or my father, God rest his soul. This was wrong, naturally, as nobody ever *made* me do anything; indeed, I was brought up to shoulder responsibility for my family, who actually acted on my advice. Later, when I was released, I told her personally that it was I who had stopped her visiting me simply because it was impossible for us to go on living together. Divorce proceedings followed.

I had finally come to know myself. I had finally come to know what I could, and what I could never, accept, and thus began to see my route ahead clearly as never before, as well as the steps I had to take along that road.

III

Nothing is more important than self-knowledge. Once I had come to know what I wanted, and got rid of what I didn't, I was reconciled to my 'self' and learned to live at peace with it. To return to my village became a beautiful dream, and to work in any field enchanting. In short, the future – both foreseeable and unforeseeable – was a joy to contemplate.

By then we were allowed to read books, magazines, and newspapers. I read voraciously, finding in every word a novelty – something that opened up new horizons before my very eyes.

I read more in English than in Arabic. When an idea, a poem, or anything in print appealed to me, I immediately copied it into a notebook that I still keep and really cherish. I call it the Prison Notebook. It includes quotations from world authors – Eastern and Western alike – who have had a marked influence on my life.

My wide-ranging reading not only broadened my mind and enriched my emotions, it also helped me to know myself better. Through reading I succeeded in overcoming certain nervous troubles which had been caused by my arrest in the small hours in the bitterly cold winters of 1942 and 1946. I had not realized the nature of these nervous 'crises' but I knew that they disturbed my deep spiritual recesses; only when I had engaged in that long soul-searching in prison did my troubles float to the surface of my consciousness.

Perhaps one week in prison would have sufficed. Still, it was thanks to an article contributed by an American psychologist to the *Reader's Digest* that I succeeded in getting over my troubles. The gist of that article (which represented the outcome of research undertaken over twenty-four years) was that a shock may occur, at any stage in a person's life, which might make him feel that all avenues in front of him are blocked, that life itself is a prison cell with a perpetually locked door.

There is more than one key to this door. First, a man should clearly recognize the source of his trouble; second, he must have faith. Faith means that a man should regard any disaster simply as a fate-determined blow which must be endured. From this stems a deliberate effort to fight away its consequences. No problem should ever be regarded as insuperable. There are always solutions to everything. What makes us think in this way is our belief that God created men to play the roles assigned to them. The God who has created us cannot be evil in any sense: He is good and beneficent (contrary to the image of God which a sheikh in our village Koranic teaching school had drawn up as a mighty and frightening Being).

Ideally the relationship between man and God should be based not on fear (or punishment and reward) but on a much loftier value, the highest – friendship. The Creator is merciful, just, and loving; He is all-powerful because He created everything. If you have Him for a friend, and establish a bond of mutual love between you, you will always have peace of mind whatever the circumstances.

The analysis contributed by that psychologist not only helped me get over my nervous trouble but also opened infinite horizons of love before me. My relations with the entire universe began to be reshaped, and love became the fountainhead of all my actions and feelings. Armed with faith and perfect peace of mind, I have never been shaken by the turbulent events, both private and public, through which I have lived.

Love never let me down. Love always had the upper hand, as is shown by my story – or part of my story – with Gamal Abdel Nasser. There were times, during the eighteen years of our close collaboration, when I could not understand him or accept his actions; but the love I bore him never diminished. He, on the other hand, had been in the grip of 'complexes' since childhood and was often motivated by them; and he, as well as many of his entourage, suffered as a result.

Some people have wondered how I managed to spend such a long time by Nasser's side. Having avoided ever clashing with him, and having been the only man among the 1952 Revolution leaders not to be harmed by him (I was the only Vice-President at the time of his death), I must have been, they concluded, either too insignificant or too cunning. Such a naïve conclusion reveals ignorance of my nature. I was not a nonentity during Nasser's lifetime, nor was I ever cunning. All there was to it was that Nasser and I had been friends since we were nineteen. When he assumed the presidency after the revolution, I welcomed it. It made me happy to see my colleague and friend become President of Egypt. I experienced the same feeling when he became the leader of the Arab world and surrounded himself with an aura of glory.

Sometimes we differed over one thing or another, and occasionally we had an estrangement that would go on for a couple of months or more. Sometimes it was caused by a difference in opinion, sometimes by the intrigues of his entourage, who had a remarkable influence on him. Nasser believed in 'reports', and was by nature inclined to listen to gossip.

Under no circumstances, however, did I ever take up a position of self-defence. It is not in my nature at all to be on the defensive, whether against Nasser or anybody else. However long, our estrangement would end when he rang me up and asked where I had been all those days and why I hadn't got in touch. I usually answered that I thought he had been too busy and so didn't wish to take him away from his engagements, whereupon we would meet and carry on again as though nothing had happened.

This was not infrequent, and I still dealt with whatever Nasser did in a spirit of genuine love. When I was imprisoned in 1942, Nasser took over command of the Free Officers' Organization and remained in charge for a very long time indeed (six years), during which I was an inmate of prisons or detention centres. When I was released, I had to be reinstated in the army so as to participate in his and his colleagues' activity – activity that I had originally started. This was done in 1950.

The revolution took place in 1952 and I played a part in it. My participation was not in itself important to me. What *was* important to me was that the revolution actually took place and that the dream I had had from early childhood was now realized. It was this that made me live with Nasser for eighteen years without ever clashing with him. I was happy to work in any capacity simply because I looked for no personal gain, and never made any demands at all. Whether as a member of the Revolutionary Command Council, as secretary-general of the Islamic Congress, as editor-in-chief of *al-Gumhuriah*, or as Speaker of the National Assembly, my feelings towards Nasser did not change. I stood by him alike in victory or defeat. And this was, perhaps, what made Nasser look around him seventeen years later to realize that there was indeed one man with whom he never quarrelled.

This is what makes me say that love ultimately triumphs. Nasser's blinkers were not easily removed when he suffered from such intractable inner 'conflicts'. As I was his friend, I am bound in duty not to reveal them; all I can say is that they existed. Nasser died without ever experiencing *joie de vivre*. He was always alert. Anxiety gnawed continually at his heart, as he regarded everybody with suspicion, whatever a man's real position was. It was only natural, therefore, that Nasser should bequeath a legacy of suspicion and alertness, both to his closest colleagues and, indeed, to all classes of our people.

Still – to repeat myself once more – love triumphed in the end. For, in fact, I cannot bring myself to hate anybody, as I am by nature committed to love. This became quite clear to me through suffering and pain, in Cell 54. Suffering crystallizes a soul's intrinsic strength; for it is through suffering that a man of mettle can come into his own, and fathom his own depths. It was through suffering that I discovered how I was by nature inclined to do good, that love was the real motivation behind my actions. Without love I really could not work at all. Love provided me with faith, full confidence in myself and everything around me. My love for the universe is derived from my love for God. As the Creator is my friend, I couldn't possibly be afraid of men ... it is He who controls their life and the entire universe.

Through that feeling which came to be an indivisible part of my very being (and which, though unconsciously, remained with me all my life) I was able to transcend the confines of time and place. Spatially, I did not live in a four-walled cell but in the entire universe. Time ceased to exist once my heart was taken over by the love of the Lord of all Creation: I came to feel very close to Him wherever I was.

God says in the Holy Koran: 'If my servants ask you about me, tell them I am near to them; I fulfil the demands of those who turn to me in prayer.' I was in no need of demanding anything in prayer; I was more than near to God. I loved and worshipped Him, in all that He created. Everything came to be a source of joy and delight. All creatures became my friends, and all are made by God – the tree which God decreed to be, and it was; the seed which God made to grow through His will, which is really His love; the flower, the mountain, the fruit, the roots, the branches, and men of all colours and qualities. Everything in existence became an object of love, for, like me, it was made and exists through God's love for it and its love for God.

IV

One of the things Cell 54 taught me was to value that inner success which alone maintains one's inward equilibrium and helps a man to be true to himself. No man can be honest with others unless he is true to himself. I do not care for socially recognizable success. I only value that success which I can feel within me, which satisfies me, and which basically stems from self-knowledge. A true believer should, if he has to call anybody to book, start with himself. What should matter to him is not material gain but his recognition of his own self-image and the extent to which his actions reflect it. Inner success is a source of permanent and absolute power, independent of external factors; outward success fluctuates in response to changing circumstances and is therefore of a purely relative value.

Most people are fascinated by outward success – their social position, financial gain, power, or, in a word, their image in the eyes of others. If their external image is, for any reason, shaken, they are inevitably shaken and may even collapse. They lack fortitude because they are neither true to themselves nor honest with others. To them the end always justifies the means. However, I was brought up to believe that how I saw myself was more important than how others saw me.

I do not hold the presidency to be of greater value than Anwar el-Sadat. To me Anwar el-Sadat is always Anwar el-Sadat, whatever his position, whatever the circumstances – a man who has no personal demands; and, if you wish for nothing, you will need nobody.

Outward success alienates a man from himself. Self-alienation, another name for self-ignorance, is the worst that can befall a man inasmuch as it leads to the loss of inner light and, inevitably, the loss of his vision altogether. A person's inability to see his way ahead makes him a prisoner within himself; it isolates him from everything outside the narrow entity of the 'self' and, therefore, annuls his belonging in humanity.

To preserve his entity as a human being, a man should maintain conscious communion with all existence. Without such communion he will be left with nothing beyond ephemeral success (or failure). He will be reduced to a slave to time and place, and his being becomes quite simply unreal.

It is only through such communion, I believe, that a man can really exist. His consciousness can then expand to encompass the entire universe, his individual entity can merge into those of others (by loving them and suffering for them), and, in a word, he ceases to exist in his individual capacity. Man can, I've been taught, conquer time and space. How many people are aware of this I don't know; the majority are not, I'm sure, as they can see nothing beyond their own little 'selves'. They judge others by their own criteria, which blind them to everything apart from outward success, and thus their souls are starved rather than fulfilled, driven to unhappiness rather than joy.

I used to broadcast a weekly talk over The Voice of the Arabs in the late 1950s. I felt that the Egyptian society should go back to its genuine values, which have maintained its unity and distinctive character down the centuries and enabled it to conquer all invaders. When it became clear that some people wanted to exploit the revolution by destroying all human values, I felt that I had to speak out against this and that our target should rather be to build up mankind. I don't know who informed Nasser of this, and I don't want to slander him. For all the information I possess and all the freedom I have pledged that the people will enjoy, I cannot – out of loyalty to him – allow anybody to slander him.

Nasser asked me about the broadcast talks. He said he came to learn that I had been paid a fee of £400. I said it was true, but didn't reveal to him that the money had been paid into a special fund – 'The Mit Abul-Kum Mosque', a charity I had established. I simply would not 'defend' myself to anybody. Nasser went on to point out that people might talk, that people's talk can do harm, and so on. Following that conversation, the talk with which I concluded the series dealt with 'inner' as opposed to 'outer' success. I explained that the former was permanent, the latter ephemeral. I dwelt on the fact that the latter appealed only to those who were not true to themselves, who could not, therefore, be honest with others but would always be slaves to their personal ambition – a principle I have always rejected.

The theme of my last talk was chosen deliberately, for I knew that one of Nasser's advisers was fascinated by outward success, and that he would convey the drift of the talk to Nasser, who would be equally upset by it, particularly my assertion that I was personally interested in the inner rather than outer man. It was just as I had anticipated, and an estrangement between Nasser and me followed. For a month or more we didn't get in touch with each other.

V

For a long time the concept of outward success reigned supreme in the hearts and minds of those in power in Egypt. One of the consequences of this was that people became unprecedentedly materialistic. A man was not judged by his good deeds or the love he bore others, but by his money or power. Amid the fighting for material gain we became oblivious of a permanent, immutable truth, namely, that a man's real worth can only be determined by the condition of his 'inner self' – an absolute, never a relative, entity. No human community can hope to survive unless this fact is firmly established in its consciousness.

God says: 'We offered Responsibility to the Earth, the Heavens and the Mountains but they declined to bear it and felt unequal to it: Man bears it' (the Koran). God has assigned to man a role which distinguishes him from all other creatures. In the Bible we are told that God created man in His own image and in the Koran that He breathed His Spirit into man. Without a vocation, man's existence would be meaningless. We have been created to bear the responsibility God has entrusted us with. Though different, each man should fulfil his specific vocation and shoulder his individual responsibility. To do this he should first recognize and be loyal to his real entity within, regardless of any external factors; for it is this alone which will enable him to belong and owe allegiance to that Entity which is greater, vaster, and more permanent than his individual self.

In Cell 54 this belief assumed the proportions of a real faith and came to constitute an integral part of my very being. If a day passed without my having done something worthy of belonging in that greater and all-embracing Entity, I took myself to task for failing to honour my responsibility through a whole day.

There can be no doubt that man's value is absolute. If it were relative it would change from one person to another, from one society to the next, and from time to time. Furthermore, if it were relative, a man's value would depend on his material 'weight' or worth and could vary according to whether people found him useful or otherwise. The same man may be viewed differently by different people and so end up without a human (absolute) entity, thus losing his very 'self'.

This is the case with all Fascist communities – Nazi or Communist – where man's value is always determined by social needs. People may be reduced to serfs or elevated to demigods; a man can be turned into an automaton, obeying orders and doing his work without thinking. A man's humanity is inevitably lost as he ceases to be an individual worthy of the responsibility and the vocation entrusted to him by God. The holy torch which he was created to bear and to use in lighting the way both for his fellow men and for posterity is then extinguished.

If human values were relative, all laws – whether those based on revealed religions or those devised by man – would become meaningless. If in a given community the sovereignty of every individual as a human being ceases to be an absolute value; and if, instead, we take 'power' as the only meaningful value (particularly if in the hands of a clique seeking outward success and using it as the only criterion in judging others), then all lofty human values and ideals will be hopelessly lost. To damage the sovereignty of the individual is to replace a community inspired by love, benevolence, and beauty by another based solely on power.

Most people today live in power-based communities, and the world has lost the lofty ideals which man has established down the centuries. Mankind has, I believe, no way out of its current predicament except the restoration of these ideals and the vindication of them in all walks of life. This is why I tirelessly advocate the adoption of the values of the Egyptian village. True, I often tend to overemphasize the importance of this, but I do believe it is the only way of removing the consequences of our experience with a power-based community – an experience that almost destroyed our ideals altogether.

In the eighteen years that preceded my assumption of the presidency, an attempt was made to turn Egypt into a power-based community. The attempt was an unqualified failure simply because, for the Egyptians, it went against the grain. It was incompatible with our nature, our temperament. We had called for a benevolent dictator, a just tyrant; but when we had one, we realized that the system, though outwardly attractive, was built on sand. It was only natural that it should collapse in no time at all. The ugliest feature of that experience, however, was neither our drained economy nor our humiliating military situation; it was the mountain of hate which accumulated in the course of the attempt to build a power-based community. (Due to the lack of human values in such communities, people are solely preoccupied with outward success. They try to secure as much material gain as possible, lawfully or otherwise, even if it involves the destruction of others.)

The frustration, the sense of loss, of young people in Egypt today is definitely to be related to that experience. The young had been led to believe in values and ideals which were totally unrelated to their real 'selves' and which went against their very nature. They were asked to believe that such a power-based monster was their New Society (the hardest and cruellest, in fact). A bitter inner conflict raged in these young hearts and minds. The lofty moral and aesthetic values implanted in their collective unconscious through a cultural heritage thousands of years old came into conflict with the new power-based community, which was imposed on them. The conflict reached its culmination, and frustration was inevitable, when young men and women actually witnessed the collapse of that power-based community while still being taught it was the best and strongest.

VI

Inside Cell 54, as my material needs grew increasingly less, the ties which had bound me to the material world began to be severed, one after another. My soul, having jettisoned its earthly freight, was freed and so took off like a bird soaring into space, into the furthest regions of existence, into infinity. So long as a man is enslaved by material needs – wanting to be or to possess one thing or another – nothing will ever belong to him; he will always belong to 'things'. A slave to things does not exist as a human being; only when he has ceased to need things, can a man truly be his own master and so really exist.

Once released from the narrow confines of the 'self', with its mundane suffering and petty emotions, a man will have stepped into a new, undiscovered world which is vaster and richer. His soul would enjoy absolute freedom, uniting with existence in its entirety, transcending time and space. Through this process of liberation, the human will develops into a love-force, and all earthly forces (even those that might perturb a man's mind) come to contribute to the achievement of perfect inner peace, and so provide a man with absolute happiness.

This is why I regard my last eight months in prison as the happiest period in my life. It was then that I was initiated into that new world of self-abnegation which enabled my soul to merge into all other beings, to expand and establish communion with the Lord of all Being. This could never have happened if I had not had such solitude as enabled me to recognize my real self. Although I didn't study mysticism, the mystics I read in prison appealed to me tremendously as I found in them an expression of such inarticulate, almost unconscious feelings as I experienced at the time.

One of the most important factors which facilitated my access to that new world wherein I enjoyed perfect peace of mind was suffering. Great suffering builds up a human being and puts him within reach of self-knowledge. And great suffering really follows from lofty human ideals. As I hold friendship to be sacred, the pain I suffer if a friend plays me false is most excruciating. Betrayal by a friend shakes my being to its foundations; and, if ever it came to it and I decided that a friendship had foundered, I would feel that part of my very being had been lost and would suffer practically unendurable pain. There would be no one I could resort to, no way of ending my grief.

Now that I had discovered and actually begun to live in that 'new world', things began to change. My narrow self ceased to exist and the only recognizable entity was the totality of existence, which aspired to a higher, transcendental reality. It was genuinely a conquest, for in that world I came to experience friendship with God – the only friend who never lets you down or abandons you. God has created you, shaped your soul, breathed His Spirit into you, and charged you with His responsibility. He is Love limitless and benignity infinite. And He wants the life He has created to be inspired with a sense of honour, beauty, and strength.

My friendship with God changed me a great deal. Only in defence of a just cause would I take up arms, so to speak. For now I felt I had stepped into a vaster and more beautiful world and my capacity for endurance redoubled. I felt I could stand the pressure, whatever the magnitude of a given problem. My paramount object was to make people happy. To see someone smile, to feel that another man's heart beat for joy, was to me a source of immeasurable happiness. I identified with people's joys. Such despicable emotions as hate and vengeance were banished as the faith that 'right' ultimately triumphs came to be ineradicably implanted in my consciousness. I came to feel more deeply than ever the beauty of love: to me it was that invisible bond which united people in my village both at work and out of work (as I had realized in my childhood). Throughout my life my mother nourished that emotion in me. She had, God rest her soul, inexhaustible resources of love; by nature she was a loving, love-inspiring woman.

What I suffered most in Cell 54 was perhaps the lack of a love relationship. For a man's life to be complete, he must have a female partner to whom he is bound in mutual love. This is indeed the greatest possible blessing. When a man's heart is animated by love, he is naturally impelled to accomplish his vocation. Without love, a man may grow very old indeed and yet feel he hasn't lived at all; he would feel he has missed a very important thing – that, however great his achievement, he has really achieved nothing.

I have always felt this. To me love has always been a lofty human ideal, and it was in Cell 54 that I discovered that love is truly the key to everything. When the heavy shackles that had bound me to my 'narrow self' were removed, I began to enjoy God's love. I felt I lived in His love, that love was a law of life. In love, life – nay, being itself – becomes possible; without love, being comes to an end.

Love helped me to know myself. When my individual entity merged into the vaster entity of all existence, my point of departure became love of home (Egypt), love of all being, love of God. And so I have proceeded from love in discharging my duty (my responsibility), whether it was during my last few months in prison, immediately after my release, as a member of the Revolutionary Command Council, or now that I am President of Egypt.

This is why I am a tireless advocate of love. Love is a human safeguard against all social pitfalls. Whoever lives in love must have spiritual fecundity. To love means to give, and to give means to build, while to hate is to destroy. The hate that had prevailed in Egypt for eighteen years before I assumed the presidency was a destructive force, which razed everything to the ground – and we are still suffering from its consequences.

O Lord! You have folded away some of my days and unfolded others! O bring me on this day closer to good deeds and further from evil! O banish on this day the shadows of wrong so that it shines with the light of right! O help me dedicate this day to your service, beginning and ending in loyalty to you! O help me to attain the certainty of faith, and inspire me with the capacity to correct it if it ever goes astray!

Thus I prayed, addressing God as a friend, during the first week after Nasser's death and before I became President.

VII

It was only natural that when I started to live in my new world – when my soul had jettisoned its mundane burdens and come very close to living with God – some of my concepts should be corrected and my outlook on life should generally be changed.

To love no longer meant to possess but rather to let yourself be absorbed into another person's soul, to give and lose yourself in another person's being. This does not mean, however, 'un-being', but, on the contrary, a superior kind of being. Love is the only force capable of pulling down the barriers which may stand between matter and spirit, between the visible and the invisible, between the individual and God. Without love we fail to recognize the otherness of others and so fail to communicate, losing ourselves by stifling the self within its own narrow confines. Furthermore, in the absence of love a man's peace of mind – the mainstay of each individual's life – is consistently eroded; his soul begins to lose its inner equilibrium, and an inner conflict ensues, never to end.

Looking back upon the first eighteen years of the Egyptian Revolution (which preceded my assumption of the presidency), I now realize that for me this was a period of intense suffering. I was not aware at the time of the reason for it, but it lurked, I am sure, somewhere in my subconscious just like the story of my first marriage. I knew, however, that it disturbed the peace of mind I had acquired in Cell 54 and was so eager to maintain. Nasser was no doubt my friend, but when I joined the Revolutionary Command Council I felt that my inner equilibrium was being upset and that my peace of mind was in jeopardy. What was I going to do about it? A man has a mind, a body, and a soul, I thought; surely, each of these elements should have its appropriate exercise if peace of mind is to be achieved. Reading provided me with knowledge and proved an adequate mental exercise – I read all the time. My faith was absolute and spiritually satisfying. And as for physical exercise, I walked $2\frac{1}{2}$ miles every morning, and still do.

That was how I tried during my days of suffering to maintain the peace of mind which I believe is essential for the proper accomplishment of man's vocation on earth. Some people may be led to believe that being reconciled to oneself (which follows from one's peace of mind) means resignation to, or at least acceptance of, reality. This is not true. As a rule I do not automatically accept whatever is there – a given status quo – but always try to change it for the better. I believe that a man should always set himself an ideal. Without an ideal it is impossible to have a vocation and, without a vocation, life would not be worth living. It would simply be meaningless.

In Cell 54 knowledge was unprecedentedly accessible. It appears that knowledge and a man's spiritual life are intimately related and influence one another – the more knowledge you acquire, the more mature your spiritual life and, consequently, the higher the quality of your knowledge becomes. It is an incessant process, which helps man enhance his self-knowledge, and the clearer his vision of himself, the easier it will be for him to transcend the confines of the 'self' and release his feelings, thoughts, and actions from the 'cell' of personal concerns to direct them towards perfection and beauty. Beauty came to be my presiding ideal – whatever I did and whatever happened. I sought after beauty in everything, and the more my aesthetic satisfaction, the more thirsty I grew for it.

Hence my idealism – which is nothing in effect but a perpetual craving for beauty. As a point of departure to everything I did, this principle has made it difficult for many people to understand me; some of my actions have appeared simply inexplicable.

Some people have asked me to define politics. I have always found it puzzling and could not provide a precise definition. I do not claim to have studied politics as a science or to have specialized in it. All I know is that I have been brought up to nurture certain values (which make up the person I am) from childhood to maturity, even to this day when I am President of Egypt, and which have been inspired by the paramount desire to save Egypt from her besetting troubles and to help her advance towards perfection and beauty.

Some people define politics as the art of the possible, which I find unsatisfactory. Indeed, if the October War is anything to go by, politics may be defined, rather, as the art of the impossible. Which is the correct definition?

I have no Ph.D. in political science nor am I academically well versed in it. I am simply a man who has come to know himself and is therefore true to himself in everything he says or does. The truth is always the basis of my relationship with people.

This is, perhaps, what has surprised many people. They have wondered how a politician could say behind closed doors the same things he declares in front of a microphone, how he could refrain from the exploitation of a given situation in gaining easy popularity and demagogic applause. The answer is simply self-knowledge. It is self-knowledge that makes a man's actions proceed from objective, rather than puny subjective, considerations.

I think that politics is the art of building up a society wherein the will of God is enacted. Our Creator has decreed we should engage in constructive work, consistently. In such a society as that, each individual should enjoy absolute freedom, subject to no other restrictions than those implicit in the genuine human values of the society itself — values which are the fruit of its indigenous culture and are therefore acceptable to all. Freedom is the most beautiful, holy, and precious fruit of our culture; an individual should never be made to feel that he is at the mercy of any force of coercion or that his will is subordinated to that of others.

Freedom may not be essential to a power-based community, but it is the mainstay of a society based on truth, benevolence, and beauty. Then people's hearts are animated by love, faith, and inner light. Constructive work can be done and principles vindicated — faith, dignity, peace, and glory. To enact the will of God, man must combine inner peace with outward security and strength.

In building such a society, leaders should not shirk their *human* responsibility — the responsibility dictated by their human consciousness and human belonging. But they should be impelled in all their actions by distinctively human 'power', rather than acting in response to personal dreams of glory or ephemeral and spurious power such as obsesses the dictator's mind and turns his head. Indeed, it would be impossible for any community under such leaders even to aspire to the ideals of truth, benevolence, and beauty. Human dignity would be shattered and man would be turned into a 'thing', insignificant and almost inanimate, deprived of his absolute power as human being.

My words are based on actual practice and on our own experience. The 23 July 1952 Revolution introduced new ideas into our life and tried to transform the Egyptian society into a modern advanced one able to keep abreast of developments in today's world. However, I must admit that we have not been fully successful in achieving our objectives, for many reasons, among them personal conflicts and the lack of a sufficiently clear vision both while the Revolutionary Command Council held the reins of power and during Nasser's presidency. By nature Nasser tended to suspect others. He was too preoccupied with his own 'security' either to have a clear vision of the future or to pay due attention to the advancement of his people *as human beings* – to that humanity which is the most precious asset of a given community. Worse still, as a result of his preoccupation with 'security' and of the doubts that preyed on his mind, the Egyptian people's horizons dimmed and their opportunities for self-fulfilment increasingly narrowed down. Regrettably, grave mistakes were committed in Egypt against man's humanity, the very asset we should have guarded most zealously.

VIII

A feeling that I had lived dangerously since I graduated from the Royal Military Academy possessed me in Cell 54. It was true, for I had indeed faced one danger after another from the day I graduated until my last moment in Cell 54. Fraught with danger were my efforts to create a public opinion in the army favourable to our cause, my attempts to protect Egypt from an imminent Hitlerite invasion (which precipitated my dismissal and arrest), my work for the elimination of the agents of British colonialism (which culminated in the Amin Osman case), and, finally, the fact of being inside Cell 54 itself. I felt that I stared danger in the face, that it was only too real ... almost inevitable.

I couldn't speculate, with any sense of certainty, about the possible outcome of our case. All I knew was that my name was seventh on the list of defendants and that my specific charge could, if proved, result in a death sentence or hard labour for life. I knew that no leniency could be exercised; we would either receive a harsh sentence or we would be acquitted altogether. But could we really be acquitted?

The Arab-Israeli War broke out while I was still in prison, late in 1948. God knows how I suffered at the time! It was agonizing to witness the Israeli air raids on Cairo, violating the sanctity of Ramadan, our holy month. But I was helpless and could do nothing about it.

Our trial was protracted; it took eight months, from January to August 1948. Once when the police wanted to escort us to the court, I remember, the guards suggested we be handcuffed. I refused and said that as no verdict had yet been handed down, it was simply unacceptable. Only if and when I was convicted would handcuffs be appropriate. As the boys followed suit, the police gave in about the handcuffs and used a huge truck to take us to court and back to prison.

Meanwhile the government became less nervy about us. We were allowed to go out from time to time. I seized the chance and asked to be taken to an army dentist, one of my acquaintances, for treatment. His name was Ahmed Ali and he had a surgery in the army hospital at Kubri al-Qubbah, while the prison was at al-Qalah, an hour's drive away at least. My wish was granted and I began to go out regularly. I enjoyed the taxi ride very much. I devoured the sights and sounds of Cairo and felt practically reborn as I inhaled the air of freedom for an hour at least each way. True, a police officer always escorted me, but it never really mattered. I asked the dentist not to touch the bad molar so that I could come out to see him more frequently. My guard always watched the dentist at work but could never guess that while he apparently dealt with my teeth, the molar itself was never touched. I still recall the pleasures of that taxi ride, brief though it was, and the free air that I breathed on the way. Sometimes I called on my father, who worked in the army hospital, and had tea with him.

It was all short-lived, however, for Hussein Tewfik unexpectedly escaped and, as an indirect result of this, we were prevented from going out under any pretext. The trial dragged on, day after day, month after month, and we increasingly enjoyed the support of Egyptian public opinion. Furthermore, my efforts at the cross-examination had adequately thrown the case into confusion, and the best lawyers in Egypt were handling it.

Early in July 1948 our trial was finally concluded and a day appointed, a few weeks later, for the verdict to be handed down. It was already August. I put on old grey trousers and a white jacket, all the clothes I possessed, to go to court. Hussein Tewfik was, naturally, first on the list. He was sentenced *in absentia* to ten years in prison, and the moment I heard that sentence, I knew I would be acquitted. Then the judge announced that Defendant number 7 was *not* guilty.

It was lunchtime, but we had, according to established practice, to stay in prison for a while before our final release. We actually returned to our cells and didn't leave until five o'clock in the afternoon.

I was still legally married and my first wife was living at my father's house. To avoid embarrassment I decided to go to Hilwan, where I stayed at a cheap *pension* whose nightly rates I could just about afford. There, grateful for the Hilwan mineral water, which was good for my damaged digestion, I just sat tight and waited.

4
The July 1952 Revolution

I

Once again I was a free man. However, having spent an
uninterrupted thirty-one months in jail I felt (it was
only natural) as though I had been reborn into another
world, completely unknown to me. At Hilwan I passed
my time in the Japanese Gardens, often relaxing on a
bench, with a book or newspaper in hand, away from
everybody. The solitude helped me to concentrate on
my situation, both past and present, and to consider what
might yet be in store for me. I deliberately shunned
human company and shied away from conversation – it
would require an effort, I reckoned, decidedly beyond my
ability. The old familiar routine of daily life now assumed
the proportions of a new world to which I had to re-
adjust, if ever I hoped to belong to it again. Indeed, I was
shocked to realize that I was no longer able, excellent as
my driving was, even to manoeuvre any car through the
regular Cairo street traffic. I did drive a car once as far as
Guiza, about a month after my release, but ended up running into another under the Guiza flyover bridge. It was
best, I thought, to confine myself to Hilwan, both in order
to recover from the traumatic experience of jail and to
profit by the mineral waters in curing my ailing stomach.
Soon, however, I had an unexpected visitor.

Hassan Izzat, my old colleague and friend, had searched
everywhere for me. Then one day, while I was performing my morning prayer, he simply appeared on the door-

step. I had practically run out of money and didn't know what to do with myself.

'What are you doing here?' he asked, as his eyes glanced searchingly over the threadbare furnishings and walls of my room. 'Come on, let's go.'

'Go?' I said. 'Where to?'

'To where I live, in Suez. Come on!' he insisted.

In no time at all I was ready to leave. I put on my white jacket and grey trousers – the same outfit I had worn on my release, and the only one I had. Hassan noticed that my trousers were showing signs of 'old age', especially at the back. I said I had no others and that even if I went to my father's place to look for some I wouldn't really find a replacement. So before we went to Suez, Hassan and I set off for Cairo, where I bought myself a few shirts and had two suits made to measure. I also tried out a new type of socks ('socket' they were called) which seemed to have been first introduced into 'fashionable Cairo' while I was in jail. Hassan bought me three or four pairs, then we drove together to Suez.

It was there in Hassan's Suez home that I met Jihan, my present wife, for the first time. She had called on her cousin, Hassan's wife, and we subsequently spent a good deal of time together. In the days that followed I came to realize that Hassan hadn't looked for me and enlisted my 'services' just for love. He was finding it difficult to deal with his partners in the business he ran – a kind of trading concern via Suez with the Saudis – and wanted to have a 'hero' of the Amin Osman case, the talk of the mass media, on his side. It obviously worked, and I did take part in some of the deals struck at the time. Although my share in the profits amounted to 180 sovereigns, Hassan gave me only 60 and pocketed the rest. But a sovereign was worth £6 Egyptian at that time – which meant I had a fortune. And, in fact, when I went back to Hilwan to resume my mineral water treatment, I deposited the money in the hotel safe. The money went quickly, all the same, to pay for the 'good living' I subsequently enjoyed.

It was all short-lived, though, for soon afterwards I moved to another *pension* downtown but had no job or any other source of income. As the burden of debt grew heavier, I asked an old friend – Ihsan Abdul Quddus – to help me get a job. We tried the newspaper *al-Ahram* but there were no vacancies. Then I suggested *Rose-al-Yusuf*, but Ihsan said the magazine couldn't afford to pay two staff members doing the same job and he was already working there as a rewriter. In fact he did the same job elsewhere – at the publishing house of Al Hilal and on the newspaper *al-Zaman*, besides *Rose-al-Yusuf*, being on the editorial staff of all three simultaneously.

It so happened, however, that Ihsan gave up his post at Al Hilal publishing house and introduced me to the proprietors, who immediately bought my prison diary and started publishing it. They apparently first wanted to make sure that it was I who had written the diary, for Shukri Zaydan, one of the proprietors, asked me one day to amplify one section of the diary to make it fill a whole column and a half. I accepted gladly, whereupon he asked me to do it on the spot.

'You must do it now,' he said. 'It's got to be out in ninety minutes – otherwise we'd be too late for press.'

So I did it and met my deadline easily. He made a point of waiting until I had finished. Then he read the instalment, thanked me, and went home.

There was no doubt in my mind that that was a kind of test and, sure enough, Shukri sent word for me to 'come and see him in connection with a job' the following morning. I did go and was more than surprised to learn that I was being offered full-time employment on the editorial staff of Al Hilal and asked to fix my own salary. It was all the more surprising in view of the fact that the entire editorial staff consisted of freelances. I took up the post immediately, replacing Ihsan as a rewriter, and continued with Al Hilal until the end of December 1948. Meanwhile I proposed to Jihan, on 29 September 1948, to be precise, and her father accepted for her.

I would have carried on with Al Hilal as I was satisfied, even happy, with the work, if Hassan Izzat hadn't approached me yet again towards the end of the year. He had fallen out with his Suez partners and moved to Cairo, and so he asked me to go into business with him. I felt that I could not turn him down. After all, it was he who had helped me get over my financial difficulties when I was literally broke in Hilwan; and over and above this, I had a soft spot for Hassan as a friend who loved me, hid nothing from me, and looked upon me as his 'conscience'.

It wasn't easy, of course, for me to quit Al Hilal. The manager thought I wanted a better salary and began to dangle a bigger carrot, but I was determined to leave and actually started to work with Hassan. We had a contract for the provision of drinking water to fifty-two villages in the province of Sharqîya, in Hassan's name. Although I was his partner, my name was not officially registered as such.

I moved to Zaqazîq – the chief town in Sharqîya – and when I married Jihan, on 29 May 1949, she joined me there. We spent our honeymoon and the following months at a modest provincial hotel there. I set myself a strict timetable, according to which the contract would be carried out in half the time expected. It worked. I used to start very early in the day, putting in fifteen to seventeen hours, then go back to my wife at the hotel in the evening.

It was all over in six months. We netted a profit of £6000 and received a letter of thanks from the government, naturally addressed to Hassan Izzat. Consequently we won bigger contracts, again for the provision of drinking water to villages in the province of Almenia, worth £60,000. Judging by our previous performance we might have cleared no less than £30,000 net profit.

Our work in Almenia would have started in November 1949. But before leaving for Upper Egypt, I told Hassan that I wanted financial stability. I wanted an apartment in

Almenia for my wife and myself, and I had financial commitments towards the children by my first wife. He first resorted to evasive tactics, then reluctantly approved, and then told me (most unexpectedly) that I had already drawn £2000 which, he alleged, I had spent in Zaqazîq. This was a stark lie. In Zaqazîq, as he must have known, I had had hardly any expenses apart from the modest hotel bill and the little I paid for my cigarettes. When he went on insisting that I had taken the money, I simply found it all disgusting. I seemed suddenly to have come face to face with reality, and began to turn away both from Hassan Izzat and from the business world altogether. Although he still owed me £3000 (my share in the Zaqazîq contract), I didn't claim it; with no more than £1,20 piastres in my pocket I said goodbye.

All I wanted was to get away – to save myself. Indeed, money would be worthless if it posed a threat to man's real entity, his inner peace and mental life. The dreams of early life, the hopes of my tender years, the battles I had fought for the liberation of land – all seemed to point an accusing finger at me. Had I done all that to end up as a businessman haggling over money – whether £3000 or £30?

Throughout the period that immediately followed my release I had felt that I was not myself. The inner man I knew, with whom I had lived and of whom I had been proud (especially in Cell 54), was a stranger to me now. I was confident 'he' hadn't gone away – not too far away, at any rate. I had a feeling that it was purely the work of outward circumstances and then, one day, I was overwhelmed with happiness when I heard that inner man inside me say to Hassan Izzat, 'How I wish you had real wealth – a hundred thousand or more – and I had nothing! You would still be inferior to me, for all that you possessed, and I shall always be superior to you, for the *nothing* that I have!'

The moment of departure saw my real self born again.

Indeed, it was at that moment that I decided to go back to the army. I felt that that was the only way in which I could accomplish the mission – the vocation – that, to me, was everything.

II

In 1941 certain units of the Egyptian Army had been stationed on the beautiful Mediterranean beach of al-Garawlah. On orders of the Intelligence Service I was posted there – simply to be out of the way – and it was there that I came to know and subsequently make friends with the army doctor called Yusuf Rashad. He lived in the next tent and our friendship seemed inevitable. He was an exceptionally fine person, highly cultivated and well read. He always smoked a pipe and he read one book after another. We grew to be more than friends; we became perpetual companions, parting only to go to bed at night. We cooked our own food and consumed it together, read and thought together, and had interminable conversations. I still remember the day he gave me John Stuart Mill's *Totalitarianism, Liberty and Representative Government*, which impressed me deeply. In the years that followed we saw nothing of each other but we remained as good friends as ever.

Now, in January 1950, that friendship still didn't seem too distant; on the contrary, Yusuf Rashad appeared to be my only hope as he had become a royal guard physician and I didn't think he'd turn down any request I might make. Sure enough, I rang him up at his home and he asked me to call on him personally. I did so, and explained everything to him. The Prosecution Office had appealed, the appeal had been rejected towards the end of 1949, and my acquittal had thus been upheld by the Court of Appeal. There was nothing really to prevent my going back to the army.

Quietly smoking his pipe, Yusuf Rashad listened attentively and politely to all I said, then promised to get in touch with me as soon as possible. Within a few days, on 10 January, he called and asked me to see El Farik Muhammad Haidar Pasha, the commander-in-chief of the armed forces. Haidar Pasha was expecting me. The moment he saw me, he attacked me. A positive spate of words ensued – 'You're a troublemaker ... You've got a black record ...' I tried to speak but was stopped. 'You needn't say anything ... keep quiet, will you? Don't say a word!' He rang the bell and instantly his private secretary came in –

'Yes, Pasha?'

'This boy ... is to be reinstated immediately as from today.'

A military decree was issued reinstating me in the armed forces as of 15 January 1950, with the rank of captain – the same rank I had had on my dismissal. My colleagues had already been promoted twice, to major and lieutenant-colonel.

III

Gamal Abdel Nasser and Abdel Hakim Amer were the first to call on me to congratulate me. From Nasser I learned that the Free Officers' Organization had spread far and wide, and was growing increasingly powerful. As though to show me just how powerful, or else to let me test its power, he suggested I immediately take my promotion tests so as to make up for the time lost. The idea was that however big the obstacles that lay ahead, the organization should either help or remove them altogether. This actually happened and I was in fact promoted to lieutenant-colonel in a very short time.

Nasser asked me not to take part in any conspicuous political activity because, due to my record in struggle, I would be watched by the authorities. He nevertheless gave me a map showing the distribution of the Free

Officers in the various army units, which enabled me to call on them and talk to them. Our conversations were merely of a general nature, totally unrelated to politics, for according to the rules of our organization, I wasn't supposed to reveal my real loyalty or to make them suspect that I knew they belonged to the Free Officers.

This was a basic rule which had been laid down by Nasser when he took over command of the organization following my arrest in the summer of 1942, namely, that the formation of each cell should remain unknown outside the cell itself. The second in command, after me, in 1942 was Abdel Munim Abdul-Rauf. He maintained our contacts with Sheikh al-Banna, the Supreme Guide of the Muslim Brotherhood, who agreed with me that the Free Officers' Organization should not be partisan or in any way affiliated to an existing political group, as it set itself the target of serving Egypt as a whole rather than a given class or section of the community.

When I was taken into detention, Nasser was still in the Sudan. When he returned to Egypt (with his battalion) towards the end of 1942, Abdul-Rauf contacted him with a view to recruiting him in the Free Officers' Organization on account of his outstanding record. This was a rule I had laid down, that only officers of outstanding performance in the armed forces should join our organization. A good officer is trusted by everybody and can be listened to willingly. Nasser immediately accepted. It wasn't difficult for him afterwards to remove Abdul-Rauf and take over command of the organization.

The way Nasser led the organization was naturally different from mine. He resorted to the creation of secret cells within the army, each quite unknown to the other, which proliferated day after day until the organization was represented in every corps, and particularly in such crucial departments as army administration, and so on. In 1951 Nasser felt that the time was ripe for the organization to have a 'regular' command, especially as many of its members were already anxious to know the man or men who led it. At the time five secret bodies were operating in Egypt: the Political Police; the Criminal Investigation Department; the Army Military Intelligence; the British Intelligence Service; and the US Central Intelligence Agency, which began to operate in Egypt immediately after World War II. Apart from these there was a further body that worked for the king and was directly responsible to the royal court – the Royal Intelligence Service.

It was therefore of paramount importance to be careful in establishing a constituent body – or council – for the organization. Nasser began to pick its members from among his immediate acquaintances – the officers he knew personally during the first Arab-Israeli War (such as Kamal al-Din Hussein and Salah Salem); his lifelong friends (such as Abdel Hakim Amer); and the original leaders of the organization (before he took over) such as Abdel Munim Abdul-Rauf, Abdel Latif al-Baghdadi, Hassan Ibrahim, Khaled Mohieddin, and me.

Nasser's decision to include me in the Constituent Council may appear to indicate a sense of loyalty on his part for, although I had originally created the Free Officers' Organization, I stayed away from it for eight years – from 1942 (when I was dismissed) to 1950 (when I was reinstated). However, Nasser was not the kind of man to be motivated by such loyalty to others – unless, of course, as the result of a firm and long-established friendship, as was the case with Abdel Hakim Amer. Although Nasser and I had come to know each other at the tender age of nineteen, I cannot say that our relationship ever exceeded mutual trust and respect; it was hardly what you'd call a friendship at all. It wasn't easy for Nasser to have anybody for his friend, in the full sense of the term, because of his tendency to be wary, suspicious, extremely bitter, and highly strung. By this I do not mean, however, that Nasser lacked all sense of loyalty; on the contrary, I mean to point out his sharpness of mind. From my record in the armed forces, and from his experience since we first met early in life, he gathered I was a man of principles and lofty values. It wasn't difficult for Nasser to realize that he could rely on me and that my inclusion in the Constituent Council would make me permanently loyal thereafter to the man who thus appeared to be loyal to me.

There can be no doubt that Nasser – naturally a cautious man – was fully confident that I would stand by him and that I would, with my rich experience, constitute a considerable loyal force to back him up in the conflicts that already raged within the Constituent Council and continued until the actual day the revolution broke out.

He always rushed to see me, whenever I arrived in Cairo on leave, to complain about the difficulties some members created for him. It is no exaggeration to state, recalling the events of that distant period, that out of a seven-day army leave five would be spent with Nasser, during which the situation within our organization and the problems that lay ahead would be thoroughly studied. Nasser always respected my experience. Once in 1951, I remember, it occurred to him to launch the revolution with a large-scale political assassination operation. He sought my advice and I immediately objected. 'It would be a mistake, Gamal,' I explained. 'Where would that get us? The effort required for such an operation should be made in the direction of the revolution itself. Let's advance to our objective directly; let's have our revolution.' Nasser showed no hesitation whatsoever. He accepted my view without question.

Nasser's attitude changed, however, after the revolution broke out and he took his place at the helm. In 1953, for instance, when conflicts rocked the Revolutionary Command Council (to the extent of actually posing a danger to the revolution and the entire future of Egypt), I called on him at home and said:

'A revolution, Gamal, can consume itself as well as its revolutionaries. Surely we don't want this to happen to us. Shouldn't you put an end to all this? Simply say to our colleagues, Let's act as a team; those who share our views may carry on with us. Those who seek to dictate to us (whatever their individual stands) are free to go. We have completed the first stage of our task, namely, getting the revolution off the ground – a remarkable and historic feat. Anyone who makes his exit now should be proud enough to have taken part in this initial stage.'

Nasser was listening very attentively. I went on, 'It's only natural for changes to take place once we come to power, but this should never be at the expense of Egypt. We have unanimously elected you chairman of the Revolutionary Command Council. Therefore, we cannot possibly differ from you. So it should be made clear to all that anyone who can co-operate with you may stay with us, and anyone who cannot may resign ...' But Nasser wouldn't let me finish. Livid with rage, he suddenly interrupted me to object, and burst into an attack as though I was against him rather than being on his side. His words were strangely bitter and the vituperation poured forth in all directions, almost as if a volcano had erupted in his chest. God knows I had no other end in view but to spare Egypt the consequences of an internal conflict between the rulers of the land that was becoming increasingly intensified. It was this that made the 23 July Revolution, for all its achievements, steer Egypt on a disastrous course culminating in the 1967 defeat which very nearly blotted out all our earlier achievements.

IV

The part I played in launching the July Revolution was not, of course, confined to giving advice to Nasser whenever possible, supporting his various stands through the conflicts that rocked the Constituent Council, or distributing Free Officers' leaflets in the areas assigned to me. Events developed at a breathless pace and I had to keep abreast of them.

In October 1951, el-Nahas abrogated the Anglo-Egyptian Treaty concluded in 1936. Freedom fighters and members of the Muslim Brotherhood started their harassment of the British base in the Suez Canal Zone. My role in these activities was to offer the fedayeen the necessary training and supply them with arms and ammunition. We could tell from the general climate in the country that our target was no longer far off, and so the Constituent Council was convened early in January 1952 and a decision taken for the revolution to start in November 1955. Then, only days later – on 26 January – the uprising and rioting known as the Cairo fire took place, taking everybody by surprise. It is not yet known who was responsible for it, but the object of the exercise was only too obvious – to weaken the position of the king. It was also a violent expression of the suffering of more than 95 per cent of the population, the broad masses who lived in great deprivation under the flagrantly capitalist and class-based system. The political parties were themselves a tool in the hands of the king and the British, allying themselves alternately with one or the other to secure the greatest possible personal gains at the expense of the people. The Cairo fire was a warning sign of impending revolution which, if it broke out, would destroy everything. It was definitely directed against the king and the whole political system. It did weaken their position.

So now we had to undertake a thorough reassessment as to precisely where we stood. Here I remembered Yusuf Rashad, who was the king's private physician and still a good friend of mine. This was the time, I thought, for me to utilize that friendship in serving the interests of the cause we all worked for. I got in touch with Yusuf Rashad, handling him very tentatively this time in his capacity as one of the king's personal friends and head of the Royal Intelligence Service.

Yusuf Rashad accepted everything I said without question. He never argued or showed any sign of suspecting my words. Well and good, I thought, for I could then easily

The author, three months after graduating from the Royal
Military Academy as a second lieutenant.

Shortly after coming out of jail in 1943.

On trial, June – July 1948.

The author at his wedding, 29 May 1949.

The author and his baby daughter with Abdel Hakim Amer (centre) and Gamal Abdel Nasser, 1954.

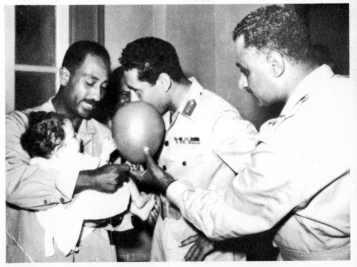

Nasser paying a visit to the author at his house on the Pyramid Road, May 1962.

With the family in Cairo in 1971, showing them Cell 54 in Cairo Central Prison, where the author had spent two and a half years. His prison number was 2151.

The al-Aqsa Mosque, 1955. The author was then visiting Jerusalem in his capacity as secretary general of the Muslim Congress.

mislead the king and keep him at bay until our organization had carried out the revolution. And this was precisely what I did. I supplied Rashad with false information and, when he confronted me with Free Officers' leaflets, I told him there was nothing in them but the fantasies of a certain officer well known for his exhibitionism and megalomania who was in fact powerless. When he did lay his hands on facts, I worked hard to cast doubts on their veracity, insisting they were at best unnecessarily magnified and so distorted. Furthermore, I always tried to obtain information of the king's plans and intentions and was, in large measure, successful.

A few days after the Cairo fire I learned from Yusuf Rashad that the king now felt he could not survive in Egypt and had even prepared a list of all those who would accompany him into exile, including Yusuf Rashad, naturally. He had also started to smuggle his gold abroad (on board his private plane) for safe keeping in banks in Geneva. Nasser and I became convinced that the Free Officers' movement would not meet with significant resistance from the king. It was obvious that his final collapse was not only imminent but had already begun. In February 1952 the Constituent Council was convened. We decided that the revolution should take place in November 1952 rather than November 1955. But why November? It was in that month that the king and government would be back from Alexandria and so we could strike our blow – a single concentrated blow – in Cairo.

Naturally, nobody apart from Nasser knew of my contact with Yusuf Rashad, who continued to be one of the best weapons in our arsenal. Not until we had achieved our objective in full did we stop using him. Early in July 1952, I remember, I was on leave in Cairo when, during a conversation, Nasser wanted to know the king's news. I drove my Vauxhall to Alexandria on the spot and headed for the Automobile Club in Sidi Bishr where, predictably, I found Yusuf Rashad. I learned that the king was worried that the Free Officers' leaflets were being distributed on an unprecedentedly large scale. I set his mind at rest and attributed the leaflets, once more, to an exhibitionistic officer. Besides, I had spun a few yarns designed to mislead the king. When I was sure Yusuf had taken the bait and conveyed them all to the king, I drove back to Cairo where I briefed Nasser on the outcome of my trip. Then, as my leave had come to an end, I returned to Rafa and Gaza, where I was posted at the time.

On 18 July 1952, we were surprised to learn that the king had cancelled the election results of the Officers Club Board, apparently because the Free Officers had won most seats on the board, thus defeating the 'Royalists'. So he had already licked his wounds and, indeed, moved on to the offensive. Meanwhile, a Wafdi journalist – Ahmed Abul-Fatah – informed Nasser (who was a personal friend of his) that the king was about to change the government and that the new War Minister would be Major-General Hussein Sirry Amer, who knew a great deal about the Free Officers, and that once in power, he would eliminate them all and frustrate their plans to show the king how powerful and loyal he was. Nasser came to the conclusion – and we all agreed – that a fight with Hussein Sirry Amer was inevitable since he knew a good deal about us and, in particular, about the members of the Constituent Council. It was either him or us. So Nasser decided that the revolution would take place before that minister took office, and before we lost the initiative.

This meant that it should be planned for July instead of November 1952.

On 21 July 1952, Nasser sent me a message with Hassan Ibrahim (who delivered it to me at Al-Arish airfield) in which I was asked to go to Cairo the next day as the revolution would take place one day between 22 July and 5 August. I did arrive in Cairo on 22 July but Nasser was not there to see me at the railway station as usual, so I thought it was too early, went home, and took my wife out to the movies. When I returned, I found a note Nasser had left asking me to see him at Abdel Hakim Amer's house at eleven o'clock the same evening. The porter who handed me the note told me that Nasser had called twice, first at eight and again at ten, when he had left it there.

I changed quickly, took my pistol, and went immediately to Amer's house. He wasn't in, of course, and I had to find him at the Al-Abbasiah army barracks. But again I failed as I didn't know the password and couldn't get in. When the guard learned that I was a colonel, I was asked to stay at home, as those were the orders for senior officers. I tried every possible trick and fought desperately to get in but it was useless.

Was the revolution about to take place before my eyes without me? I had worked all my life for this moment; I had struggled, suffered, and devoted my very existence to this glorious hour. What would be the meaning of my struggle – of the very man I call myself – if I were to be reduced to a spectator when my *raison d'être* was taking shape?

I tried again and again, relentlessly, until at last I spotted Abdel Hakim Amer in charge of the army traffic. I called out to him and, although he could not see me, he recognized my voice. He told me that Army Command Headquarters had fallen, that it had been stormed by our forces advancing from Huckstep Camp (a US camp during World War II, which had been named after an American) under Amer himself and Yusuf Siddiq. The Chief of Staff, Hussein Farid, had been put under house arrest, he explained, while other commanders were being taken for detention to the Royal Military Academy, again by Amer personally.

I drove in my own car to the Army Command Headquarters where I found Abdel Nasser. He asked me to call each of our unit commanders on the telephone to see if everything was going according to plan. I went to the telephone room on the ground floor but nobody was there. I called the NCOs but none would emerge, but I persisted until some of them turned up. Recognizing me, they were reassured. More came in. Gradually they calmed down and started to work under me. We telephoned all army units – in Sinai, the Western Desert, Alexandria, Al-Qantara East, Al-Arish, Rafa, and so on.

As it happened, Haidar Pasha (who was the War Minister) rang up and wanted to get through to the night-duty officer. I put him through to Nasser. Although I didn't overhear their conversation, Nasser told me he pretended to be the night-duty officer and, answering Haidar's questions, said there weren't any unusual movements in the army, that everything was under control. A little later Haidar telephoned again and wanted to be put through to the Armoured Corps. This time I ordered the NCOs to ignore the request.

It was already three o'clock in the morning when I received the 'all signals go' from all units. I informed Nasser and the members of the Constituent Council. The moment Nasser heard from me he rang up Muhammad Naguib at his home in Hilmiah al-Zaytun, then sent an armoured car to fetch him.

Naguib arrived at dawn.

With the soft hues of another day already suffusing the eastern sky and a gentle summer breeze blowing against my face, I stood in the terrace of Army Command Headquarters looking down the vast, wide, and almost endless road that ran along the barracks. I watched our forces as they poured into it from Heliopolis and Manshiat al-Bakri and headed for the centre of Cairo – the artillery, the infantry units, and the tanks. It was as calm as ever so early in the morning, but there it was . . . the revolution had begun.

The dream on which I had lived for years – a dream to which I devoted my entire life – had finally materialized. It was now a reality surging in my heart, possessing my being and dwarfing it. Everything else paled, was pushed into the shadows, while that reality alone shone bright, rising high and majestic and towering above all else.

Such was my joy – so beautiful, so overpowering – that I could not bear it alone. At daybreak on 23 July I made my way to Broadcasting House to announce the birth of the revolution to the Egyptian people and to let them all share my jubilation.

As I came out of the broadcasting station and drove up to our headquarters in the north of Cairo, I saw the streets of the metropolis crowded with people as I had never seen them before. Men, old and young, women and children, were kissing each other, shaking hands, coming together in small clusters or large circles – but all the time in total silence. No shouts were heard and I presume hardly any words were uttered or exchanged. It was clear that what mattered to them was to wait together for the one thing for which they had waited so many years separately, individually, and perhaps sometimes quite hopelessly. Now it had come at last and the realization of their dream was beyond words; it was best expressed by this festive silence and by the feeling of togetherness which they all shared.

V

The wheel of time keeps turning and history marches on – there is nothing you can do about that. What you can do is be at the helm, take control, and try to make sure it moves in the right direction. This was what we did or, at least, what we tried our best to do.

Before I announced that the revolution had taken place, we considered getting in touch with the Americans (even at dawn on 23 July) to give them an idea of the objectives and nature of our revolution. The image of the United States was closely associated in our minds with championing the cause of freedom and supporting liberation movements. Besides, by establishing such a link we sought to neutralize the British. But how could we do so when we knew nobody at the US Embassy? We eventually found an officer in charge of Air Force Intelligence called Ali Sabri who was friendly at the time with the US military attaché. We summoned him and gave him a message to convey, through his friend, to the US ambassador, Mr Caffery. It was actually delivered early in the morning, on 23 July.

The US ambassador thought this was a nice gesture, particularly as he was one of King Farouk's personal friends (at least, that was what the king thought). Indeed, our contact with him marked the start of a good relationship, so much so that while the British were trying hard to identify the members of the Constituent Council, the US ambassador invited us to have dinner with him at his place and we all accepted.

It was obvious that the country was ready for the revolution: people had lost confidence in the political parties and their hostility to the king and the British was at an unprecedented peak. It was only natural for our tanks to be welcomed everywhere, to be hailed by citizens who chanted and danced about them in great happiness. We were conscious of this and the responsibility it entailed. Our first task was to form a government to handle public affairs satisfactorily. But who could possibly head it?

We agreed, after a reasonably short discussion, that Ali Maher was the best available candidate. He had no partisan affiliation and was well known for his firmness. 'Anwar,' said Nasser, 'you've always been in politics, haven't you? Go find Ali Maher and ask him to form a new government.' I didn't even know where Ali Maher lived. Ihsan Abdul-Quddus, a journalist who had launched many a campaign in the press that paved the way for the revolution, and a friend with whom I had worked when I was a journalist, called on me at Army Command Headquarters. He knew the address and so we went together.

Ali Maher welcomed us and took us upstairs. We sat together on a second-floor balcony where a cool breeze tempered the summer heat. There I told him that the Constituent Council had entrusted him with the formation of a new government. He fell silent. He was obviously embarrassed as it was the king who should make such a demand and he wasn't certain our 'movement' would come off. I began to reassure him and told him we were already in control. Meanwhile four bombers flew overhead at a low altitude. 'Do they belong to you?' he asked.

'They do indeed,' I answered. 'Haven't I told you we are in control of everything? We have had control of the armed forces since dawn, and have since secured control of all the vital services; everything is in our hands now. We ask you to be the new prime minister. This is an order from the Constituent Council, which alone wields all power in Egypt now.' He asked what we planned to do with the king. I said it was up to the king to decide what he deemed fit and that he would then be dealt with accordingly.

At that very moment the telephone rang in the next room. Ali Maher was away for a few minutes. When he came back he said the king had telephoned, that he approved of his appointment at the head of a new government, and that he would receive him in the evening of the same day in Alexandria. 'Congratulations,' I said, and went back to my colleagues at Army Command Headquarters to report what had happened.

We entrusted Ali Maher with the formation of a new government instead of doing it ourselves – that is, instead of having a government of army officers – because we had not prepared ourselves to take over power. Our object was to have a healthy political life in the country, to get rid of the king, the various political factions, and the British.

We had, by then, won the first round. There were others, naturally. To begin with, military forces had to move from Cairo to Alexandria where the king spent the summer months every year, which needed time. Playing for time and so that the king wouldn't suspect our intentions, we pretended to have 'demands' and asked Ali Maher to convey them to the king, when he left on the afternoon of 23 July to see him in Alexandria.

The only real demand we had was for the king to leave the country altogether, but we couldn't possibly declare this at the time. We had to wait until our forces had arrived quietly in Alexandria. Consequently, we faked up a number of trivial demands – six in all, I remember – and took them (Nasser and I) to Ali Maher. He then left for Alexandria in the afternoon to see the king. Later that night I had a telephone conversation with Ali Maher. He had already submitted our demands to the king, he told me, and the king had agreed to all of them. We were surprised, as we had expected a 'dialogue' with the king to begin with. Ali Maher suggested that two members of the Constituent Council should come over to Alexandria to sign their names in the Royal Ceremonies Book, 'to thank the king for granting the army's wishes'. 'I'll discuss the matter with my colleagues,' I said.

The whole of the 24th was taken up in preparing for the military advance to Alexandria, and in the morning of the following day our forces actually started to move. The king learned of this and got in touch with Ali Maher, who in turn contacted me to enquire about it. I told him the forces were going to Alexandria to 'safeguard' the vital services just as had happened in Cairo. The king needn't worry, I said; besides, I would personally arrive in Alexandria later that evening to do what had been agreed on.

'Listen, Anwar,' Nasser said, as we stood in the main hall of Army Command Headquarters, 'let's get rid of this guy as soon as possible. Will you handle this, please? Give him an ultimatum and make him go! We want to get him out of the way quickly in order to have stability.'

'All right,' I said. Muhammad Naguib happened to be passing by and, when he knew what we'd been discussing, he asked to accompany me. We agreed.

Naguib and I took an aircraft, a small military Dove, and landed at al-Nuzha airfield, Alexandria. We went straight to Bokly (the premier's official office quarters during the summer in Alexandria) where we saw Ali Maher.

He was apparently perturbed to hear of the forces advancing on Alexandria. Once again I reassured him and emphasized that the forces were needed to 'safeguard' the vital services, as well as public and private property, especially as many foreigners lived in Alexandria. Some of them, I said, might try to jeopardize public security. We had to be prepared, particularly, for any action by the British Intelligence Service.

When I left, the hall outside the premier's office was swarming with journalists of all nationalities. They gathered around me asking for news. 'No news,' I said. 'I shall see the premier again at six this evening.'

I don't know whether it was my good fortune or otherwise that I was the only member of the Revolutionary Command Council who *had* to be in the thick of events from the moment I announced the birth of the revolution to the actual departure of King Farouk from Egypt. This was what first aroused the jealousy of my colleagues in the Council, especially as I was the only name familiar to the public due to my long political struggle and the fact that the mass media had turned me into a mythical hero over the Amin Osman case.

I was not conscious of such jealousy in the beginning. I behaved naturally and happily, impelled by the joy of a man who had started a great project and wanted to complete it regardless of who took part. I always felt that way and acted in that spirit. Still, I did suffer a lot from a situation I had played no part in creating. I was even unaware of its existence; it was purely the work of our peculiar circumstances.

Now I don't know what makes me recall these jealousies. They certainly never troubled me, even when I came to recognize them fully and clearly. But in the years to come they did, however, affect others so much that the situation nearly exploded on more than one occasion with possibly disastrous consequences to the fine work we had done. That is why I believe that we should bring up our children to disregard all personal considerations in whatever they undertake to do and to adopt a purely objective approach. In other words, a man who builds a house should take secondary importance to the building of the house itself; indeed, the only thing of any importance at all is for the house to be completed, once its foundations have been laid.

VI

When I left Ali Maher I made my way to Mustafa Pasha Barracks, the Armed Forces Headquarters in Alexandria, where Zakaria Mohieddin had been waiting. Only part of our forces had arrived; the rest were expected later in the day. Zakaria explained that he wouldn't be ready to besiege Ras al-Tin Palace and the other palaces of the king, prior to giving him an ultimatum, before seven o'clock the following morning (26 July 1952). The rest of the forces would not arrive, he said, before six in the evening and, after such a long and arduous trip, they needed a rest and a hot meal. Six p.m. on 25 July was, as I have said, the time fixed for another meeting with Ali Maher, at which I was to convey to him the Constituent Council ultimatum.

The meeting had to be postponed – there was no way out. I got in touch with Ali Maher and asked for our meeting to be delayed until nine o'clock on the morning of the 26th. Just before I met him, however, Zakaria had deployed most of the forces around Ras al-Tin Palace, the royal summer residence, and laid siege to it. The royal guard engaged our forces and a battle ensued in which a number of guards were wounded. The king panicked, withdrew the guard, got in touch with Ali Maher, and then he asked the US ambassador for help, as he feared for his life. The ambassador acted cautiously, however, and sent him only his private secretary – Mr Sampson – first, because he didn't want to antagonize us, and second, because he knew that the king was unpopular and that he had lost the encounter.

At nine o'clock in the morning of 26 July Major-General Naguib and I went to Bokly. Once again the hall outside the premier's office was swarming with journalists and once again they pressed me for news. All of a sudden I was approached by a man who introduced himself as a US Embassy counsellor and, in great agitation, asked me why our forces had besieged Ras al-Tin Royal Palace, how come there had been an exchange of fire, and so on. I looked at him indifferently and said curtly that it was none of his business, whereupon he quietly withdrew. I was then approached by another man, an Egyptian, who whispered to me, 'It's important, sir! Dr Yusuf Rashad is on the phone and insists he must talk to you before you see Ali Maher.'

It was obvious the king wanted reassurance and still believed that I, as Yusuf Rashad's friend, could help him. I turned to the man and said, 'Ask Yusuf Rashad to wait; the wheel has turned and can never be put back again.' Dr Yusuf Rashad was a dear friend whom I had used in misleading the king. Because the issue now at stake was greater than friendship, I refused to talk to him until the battle for the removal of the king was over.

When the king had gone and we took control of everything, the situation changed. Then once again Yusuf Rashad was my good friend, whom I loved and whose support for me at any hour of need I acknowledged. That was why when members of the newly formed Revolutionary Command Council demanded, after the removal of the king, that Yusuf Rashad be arrested, they were surprised to see me turn up at the meeting carrying my suitcase. I told them: 'This Yusuf Rashad, well, he had done so much for us ... He had, well, Nasser knows all the details. So, if you have to arrest Yusuf Rashad you'll have to arrest me as well. As you see, I have my suitcase ready and I'm ready for it. This to me is a matter of ethics and principles.' Yusuf Rashad was left alone until the day of his death.

In Ali Maher's office I wasted no time. I opened my briefcase and produced the official ultimatum which was in my handwriting and addressed by the Constituent Council to the king. I read it out. It demanded that the king should leave Egypt by six o'clock in the evening on 26 July 1952. If he failed to do so, he would have to bear all the consequences. Ali Maher's sense of shock was all too obvious. He soon recovered his composure, however, and took the ultimatum so as to convey it to the king.

At 10.30 a.m., one and a half hours after receiving the ultimatum, Ali Maher got in touch with me from his office, having seen the king, and told me the king had accepted the ultimatum. He begged me to come and see him to help draft an abdication statement (the ultimatum demanded that the king abdicate his throne in favour of his son Crown Prince Ahmed Fuad).

I went, with one of our colleagues, the late Gamal Salem, to see Ali Maher in his office. There we approved an abdication statement which provided for a regency due to the new king's minority. It was sent to the king, who signed it. I immediately got in touch with the captain of the *Mahroussa*, the royal yacht, and asked him to have the boat ready to sail the royal family into exile at six o'clock that evening. He was to return the boat to Egypt when the royal family had been taken to their destination.

In Mustafa Pasha Barracks some of my Constituent Council colleagues and I were busy receiving congratulations from well-wishers – party leaders, pashas and beys, and big feudalists – when, to our great surprise, the British chargé d'affaires and the British military attaché (the British ambassador was away on leave) asked to see us. The British military attaché was formally dressed in the old imperial manner the British used to frighten their colonies' leaders. We received them. The chargé d'affaires submitted a note to us, which he read aloud, to the effect that the British, being our friends and allies, wanted to know the revolution's attitude to the Muhammad Ali ruling family and its historical rights, and that they demanded the imposition of a curfew for the protection of foreigners.

This was the first instance of friction with the British after the revolution had taken place. I thought it afforded a good opportunity for us to teach them a lesson, which we had always longed to do. Turning to the two men, I said: 'Item One: The Muhammad Ali ruling family and its historical rights. Surely it's nothing to do with you? It's not a British ruling family, is it? You're an odd lot, I must say. As for the protection of foreigners, you should remember that this is *our* country. As from today nobody should ever claim responsibility for it except us, and us alone ... is that clear? Besides, we would like to know whether your note is official. If it was, we would like it to be in writing and addressed by the British government to us so that we can adopt an official stand on the matter *vis-à-vis* your government.'

The British chargé d'affaires immediately retreated. The piece of paper he was reading was not official and his government knew nothing about it or, indeed, about their 'visit'. He had called only as a friend, he said, not in any other capacity. He begged me to forget all about it – 'It's as though it never took place,' he said. In short, he beat a hasty but very smooth and apologetic retreat.

As soon as he had left, I informed my colleagues at the Cairo Command that our first confrontation with Britain had taken place at midday on 26 July 1952, and that it would end in Britain's complete retreat.

I then contacted the port. I learned that everything was going well on the royal yacht, and arrangements were being made for the king to sail. I ordered our coast artillery to leave the *Mahroussa* alone, and our air force to get a few aircraft ready for a flyover salute to the king when the boat sailed out of Egypt's territorial waters.

Thus, at six o'clock in the evening of 26 July 1952, King Farouk left Egypt. He was seen off on board the royal yacht by members of the Constituent Council – Muhammad Naguib, Gamal Salem, and Hussein el-Shafei (who was not yet a member of the Revolutionary Command Council). I stood on board the warship *Ibrahim* – the flagship and the biggest we had at the time – in the harbour watching our aircraft as they circled overhead. It was a simple gesture, I thought, but sufficiently implied our self-confidence, pride, and tolerance – the emanation of the spirit of Egypt down the centuries.

5

Revolutionaries in Power

I

On the evening of 27 July 1952, one day after the king had left, Nasser called a meeting of the Constituent Council at Army Command Headquarters in Cairo. He began by saying that the first stage of our revolution had been successfully completed with the king's departure on the previous day and that we were now in complete control. Consequently, a decision had to be taken on a very important question. However, he said, he felt that it was his duty first to resign as chairman of the Constituent Council which, with the successful launching of the revolution, had ceased to exist as such. Our Council was to be renamed, as from that day, the Revolutionary Command Council.

Nasser's words didn't make sense to me. Why should he resign? What difference could there be between the chairman of a Constituent Council and the chairman of a Revolutionary Command Council? The revolution had succeeded. Nothing else mattered. Why give different names to things – what's in a name?

It was difficult for me then to grasp what Nasser was after. As far as I was concerned, the success of the revolution and my membership in the Revolutionary Command Council were the embodiment of the dream I had always known – in boyhood when, lying on top of our stove in Mit Abul-Kum, I listened to the ballad of Zahran; in early youth when I moved from one detention centre to another, and in manhood when I was dismissed from the army and spent years in prison, on the run, and in search of a livelihood. To me it was the climactic point of a whole lifetime of suffering and struggling for a vocation. It would not be an exaggeration to say that without such a vocation, life itself could have no meaning for me. Now that the mission was accomplished; now that I personally had taken part in it by announcing the birth of the revolution, getting the king out of the country, and confronting Britain, the people's public enemy number one, to teach them a lesson I had always dreamed of – what else could I want? Could anything else matter? Even if I had not been made a member of the Revolutionary Command Council, even if I had not played any part in launching the revolution, I would have been content to see the revolution take place – my lifelong dream.

This was how I really felt from the start. The revolution did take place; it had to be in the interests of Egypt, and it was bound to vindicate the lofty principles (justice, benevolence, etc.) which had guided my steps from early boyhood. Let the revolution, therefore, take its own course. Let its leaders take the decisions they deemed fit. The outcome must ultimately be the good of Egypt and all Egyptians.

Hence my surprise when Nasser proposed to resign. I objected, but he insisted and did resign. He was subsequently re-elected by a unanimous vote as chairman of the Revolutionary Command Council. Since Nasser, I knew, would never say or do a thing without reason, I wanted to know why he had to do that. Nasser was not in any sense an idealist; on the contrary, he was practical in the extreme, often suspicious, and so bitter as to be wary in every step he took. There had to be a reason, I was certain, for his insistence on resignation and re-election as chairman of the Revolutionary Command Council. He had, I remembered, fallen out with some members of the Constituent Council (due to their well-known power struggle), but now that the revolution had taken place, what could they possibly quarrel about?

I asked myself that question over and over again until I finally succeeded, not in finding an answer but in finding a means of understanding what went on around me. If I may repeat myself, the revolution to me meant something entirely different from what it meant to all the members of the Revolutionary Command Council. To me it was the culmination of a lifelong struggle, and, in terms of my own values and ideals, the moment it came off I felt I needed nothing more – nothing else was of any real value to me – and that was why I could then stand easily aside from all squabbles. My conduct was interpreted as implying indifference, lack of interest, and indecision. It never occurred to my colleagues that I stood aloof because I felt far above their petty conflicts, rather than being incapable of taking part in them. I did it not because I had nothing to contribute but because I felt self-sufficient, although I *was* afraid for the revolution. I was eager for the team to maintain its unity as this must reflect, I felt, on the future of our country. And the petty things I felt one needed to rise above included power. I was firmly convinced that since we had launched the revolution, nothing else mattered; while they were in a vastly different position.

My colleagues on the Revolutionary Command Council had been sitting – only three days before – as a group of young officers at their desks in Cairo like many other members of the armed forces. They had never known what homelessness and destitution meant, never served time in jail or detention centres, never gone through the chastening cycle of hope–expectation–frustration. All they knew was that they found themselves, in a matter of days, transplanted from their army offices into a position of absolute power as the sole rulers of Egypt. Hence the power struggle in which they were now engaged.

If I had not witnessed it all I would hardly have believed it. But Nasser's reaction was very different. He was fully conscious of the power struggle and made sure he was prepared for it. Having secured re-election as chairman of the Revolutionary Command Council, he raised a question which he described as of vital importance, namely, whether to keep the old 'democratic' system of government or to opt for a dictatorship.

Whatever has Abdel Nasser got in mind, I thought; had he gone mad? I was certain that all of us, the people who gave their massive support to the revolution and Nasser himself, had lost faith in the existing 'democratic' system, which had been thrown into disarray by the old political parties in their power struggle and subservience to the king and the British. Furthermore, being army officers brought up on quick decisionmaking and prompt performance, we all sought to achieve the objectives of the revolution (that is, to improve the situation in the country) in as short a time as possible.

The question was put up for discussion. To be absolutely fair, I must record that Nasser insisted throughout on rejecting dictatorship because, as he put it, it marked out a bloody path ahead and, he argued, if you began with bloodshed you inevitably ended in bloodshed. He said he'd rather have back the old 'party-based' Parliament and hand over all power to the parties, even though the people utterly rejected them, than resort to a dictatorship. It would be senseless, he said, to rid the country of a dictatorship exercised by the old political parties only to plunge it in our own brand of dictatorship. Indeed, this would be worse, as the old factions feared the king and the British, but we had absolute power and feared nobody.

Everybody took part in the discussion. I was perhaps the most ardent in defending dictatorship, stemming from my eagerness to serve Egypt's interests – for what may be achieved 'democratically' in a year can be accomplished 'dictatorially' in a day. It never occurred to me at the time that the whole exercise was a trial of strength, that Nasser simply wanted to prove to everybody at the beginning of his term of office as chairman of the Council that he could impose a decision.

As the conflict intensified, I felt we were about to have a serious split and that I had to take the heat off the discussion. I began by summarizing what my colleagues had said, but Nasser interrupted me angrily and said very sharply: 'You're just summing up what the Council members have said ... You don't make sense ... You're acting as though you're the chairman of the Revolutionary Command Council ... What do you think you're doing?'

I was astonished by this but replied quietly, 'Sorry, Gamal. I was trying for a compromise ... I'm not the chairman of the Revolutionary Command Council, or anything of the sort.'

After this sharp exchange the motion was put to the vote. The result was seven against one – seven for dictatorship, and one for democracy, the one being Nasser, of course. Whereupon he stood up and shouted: 'I cannot accept this decision, this opting for a dictatorship. It's a dangerous path, both for the revolution and for our country. I hereby resign all my posts!'

Although the topic was discussed again and the motion again put to the vote, the result didn't change: seven for dictatorship and one – Nasser – for democracy.

Nasser collected his papers, declared he had resigned all his posts, and wished us success although, he insisted, dictatorship was dangerous for the country and we'd soon come to realize how wrong it was.

He left for home at two in the morning of 28 July. We were all at a loss. When Nasser had left, we sat still in deep silence around the table.

Then the discussion was resumed, in the absence of Nasser this time. Our desire for unity made us overcome our differences, our conflict, particularly as Nasser was the motive force without which we could envisage no real start to our reconstruction effort. At the end of this discussion we took a decision that Nasser should be reinstated, and that we had full confidence in him. Two of us went to see him at home and inform him of this.

At dawn Nasser came back. He had won, by our consent and *authorization*. However controversial it may be, that was a historic decision.

II

The first decision we took for the exercise of democracy was to ask the political parties to purge their ranks. The Revolutionary Command Council issued an Act for the Reorganization of Political Parties. We subsequently asked the old parties to approve the Agrarian Reform Law, which was a basic principle of our revolution insofar as it promised a restructuring of the Egyptian society – our professed goal.

The Revolutionary Command Council also issued a decree fixing February 1953 as the time for holding general elections – that is, just seven months after the revolution took place. When Ali Maher, the 'revolution's' premier, whom we had imposed on the king, attacked the parties in a statement which didn't specify the date of the general elections, we prevented the printing presses from releasing the day's editions of the national newspapers until a statement by the Revolutionary Command Council confirming our commitment to the holding of democratic general elections in February 1953 was published instead.

It was a slap in the premier's face. Regarding the first point, the political parties seized the opportunity to carry out a typically partisan and purely formal exercise: the powerful members in each party got rid of the weak ones and declared the purge complete. As for the Agrarian Reform Law, it was rejected by all parties, as well as by Ali Maher, the head of the first revolutionary government.

New measures had to be taken, particularly after the

Act for the Reorganization of Political Parties had been passed. But what came of it? We received applications for the formation of new political parties from the old parties themselves and from twenty-one other groups! Meanwhile, with the revolution barely three weeks old, the conflicts within the Revolutionary Command Council had intensified so much that new and 'neutral' elements had to be introduced (at least to help ease existing tensions). Indeed, we accepted five new members, apart from Major-General Muhammad Naguib, who was appointed chairman of the Revolutionary Command Council at Nasser's request in view of his seniority. The Council membership, at fourteen, was the biggest on record.

It was obvious that we hadn't prepared ourselves, when we carried out our revolution, for taking over government posts. Our highest hope was for our revolution to succeed, for the political parties to be purged, for a 'clean' and genuine machinery of government to be established, and for a new team to hold the reins of power – a team with different views and different methods of approach. As army officers we had envisaged a role in the background. We simply wanted to keep an eye on the situation until the country had achieved its goals, when freedom and independence had been firmly established in the land and neither monarchs nor colonial powers posed a threat to the country's progress. We had no ambition to be government ministers. We had not envisaged that and had not even drawn up a specific government programme.

What happened, however, was that at one of our meetings it was suggested that it was 'high time we began to follow up the work of government ministries', in other words, that each one of us should be responsible for one or more ministries to give a fresh impetus to government performance. So each began to make a case for this or that ministry to be taken over by him, defending his aptitude for the task. When it was my turn to speak, I said, 'I don't think I want a portfolio; I know very little outside politics.'

Salah Salem asked me sarcastically, 'And what is the "politics" you say you know?'

'By politics,' I answered, 'I mean how to realize Egypt's hopes as quickly as possible. We want to usher in a new era in Egyptian history. Well, this is my view of politics.'

The moment I had finished I felt as though I had committed a crime. Salah Salem leapt to the offensive at once, with others joining in, led by Nasser. Salem's attack didn't bother me much as he was well known for his exhibitionism and aggressive insolence; but I was shocked to see Nasser join forces with him when we had been bound in mutual respect for one another since the age of nineteen. I simply saw no justification for his sudden attack on me. I had done all I could, both before and after the revolution broke out, to maintain our relationship, whatever the cost to me. Why did they attack and ridicule me, as though I was an outsider who wanted to usurp their rights or a stranger who spoke a different language?

I was sad. I felt sorry not so much for myself as for Nasser and for them. From that moment on I withdrew, taking up the position of a detached observer watching their conflicts as though from a window in an ivory tower, laughing but wondering all the while. What were they fighting about? I kept asking myself. Eventually I realized that we were only human – we were ordinary mortals. This realization did not prevent me, however, from putting them – any one of them – before myself, proceeding from a belief in the friendship that united us and the joint action we had carried out for the good of millions of Egyptians. Still, hard as I tried to merge into the 'pack', subordinating my individual entity to that of the team (guided by the values and ideals I had been brought up on), the question why Nasser in particular had attacked me, and why the others had supported him, could not be satisfactorily answered.

It wasn't until much later, in fact, that I came to know the answer, or part of it. In the early days of the revolution, the only revolutionary leader known to the public was Anwar el-Sadat, the 'hero' of the Amin Osman case. The press and other mass media created a very impressive image of that 'hero' and expatiated on his patriotism and long history in struggle. Did my record and the various stages of my struggle constitute an offence for which Nasser and some of our colleagues wanted to punish me?

I hadn't as yet realized all the facets of Nasser's character. My love for him blinded me to the truth. Besides, one tends to judge others in terms of one's own character. I naturally trust everybody until some definite fact warrants a change of heart. Nasser (I later came to realize) suspected everybody and everything until there were facts to warrant the contrary; although in the circumstances of the complex life we lead, the contrary is rarely proved.

The experience of years enables me today to state this. At that early stage, however, it wasn't easy for me to accept or even imagine that Gamal didn't trust me – the only man who had never fought him, never demanded anything for himself. Consequently, with the revolution so young as yet, I found myself forced by the events *at that level* to withdraw to a solitary distance from which to watch them. When differences arose, I tried to reconcile them; otherwise, I felt there was nothing that deserved bothering too much about. They repeatedly tried to find out why I adopted that stand, putting it down to weakness, inexperience, or indifference. They could not have been further from the truth. 'I discovered my real self in Cell 54, Cairo Central Prison,' I thought. 'I have, since then, realized that my real self is a greater entity than any possible post or title. Why be surprised, then, to see me shun such human conflicts?'

III

By 9 September 1952, the contours of the picture had emerged very clearly. The Agrarian Reform Law had been rejected by Ali Maher, the revolution's premier, as well as by the political parties; and the purge the parties had formally carried out was anything but real. Obviously, we had to take over power ourselves. Nasser, Gamal Salem, and I called on Ali Maher at his office and told him, 'Thank you, you've done a wonderful job,' whereupon he resigned and Muhammad Naguib was appointed premier. All other ministers were to be civilian.

That was how we started to take over government posts. The idea in appointing Naguib chairman of the Revolutionary Command Council had been that it would put an end to the conflicts that raged within, in view of the fact that we were all young men, practically the same age, while he was many years our senior. Unfortunately, what happened was directly the opposite. New conflicts started, in which Naguib was involved. A 'campaign of rumours' against me was suddenly launched by Naguib (as Nasser told me at the time). It didn't bother me in itself too much; but there were further developments in store.

Only six months after the revolution took place, we were surprised to learn that some party leaders had established links with certain members of the armed forces. There was a simple explanation for this. The political parties which had in their past power struggle sought the support of the king, the British, or both, discovered in the first three days of our revolution that the king had been removed, that the political influence of the old British Empire had been neutralized, and that all power was in the hands of the Revolutionary Command Council, which consisted of Egyptian officers in the Egyptian armed forces. So, insofar as power was now in the hands of the armed forces, the old political parties decided to approach and seek the support of army officers who had wrested power from the king and the British.

When we, the Council, learned of this, we had to take certain measures to make the politicians and the parties understand that the armed forces were not partisan or sectarian but served the whole country. An immediate measure had to be taken to drive that point home. The politicians were taken into detention, while the army officers who tried to hatch a plot against the revolution in co-operation with those party politicians were court-martialled. On 16 January 1953, we disbanded all political parties. In accordance with a decree issued by the Revolutionary Command Council, both the legislative and executive powers would be exercised by the Council for a transitional period of three years, ending on 16 January 1956.

It was then that the Muslim Brotherhood openly declared war on us, with the obvious intention of overthrowing us and taking over the rule of Egypt. So, the Revolutionary Command Council issued a decree disbanding that society. Their activities continued, however, until March 1954, when one of their plots was uncovered, and October 1954, when they made an attempt on Nasser's life in Al-Manshiah Square, Alexandria.

At any rate, all political parties were banned and all power was concentrated in our hands for three years, after which, we promised, Egypt would have a Constitution. Indeed, on 16 January 1956, an Interim Constitution was declared – though why we chose to call it 'interim' I cannot tell.

Recalling those days, I can still see myself writing my letter of resignation from the Revolutionary Command Council and asking for passports for my wife and me to leave and settle in Lebanon. Why Lebanon? I had always heard of its natural beauty, its attractive scenery, so, as a lover of beauty and nature, I chose Lebanon. The reason for my decision was Muhammad Naguib and the unabated war he had declared on me. It went on, both openly and secretly, without apparent reason (at least as far as I was concerned) for a very long time indeed. I later came to know, from the Intelligence officers who had taken part in the campaign against me, that the reason was, in fact, just as I had suspected – that the people were conscious of my long history of struggle. This was used by more than one member of the Council (as those officers later admitted to Nasser) in making Naguib wrongly believe that I wanted his job. I hate conflicts. I don't believe there is anything important enough to warrant a conflict with my colleagues. So, to work with him on the Revolutionary Command Council came to be simply intolerable. I had to withdraw; what else could I do?

It was we who had appointed Naguib chairman of the Council and introduced him to the public as such, so there was no chance of going back on the decision, particularly at that advanced stage. It was decidedly better for me to quit and live in peace, I thought. But Amer got in touch with me, and then it was Nasser's turn, and I was persuaded to withdraw my resignation.

That wasn't all. The same thing happened with Rashad Mehanna, a member of the Regency Council, who imagined that being a regent (due to the minority of Crown Prince Ahmed Fuad) meant wielding total power.

Mehanna now joined the faction against me. Nasser told me that, when they met to talk things over, Mehanna said that if any understanding was to be reached, Anwar Sadat had to quit the Revolutionary Council. I again marvelled at that attitude, particularly as I had never competed with anybody for a post, never engaged in a power struggle at all. It is quite extraordinary how people can live with delusions big enough to transform illusions into reality, reality into illusion. Was there a way of putting things right? We had to do something sufficiently decisive and irreversible. And this Nasser did, in March 1953, by convening the Revolutionary Council and taking some historic decisions.

At a stroke Nasser promoted Abdel Hakim Amer from the rank of major to major-general and appointed him commander-in-chief of the armed forces; and on the same day, Egypt was declared a Republic. We thus got rid of the Regency Council, confiscated the private property of the royal family, and decided to appoint Muhammad Naguib President, having been forced by the Revolutionary Command Council to abandon the command of the armed forces. For the first time Nasser held a government post as deputy premier and Minister of the Interior and, to put an end to all conflict (especially after Amer had been appointed commander-in-chief of the armed forces), some of us were appointed ministers.

Taken together, these moves constituted an important opening chapter for 1953. They show that in less than a year Muhammad Naguib was at loggerheads with the rest of the Council members, and demonstrate a fact of which I, at least, hadn't been conscious before – that power is dazzling. It could sway and turn the heads of men, even 'revolutionary' young men. It was only human, I suppose, but, thank God, it wasn't and won't ever be so with me. When the inner man is more important than anything else, a person is in need of nothing.

IV

The year 1953 was an eventful one, its events variegated. They were mostly the fruit of a revolutionary impulse which was by its very nature (and is almost by definition) young and strong. One event I recall clearly was our request for weapons from the United States. The US ambassador, Jefferson Caffery, being our friend, welcomed our request and immediately got in touch with his government. The answer we received was that the United States would be willing to hold a Mutual Security Pact with us – a formula devised by the Americans after World War II to enable them to fill the so-called vacuum by replacing Britain and France in those countries where they used to have an 'influence'.

The version of that formula delivered to us stated that the United States was prepared to provide us with weapons, free of charge, on one condition: a number of American experts would have to come in with the weapons, and the weapons must never be used against a US ally.

We gave the paper back to the US ambassador and said, 'Thank you, we wanted to buy weapons with our own money; we don't want them free of charge. We also reject the Mutual Security Pact because it affects our independence, which we value as highly as life itself.'

We continued the dialogue with the United States, though unenthusiastically. The Americans agreed to receive an Egyptian military mission in Washington to negotiate an arms deal with us. But when it arrived in Washington, the Americans ignored the mission completely, which hurt us a great deal and left us in no doubt whatsoever that they didn't want to sell us any weapons, and that the whole exercise was merely a tactical manoeuvre.

The Americans tried afterwards to persuade us to join one pact after another – the pacts initiated by John Foster Dulles within the framework of his 'containment' policy, intended to contain the Soviet Union by surrounding it with a belt of bases and pacts. It began with NATO/ SEATO and ended with the Baghdad Pact, which should have linked the two. We gave them a clear and categorical answer. Our will had been competely 'liberated' the minute the revolution was carried out; pacts and maritime bases were out of the question.

The country's budget at the time was £200 million but our economic situation wasn't bad. When the Americans turned down our request for weapons we contacted the Russians early in 1953, while Stalin was on his deathbed, but they in turn refused; Stalin's principles prevented him from supplying weapons to non-Communist states. However, following a meeting during the Bandung Non-Alignment Conference in the spring of 1955 between Nasser and Chou En-lai, a mediation effort was made and the Soviet Union, on Chou's recommendation, accepted it. In September 1955 the first-ever arms deal was concluded between us on the one hand and the Soviet Union and Czechoslovakia on the other.

This reminds me of an incident that took place many

years later. When Nasser died, I sent emissaries to every country. Our envoy to China – the Speaker of the People's Assembly – was asked by Chou En-lai: 'Do you know who killed Nasser at the age of fifty-two?' The Speaker of the People's Assembly was silent. Chou answered his own question: 'The Russians.' And I believe it is true. Nasser liked to have elbow-room for his manoeuvres; given such room, he could perform very well. What happened, however, was that he broke off relations successively with the United States and the West, the Arabs and Iran, and was left with no friend apart from the Soviet Union. This deprived him of all freedom of movement, particularly as the way in which the Soviet Union treated him could never be described as either generous or dignified, and that consequently had an adverse effect on his health. It was undoubtedly one important reason why his morale deteriorated and so precipitated a terminal heart condition and diabetes. How and when a man dies is, of course, preordained by God – but Chou was right.

Two months before he died, Nasser had spent twenty-one days in the Soviet Union. I asked him on his return about the outcome of his visit. His answer consisted of two words in English: 'Hopeless case.' He told me he was so annoyed that he told the Soviet leaders at the end of unsuccessful talks that he would immediately declare he'd accepted the Rogers Plan which the United States had submitted a month before. Nasser in fact did not declare his attitude to that plan until then – when he sat around the conference table in the Kremlin in July 1970. Nasser told me that Brezhnev got excited to hear him state this and asked him angrily: 'Does this mean that you'd accept an American solution?' To which Nasser replied: 'After what you've done to me I would accept a solution even if it came from the Devil himself.'

V

To avert clashes and any possible duplication of work between the Revolutionary Command Council and the Council of Ministers, we set up a body comprising the members of both councils, which was described as a Joint Congress. Apparently ideal, this formula turned out in fact to be far from satisfactory. There were far too many members, and discussions went on for longer periods of time in all directions. Everybody resorted to muscle-flexing and the differences often made it impossible to reach a decision. We were bogged down by such conflicts at a time when every minute counted, when we could ill afford to waste time and our projects for the good of Egypt could not wait. In view of this odd situation, I was forced to take the floor during one meeting and point out, frankly, that due to the incessant manoeuvres that had come to constitute a permanent feature of the Joint Congress, our progress was being obstructed. The method must be changed and another found.

New councils were then set up, one for production, the other for services.

The property of the royal family was confiscated and totalled £70 million, and this we spent on the establishment of rural health centres, hospitals, and schools. The rate was breathtaking – three schools every two days. I remember that in one year we had as many new schools as had been built in Egypt in the previous twenty years. The Council for Production started by establishing the KIMA fertilizer project. Recalling those days I can still see a Greek engineer, with shaggy hair and wild eyes, who was always calling on us at the Abbasiah Command Headquarters. He just called whenever he chose, without prior appointment. His name was, if I remember rightly, Daninos. Every time he stormed our premises, he raved about one unchanging idea – a high dam had to be built on the Nile at Aswan.

The way he harped on this, appearing to be quite haunted by it, and the sparkle of obsession that lit up his face as he talked, implied madness. However, the faith he seemed to have in it (which was almost religious) made us direct the Production Council's adviser, the engineer Mahmoud Yunus, to study it. After a short time he came back with results. From the research and field study he had undertaken, he concluded initially that the idea was excellent but that further riverbed research was needed. He asked us to give the green light for such research, to be undertaken in co-operation with specialized international bodies. We agreed.

The idea of the Aswan High Dam thus began to take shape. Like all great ideas it was the fruit of faith, enthusiasm, and penetrating insight. The establishment of a hydroelectric station on the old Aswan Dam was a project that had been delayed for twenty years by one government after another. We started work on that in 1953; by 1960 it was completed and the power generated from it helped us to start work on the High Dam.

But the one project which, more than any other, helped to change the countenance of the Egyptian community and gave our movement the character of a genuine revolution (rather than a mere *coup d'état*) was perhaps the Agrarian Reform Law. When Ali Maher resigned in September 1952 and Muhammad Naguib took over as premier, the new government immediately began to put into effect a law to limit land ownership to 200 feddans* per person. I should state, for the record, that the architect of that law – the man totally responsible for it – was the engineer, Sayed Marei, present Speaker of the People's Assembly. Sayed Marei was a very prominent figure in the Saadi Party but, on the strength of his work on that

* 1 feddan = 1·038 acres.

project, he took office as Minister of Agriculture and Irrigation (and subsequently deputy premier) to follow up its implementation. Again, it was Sayed Marei who introduced the second and third Agrarian Reform bills which, as amendments of the first, further restricted the size of land ownership and so provided more equality and social justice.

On the political front the banning of all political parties in 1952–3 produced a vacuum which we had, naturally, to fill up. We created a body which we called *Hay'at al-Tahrir*, which meant literally Liberation Corps. It adopted for its slogan, 'Unity, Discipline, and Work.' When this proved ineffective, it was succeeded by another body, *al-Ittihad al-Qawmi* (The National Union) which was equally a failure. The re-formed *Ittihad Qawmi* didn't fare any better; it was duly disbanded and replaced by *al-Ittihad al-Ishtiraki* (The Socialist Union). This was similarly re-formed, and the second Socialist Union finally managed to survive for a time.

All these formulas had been borrowed from Yugoslavia, due to Nasser's close personal relationship with President Tito. Nasser had interminable conversations with him and always showed admiration for his views. The structure of the National Union, at both its stages, was very similar to the Union of Socialists which Tito had established in Yugoslavia after his victory in the liberation war through the well-known partisan movement (during the Second World War), which combined all the nationalist forces throughout Yugoslavia – not only the Communists. Although the League of Communists was kept as the nucleus of the new body, all parties in the five Yugoslav republics were represented.

Nasser modified the Yugoslavian model into that of our Socialist Union. This was done through a National Congress held later, after the breakup of the union with Syria which made people feel so frustrated and sparked off open and violent criticism of the regime. The Socialist Union was based on the alliance of the five 'working forces of the

population' – the peasants, workers, soldiers, intellectu[als]
and national capitalism. The model was submitted to, an[d]
approved by the National Congress; it was then include[d]
in a so-called National Charter which Nasser himself presented to the Congress.

But this Socialist Union was destined ultimately to fail
just as the National Union had; in both cases, the formula
was that of a one-party system. The trouble arose when the
Socialist Union (the one party) later turned into an instru-
ment for wielding absolute power and exercising control
over everything, even people's livelihoods. Nasser's assistants and those who devised theories for him borrowed
Marxist concepts for application in Egypt. They imposed
state 'custodianship' on people's private property, confiscated private capital, put people in detention centres,
and so dealt a fatal blow to the private sector, on the pretext that they had to liquidate capitalism. They disregarded the fact that the National Charter on which
they based their theories actually allowed national capitalism to exist as one of the five forces in the alliance.
Economic disarray was inevitable; it was followed by the
humiliating defeat of 5 June 1967.

Having got over the initial shock, the people began
to direct serious criticisms at the regime. Popular fury
erupted in February 1968 when light sentences were passed
on the air force commanders who were regarded as the
main culprits behind the humiliating June defeat. The
people found out too that the so-called Charter had neve[r]
been applied, that it was introduced only to 'absorb' thei[r]
wrath after the setback they had suffered when the uni[on]
with Syria broke up. Nasser then issued a statement, wh[ich]
came to be referred to as the 30 March Statement. It [had]
really been prepared by his assistants, who were intere[sted]
in nothing but maintaining their power through ab[solute]
autocracy. Indeed, the people soon found out th[at the]
30 March Statement simply maintained the regim[e's dic-]
tatorial grip: it upheld the right of arrest witho[ut prefer-]
ring charges, and promised a permanent Co[n-]

only when the consequences of the Israeli aggression had been removed. This was a disappointment: the people had expected that Statement to usher in an era of democracy, but found that it, too, was designed simply to 'absorb' the wrath of the masses.

I suffered a great deal afterwards from that policy of 'absorption'. My method is to change rather than absorb, to give treatment rather than a soporific dose. I would like everything to be as clear to the people as it is to me. Approaching a given problem, I do all in my power to provide a radical and final solution rather than a temporary one. Still, people *are* different.

Applying the 'temporary solution' technique, Nasser tried to resolve the conflicts that had raged in the Revolutionary Command Council since the early days of 1953: he appointed its members, one after another, to ministerial posts. Before 1953 was through, all 'revolutionaries' had been appointed ministers except one – me.

But could Nasser thus resolve all conflicts?

VI

In 1954 the struggles for power had reached an unprecedented level, particularly those the revolutionaries were conducting against Muhammad Naguib, against the Muslim Brotherhood, and, finally, against a handful of figures from the old political parties who had thought that by supporting Naguib and hatching intrigues they could achieve something.

By March 1954 all this dissension had come to the surface and could no longer be ignored. The Revolutionary Council held a meeting after which we declared that we relinquished all power. However, certain events in the days that followed made us change our minds.

Apart from Muhammad Naguib and his supporters, Khaled Mohieddin – a Marxist and a Communist – was involved in a further development of the conflict. By

using the strength of his Cavalry Corps, Khaled thought he could impose a dictatorship of the left (under the pretence of wanting to restore democracy and the party system), turn human beings into cogs in a wheel, and deprive man of his most distinctively human quality – the God-granted life of the spirit. But the Free Officers exploded the claims of certain officers and politicians to super-patriotism, and the Cavalry Corps mutiny was crushed. We sacked Naguib, then reinstated him soon after. Meanwhile the process of negotiation with Great Britain for evacuating the Canal base had started, accompanied by a remarkable harassment effort against the British base itself. All the hostile elements tried to exploit the rift with Naguib, not because they liked or supported him but because they wanted to put an end to the revolution and take over power. There were Muslim Brotherhood demonstrations in the streets of Cairo. Waving napkins stained with blood and chanting slogans against the revolution, the Brotherhood demonstrators marched to the Republican Palace in Abidin.

In view of all this we had no option but to take decisive action, and Naguib was finally dismissed in October 1954, after the conclusion of the Anglo-Egyptian Evacuation Agreement signed with Britain earlier that month (on 19 October), according to which the seventy-five-year British occupation of Egypt came to an end.

Nasser led the Egyptian side in the negotiations. The British position was that they were prepared to evacuate the base in twenty-four months but would retain some of their stores and some 1200 civilian experts for a period of seven years, after which the stores and everything else in the old base would be given to Egypt in full.

Nasser convened a meeting at the Pyramids Resthouse. He submitted the negotiated agreement to the Revolutionary Command Council and wanted to know the views of each member, individually, while he took down notes.

As always, some of us objected to the draft agreement. There were the usual exercises in oneupmanship and the usual conflicts. I was amazed to hear the views of the 'opposition'. When it was my turn to speak, I burst out: 'I accept the draft. We needn't go into any further discussions. What is there to be discussed? The British want to retain some 1200 non-military experts who would thus be guarded by us, the Egyptians; will such experts frighten us? Let Britain retain 10,000 rather than 1200; and let them stay for 10 rather than 7 years! Could we attach any value to them now we have attained independence and liberated the Canal? Only a stupid politician could reject such a solution to a problem that is over seventy-five years old ...'

The Evacuation Agreement was signed in October 1954. The first steps on the road to independence had been taken. A previous agreement on Sudan's self-determination had been reached – Sudan could either opt for union with Egypt or attain independence. Our withdrawal from Sudan was completed, however, before the time fixed in the agreement, which enabled Sudan to decide her own future. Britain was thus forced to follow suit, so that in fact Sudan attained independence before the British left Egypt.

VII

The years 1953–6 marked a transitional period. They witnessed many important events, most of which may be regarded as turning points in the history of Egypt and the revolution. The Evacuation Agreement was signed in 1954 and the last British soldier left Egypt on 19 June 1956 – the Egyptian flag thus flew high at last over the old British base in the Canal Zone, following a struggle of more than seventy-five years. It was during that transitional period, too, that we finally got rid of Naguib and put an end to the conflicts which the professional politicians tried to exploit to regain power but which could have adversely affected the political life of Egypt. Nasser assumed both the premiership and the chairmanship of the Revolutionary Command Council so that all power was concentrated in the hands of the revolutionaries. Although I had been for a long time reluctant to take part in the executive, I accepted the post of Minister of State in the government Nasser founded in September 1954. For over a year I had been the only member of the Revolutionary Council outside the government. Nasser used to refer to me as a 'getaway man' – a military term for the member of a patrol who remains outside to ensure security.

One of the salient events of that period was Eden's call for the creation of the Baghdad Pact, shortly after the signing of the Evacuation Agreement, on the pretext that a vacuum had arisen in the Middle East and must be filled. Turkey, Iraq, and Pakistan joined the pact. Our revolution was, naturally, opposed to the pact. How could we agree to be members of such an agreement when our predecessors had turned down the idea of bilateral treaties? Besides, having just put an end to British occupation in October 1954 we could hardly be expected to tie Egypt down to a British-controlled pact or to any other foreign power. But our opposition to the Baghdad Pact went further than this: we made concentrated and successful efforts to prevent some countries in the Arab region, such as Jordan and Lebanon, from joining it. This angered Britain and the United States, and resulted in the Anglo-American-inspired 'retaliation' raid by Israel on Gaza of 28 February 1955.

That date – the last day of February 1955 – was of historic significance. It marked, in effect, a turning point in the history of Egypt, the revolution, the Middle East, and Third World countries, inasmuch as it made us realize how urgently we needed weapons and thus led, eventually, to the first-ever arms deal with the Soviet Union (following the mediation effort by Nehru and Chou En-lai, as I have said). That deal helped to pull down the barriers that had been erected between us and the Soviet Union, and effectively raised the morale of the Third World countries, whose members began to feel that there was somebody they could resort to in their effort to liberate their national will from the colonial hegemony under which they had lived for centuries – even if this took the form of straightforward business transactions.

One of the remarkable achievements of that period, at both national and international levels, was the Asian-African Bandung Non-Alignment Conference of 1955. As the first of its kind, it consolidated the position of the non-aligned countries by enabling them to stand side by side with the two superpowers as a third power to be reckoned with. Non-aligned countries constituted a haven for small countries and an example to be followed. On the local level the Bandung Conference boosted Nasser's popularity inasmuch as he was able to cut a fine figure alongside world leaders (such as Nehru and Chou En-lai). He actually won their admiration, although he was much younger than many of them and decidedly less experienced.

VIII

Where did I stand in all this? How much part did I take in these events, and how did I view them?

In December 1953 I had established a new newspaper – *al-Gumhuriah* (*The Republic*) – and assumed the post of editor-in-chief. It was to prove the organ of the revolution and play a significant role in thwarting the Baghdad Pact. Although uninterested in power for so long, I had accepted the post of Minister of State in the government formed by Nasser to help him expedite certain projects. In January 1955 the Islamic Congress was established, with me as secretary-general. This post necessitated many visits to the various countries of our region, as I had to work for closer links between Arab and Muslim countries as well as for certain political objectives in the interest of our national cause. It is no exaggeration to say that I played an important part in the frustration of the Baghdad Pact. In Jordan, for instance, although the king belonged to the same ruling family that ruled in Iraq, I was able to persuade him not to join the pact. One important consequence of this was the dismissal of Glubb Pasha, the British commander-in-chief of the Jordanian Army. It was the decision of King Hussein. In Lebanon I met President Camille Chamoun and succeeded in keeping Lebanon out of the pact, utilizing the old irresolvable hostility between Chamoun and his family on the one hand and the Turks on the other. In Baghdad I met Nuri al-Said to try to persuade him not to join. Our meeting lasted perhaps too long, for the sly politician told journalists that Anwar el-Sadat was negotiating with him about Egypt's accession. When the meeting ended I was surprised to hear this from the journalists. Of course I denied that anything of the sort had happened and explained that it was just one of Nuri al-Said's well-known tricks.

So much for my role during the eventful transitional three years. But there was another, darker side to the picture that must be mentioned: the continued power struggle between the members of the Revolutionary Command Council – a struggle which took a turn for the worse, and was brought out into the open, after Naguib was dismissed as chairman of the Revolutionary Council, and Nasser attained his Bandung Conference popularity.

One instance I remember concerns Gamal Salem, a member of the Council. Before Nasser went away, he appointed Salem acting chairman. Salem was hot-tempered, extraordinarily nervous, and of completely unbalanced character. Finding that he couldn't win people's hearts (if only because he rode roughshod over everybody), he began to make trouble here and there, sometimes with reason, sometimes without. When Nasser returned, the 'trouble' had developed into sharp conflicts. An additional factor was that in Nasser's absence Gamal Salem had taken some measure or other against one of

Nasser's uncles. Nasser was oversensitive with regard to his relatives. It was enough for him to be told that someone had criticized a relative of his for him to order the arrest of the 'slanderer' and take any number of arbitrary measures against him.

This was one of Nasser's weaknesses, which the leaders of the power bloc and their men exploited shamelessly in order to curry favour with him and, at the same time, eliminate their enemies. As a ruler, Nasser should have realized that such was the nature of power, and such was human nature; an Arab aphorism says that a ruler is *naturally* opposed by half of his subjects, if he happens to be just, which, I believe, is true. A ruler is a solo performer on the stage, as it were, and, with the spotlight on him, people can see him very clearly but hardly notice anybody else. Any citizen with troubles, problems, or even trivial daily complaints will naturally blame them on the ruler, even if he is the most fair-minded and even-handed man possible and is not in fact responsible for any of the problems or complaints in question. This conclusion was all the more appropriate in the case of Nasser, who had concentrated all power in his own hands and thus made the people believe, perhaps rightly, that he *was* solely responsible for whatever happened to them.

Personally I believe I am diametrically opposed to Nasser as far as this is concerned. Indeed, one day I wanted very much to tell the people: 'Now that I have put an end to arbitrary arrests and detention centres for ever; now that I have restored the rule of law to you; may I ask you to grant the President the right to use the detention weapon against his relatives – and *only* against his relatives? Power, together with the paraphernalia of power, does not turn my head, but how do I know it does not turn the heads of my family and relations? Surely they could behave unjustly towards others without my knowledge?' Hence the only detention order I ever issued throughout my term of office concerned my elder brother – the man who had helped and stood by me while I was in prison and detention centres, and who helped me through all the other crises I faced, but who shortly after I became President behaved arrogantly towards his neighbours.

This does not mean that I could ever turn against or show the least lack of loyalty to my family, since this is in sharp contradiction with the family values I was brought up on – the values that continue to sustain my lifeblood and determine my mental life more effectively than anything else. Indeed, the faith I have in these values deepens day after day, so much so that I have come to believe that only adherence to such values can save society – that there can be hope only for a society which acts as one big family, and not as many separate ones.

One of my rounds in the region as secretary-general of the Islamic Congress took me to India, shortly before the Bandung Conference was to take place. Nehru accorded me a very cordial reception and gave a reception in Delhi in my honour. He introduced his guests to me, including a member of the Indian Parliament and his wife (who was also an MP). Both were Communists and very much opposed to Nehru, I knew for sure, as I had met them in Cairo and made friends with them. That was why I was surprised to see the man kiss Nehru on both cheeks, and his wife following suit. Nehru didn't know that we knew one another, so he said, jestingly, 'Be careful, Mr Sadat! They are Communists; I hope they won't be able to convert you!' The tone was marvellously paternal, his smile radiant with tolerance and love. The two MPs laughed and said, in the same spirit of love and filial respect: 'It's all right. We shall reply to you in Parliament!'

I was very impressed by what I saw and heard. Beauty can overwhelm me, sweep me off my feet – and that scene was beautiful, animated with love, with the human values I was brought up on in my village, where people live together as one family, where the young respect the old regardless of their differences of opinion (insofar as the old man is the head of the family), and where elders respect the young, because an older man is primarily a father and no father can hold a grudge against his son, even if they differ on one thing or another, for no father can really turn against his son.

I left the reception that day in Delhi feeling very happy with the scene I had witnessed. It continued to thrill me whenever I recalled it, and glowed in my mind as a paragon of excellence until I arrived back in Cairo – where I was brought face to face with scenes of conflict that stood in sharp contrast to it. Everywhere I looked there was tension. My colleagues in the Revolutionary Command Council were quarrelling about everything, however trivial. Naturally I could not take part in these quarrels but remained aloof watching them, sometimes in amazement, sometimes in disgust, but always with deep pain.

The human soul can sink very low indeed when personal interests take over and act as blinkers, distorting its vision of the truth. Those men were jealous of Nasser because he had scored a great success in Bandung and gained remarkable prestige in the eyes of the world. Well, wasn't his prestige also Egypt's? Didn't his success belong to all of us? How could they be so blind?

Under the title 'A Dear Friend Is Back' I wrote a small article (published in *al-Gumhuriah*) welcoming Nasser back from Bandung. Given the same circumstances, I would do it again. The basic element in my natural constitution being love, I find perfect satisfaction in the love I bear others and through it can solve any problem, whatever its magnitude. Without love I would literally lose my balance ... a devastating sense of impotence would overwhelm me. It is only through love that I can function, so to speak, in my full capacity as a human being.

It became increasingly difficult for me, however, to maintain the position I had assumed as a spectator in an ivory tower. The conflict between that image of family love I had carried back in my mind from India and the hate and power struggle that so clearly prevailed in the Revolutionary Command Council in 1955 made it impossible for me to continue. The letter of resignation I now submitted to my colleagues in the Council described that scene, which had impressed me so much in India.

This was the second time I tried to resign – the first having been in 1953.

When I recall those distant days I can see very clearly that the second resignation attempt had the same motive behind it as the first. Both were a direct protest against the conflicts that dominated the Council; each was an equally direct call for 'correcting the course' of the revolution when hatred and jealousies rocked it and caused it to deviate from the line we had professed to take.

Being so deeply engaged in their power struggle, the leaders could hardly be expected to show interest in the people's welfare; their own interests were of paramount importance to them and always came first. A situation arose in which it became difficult to distinguish those who were efficient from those who weren't. A person could easily be punished for another man's crime, or for no crime at all; and something no more positive than a rumour could spell the end of anyone.

That terrible state of affairs was exacerbated by the leaders' conviction that they were entitled to impose anything they wanted on the people, proceeding from the premise that they were 'benevolent dictators'. They found that perfectly plausible insofar as they had created the revolution. Their heads turned by such power, they divided the country into 'spheres of influence' for their own benefit and that of their followers – both relatives and friends. A living example of this was the Foreign Ministry, with which the revolution played havoc. Abdel Hakim Amer appointed cashiered officers in Foreign Ministry sinecures until they reached the civilian retirement age of sixty.

This was typical of the period. The criterion applied was not whether a given project would be useful to the country or not, but whether it could be utilized for illicit gain by the relatives, friends, and satellites of the rulers.

Values were shattered and people lost all sense of security; they couldn't tell what tomorrow would be like or even how today would end.

The Revolutionary Council was formally dissolved on 22 June 1956, when, following a plebiscite, Nasser was elected President. By then, however, fear had reigned everywhere, and, to be gripped by fear is, I believe, the most degrading of all emotions for a human being. In fear personality disintegrates, the human will is paralysed, and man acts as an automaton.

Did the members of the Revolutionary Council realize what they were doing to the people of Egypt? I don't know. What I do know is that the people fully understood what their rulers were doing both to the people and to themselves. A common joke at the time eloquently expressed what the people thought of their leaders:

Once upon a time an Egyptian fox crossed the border into Libya. He was stopped for questioning.

'Why did you leave Egypt?'

'Well, in Egypt camels are being taken to detention centres.'

'But you are a fox, aren't you?'

'Ah, well, God knows how long it will take them to realize that!'

This joke was passed on to us in the Revolutionary Council and amused us a great deal. But rather than laughing, we should have realized that it implied a condemnation by the people of Egypt; we should have done something about the situation in our country before it was too late.

Was that possible? Could we really have done anything about it when human factors had blotted out the idealism which gave birth to the revolution, and blinded us to the reality of everything, even ourselves? Again, I don't know. But I do know that I was happy to see the Revolutionary Command Council dissolved. Indeed, on the eve of his election as President, I called on Nasser and asked him to leave me out of the government he was about to form. I was, I said, still available for any exchange of views as we were still friends and would always be so.

The conflicts I had witnessed over four years proved a terrible burden; they weighed so heavily on my soul that I very nearly succumbed. For, as always, a place lacking in love is no place for me!

6

The Powerlessness of Power:
Egypt under Nasser from July 1956 to June 1967

I

On 22 June 1956, Nasser as President assumed full and complete responsibility for both domestic and foreign policies in Egypt.

On 19 July of the same year the US Secretary of State, John Foster Dulles, declared that the Egyptian economy was bankrupt and that the United States and the International Bank were withdrawing their offer to finance the High Dam. Shipolov, then a rising star in Soviet politics and a foreign minister of the Soviet Union, arrived in Egypt to attend the 23 July Revolution celebrations. He told Nasser that the Soviet Union was prepared to carry out the High Dam project.

This, naturally, boosted Nasser's morale as he was getting ready to leave for Alexandria for the usual 26 July celebrations. He rang me up in the morning of the 26th and asked me to leave with him for Alexandria, where he expected to make a speech in Al-Manshiah Square. But as I was unwell, being immobilized by an acute attack of gastro-enteritis, I asked to be excused. 'It's all right,' he said, 'but please listen to my speech on the radio.' I said

I would certainly do that, though I was surprised at his request. It was only natural for me to listen to the speech. I wondered what had made him make such an odd remark.

I didn't think too much about it until he started actually to deliver his speech. It was a long one, as usual, and contained nothing out of the ordinary until, halfway through, he began to talk about Ferdinand de Lesseps, the Suez Canal engineer. I realized then what he was about to do. Minutes later Nasser declared that the Suez Canal Company had been nationalized in retaliation for the action taken by John Foster Dulles and Anthony Eden, the British prime minister and leader of the Conservative Party.

I did in point of fact feel proud. For there it was: Egypt, a small country, was at last capable of speaking loud and clear in defiance of the biggest power on earth. It was a turning point in the history of our revolution, and in the entire history of Egypt. The nationalization decision had vast repercussions both inside and outside Egypt. From that moment on, Nasser turned into an Egyptian mythical hero. The Egyptian people had been yearning for such a moment of proud achievement and self-fulfilment, after nearly a century of humiliation and oppression at the hands of British colonialists.

The following day Nasser came back to Cairo by train to find the entire Egyptian people waiting with a hero's reception for him. He went to Government House, and stood out on the balcony to salute the demonstrators, then made a speech which further fired their enthusiasm. When he had finished, he came into his office, where I was waiting for him.

'Listen, Gamal,' I said.

'What is it?'

'You never told me about that decision and you've already taken it, so that's that. But I'd like to tell you something.'

'Go ahead.'

'If you had consulted me, I would have told you to be more careful. This step means war, and we're not ready for it. The weapons we have, we've only just received from the Soviet Union. The arms deal was concluded last year – in September 1955, as you know – but actual delivery didn't start until October, even November, and we've not been adequately trained to use the new weapons. Our training has been British, and we haven't had time to change our military thinking, our military orientation, from Western to Eastern. If you'd asked me, I would have told you to be careful. But now that this decision has already been taken, of course, we should all support you. And I shall be the first to do so.'

Indeed, from 27 July 1956 on I started to attack Dulles and the United States most fiercely in my *al-Gumhuriah* editorials. The Soviet Union was extremely happy with this because it had found somebody to fight its battles for it – somebody to wake up the Third World countries and the colonies for a small price, indeed: the Soviet weaponry for which we paid in full. It seems the Soviet Union liked that game, for the Russians made a practice of letting us fight their battles for them, as happened in the Yemen and elsewhere. They provided us with weapons, received their price, and lost nothing. In fact, as it later transpired, only the Soviet Union stood to gain. The Soviet weapons are usually more expensive because less old, than the Western ones, and, if we add the $2\frac{1}{2}$ per cent interest rate charged by the Soviet Union on its arms deals, the Western weapons turn out to be less expensive in the long run.

Anthony Eden heard of the Suez Canal nationalization at a dinner he was giving in honour of King Faisal of Iraq and Nuri al-Said, the Iraqi prime minister. He interrupted the dinner to contact Guy Mollet, head of the French Socialist Party and prime minister, and David Ben-Gurion of Israel. At the time British forces had evacuated the Canal Zone, but the British and the French owned all shares in the Suez Canal Company on a 50/50 basis.

This wasn't the only reason the British were angry. With

his traditional colonialist mentality, Eden found it difficult to accept Nasser's attitude when, having thrown a
monkey wrench into the works when the British tried to
create a Baghdad Pact, he now proceeded to nationalize
the foreign Suez Canal Company.

Eden agreed with Guy Mollet and Ben-Gurion to resort
to force of arms. They didn't declare this, however. Instead, they applied a variety of camouflage tactics such as
the convening by Eden of an international conference on
the Suez Canal in London, the setting up of a Suez Canal
Users Association, and, finally, the referral of the dispute
to the United Nations. It was agreed that Dr Mahmoud
Fawzi, then Egyptian Foreign Minister, would meet his
British and French opposite numbers on 29 October to
draw up a peaceful settlement and decide on the financial
compensations incurred.

The meeting never took place, of course; for that very
day, 29 October 1956, was the date fixed by Eden, Guy
Mollet, and Ben-Gurion for the implementation of the
plan on which they had agreed at their secret meeting in
Sèvres in France (as it was revealed afterwards). Sure
enough, Israel attacked Sinai and air-raid sirens were
sounded in Cairo at last light on the 29th, the date fixed
for a UN peaceful settlement. Nasser was at home. He
went up to the roof of his house and saw with his own
eyes foreign aircraft, bearing British and French markings,
as they bombarded Almaza airfield – which wasn't far
from his house. He realized that the plot had begun. The
same evening, he went to Army Command Headquarters
and issued orders for the immediate withdrawal of our
forces from Sinai, to avoid falling into the trap prepared
so carefully – for the Israelis were attacking our front, the
British and French our rear. The orders were carried out
most meticulously over three days, which saved two-thirds
of our armed forces. We should, therefore, recognize this
decision by Nasser as a stroke of genius. True, all our
aircraft (which we had bought from the Soviet Union less
than a year before, and in which we took great pride) were

destroyed on the ground at one blow, but nobody, Nasser or no Nasser, could have done anything about that. Britain and France made a surprise attack on us. They sent us an ultimatum – which I described in my *al-Gumhuriah* column as 'dirty' – on the very day they committed that act of aggression against our airfields.

The Anglo-French ultimatum gave us only twelve hours to act and so perturbed some of the old-guard politicians in Egypt that they decided to approach Nasser so as to persuade him to accept it in an attempt at a desperate salvaging operation. When Nasser heard of this he ordered a presidential guard firing squad to take up its position in the Government House courtyard. Anyone who suggested that the ultimatum should be accepted would there and then be executed.

Nasser proceeded, of course, to declare to the world that Egypt had rejected the ultimatum and was determined to fight on, happen what may. This declaration came in a speech he made in al-Azhar Mosque on 2 November 1956. The entire people supported him – he rode to al-Azhar and back in an open car. Meanwhile the British people were throwing stones and tomatoes at 10 Downing Street, the British premier's residence, in protest against the unethical action he had taken.

Having rejected the ultimatum, Nasser summoned the US ambassador (Mr Raymond Herr) and gave him a message to convey to President Eisenhower: 'Will you please deal with your allies – Britain and France – and leave us Israel to deal with?' Eisenhower replied that he would do all he could.

In the thick of the fighting, between 29 October and 2 November, Shukri al-Kuwatli, the then Syrian president, was on an official visit to the Soviet Union. He spoke to the Soviet leaders about the Canal battle and asked them to extend a helping hand to Egypt. However, they refused point blank, whereupon al-Kuwatli sent word to us to that effect and advised us to rely on ourselves, as no hope at all could be pinned on the Soviet Union. This made me believe, from that moment on, that it was always futile to depend on the Soviet Union. On 5 November Eisenhower intervened and asked Britain and France to withdraw at once.

When the Soviet Union learned that Britain and France had responded to the US President's request, it addressed a warning – known as the Khrushchev–Bulganin Ultimatum – to both countries. It was nothing in effect but an exercise in muscle-flexing and an attempt to appear as though the Soviet Union had saved the situation. This was not, of course, the case. It was Eisenhower who did so. Both Britain and France obeyed his orders and withdrew their forces by 23 December. Israel followed suit. All her forces were withdrawn by March 1957, after Golda Meir, then Israel's Foreign Minister, had declared to the Knesset that Sinai had been annexed to Israel and that Sharm al-Sheikh had been given a new name. Ben-Gurion's famous dictum, 'What must be feared, must be feared,' was made at the time. He had the United States in mind, actually; for Israel couldn't afford to lose the support of America as the world's greatest power.

We must pause a moment at this point, perhaps go back in time a little, to have a clear view of Israel's line. Israel has always had to seek the support of the world's biggest power. Between the wars Great Britain was such a power, and the Israelis sought her support; after World War II Britain and France lost their position and the United States emerged as the most powerful country in existence. And so Ben-Gurion worked hard to transfer the activity of the Zionist movement in full to the United States. Indeed, he did everything in his power to keep the weight of America's support behind him alone, and would not allow the Arabs to have firm friendly relations with the United States. This policy since the advent of the Egyptian Revolution had been based on the necessity of maintaining bad blood between Egypt and America. Ben-Gurion was deeply perturbed, as I have said, when we set about cementing our relations with the United States in the early days of the revolution. He in fact decided to sabotage US-Egyptian relations through the well-known Lavon affair: A secret operation was planned by Ben-Gurion and Pinhas Lavon, then Israel's Defence Minister. Israeli agents would be sent to Egypt to strike at US interests or US 'centres' in Egypt. So, in 1953, attacks were made on the US-owned Cinema Metro in Cairo and the US Consulate in Alexandria. The Egyptian police seized the culprits – two Israeli young men who gave a full confession on their part in the Lavon plot. They were tried and sentenced to death but committed suicide in prison. It was a big scandal and we informed the United States of all the details. Lavon, then, differed with Ben-Gurion and resigned. His resignation is known in Israeli history as the Lavon affair.

Nasser should have learned a lesson here, namely that Israel's strategy is based on creating a rift between the United States and Egypt. But Nasser did exactly the opposite to what he should have done: he attributed the failure of the 1956 tripartite aggression to the Russian 'warning', and praised the role of the Soviet Union, in complete disregard of Eisenhower's efforts and his direct orders to Britain and France to withdraw from Egypt. This was absurd because it was the US attitude, as I have said, that turned our defeat into victory. Besides, as a professional politician, Nasser should have seized that chance to consolidate US-Egyptian relations, if only to frustrate the Israeli strategy which sought the reverse.

But that was Nasser's nature. His vision would be blurred, and he would lose both insight and foresight, above all because he was so greatly influenced by the reports his entourage submitted to him. His men were not honest in giving him advice; all they were interested in was magnifying Nasser's self-image in his own eyes and so maintaining their own posts and power.

Up to 31 December 1956, the Anglo-Egyptian treaty was still officially in force. During the fighting the British experts retained in the Canal Zone were, naturally, put in custody. According to that agreement, they would have been retained for seven and a half years beginning in 1954, when the treaty concluded.

Now the invading British forces withdrew by 23 December 1956, on Eisenhower's orders, and on 1 January 1957, Nasser declared the abrogation of the Anglo-Egyptian Agreement. Our commitments under it had thus been lifted, and the experts we had detained became prisoners of war, who were later exchanged for our own POWs. On the same day Nasser declared a more important decision – the Egyptianization of the Egyptian economy in retaliation for the damage caused by the Anglo-French air raids. This was a big blow to the capitalists since until then all insurance companies, banks, and major business concerns had been French, British, Belgian or – in a word – European.

This was followed by the payment of debts to all shareholders in the old Suez Canal Company. The debts, which all told did not exceed the annual revenue of the Canal, were paid in instalments. In return, Britain released an Egyptian foreign reserve currency totalling £400 million that had been frozen in retaliation for the Canal nationalization.

So, in 1957 we started having complete control of our economy, and were in possession of all our own economic resources and hard currency assets, as well as the £400 million released by British banks.

This should have been a point of departure indeed. Assets were available; we had adequate revenues; and everything was ready for a plan that might help us carry out vast domestic reconstruction projects to make up for the time lost under foreign occupation.

Unfortunately, nothing of the sort took place, for Nasser was preoccupied with the fable which came to be associated with his name both in Egypt and the Arab world – that he was a hero who had defeated the armies of two great empires, the British and the French. Having completely disregarded the real part played by Eisenhower to that end, which turned military defeat into political victory, he became the first to believe that he had won. He could never see that he had in fact been militarily defeated.

Thereafter followed a few attempts by Dulles to create a hero out of King Saud of Saudi Arabia, to elevate him to the position of a leader of the entire Arab world, so as to destroy Nasser, isolate Egypt, and eventually destroy her as well. These attempts came to grief, however, in spite of Dulles' efforts to frighten King Saud and warn him off Nasser and all Nasser's friends. King Saud once showed me a report by the CIA which alleged that I was Soviet agent number one in Egypt. The reason it gave was that I contributed a daily column in *al-Gumhuriah* attacking the United States for trying to obstruct the advance of our revolution. My purported attack focused on John Foster Dulles, the Secretary of State, whose brother, Allen Dulles, was director of the CIA.

This shows that the CIA could rely for its information on unreliable and flimsy sources much like the sources the Soviet Union relies on today for its information.

III

Dulles did not give up, even when his efforts to isolate Egypt and destroy Nasser had completely failed. He prompted Turkey to build up huge army concentrations on the Syrian border, and the situation rapidly deteriorated. At the time an Egyptian-Syrian Common Defence Agreement was in force. Then, one morning, the world woke up to hear that an Egyptian warship had arrived at the Syrian port of Latakia, and that 5000 Egyptian soldiers had disembarked there, complete with arms and ammunition. Both the United States and Turkey were taken by surprise – and genuinely so – for the Egyptian naval force had sailed from Alexandria to Latakia in secret, in spite of the fact that the US Sixth Fleet and the Israeli Navy still patrolled the eastern Mediterranean.

That gesture inflamed the enthusiasm of the Arab world. Nasser towered even higher as an unstoppable national – Pan-Arabian – hero, and the idea of a Syrian-Egyptian union was born.

After this we began to prepare for National Assembly elections. Two points loomed large at the time. First, the Revolutionary Command Council reserved the right to object to certain candidates. And, indeed, when nominations were made we did object to many, either because they belonged to the old political parties or because they opposed the revolution. The second was that some of the Free Officers who had left the army and engaged in political civilian activity had 'closed' constituencies. Out of 350, 60 constituencies were thus given to them. Elections took place and the first-ever Parliament under the revolution met in 1957 – that is, five years later.

Three days before the opening session I was with Nasser at the Borg al-Arab Presidential Resthouse. I was surprised to be asked to act as Speaker of the Assembly, but I agreed. Two days later, however, Nasser convened a meeting of the Revolutionary Command Council members in Cairo at which he said he was thinking of appointing Abdel Latif al-Baghdadi Speaker of the Assembly because he was most senior. Why did Nasser change his mind in no more than two days? I still don't know. However, as he could often change his mind at the last minute, some of us were careful not to divulge a decision taken by Nasser (or even an opinion) until Nasser himself declared it to everybody.

I didn't care really about Nasser's change of heart. It

didn't worry me not to be Speaker for I was a member all the same, and, throughout my career, I never sought power or a position in the government. I was the first, as I have said, to apologize to Nasser on his election as President for not accepting a government post; indeed, I genuinely asked him not to entrust me with any official state portfolio.

As one of the Free Officers had to be appointed Deputy Speaker, Nasser offered the post to more than one person and each in turn declined. He was then left with no choice but to approach me ... and I accepted. My colleagues wondered how I could agree to work under al-Baghdadi, when we were simply colleagues in the Revolutionary Command Council and there was nothing to choose between us. This was not, of course, how I looked at it. Never in my whole career did I prefer one post to another on account of 'power'. I would serve in any capacity as long as I knew it was for the good of Egypt – Speaker, Deputy Speaker, or member were all the same to me. What counted was what I did, not the post I held.

Towards the end of 1957 we received an invitation from the Syrian Parliament, under Akram Hourani, to visit Damascus. Nasser agreed with al-Baghdadi that I would head the delegation. We left in November for Syria, to find events developing at a breathless pace. Shukri al-Kuwatli was president, but he did not enjoy the support of the whole army. The army was itself divided, and each faction had to have a separate camp for fear of a *coup d'état*. Nobody trusted anybody.

Early in February 1958, a bigger surprise yet was in store for us. Five Syrian Army commanders arrived in Cairo, met Nasser on the same day, and asked for an immediate Syrian-Egyptian merger. Nasser tried to change their mind. No union, he said, could take place just like that, suddenly and without preparation, if only because of the many differences between the two countries. But it was useless. On the third day of the talks, faced with their unyielding insistence, Nasser had no option but to accept. The official union between Egypt and Syria was declared on 22 February 1958, under the title of the United Arab Republic (UAR). Nasser was named as President of the Republic.

Most Arab countries were not happy to hear this. Saudi Arabia in particular wanted Syria to remain neutral, as the Saudis shared a common border with Syria. Saudi Arabia had, in fact, paid regular 'salaries' to some Syrian party leaders, heads of government, and ministers to maintain the status quo. Now that Syria had joined Egypt, other Arab countries grew increasingly afraid lest Nasser should do the same to them. That was the way King Hussein of Jordan, King Faisal of Iraq, and President Chamoun of Lebanon all felt. Everybody became apprehensive of the new power which had emerged through the Egyptian-Syrian union to disturb the balance in the region – and not only the Arab countries but also Israel and the representatives of Western imperialism.

As it happened, King Faisal of Saudi Arabia (God rest his soul), who was then Crown Prince, was on a visit to Egypt at the time. We were good friends and he made a habit of taking supper with me at my house near the Pyramids. As we were eating one evening, he said to me: 'Which way are you going?' referring to our union with Syria, of course.

I answered, 'It's too late now to do anything about it.'

'I beg you,' he said, 'to tell Brother Gamal that that country [Syria] is tribalist and factious. We know it better than you do. This union won't survive – it won't fit in with the political current over there and will do you harm. I'm confident of this. I'm talking to you as a friend and a brother. You'll be dealt a blow in the end.'

I listened to King Faisal very carefully. He was sincere in giving advice and was always a rational and stable character and, above all, a real friend. But what could I do? It was 20 February 1958. Finally, I said, 'It's all over, Faisal. Al-Kuwatli will be here in two days' time for the

union to be officially declared. The decision is irreversible.'

'I'm telling you this,' Faisal said 'just to clear my conscience. You can be sure this union will end in disaster.'

He was right.

On 22 February Nasser and al-Kuwatli made speeches
in Cairo from the Government House balcony in which
they declared the birth of the Egyptian-Syrian Union.
Minutes before, they had signed the relevant document
which, at Nasser's request, I also signed, even though I
did not at the time hold any government post.

The National Assemblies in both Egypt and Syria were
subsequently dissolved, prior to the formation of a single
Assembly for both countries. Nasser and I took one of our
regular Comet airplanes and flew to Syria in great secrecy;
we were afraid lest Israel should hear about it. Israel felt
our union was catastrophic for her, so much so that Ben-
Gurion could not conceal that Egypt and Syria had now,
as he put it, got Israel in a nutcracker.

We arrived in Damascus and spent a whole week in the
Presidential Guesthouse. I really feel incapable of describing that week. It was like a constant delirium – a stream
of talk that flowed day and night, Nasser making a speech,
followed by al-Kuwatli, then by me, then by Nasser again,
ad infinitum! We were joined in that speechmaking
marathon by some Syrian leaders and we simply couldn't
stop, for our Syrian audiences wanted more and more.
The crowds couldn't get enough and seemed to grow increasingly frenzied. All that was said was hailed, applauded, celebrated. People chanted and screamed and called
for more. For a whole week the crowds besieged the
Guesthouse. They camped outside in the wide square, eating, drinking, and sleeping in the open air.

It was from the same balcony that the Interim Constitution was declared at the end of that week. I read it out
myself article by article to the people in the square, who
were literally drunk with enthusiasm – applauding every
clause, every word, every syllable.

IV

On 14 July 1958, while Nasser was on the way home from the island of Brioni, Yugoslavia, where he had met Marshal Tito, he received a message from Abdel Hakim Amer – the acting President – that a revolution had broken out in Iraq. He received another message from Tito advising him to interrupt his trip and return to Brioni lest, on account of the Iraqi Revolution, the US Sixth Fleet in the Mediterranean might do him harm. Nasser asked Tito immediately to prepare a special aircraft for him at Paula airport. He took the cruiser that had guarded his yacht back to Brioni, while the yacht, with Nasser's family on board, sailed on to Alexandria.

Nasser himself flew from Paula airport in Yugoslavia direct to Moscow, where he met Khrushchev and asked him to support the Iraqi Revolution against Western pressures, intrigues, and armed attacks (such as the aggression committed against Egypt in 1956). Nasser told me personally that he did all in his power to persuade Khrushchev, in sixteen hours of talks, to help the Iraqi Revolution, but it was no use. Khrushchev refused to render any kind of assistance. It was a repetition of what had happened in 1956 when Shukri al-Kuwatli urged the Soviet Union in vain to help put an end to the tripartite aggression against Egypt.

Nasser was extremely saddened by that meeting. He informed nobody of this, apart from Amer and myself. He went to Damascus, where he made a speech in which he declared to the Syrian people and to Arabs everywhere that the Soviet Union stood by the Iraqi Revolution. His purpose was twofold: he wanted to cover up for the Soviet Union and at the same time make the West think that the Iraqi Revolution *was* being backed. Nasser remained in Damascus for a while until the new revolutionary regime in Iraq stood firmly on its feet, then returned to Cairo.

While on another visit to Damascus in 1959, Nasser was surprised to learn of a fierce attack by Khrushchev on the Egyptian-Syrian Union. It was dictated by the well-known Communist detestation of nationalist or even patriotic sentiments. Nasser attacked Khrushchev in return and contacted me in Cairo for a similar attack to be launched in Egypt. I was secretary-general of the National Union, the only political organization in Egypt at the time. I made an anti-Soviet speech at Abidin Square in Cairo, then went to Alexandria where I made another, renowned for its fierceness at the time, in which I had unprecedented success in arousing anti-Soviet feeling. On his return from Damascus, Nasser told me that when he started his attacks on the Soviet Union the CIA got in touch with him and said they were at his service and that the United States was willing to give him any assistance he required. He told them, he said, that he'd fight his battle on his own and that he just wanted America to help him with wheat and oil supplies, and so on. Indeed, US aid had an important role to play at the time, for it helped us to run a comfortable budget. When it was stopped in 1965, the effect on the Egyptian economy was considerable.

A little while after the Iraqi Revolution broke out, Abdul-Karim Qasim took over as Iraq's only strong man. Qasim was a Communist agent and his name was on the list of Communist Party members. The Soviet Union naturally gave him its support and he, in fact, was one of the reasons why the Soviet Union intensified its campaign against us in general and against our union with Syria in particular. When we attacked it in return, Khrushchev gave us his famous dictum (based on an old Russian popular proverb): 'Don't spit in your own well; you're bound to return to it for a drink.'

V

With the end of the 1950s and the beginning of the sixties the revolution entered an era of painful experiences, defeats, setbacks, and some of our gravest mistakes. I have always maintained that while the fifties saw the 23 July Revolution realize colossal achievements, the sixties saw it making colossal mistakes.

The only bright spot in 1960 was the completion of the old Aswan Dam hydroelectric station, and the start of work on the new High Dam. The detonation signalling the latter event was witnessed by King Muhammad V of Morocco. Apart from this, one could record nothing on the credit side. Conflicts between members of the old Revolutionary Command Council had come to the surface as Nasser, for reasons at the time unknown to me, always left a trail of hatred – in fact a huge legacy, so to speak, of hatred. That wasn't true in my own case. I don't recall ever having a grudge against Nasser. Some of my actions could be unfavourably interpreted, of course, but as I never coveted anything myself, I simply never hated anybody. But of the others, I knew for sure that each one bore, and still bears, Nasser a good deal of hatred. Even Abdel Hakim Amer, who was Nasser's only lifelong friend, saw his relationship with Nasser deteriorate towards the end of his life into a terrible exercise in hate.

As the grudges and the hatred came to the surface in the sixties, the unity with Syria began to disintegrate – much to our dismay. Only one and a half years after the United Arab Republic had been formed, it became clear that things were going seriously wrong. Political parties had been disbanded in Syria, including the Baath Party which, alongside of other parties, had hoped that it could achieve its ends through the union and had therefore not objected to the disbandment. But when they realized that that wasn't possible, the Baathists began to crack jokes about the National Union and to intrigue against our unity.

Nasser realized what was happening in 1960, yet he couldn't prevent it. He felt he was in a blind alley, and that he was helpless. He became convinced that something would happen to strike a blow to the union – and perhaps to the situation in Egypt as well. It was in that year that Nasser contracted diabetes, as a result of the state of despair and helplessness he was in. It was a strange co-incidence that I had a heart attack on 15 May of the same year, as a result of my exhaustion over many successive years but particularly at that point, following a trip to Conakry in West Africa to chair the Afro-Asian Solidarity Conference at which the dispute between the Soviet Union and the People's Republic of China came to the surface for the first time.

Before leaving for Conakry I had resigned from the National Union. I had felt that Nasser had turned rather cool in his relationship with me, perhaps as a result of slander. He was always listening to gossip and 'reports', and if a slanderer touched on his own person, his family, or his security, he could be very easily influenced. As usual in such circumstances, I remained cool. (I generally kept away from him until the cloud had passed and he decided to approach me again to put an end to our estrangement.) So, when I returned from Conakry and fell ill, he came to see me. Salah Salem had started a rumour to the effect that Nasser was behind my heart trouble, and Nasser wanted to know if this was true. I denied it, naturally; I said that the reason was probably my exhaustion over long years of hard work both before and after the revolution, added to the extremely hot and humid climate of Conakry, from which I suffered badly.

VI

In the summer of 1960 Nasser asked me to stand for election as Speaker of the Federal (Syrian-Egyptian) National Assembly. I did so and was elected. It was my first post in public life after recovering from the heart attack. At about the same time Amer was appointed commander-in-chief of both the First and Second armies (that is, the Syrian and Egyptian armies) with the rank of field marshal. Nasser bestowed on him the title of Vice-President as well.

In 1961 the predicament of the United Arab Republic was getting even more serious. All the political parties had resumed activity, and dissatisfaction spread far and wide. Nasser had relied on one person in Syria, Abdel Hamid al-Sarraj. The Syrian people had been suffering before the union from the same conditions we had known only too well in Egypt until a few years before: suppression of freedom, mass arrests, detention, torture, abuse of individual powers, and the physical liquidation of opposition – often in the form of murder. Now, after union with Egypt, the Syrians hoped the situation would change, but this, of course, never happened. People in Syria began to show resentment, and increasingly aired their grievances. Nasser consulted us about sending Amer to Syria – in his capacity as second in command and commander-in-chief of the armed forces of the new state – in the hope of improving the situation and salvaging the union. We agreed. Amer did leave for Syria, though Nasser still left al-Sarraj in his old position – a big mistake insofar as al-Sarraj believed he was more entitled to rule Syria than Amer was.

Aside from Amer's other mistakes, he simply never could choose the right assistants. But even more important than this was his sectarianism, for he just stood by his assistants, regardless of whether they were in the right or no.

As a result a secret conflict between Amer and al-Sarraj arose. It grew in intensity until finally even the man in the street in Damascus was involved. As usual Nasser supported Amer, regardless of whether he was right or wrong. Added to this, King Saud paid £7 million through King Hussein of Jordan to the rebels in Syria, and Nasser on 23 July 1961, issued the socialist laws which had an undeniable effect on the Syrian community, based as it was on free enterprise and business. Clearly, the Syrian people were very dissatisfied with both Nasser and the union. The situation came to a head when people in Damascus woke up on the morning of 26 September to hear that units of the Syrian Army had besieged Army Command Headquarters in Syria.

Amer lived in a house nearby, so he rushed over to the command headquarters. The Syrian Army representatives started to talk to him through a loudspeaker, bellowing and threatening. Then the rebels began to issue military communiqués (complete with numbers) as though the country was at war. When Nasser learned of this, he tried to save the situation. But it was all in vain. Amer was seized and sent to Egypt by air. Egypt and Syria were separate once again. The union was gone – it was as though it had never taken place.

Faisal's prophecy had come true.

VII

Among the revolution leaders the breakup of the union led to a deep dissatisfaction *vis-à-vis* Nasser and Amer; among ordinary people listlessness reigned supreme. Questions were in the air: Why did it happen? Who was responsible? The breakup of unity had been preceded, it is true, by certain socialist laws designed to serve the interests of the masses but the bulk of the population still lacked one very important, even essential, factor – freedom. And nothing can make up for a man's lack of

20

personal security.

This was something that Nasser never understood to the day of his death. He imagined that people were happy and satisfied with his method of government; but he forgot that deep down in every citizen's heart – even among the classes he imagined he was serving – a paramount need for freedom had always burned.

On Amer's return from Syria he told Nasser he could not carry on as commander-in-chief of the armed forces on account of the humiliation he had had at the hands of the Syrian Army. His pride simply wouldn't allow it.

Nasser was delighted to hear this. He had expected it, or hoped for it, from the days of the 1956 War, when Amer adopted an irresolute stand and the armed forces were in as poor a shape as they were on the day the Syrian-Egyptian union broke up. But he could not show Amer that he welcomed his resignation; he dared not, in case Amer should change his mind. They knew each other too well, and lay in wait for one another all the time.

For a whole week Amer didn't turn up at his office in Army Command Headquarters, while Nasser worked on the speech he wanted to make – the speech in which he was to declare that since Syria had chosen that road, may God bless her voyage upon it, and everyone should respect her will and solitary way. Then he finally made the speech, which was well received in the Arab countries, and two days later he was surprised to receive from Amer certain requests regarding armed forces equipment and so on which meant that Amer was simply carrying on as commander-in-chief. Nasser was at a loss. Behind Amer's change of heart were advisers, such as Shams Badran, and some of his relatives and friends who exercised a bad influence on him. There was also his determined belief that he was Nasser's partner; as long as Nasser remained in power, Amer had to continue as commander-in-chief.

Not only was he at a loss, Nasser was furious. But he concealed his feelings and called a meeting – attended by all of us – at which the subject was raised. We told Nasser there was no need for further discussion: we believed that Abdel Hakim should have left the command in 1956 rather than 1961. He was a nice man, no doubt, and a gallant one, but he was unfit for military duty. In a word, we told Nasser that Amer's removal from the army was a foregone conclusion and should not be brought up again for discussion.

This didn't prevent us, of course, from wondering between ourselves about the reasons for convening that meeting. It would have been only natural for Nasser, in his capacity as President, to issue a decree, immediately the union broke up, appointing another commander-in-chief and perhaps keeping Amer as Vice-President. Only later on did we come to realize that Nasser wanted to establish our opposition to Amer as that of *public opinion*. As we saw it, the situation hardly called for this. We were not the ones to be regarded as public opinion, and the people as a whole were actually demanding the head of the man responsible for all this.

When we left, Nasser summoned Amer and started a lengthy conversation, which was protracted over many meetings – after which Amer vanished. Nasser called another meeting with us in which he said he had told Amer about our decision but that Amer didn't respond. Amer had now disappeared, Nasser said, and his whereabouts were unknown (he was, it later transpired, in Marsa Matruh). Our reply was that if Nasser took back his decision – which had our unanimous support – he would be acting against the interests of Egypt. We further remarked that he needn't consult us on this as the responsibility was solely his as President of Egypt.

Meanwhile, just to spite Nasser, Amer submitted the letter of resignation that came to be famous (when it was published in 1967) in which he said that he was resigning for democracy! He deliberately mentioned things he knew would enrage Nasser. He said, for instance, that he would not accept a system of government that did away with political parties and relied on an absolute dictatorship. Amer knew very well that Nasser would never allow the contents of that letter to be made public for, as the whole people called for democracy, to accept the resignation would have turned Amer into a national hero – the last thing Nasser wanted.

Nasser called another meeting and submitted Amer's resignation to us. We said that he was the President of Egypt and needn't have asked us now or before for an opinion. Nasser then sent for Amer again and had yet another meeting with him. A big question mark emerges at this point and hangs even now over the special Nasser-Amer relationship. What happened was the exact opposite of what we had anticipated: they agreed that Amer should resign as commander-in-chief of the armed forces but that he should be reappointed deputy supreme commander, for the supreme commander should always be the President. Although an honorary post, the supreme commander does exercise his power at time of war. He has to sign the Fighting Order, as well as the Strategic Order which defines the strategy of war for the commander-in-chief of the armed forces. Notwithstanding this, Amer insisted on remaining in actual command by preventing the appointment of another commander-in-chief in his place. Nasser granted him his wish but intended to appoint General Mahmoud Fawzi by 23 July 1962 (we were then in December 1961).

The appointed date saw the situation unchanged. On 23 July 1962, Fawzi was still Chief of Staff, and all the high-ranking officers who supported Field Marshal Amer still kept their posts. We again wondered why Nasser convened those meetings with us and repeatedly asked us for advice. Everything was now back to normal between Nasser and Amer; it was as though nothing had ever happened – except, of course, that Amer had been promoted to deputy supreme commander, and thus kept the powers of the commander-in-chief. And the situation continued this way, unchanged, right up to the 1967 disaster.

Nasser told Amer that the decision to remove him from

his original post had been taken by his colleagues – the members of the old Revolutionary Command Council – which naturally disturbed our relations with him. But having considered the matter rather more closely, Amer came to the conclusion that we couldn't have taken such a decision by ourselves, that Nasser must have asked us to take it. He came to know, of course, of the meetings Nasser had held with us in his own home. So, from that time on, Amer began to be wary of Nasser, just as Nasser was perpetually on his guard, always watching out and moving cautiously instead of acting with the firmness and resolution of a true President.

That was how the first power bloc against the established regime came into being, and it exercised its power quite openly. For Amer's prime concern was to secure his position. He felt he must make sure that he was unharmed by Nasser now that the belief (which he had always held) that a gap of distrust and conflict separated him from Nasser and the rest of Council members had been confirmed.

So the conflict that emerged in the early sixties widened and the disintegration intensified. Hatred now dominated Nasser's relationship with Amer, Nasser's relations with other Council members, and Amer's relations with them. I looked on at this with a broken heart.

That situation was the earliest prelude to the 1967 defeat. Amer's efforts were devoted to the consolidation of his position, not only within the armed forces but on the level of Egyptian life at large. And Egypt was thus plunged into the worst turmoil imaginable.

The armed forces were faced with the breakup of unity while unprepared, and negligence made the situation worse. The Yemeni Civil War of 1962–7 ensued. Instead of being an opportunity for our armed forces to gain more experience, training, and equipment, it turned into an occasion for personal gain which Amer's men exploited. Amer didn't stop them, however. To entrench his position in every sphere, he appointed officers and ex-officers as board chairmen in civilian establishments, as chairmen of town councils, and in all the civic institutions throughout Egypt. The army officers even had a say in the renting of government-owned apartments.

He imagined that in this way he could make himself popular, but what happened was the opposite. Amer's behaviour made people more dissatisfied with him personally and with the regime in general. As a result of the suppression of freedoms and the lack of any sense of democracy in the period that followed the breakup of the union with Syria, dissenting elements were active, and the people grew increasingly restless. Amer portrayed this to Nasser as a counterrevolution, and consequently the property of many old politicians was put under state custodianship. But the measure was scarcely effective; instead of neutralizing popular dissatisfaction, it intensified it. In view of this Nasser resorted to the trick of setting up a Constituent Committee of 200 (also called a 'Consultative Committee'), consisting chiefly of intellectuals, with me as secretary-general. We met at the National Assembly. Nasser attended most meetings and took part in our conversations, which were later published in the press. The whole thing was designed to make Nasser appear as though he was interested in and wanted to solve people's problems. He therefore welcomed the conclusion reached by the Committee – to issue a charter which would define the line, goals, and policies of the revolution.

This appeared to work, as most intellectual members of the Committee had primarily objected to the lack of any definite programme for the revolution. The charter was drafted and Nasser submitted it to the 'expanded' National Congress held at the time. He read it out article by article; it was endorsed by all those present, and did serve its purpose. The people were kept busy trying to understand it and fathom its ideological implications.

At the time our Political Organization was still in existence but, as the members were not elected but appointed, they were lame and practically helpless. They could not, for instance, put the charter into effect. The charter was issued, it is true, and it was being taught in youth groups and universities; but no part of it was ever actually implemented.

VIII

In the summer of 1962 Saudi Arabia, Syria, Jordan, Iraq, and Lebanon held a conference in Shutura with a view to attacking and isolating Egypt, and dealing a blow to our regime.

It was very unfortunate. However, the Yemeni Civil War broke out on 26 September 1962 (the first anniversary of the breakup of unity with Syria), and that was a good opportunity to teach King Saud a lesson. He had financed the breakup of the union with Syria, and led the campaign against Egypt, while his country had common borders with the Yemen. So when the Presidential Council met in Cairo to consider the Yemeni request for assistance, I was the first to support it. I convinced the Council of the necessity for supporting the Yemeni Revolution, and we did so.

While I was responsible for the political side of the Yemeni Civil War, Amer was, naturally, responsible for the military side. As usual he took the wrong actions throughout. Instead of using the Yemen as a battlefield for training our forces in guerilla warfare and new tactics, he turned it into an opportunity for personal gain. It offered Amer the chance to establish his feet more firmly in this new territory, and to spread his influence in such varied directions that nobody would be able to shift him from his entrenched position as head of the leading dissident power bloc in Egypt. Quite apart from this, his military involvement steadily grew. The one Egyptian brigade initially sent to the Yemen multiplied until one day the Egyptian force in the Yemen numbered 70,000. These were not withdrawn until after the 1967 defeat, when King Faisal and Nasser met at the Khartoum Conference and agreed on that.

The Yemeni War was a military failure for Egypt. We had a regular army fighting an enemy well versed in guerilla warfare. Still, I cannot say that our sacrifices were made for nothing. The Yemen got rid of the Imam's regime, which was worse than anything in the Middle Ages, and as a result of the Yemeni War Aden attained independence. The war, it is true, used up a large portion of our hard currency reserves; it also prevented two of our best divisions from taking part in the 1967 War. But to state this is not to deny that intervention in the Yemen was a necessary political coup. It was one of the factors that curbed King Saud's aggressiveness and affected his position at home and within the Saudi ruling family, since it precipitated his removal and Faisal's takeover – a remarkable gain not only for Saudi Arabia but for the entire Arab world.

IX

In 1965 the domestic situation in Egypt had become truly pathetic. Ali Sabri, then prime minister, would not take a decision on anything. He was by nature afraid of responsibility – which may have been the reason why Nasser picked him for the job. Dictatorial by nature, Nasser didn't really want a premier but a secretary, who took no action beyond the implementation of orders. And Ali Sabri was like that. If we add to this his natural inclination to spy on people, hatch intrigues, and play underhand games, it is easy to understand why people resented him. Indeed, what could Egypt gain from a government like that?

The situation grew worse as the problems we encountered in our public services – telephones, transport, housing, etc. – were not solved on the spot but were actually shelved as of 1962, under the pretext of having to be handled within the framework of certain ambitious plans that were simply impracticable. These problems intensified and accumulated over the years, so much so that it has become very difficult to solve them now. The pretext used by our officials at the time was that such public services and utilities could be sacrificed for the establishment of productive firms in co-operation with the Soviet Union.

In the same year, 1965, President Johnson cut off US economic aid to Egypt and so put us in a very critical position. Our plans were thus jeopardized, since we had relied heavily on our imports of US wheat, for which we paid in local currency and so saved about £80 million that could be spent on other projects.

With US aid cut off, we had no option but to approach the Soviet Union. So Nasser, Zakaria Mohieddin, and I paid a visit to Moscow in September 1965. The Soviets had already removed Khrushchev, on whom we had looked as a friend, if only because he was a firm, genuine, and straightforward man, who never applied the evasive tactics of his predecessors. The new leadership sent us the man who had led the coup that toppled Khrushchev – one by the name of Shilipin – to pave the way for reconciliation. When we arrived in Moscow, we found that the new leaders did their best to satisfy us, first in order to counter the effect on us of their removal of Khrushchev, and second, to neutralize the consequences of Chou En-lai's two-week visit to Egypt. Chou was in fact waiting to see what might happen to the Afro-Asian Solidarity Conference, which was supposed to be held in Algiers. In fact, because of Boumedienne's coup just beforehand – in which Ahmed Ben Bella was removed – the conference was cancelled.

The object of our Moscow trip was to persuade the Soviet Union to put off for a while the remittance of a few instalments that were due in repayment of our debts to the USSR. We needed the cash to make up for the cut-off US aid and to carry out our ambitious plans. In fact, the Russians responded to our requests in a manner we had never anticipated. They decided to write off 50 per cent of our debts, which had totalled £400 million, so that we had only to repay £200 million. The instalments were cut in half.

X

In response to popular sentiment towards the end of 1965, Nasser removed Ali Sabri and appointed Zakaria Mohieddin as premier. He, however, soon fell out with Nasser and could not survive in office for more than a few months. Amer was behind their clash, as he hated Mohieddin and wanted one of his own men to be premier. He now got his wish with the appointment of Sidqi Sulayman.

Amer grew increasingly powerful. A time came when he put the armed forces and the military police in charge of all, or nearly all, public affairs. When public transport was in need of 'attention', for instance, the armed forces took it over; and the same happened to many other government-owned establishments. When, in 1965, it was reported that the Muslim Brotherhood were hatching a plot against the regime, the military police were put in charge, with Shams Badran, Amer's most eminent assistant, directing operations. It later transpired that acts of cruelty were committed – torture, humiliation, and the shattering of human dignity. I cannot state categorically that Nasser knew what was happening, but at the same time I cannot absolve him of responsibility for it. Whatever his own intentions may be, a President is always held responsible for the mistakes of his assistants.

As usual Nasser looked on any protests, any objection or criticism, any attempt at fact-finding or the least expression of resentment, as a counterrevolutionary reaction that must be ruthlessly crushed. So, in the Muslim Brotherhood affair, certain countermeasures had to be taken. And, as it happened, these measures proved to be the most ruthless and savage Egypt had ever seen. First, a committee was set up. It was called the 'Committee for the Liquidation of Feudalism', and was headed, of course, by Amer.

The Committee for the Liquidation of Feudalism practised the worst types of terror, repression, and humiliation. Its members played havoc with life in Egypt everywhere, their gravest and most heinous crime being the shattering of human pride – which our people could never accept. The Egyptian people may endure poverty, deprivation, even starvation, but they can never accept a hurt to their pride. Certain instances of the Committee's behaviour were brought to my notice at the time; but perhaps because of their very enormity, I was reluctant to believe that they were true. Then one day I saw the Committee literally at work.

I was on a visit to my home village, Mit Abul-Kum, when I was asked by a young agronomist whether I had seen the verdict of the Committee for the Liquidation of Feudalism on the nearby township of Tala. I said I had not. He then showed me one of the daily papers in which that 'verdict' was published. I was shocked: a number of local mayors and eminent, honest citizens had lost their jobs and their property had been put under state custodianship. I knew them all well, and was certain they were good people and that they definitely supported the revolution.

I hadn't thought the situation had reached that dismal point. I drove straight back to Cairo in a rage and spent some time locating Amer's whereabouts. Then I rang him up. 'How could you allow this to happen? You're tampering with people's private lives ...' His reply was maddeningly quiet: 'Don't get worked up. We'll cancel the verdict.'

Sure enough, the decision was cancelled on the same day it had been issued. (That was the only decision to be taken back by the Committee for the Liquidation of

Feudalism on the same day it was issued.)

This was my own personal experience with the Committee. I heard many stories afterwards which revealed how those in power, in order to gain more power, humiliated the Egyptian people and the values we had all been brought up on. They used to storm people's private homes by night, arrest the men, and drive out women and children who wandered about in the streets looking for shelter.

XI

This was what the domestic situation in Egypt was like by 1966. In foreign relations we were now at a point of direct confrontation with the United States and, as Nasser always went to extremes in conducting a dispute, he pushed this one right to the point of no return, relying as he did on Soviet support. It so happened, however, that the US government extended an invitation to me, in my capacity as Speaker of the National Assembly, to visit America – perhaps with a view to a rapprochement.

Nasser welcomed the idea. He was beginning to feel that he had 'wronged' the Americans too much, especially when he said in one of his speeches, 'If the Americans don't like it, they can go jump in the lake' (the Arabic equivalent of the idiom is, literally, 'They can drink from the sea'). 'And if the Mediterranean isn't big enough,' Nasser went on, 'there is the Red Sea as well!' I accepted the invitation and left with my wife for the United States where we were accorded a good reception. When I visited the Congress I was given the chairman's seat – I sat there again during my 1975 visit.

However, in the course of an official dinner held in my honour by Mr Averell Harriman, the chief adviser to the President, an American woman journalist surprised me with a question I had never anticipated. She held a newspaper in her hand and, pointing to a column, said: 'What do you think of this statement?' 'Which statement?' I asked. Whereupon she read a most strongly worded attack on the United States by Nasser. Dumbfounded, I said: 'No comment.' Of course I wondered why Nasser had done that when we had agreed to improve our relations with the United States and he had encouraged me to make the visit. If he was against improved relations, why did he approve of the visit in the first place?

It was strange, to say the least, and could hardly be explained away – let alone justified. Still, my visit was not affected too much by the incident as the Americans did everything in their power to make it a success. Indeed, while we were in San Francisco the chief of protocol was a Jewish lady who wanted to be excused for not receiving and accompanying my wife on account of a genuine illness. But she was prevented by the State Department, who ordered her to do her duty first, then go into the hospital!

XII

The last days of 1966 saw the Nasser-Amer conflict deepen even further. Each now lay in wait for the other almost daily, especially as Amer's power increased each day. Working through the Feudalism Liquidation Committee and on the pretext of having to crush the counterrevolution, Amer got rid of all opposition and appointed (or dismissed) whoever he wanted in all public institutions and government departments – even sporting club boards. The complaints of individuals and public establishments alike were referred to the armed forces for adjudication. So much power had accumulated in Amer's hands that he came to control people's lives and all public events.

How did this strike those revolutionary leaders who still officially 'ruled' the country?

Zakaria Mohieddin had resigned the premiership sadly at the beginning of 1967. He was a reticent man by nature and refused to say anything about it. Nasser watched what

Amer was doing with bitterness and a paramount sense of helplessness. He felt he could do nothing at all about it. The day came when Amer actually wanted to take over the government so as to be absolute ruler.

In the early part of 1967 the gloom in Egypt was all-pervasive. The country was bankrupt; the economic development plan was too ambitious and no funds were available to finance it. The deficiencies in public services were getting worse – Ali Sabri had put off all attempts to deal with them since 1962 simply to show Nasser that he had higher and more important goals to achieve, industrial projects that were in effect baseless. But graver than all this were the conflicts which now reached an unprecedented level among both the rulers and their lackeys.

One Friday in February 1967 I called on Nasser at home without prior appointment as I was wont to do. I asked the officer on duty whether Nasser was up. He said he had woken up some time ago and that he was now in his study. I entered the room to find Nasser holding his head in his hands and looking very sad and worried. I stood there for a while looking at him before asking: 'What's the matter, Gamal? Are you all right?'

He turned to me in surprise – for he obviously hadn't noticed me coming into the room – and said: 'Why did you come today, Anwar?'

'It's Friday today,' I answered, 'and as I haven't seen you for some time I thought I'd pass by and have a chat with you. I knew you'd be alone on a Friday.'

'Thank you. That's very good of you,' he said quietly. 'Please sit down.'

I sat down, then again asked him: 'Gamal! You look as though you're very worried indeed. What is it?'

'I *am* worried,' he said. 'My dear Anwar, the country is being ruled by a gang of thieves ... you know ... and I cannot carry on like this. I cannot continue to be President, to hold such a serious responsibility, while it is Amer who actually rules the country and does precisely what he wants. I think it is better for me to go, and perhaps concentrate on my duties as chairman of the Arab Socialist Union [the only political organization]. I'm willing to hand the presidency over to him and to answer for everything that has taken place up to the minute of my departure. I'd give answers to all questions ...'

It was obvious that Nasser knew everything that was happening in Egypt – the problems that had been accumulating since 1962, the unbridled behaviour of the Feudalism Liquidation Committee, and the ferocity of the corrupt power bloc – headed by Amer, Sharawi Gomah, Sami Sharaf, and Ali Sabri – particularly their suppression of freedom and monopolization of all privileges of power.

I then said: 'It would be unreasonable for you, Gamal, to quit the presidency and concentrate on the Socialist Union. Amer and his assistants would be in sole control of Egypt. You know that Amer is the worst person to choose his assistants. It has actually transpired that they were behind the breakup of unity with Syria. Yet Amer supports his assistants blindly. When he was told we wanted to remove Air Force Commander Sidqi Mahmoud he said, "Over my dead body!" He's just like that! I believe it would be best to summon him for a private conversation and perhaps you'll be able to reach a solution between yourselves.'

Gamal said gloomily, 'It looks very bad, Anwar; I feel we're heading for disaster ...'

A few days later I went to see Nasser again but was told he had a visitor and so had to wait in the study for a while. At length Nasser came in. The moment he saw me he asked: 'Can you guess who's been with me?'

'Who was it?'

'Shams Badran! Do you remember our recent conversation and my reference to a "gang" and so on?'

'I do indeed,' I said.

'Well, things have come to a head. Shams Badran was here to make a formal request for Amer to be premier. Do you know his reasons for it? He says there are complaints

– that people are complaining! Doesn't he realize that it's all because of his and his men's behaviour?'

'What did you say?'

'I took it calmly,' Nasser said. 'I told him I had no objection. I was willing to give him the premiership provided he left his post as head of the armed forces. I said I could find none better than Abdel Hakim to head the government.'

'Gamal, I still believe you should see Amer personally and discuss the matter with him. You know that he'd accept the "unacceptable" if it came from you. In this way the affair could be contained and a solution found.'

'No, Anwar!' he said vehemently. 'The whole thing is going in the wrong direction.'

Amer's reply to Nasser's suggestion to exchange his proposed premiership was utter silence. Amer regarded the command of the armed forces as his natural right and wouldn't give it up for the world. It provided him with an infinite source of power.

This was followed by grave developments in the work of the Committee for the Liquidation of Feudalism. The most ferocious period was from March to May 1967, when the Committee was actually attempting to liquidate the assets of all rich families. I thought this very serious indeed, and I believe, although nobody knows for sure, that Nasser's advisers encouraged this tendency in him. Most important among them was his press adviser, who hated big families and longed to see their downfall. It gave him great pleasure to strike at established Egyptian families and humiliate them. When put under state custodianship, the property of an individual was run by the state and the head of a family given a meagre stipend in compensation which was referred to as 'alimony'. Potential victims in Upper Egypt hated this word like the Devil. If he was unfortunate enough to be put under state custodianship he would scream in protest, 'Am I to receive alimony like a divorcée?' – it simply hurt a man's pride.

The situation continued unchanged until the middle of May when it was planned to strike at all the big families, province by province, beginning with al-Buhairah. It so happened, however, that the vast shadow of late May–early June 1967 was cast to stop all those measures. A disaster can have a bright side or, as Milton says, a 'sable cloud (may) Turn forth her silver lining on the night'.

During the same month, May 1967, I left for a trip to North Korea, and then went on to Moscow where I listened on the radio to Nasser's May Day speech in Cairo. He spoke of counterrevolution and feudalism, citing as example an incident that had taken place in a village close to mine. I heard him mention my name and wondered how reports would be transmitted like that to Nasser and how he could pass judgement before examining such reports.

The village in question was Kamshish, and it was the scene of a brand of feudalism actually unprecedented in our country. Indeed, the people Nasser referred to and cited were worse than the feudalists: they were Communists and Marxists who wanted by their attack on feudalism to substitute a Marxist system. To that end they shattered the dignity of citizens in an even more despicable manner than the Feudalism Liquidation Committee. All this was quite unnecessary in any case as we had liquidated feudalism in that village years before and distributed the land to the peasants.

But the village of Kamshish was at the time a centre for Communist activity in the Nile Delta. The Communists even invited Jean Paul Sartre to visit Kamshish to show how proud they were of their achievements.

I was annoyed by the speech. Nasser had accompanied me, two years before, on a tour of al-Munnfiah, during his presidential election campaign. I explained to him at the time the reality of the uproar raised by the Communist elements and he actually told off his assistants about it after 15 May 1967. But no meetings were ever held by the committee concerned because after 20 May trouble of a different nature was brewing – the opening acts of the 5 June 1967 disaster.

XIII

I was seen off at Moscow airport by Mr Semenov, the Soviet Deputy Foreign Minister, who was accompanied by the Speaker of the Soviet Parliament. The plane was more than an hour late, which gave us a chance to talk at length, mostly about the Syrian situation. They told me specifically that ten Israeli brigades had been concentrated on the Syrian border. When I arrived back in Cairo, I realized that the Soviet Union had informed Nasser of this. Levi Eshkol, then Israel's premier, subsequently stated that the Israeli forces would, if need be, occupy Damascus.

At the time we had a Common Defence Pact with Syria. Furthermore, the Russians were trying to set the Arab leaders by the ears (as they had done during their agent Qasim's rule in Iraq) and to provoke Nasser by claiming that the Syrian leadership was more progressive. Nasser therefore ordered Field Marshal Amer to concentrate the Egyptian forces in Sinai. Although his real aim was to deter Israel, the situation soon got out of hand.

At the time many Arab brothers criticized Egypt for leaving the Tiran Strait at the Gulf of Aqaba, Israel's only outlet to the Red Sea, open to international, particularly Israeli, navigation. Once on a visit to Pakistan, Amer felt so irritated by Arab exercises in oneupmanship exploiting this question that he sent us a cable demanding that the Tiran Strait be closed to Israeli navigation. At any rate Nasser convened a meeting of what he called a Supreme Executive Committee towards the end of May 1967, which was attended by Amer, Zakaria Mohieddin, Hussein el-

Shafei, myself, Ali Sabri, and Sidqi Sulayman – the prime minister at the time. Nasser said: 'Now with our concentrations in Sinai, the chances of war are fifty-fifty. But if we close the Strait, war will be a one hundred per cent certainty.' Then, turning to Amer, he asked: 'Are the armed forces ready, Abdel Hakim?' Amer pointed to his neck and said: 'On my own head be it, boss! Everything's in tiptop shape.'

We all knew that our armaments were adequate – indeed, infinitely better than in the October 1973 War. When Nasser asked us our opinion, we were all agreed that the Strait should be closed – except for Sidqi Sulayman, who pleaded with Nasser to show more patience, to take into account our economic situation and the ambitious development projects that were now mostly frozen, particularly after US aid had been cut off, and so on. Nasser paid no attention to Sulayman's objections. He was eager to close the Strait so as to put an end to the Arab manoeuvrings and maintain his great prestige within the Arab world. Orders were thus issued for the Tiran Strait to be closed and the United Nations Emergency Forces to be withdrawn.

All this was in fact overdramatized by Nasser, while the Soviet Union consistently warned that the tempo of events was moving faster than it should. Nasser was carried away by his own impetuosity. And for a curtain to that tumultuous drama he chose a world press conference in Cairo in which he showed himself at his most defiant and violent.

The international situation was thrown into confusion as a result. The Soviet Union, so as to avoid getting involved (as is its usual practice), deliberately further confused world public opinion. At the same time Israel resorted to her familiar tactics, pretending to be weak, in need of help, the side that had been 'wronged'.

With the Tiran Strait closed, war became a certainty. We held daily meetings at Army Command Headquarters with all commanders of the armed forces. Our forces were concentrated in Sinai. Meanwhile the Soviet Union asked to see an Egyptian envoy and Shams Badran, in his capacity as War Minister, was sent to Moscow. In the Kremlin he was asked what Egypt would do if the US Sixth Fleet intervened in the fighting. He answered without hesitation: 'We have a weapon that can deal it a lethal blow.' He had in mind the rocket-carrier TU-16 bomber which, loaded with its rocket, can go no faster than 310 mph, that is, half the speed of a civilian Boeing. The joke amused them a great deal in the Kremlin, just as it amused us in Egypt.

The War Minister returned from the Soviet Union, having concluded an arms deal – with no delivery times specified, which was normal for the Soviet Union. As always, the Russian leadership wanted to complicate the situation but, more important, they wanted to fix the times themselves and so secure their control of the situation. (This was, incidentally, why I took my later decision to expel the Soviet military experts from Egypt, among many other decisions. I know my country's interests better than the Soviet Union, and I cannot accept that a guardian power should manage our own affairs.)

On Friday 2 June 1967, Nasser endorsed the defensive War Plan in his capacity as President and supreme commander of the armed forces, as well as being an excellent soldier who had served in Sinai and knew it thoroughly. On that day, I remember, Nasser told Air Force Commander Sidqi Mahmoud that the air force would be dealt the first blow, whereupon the latter turned to him in obvious nervousness, and said: 'We've taken that into account, sir; we shan't sustain any losses beyond the calculated ten per cent.'

On the same day Nasser said that Israel would attack us on Saturday or Sunday or, at the latest, on Monday 5 June 1967. There was a change of government in Israel. A coalition government had been formed, with Moshe Dayan as Defence Minister. Dayan joined Eshkol and Lyndon Johnson in a deliberate camouflage operation designed to make the Arabs think that Israel didn't intend to fight a war against them. The situation was too obvious, however, to be camouflaged in this way.

On the day of the disaster itself – 5 June – as I learned afterwards, the plan which had been endorsed by Nasser had been completely changed by Amer. That too was obvious, for Israel was able to occupy Al-Arish in the evening of that day while she could not do so in 1956 when our forces were vastly weaker than in 1967.

On Monday 5 June Amer, accompanied by all commanders, took an aircraft and flew off on a 'tour of inspection' to Sinai. It was only natural that when the commander-in-chief was in the air, orders should be issued to all SAM and anti-aircraft batteries to hold their fire. And it was during that tour that Israel attacked all our airfields and hit our aircraft on the ground. We can thus say that the war began and ended while Amer was in the air.

How did I learn of the disaster? I knew from broadcasts on the morning of 5 June that Israel had started the attack, and so I thought, 'Well, they'll be taught a lesson they won't forget.' I was quite confident, so I had a shave, took my time changing to go out, then drove myself to the command headquarters. I had been there when the War Plan was laid down and had unshakable confidence in our victory. Our equipment was more than adequate and the plan superb. I arrived there at about 11.00 a.m. The Soviet ambassador's car was ahead of mine, so I thought that he had called to congratulate us. 'What's the news?' I asked. Some officers said we had shot down forty enemy aircraft so far. 'Splendid!' I said.

I went into Amer's office to find him standing in the middle of the room, looking about with wandering eyes. 'Good morning,' I said, but he didn't seem to hear me. I said 'Good morning' again, but it took him about a minute to return my greeting. I immediately realized something had gone wrong. I spoke to those present and was told that our air force had been completely destroyed on the ground. In a while Nasser emerged from another room. Amer began to talk, putting the blame entirely on the Americans; it was the US Air Force, not the Israeli, that had dealt us that blow. Nasser replied: 'I am not prepared to believe this, or to issue an official statement to the effect that the USA has attacked us, until you've produced at least one aircraft with a wing showing the US ensign.'

Nasser's insistence on this was firm and unyielding. Having realized the magnitude of the disaster, however, he changed his mind and issued a statement in which he accused the United States of attacking Egypt as a political cover-up for domestic consumption.

Another odd incident of the ill-omened 5 June events concerns Amer's reaction. The minute his aircraft landed and he was informed of the disaster, Amer summoned the Soviet ambassador to demand a cease-fire, although the war had broken out exactly one hour before. And this was why the Soviet ambassador had called at the Ops. Room in the morning of that day.

What could I do? I just went home and stayed in for days, until 9 June, in fact, when Nasser was due to address the nation on radio and television at 7.00 p.m. I was in constant contact with both Amer and Nasser. In the evening of 5 June I rang up Amer. He told me dryly and irritably that the Israelis had reached and captured Al-Arish. It was too much. I didn't know what to do with myself. I was in the habit of walking about 2½ miles a day, but in the days after 5 June I simply didn't know how far or for how long I walked. I walked and walked, losing any sense of time or distance. Perhaps it was 6 miles or more – perhaps less – I simply didn't know. I was dazed and unable to locate myself in time or space.

I grew even more dazed and broken-hearted as I watched the crowds flocking in from al-Tahrir Province in big trucks, or filling up the vast Pyramids Road as they marched in 'companies', chanting, dancing, and applauding the faked-up victory reports which our mass media put out hourly.

The fact that they were rejoicing in an imaginary victory – rejoicing in what was in effect *defeat* – made me feel sorry for them, pity them, and deeply hate those who had deceived them and Egypt as a whole. Watching those 'victory' processions I wished I could have a heart attack, like the one I had had in 1960. I wished I could pass away before these good and kind people woke up to the reality – before they realized that the victory they had been sold was in fact a terrible disaster.

On 7 June I rang up Nasser at home. He was there, following up the reports submitted to him by the command on the progress of the fighting. I was in fact astonished. Why didn't Nasser take over the command personally on 5 June? True, we had lost our air force, but we could have withdrawn and established ourselves at the Sinai Passes line of defence. Why didn't he do anything about the order Amer issued directly to our forces to withdraw to west of the Suez Canal in twenty-four hours? No withdrawal could really be conducted in this manner. It is common military knowledge that a withdrawal order is channelled through the director of operations, who should himself draw up the necessary plan and timetable for it that is subsequently conveyed to all the units, so that each arranges for its own withdrawal in accordance with the set plan and timetable. But nothing of the sort took place. The withdrawal order given by Amer was in effect an order to commit suicide.

Militarily the situation was quite clear in Nasser's eyes. Why didn't he do anything about it? Why didn't he intervene – I must repeat this – dismiss Amer on 5 June, and take over command himself, or perhaps appoint another commander? We have no answers – only the huge question mark that looms large whenever Nasser had dealings with Amer.

This time I was completely frank with Nasser. I said to him on the phone: 'Gamal, why don't you attempt a salvage operation? It's you who'll be ultimately responsible, at any rate. Why don't you ask Amer to stay at home and take over the command yourself?'

'Well, Anwar,' he said, 'I knew that he had given a withdrawal order and I asked him, "How could you do this, Abdel Hakim, when you could have established yourself at the Sinai Passes?"' Amer's answer apparently was that the Passes defence line was not ready. The Israelis had three lines of defence to retreat to if the fighting went the wrong way for them – we had seen aerial photographs showing those lines when we visited command headquarters before 5 June.

So, even the line right down the middle of Sinai – a line that should have been ready at all times, peace or war – was not designed to be operational.

On 8 June I rang up Nasser once again. He said: 'It's all over! The Israeli forces are on their way to Al-Qantara East, now they have captured Al-Arish. The road is open and they are meeting with no resistance whatsoever. It's just a question of a few hours and Al-Qantara will be taken too. Our forces in Sharm al-Sheikh have been ordered to withdraw to avoid destruction. Israel has begun to attack Sinai from the south as well.'

That same day I also learned from Nasser that our Fourth Armoured Division – the best we had – had crossed from the west to the east in accordance with Amer's orders, only to be destroyed. This spelled the end for our armed forces. What ensued was chaos. Soldiers left their tanks and vehicles behind and fled west of the Canal; some of them actually got as far south as Aswan, still chased by enemy aircraft which harassed them and increased their panic.

On 9 June, still bewildered, I listened to a communiqué on the radio, issued by the general command, which said that the Israelis had crossed to the West Bank of the Canal and appealed to the world to judge this move. The communiqué implied such disgraceful helplessness, submissiveness, and humiliation it made my blood boil. I rose at once, put on my 'resistance' overalls, took my rifle with the telescopic lens, got into a small Fiat I had borrowed from Intelligence, and drove away to fight my own battle. It seemed much more honourable to die on the battlefield than to stay idle at home. As I was Speaker of the National Assembly, I gave instructions to the Assembly's secretary-general to inform all members with military background that they should each call up between 100 and 200 men within the constituency and prepare them to fight the Israelis at the places to be fixed by me. After this I went to see Nasser. He was in his office at his Manshiat al-Bakri home. I said: 'What are you doing here? Come on ... What are you waiting for? Gamal, we shall have to send you to Upper Egypt. It's from there that our resistance must continue. Even if Cairo falls, we shall have to carry on with the resistance until we all die!'

I proceeded to tell him what I had done at the National Assembly, how I prepared the members for resistance, then asked him: 'Haven't you heard the latest communiqué issued by our command?'

Nasser looked at me all the while but wouldn't say a word. At last he pointed to a chair beside him and said: 'Sit down, Anwar. Please, sit down!'

'How could I?' I burst out. 'Gamal, you're not supposed to be here. You must be in Upper Egypt – you will be the symbol of resistance. Just as I told you, we must fight them to the end. Either we'll destroy them or perish ourselves. Don't forget, our densely populated country is itself a very powerful weapon in our hands.'

'Poor Anwar!' he said. 'You're just like the people. Did you really believe the communiqué? Look. I know how these communiqués are issued. Rubbish! The Jews never crossed to the West Bank! When I heard that communiqué I asked Zakaria to go to the command to verify the matter, because I knew that the command had crumbled, collapsed – finished! Zakaria came back to tell me that some of our officers who had crossed to the West Bank were enraged to realize that the Jews were there on the other side, couldn't control themselves and fired a few mortar shells on them. The Jews retaliated by bombing a paint factory in Ismailia. Sit down, Anwar ... Sit down, please! There's no need for you to fight, it's all over. The scenario prepared by the United States and Israel has been carried out meticulously. The Jews would reach the Eastern Bank but not cross to the West for many reasons – most importantly the risks involved in landing in a densely populated area. Anyway, how could they hope to humiliate us more than they have already done? Please stay with me until I've finished the statement I'm broadcasting this evening.'

I did stay and was the first to read the statement. Meanwhile Amer rang up Nasser and said: 'I want to be in your statement; with you.' Nasser said: 'Abdel Hakim, let me do this last thing on my own. I'm discharging my responsibility. If you want to resign later on, you'll be free to do so.'

I didn't at the time grasp the real motive behind Amer's strange request. Later, I came to realize that he was afraid lest Nasser should absolve himself in the statement and so let Amer bear sole responsibility for what had happened.

Amer's expectations were wrong. The statement said clearly that, as Nasser saw it, a big power – namely, the United States – wanted to be in sole control of the world and to 'rule' Egypt into the bargain. As Nasser could not grant this wish, he had no option but to step down and hand over power to his colleague Zakaria Mohieddin.

The minute Nasser ended his short statement, the streets of Cairo were crammed with people – men, women, and children from all classes and walks of life, united by their sense of crisis into one solid mass, moving in unison and speaking with the same tongue, calling on Nasser to stay on. All at once, the wheel of time had been turned back and the days of occupation by a big power were back again – only it would be the United States this time, not Britain. This was the clear implication of Nasser's address, which moved the people deeply, arousing their patriotic ardour, and restoring to them their capacity for rejection – their sharpest weapon down the centuries. The people were out to defy defeat, to declare their unwillingness to submit to any foreign power, however mighty; their armed forces had been defeated, but their *will* had not and could not ever be conquered. For seventeen hours the people wouldn't leave the streets of Cairo. They had forgotten everything – even food and drink and sleep – and could think of nothing except to adhere to their unity and defy the will of the foreign power that had attempted to control them.

I rang up Nasser several times. Every time I felt he was worse; his voice was that of a man who belonged in the past – a dark, hollow, distant past. He must be in bed, I thought; he must be suffering very much. His pride, his most treasured asset, had been hurt as never before. Only a few days earlier the world had waited, tense and expectant, for every word he uttered at his famous press conference. Now people everywhere sneered at him and made him a laughing stock. The events of 5 June dealt him a fatal blow. They finished him off. Those who knew Nasser realized that he did not die on 28 September 1970, but on 5 June 1967, exactly one hour after the war broke out.

That was how he looked at the time, and for a long time afterwards – a living corpse. The pallor of death was evident on his face and hands, although he still moved and walked, listened and talked.

7
Interlude: A Struggle for Survival

I

Although externally uneventful, the period from June 1967 to September 1970 was one of intense suffering, unprecedented, I believe, in the entire stretch of Egyptian history. The suffering was engendered by a sense of frustration on the national, political, and military levels – so much so that a struggle for survival was the period's most distinctive feature. It is a man's sense of frustration that makes him, more than anything else, fight for survival.

While the forms of this struggle were varied, they clearly shared the following pattern: one force or another fought to re-establish itself, to recover its old identity against great odds, and so survive. The lines which the struggles of these forces took often intersected, often blended together (even when the forces were opposed to one another), and were also often difficult to distinguish.

Nasser now fought, for instance, to maintain his image as a great hero, just as he had wrestled before the June defeat with Amer's determined effort to stay on as c.-in-c. of the armed forces. This new fight interacted in turn with Nasser's desire to rebuild the Egyptian armed forces and the Russian determination to remain in control by showing us that it was up to the Soviet Union to give us, or deny us, what we needed. Again, the Egyptian people's demonstration of support for Nasser on 9 and 10 June 1967, their insistence on restoring him as President, was in effect one form of our struggle for survival, the survival of Egypt – land, people, and will – in spite of everything. How far did Egypt succeed in her struggle for survival? And how far did her will to survive conflict with the wills of others likewise struggling for survival?

II

Around midday on 10 June I heard the noise of nearby explosions from my office in the National Assembly. I was told that the police were using tear gas to disperse the crowds, who had for some time besieged the US Embassy and tried to set it on fire. I immediately got in touch with Nasser, let him hear the noise for himself, told him what had happened, and then said: 'These crowds have been out in the streets of Cairo for over seventeen hours. Gamal, do you want to see a repeat of the Cairo fire of 26 January 1952? It's about to happen now. You must stay on. The people are determined to stand fast in the face of adversity. This is a responsibility you cannot afford to shirk.'

Nasser was convinced and said he would stay on, but his voice seemed to come from far away, almost from the depths of the grave. Not long after our telephone conversation, his press adviser rang me up to give me a statement to the effect that Nasser had decided to stay on as President. I took it down and ordered the bells to be rung for a meeting of the Assembly, to be held immediately.

The Assembly had decided not to accept Nasser's resignation. Now, when they met again and I told them that Nasser had agreed to stay on in response to popular demand, and that he had wished to read out his statement to them personally but couldn't, they could hardly contain themselves for joy. They applauded, screamed, chanted, and wept.

A little while later I contacted all my colleagues at command headquarters and told them that we should all resign – me included – so as to give Nasser the chance of picking his assistants, and perhaps different ones, at that critical stage in the life of Egypt. Only thus, I said, could we hope to put an end to the old conflicts which had landed us in such defeat and frustration. They all agreed. I rang up Nasser and told him that I had all my colleagues' letters of resignation ready, except for Amer's. Amer had promised, I said, to send his letter of resignation direct. Nasser asked me to put off the resignation announcements for a while. He said that if we announced our resignations at that time he would personally feel that the whole world had collapsed, and that the people would feel that way too. I wasn't convinced, so I argued the case for resignation while he pleaded with me to put the whole matter off until he knew – as he put it – where to begin. After all that had happened, he insisted, he could see no 'point of departure'; he just needed time.

On 11 June Nasser rang me up and said he had at last found his starting point, which was to rebuild the armed forces. He was soon surprised to find his home swarming with officers who had called to demand that Amer stay on. Nasser tried to get in touch with Amer but the man had vanished. The officers were sent away. Some time later Nasser received information to the effect that the military police force stationed at al-Hilmiah Barracks was marching on Nasser's home to demand that Amer stay on. At the time Nasser had no guards ready, because the Presidential Guard which had been sent away to take part in the fighting had withdrawn to Ismailia, but had not yet arrived back in Cairo.

I have said that Nasser was known to be suspicious by nature, especially when it came to his personal security. His pathological view of personal security was perhaps responsible for all the emergency measures taken at that time on an interim basis but later established and magnified into the rule rather than the exception. They came to constitute a nightmarish burden for the people.

Now when Nasser heard that the military police were coming, he told me, he took out his revolver, put it beside his bed, and sat down to wait. He tried to ring up Amer once more but to no avail. He then rang Mahmoud Fawzi, Chief of Staff at Army Command Headquarters. Fawzi told him that 600 officers led by 4 lieutenant-generals were assembled at headquarters demanding that Amer stay on. Nasser immediately gave orders that Fawzi be appointed c.-in-c. of the armed forces, the lieutenant-generals forth-with relieved of their duties, and the 600 officers dismissed or arrested on the spot, as Fawzi saw fit.

Fawzi carried out the orders and informed Nasser that he had done so. Nasser then asked him to come to see him, with Abdel Munim Riyad, on the evening of the same day. Together they laid down a timetable for rebuilding the armed forces. It was Nasser's first job after resuming his duties as President – a manifestation of his determination to survive.

III

I myself was completely overwhelmed by our defeat. It sank into the very fabric of my consciousness so that I relived it day and night. As its real dimensions were daily revealed to me, my agony intensified – and my sense of helplessness. I shut myself up for three whole weeks at my home near the Pyramids, concentrating on the recent events and trying, with all the fortitude I possessed, to weather the fierce campaign of denigration launched by both friend and foe against our armed forces.

Doubts were cast on our fighting ability. It was alleged that the Egyptians were not fit for fighting, that no further wars could ever be fought for the recovery of our land and the restoration of our honour. If it were true, I thought, it could mean death and destruction for our people for thousands of years to come – we might even end up in the same predicament as the Red Indians of America. What a disgrace and humiliation ... I was brought up to love and believe in Egypt, and to have infinite faith in the Egyptian man. Would all this now go overboard? If it did,

I would too. For in that case I could never recognize the man I call myself, never know who I really was, but must live without identity – a stranger among strangers. Would such a life be worth living?

I had to break out of the moral dilemma in which I found myself so suddenly. That Egypt should survive became my dominant passion. I wanted to ascertain whether we were able to fight or not and indeed could think of nothing else. So I rang up Maadi Military Hospital and asked the commander whether any of the men who had fought in Sinai were getting treatment there. A Major-General Kamal Hassan Ali, who was about to be operated on, was there, he said; and there were also some of the officers General Ali had commanded on the battlefield. 'I'll be with you in a minute,' I said. Whereupon I drove directly to the hospital to talk to General Ali.

'Tell me frankly, Kamal,' I asked, '*did* you fight in Sinai?'

'I did indeed, sir. I launched a counterattack on 7 June.'

'Tell me honestly. Were we deficient in armaments?'

'On the contrary, sir,' he said firmly. 'We had excellent weapons. When we fired at a tank the shell not only hit it, it turned it upside down!'

'Tell me about the counterattack.'

Pointing to two junior officers who had been waiting with him to see me before he was operated on, General Ali said: 'Let my men tell you about their experiences and their achievements. It was they who did everything. I only gave the orders.'

I had in fact heard of the counterattack launched by an Egyptian brigade on 7 June. It was spoken of highly in all the international papers (and Moshe Dayan himself wrote about it), but it was regarded as an individual effort – an exception that should not be regarded as representative of the real strength or fighting capacity of our armed forces. However, after my long conversation with the commander and officers of that brigade I was convinced that their acts of heroism should have been the rule, and everything else

223

an exception, if the army command hadn't been so confused and so weak. It transpired that as a result of the indecisive and conflicting orders issued by the command, that brigade itself was forced to cover a distance of 620 miles in fruitless movements which severely reduced its tanks' capacity. In spite of this the brigade was able to shoot down seven enemy aircraft and, for all Israel's absolute mastery in the air, the brigade lost no more than twenty tanks – one-fifth of its strength – over three whole days of fighting.

The drift of my speech to the commander and his officers was that 'in the 1967 War we lacked neither training, good tactics, weapons, nor fighting ability, thank God. It was all a question of negligence on the part of the command.' I left them in the good hands of our hospital doctors, and went out to spend one of the very few happy days I was to enjoy between 5 June 1967 and 6 October 1973. I was happy because I knew the truth.

Some time later on, on 21 November 1967, to be precise, I learned that our soldiers had already been fully trained to use the weapons sent us by the Soviet Union after the defeat. Our 'assimilation' of the new weapons took exactly five months, although the Soviet Union had calculated it should take three years, during which time, the Russians reckoned, the situation would have calmed down. It was not part of the Soviet leaders' plan to have Nasser fight another war; they supplied him with the weapons as a courtesy gesture (in recognition of his anti-American and anti-imperialist stand and in an attempt to secure Soviet presence in the region) but never intended them to be used. The Soviet Union, like many powers, had a big disappointment, for, when Nasser appointed Fawzi c.-in-c. of the armed forces, Abdel Munim Riyad Chief of Staff, and Ahmed Ismail commander of the front, our training centres became active at once and produced excellent results. This was a glorious chapter in the history of young Egypt. It was far from easy for an army that had been defeated in that way to master such a vast amount of weaponry in less than six months and so proceed to establish a complete defence line, 110 miles long, from Port Said in the north to south of Suez, ready to repel any attack.

I was delighted with these results. They confirmed my belief that our armed forces were indeed the victim, but never the cause, of the June 1967 defeat. One concrete piece of evidence was that our military 'death' did not last more than one month, and perhaps only a few days. For in August 1967 the Ras al-'Ush battle took place, in which our Egyptian commandos engaged Israeli Special Service forces and destroyed them so that the Israelis were prevented from advancing to Port Fuad (at the northernmost tip of the Canal facing Port Said). Teams of American TV cameramen witnessed that battle; they had been invited by the Israelis to record on film their capture of Port Fuad. What happened was that, following the intensive attacks by our forces and the heavy losses inflicted on them, the Israelis took refuge with the TV cameramen to stop the fighting. At the time we had not as yet, of course, recovered our full strength but the fire in our hearts was never extinguished. Indeed, on 21 October in that same year our light-missile-equipped boats sank the Israeli destroyer *Eilat*. She was split in half and sank immediately near Port Said. She is still there on the seabed.

But long before the Ras al-'Ush battle and the sinking of the *Eilat*, I had come to recognize with increasing certainty and joy that I still belonged in Egypt – to my people and my good land, without which I couldn't hope to survive – and that it was my duty to struggle for her survival, not just because Egypt was my country, but because she actually deserved to survive.

IV

Two instances of the struggle for survival during that period – for all their different characteristics – can be grouped together here.

The first concerns the Soviet Union and its military assistance to us after the defeat. The weapons sent us were mastered by the Egyptian Army in five months, as I have said, but they were not enough. The rearmament programme had been conceived in terms of weapons supplied over a period of at least three years, to enable us to defend our country against any attack. Nasser now asked the Soviets for more assistance. He made one request after another without the least sign of response. The Soviet Union had planned to provide us with just enough to meet our most immediate needs and at the same time maintain its role as our guardian and ensure its presence in the region – a more important goal from the Soviet point of view.

It was August 1967 and Tito was on a friendly visit to Egypt. As a personal friend of Nasser's, Tito wanted to make a gesture of solidarity with us in our darkest hour. I was therefore surprised to see Nasser, having lost faith in the Soviet Union, lose his temper at one of our meetings with Tito. Nasser said to him: 'Please tell the Soviet Union that I would be more willing to accept defeat – *anything*, in fact – than to be treated like this.'

I didn't know the outcome of Tito's good offices but I do know that the Soviet leaders never changed their attitude. All they were interested in was maintaining the Soviet presence in our region, and they succeeded.

The other instance is more cheerful. It concerns the Arab Summit Conference held in Khartoum in the same year, 1967. I hadn't pinned any great hopes on it but was surprised – and the world was equally surprised – by its results. The Sudanese people took to the streets to greet Nasser no less impressively than in the Cairo scenes of 9 and 10 June. The people were of course out to greet other Arab kings and presidents as well, but the welcome accorded to Nasser beggars all description. One American magazine – *Time* or *Newsweek*, I cannot remember which – had a picture of Nasser on the cover, with a caption that read: 'Salute for the Vanquished.' The journalist responsible for this hardly understood why the Arabs had such a high esteem for Nasser. To them, Nasser's role was symbolic of the entire Arab world's efforts to repel foreign intervention and oppression.

So far hostility had characterized our relations with most Arab countries, particularly Saudi Arabia. Nasser, having attacked King Faisal in many public speeches, found the situation very embarrassing. For in his defeat and humiliation Nasser now ultimately resorted to his Arab brothers, and Faisal was only too conscious of this. When in the course of the conference's deliberations the subject of compensating Egypt for the lost Suez Canal revenue was brought up, it was Faisal who took the initiative and decided that Saudi Arabia would pay Egypt £50 million per annum. It was also decided that Kuwait would pay £55 million, and Libya £30 million.

Aside from this, the conference decided that there would be no peace, no recognition, and no negotiations with Israel; the entire Arab world had resolved to stand fast against its enemy.

This was the first time in modern history that the Arab nations unanimously decided to struggle for survival.

V

Nasser's appointment of Mahmoud Fawzi as c.-in-c. of the armed forces was the only decision he managed to take in many years of conflict with Amer. The decision was not, of course, welcomed by Amer. When he met Nasser immediately afterwards, Amer turned down Nasser's offer of a vice-presidency to him, and insisted on staying on as c.-in-c. – which Nasser could never accept.

On the advice of good friends Amer was persuaded to go to Astal – his Upper Egypt home town – and stay there until he had completely regained his composure. He actually stayed there for only a week, then came back to his Giza home and immediately started to contact certain officers in an effort to set up what might be termed an opposition front against Nasser. He didn't stop there; he filled his house with weapons, and held long sessions with his officers, in which he talked about the defeat, absolving himself of all responsibility for it, the internal situation, and the emergency measures by which the people had been so humiliated that they resented the entire regime.

It wasn't easy to believe him. Everyone knew that Amer was behind the notorious Committee for the Liquidation of Feudalism, and the military police – the two bodies that had shattered men's dignity and whose evil work maintained its malignant growth until temporarily stopped by the defeat. Even so, some people did listen to him, while others just flattered him. As a result he widened his contacts with both army officers and National Assembly members, and the latter grumblingly reported it all to me. I had no option but to get in touch with Amer and advise him to desist from such activity for the sake of Egypt, to maintain the unity of our ranks, and to spare Nasser further troubles now that he was in such a pitiable situation.

I invited Amer to have supper with me at home. I welcomed him, and my family treated him as cordially as we had always done on his previous visits. But I noticed that he had completely changed. He had lost his self-confidence, and with it his *joie de vivre*; he had in fact become a shaky character whose very soul was destroyed. It was acutely painful for me to see him in that condition, especially when he suddenly turned to me while my children were being as playful with him as usual and said, 'You're being too nice to me, my friends. Should you still be so kind to me?'

'What do you mean, "still", Abdel Hakim?' I exclaimed. 'Do you mean now you're no longer commander-in-chief? Was I your friend because you were commander-in-chief? What sort of rubbish is this?'

Towards the end of his visit I asked him to accept the vice-presidency offered by Nasser. But he said roughly,

'No! As long as Nasser is President I shall have to remain c.-in-c. of the armed forces. It's that or nothing.'

During Tito's visit in August Nasser wanted to see me, while we were all staying at the Qasr el-Tin Palace, in Alexandria. When I went to him I noticed that he looked very worried. 'Well, Anwar,' he said, 'I'd like to talk to you about an important subject ... I am very worried about the Amer affair. I have spoken to Tito about it, and, in fact, told him the whole story. Tito said I had to take a decisive measure as any internal conflict, particularly one involving the armed forces, might get out of hand now that the country has been so severely hit and develop into a major conflict.'

'Listen, Gamal,' I replied. 'You have already heard our views on this matter. I quite agree that you in particular have to confront Abdel Hakim, face him with what he's been doing, and take decisive action to put an end to it, once and for all.'

'You're right there ... I should take certain measures.'

Our conversation took place on 13 August. Nasser didn't spell out the kind of measures he had in mind. As it happened, he did not move until the 25th. Why did Nasser hesitate to make any move in spite of the gravity of the situation? Again that huge question mark looms over the Nasser-Amer relationship.

Amer knew that nothing irritated Nasser more than a discussion of democracy and a reference to his dictatorial rule. He therefore had the letter of resignation which he had submitted to Nasser in 1961 printed up in pamphlet form and distributed on the widest possible scale. That letter, as I have said, came to be famous for its ironical nature, for in it Amer said that he was opposed to a one-man rule and that he supported a return to the political party system, and so on, when he couldn't have been further from believing this himself. Even so, the letter had a damaging effect on the people: rumours concerning the country's instability were rife, and talk of a *coup d'état* was in the air. Indeed, when Jacob Malik, the Soviet delegate at the UN Security Council, visited Egypt at the time he saw Nasser to warn him that a military coup was imminent.

Meanwhile, Amer had turned his Giza house overlooking the Nile into a veritable castle. Nasser decided that Amer must be put under house arrest and all his weapons taken away. Nasser summoned him for a meeting at his home on the evening of Friday the 25th. Zakaria Mohieddin, Hussein el-Shafei, and I were also present when Nasser began to talk. 'Now, my friends,' he said, 'I'd like this to be a confrontation session, in your presence.'

Nasser had arranged that the moment Amer arrived and came into the living room, his armoured car would be quietly taken away to be replaced by a civilian one, and all his guards would be arrested. The civilian car would take him back to his home, where he would be put under house arrest. Nasser had also ordered Fawzi, the c.-in-c., and Riyad, the Chief of Staff, to remove all weapons from Amer's house – together with all the officers and soldiers on duty – so that on his return Amer would find only his family and the officers ordered to guard him. It all went according to plan. Amer called at 8.40 p.m. and was surprised to find us there. The conversation, in which neither Mohieddin nor el-Shafei took part, was lengthy. Amer denied everything. Nasser produced the pamphlets Amer had issued and confronted him with certain irrefutable facts – such as the number of officers stationed in his house, the kinds of weaponry he had, and so on – but Amer persisted in his attitude so that the session went on until about 2.00 a.m.

A few minutes before the session ended 'formally', Amer suspected that something unusual was up and decided to go home. When he tried to leave he was surprised to be prevented by the night guards, and to find that while the armoured car had vanished, another car with a different set of guards waited for him outside. He realized he would be arrested and so came back to us.

Whether he was actually tired, or because he was afraid

of taking back his decision, Nasser withdrew to his bedroom. There he was, I think, joined by Mohieddin and el-Shafei. I found myself alone with Amer. He said he wanted to go to the toilet and I took him there. When he came back to the room, however, he said he had taken cyanide, to commit suicide. I was amazed, for I knew that cyanide was an instant killer. However, I sent for a doctor and he administered treatment on the spot.

It was a very difficult situation. I found it painful to see Amer in that condition; and even more painful to see him trying to evade the trap into which he had stepped voluntarily, hoping to get back to his 'castle' – not knowing that there had been some changes there too.

It was a night of mental torture. The pain I went through was truly excruciating. Throughout the night I watched Amer in agony but was unable to extend a helping hand.

At 6.30 in the morning Mohieddin and el-Shafei came down and took Amer away. He was put under house arrest.

Why did Amer respond to Nasser's invitation to see him at home? Apparently he imagined that Nasser wanted to make it up with him, as was their usual practice after each estrangement. Amer was confident of this. He was certain that Nasser would grant him his requests and take him along to the Khartoum Summit Conference, which was actually held two days later. Nasser had known all about this from telephone conversations between Amer and his friends which Nasser himself had ordered monitored and taped.

By September the cross-examination of some of Amer's assistants began to assume the proportions of a court case. Certain reports reaching Nasser still spoke of contacts being made between Amer and some of his assistants and followers through Amer's children. Nasser then entrusted Fawzi and Riyad with the task of taking Amer away and keeping him in custody *away from home*. But when they went to arrest Amer, Fawzi and Riyad found he was in pain and so took him to Maadi Hospital. According to the medical report, a narcotic drug was extracted from his mouth. He was then taken to a villa on al-Mariutiah Canal which had been prepared as Amer's detention centre. It was surrounded with barbed-wire fences and guarded in many other ways.

Having made sure that Amer was now in detention, Nasser left for Alexandria (he stayed at al-Mamurah Beach) and I moved to my apartment at Stanley Bay Beach nearby.

On Tuesday 12 September Nasser rang me up to tell me that Amer wanted to see me 'today or tomorrow, Wednesday, at the latest'. I said I ought to see him; I must go to him. 'Think about it again, Anwar,' Nasser pleaded.

'No, I'm quite adamant on this,' I replied, 'although I believe we should order the men in charge of the case to send me a copy of the cross-examination files by tomorrow morning. I'd like to read them through. I want, you see, to be armed with enough knowledge of everybody's statements to enable me to confront Amer effectively. I'll see him in detention on Friday.'

Nasser agreed, and the files were sent to me on Wednesday morning. They ran into thousands of pages and took me two days to study – the whole of Wednesday and all day Thursday.

At the meeting with Amer on Friday I meant to advise him to make it up with Nasser. We had enough problems, and the disaster that engulfed us was more serious than any personal disputes. I was also determined to stay with him in detention until the situation was resolved, whether by a reconciliation or legal action.

On the Thursday evening I had my supper and, still preoccupied with the expected Friday meeting, heard the telephone ring. It was Nasser.

'Anwar!'

'Yes, Gamal. What's up?'

'Anwar . . .' He was silent for a minute, which surprised me.

'Gamal! Are you still there?'

'I'm here.'

'Why don't you say something? What's the matter?'

'Abdel Hakim Amer has killed himself; he died at seven p.m.; it's just been reported to me from the detention centre.'

'Well, if this really has happened, it's the best decision Amer has ever taken as a commander who's lost a battle. If I were him I would've done it on 5 June.'

Nasser was silent for a while, then he said: 'How could you take it like that, Anwar?'

'Well, according to military tradition,' I said, 'a defeated commander usually does this.'

Before ringing off, Nasser asked me to get in touch with el-Shafei and Ali Sabri and ask them to accompany me to al-Mamurah, and then Cairo, without giving them the reason. Zakaria Mohieddin was already in Cairo.

We reached Cairo after midnight. Gamal went to his home in Manshiat al-Bakri but I went straight to the house where Amer had been detained – a five-minute drive from my Pyramids home. I found representatives of the Public Prosecution Office, the Forensic Medicine Department, and Amer's full brother (who was a civil court judge) all assembled there for an initial investigation. An inquest followed, and I took part in it, (the coroner actually put down my name on his list). The inquest over, I put a few questions to the physician who had been assigned to stay with Amer in detention, Dr Bataata (who is, incidentally, my private doctor). Dr Bataata said that while in the bathroom, Amer had a kind of attack and collapsed. He was carried to the very bed I saw him on now. Attempts were made to save his life without success; it transpired that he had actually died the moment he fell to the floor. There was nothing unusual about the body, except that the forensic physician noticed during examination that two tables were fixed with sticking plaster to his body at the top of his left thigh. I believe the forensic physician's report specified what the drug was.

I looked at Amer's face before I left the house – there was no pallor of death, but a natural living colour as though he was fast asleep. There was no expression of any kind on his face, no convulsions, nothing. On the contrary, his face was serene and sweet; I felt I was looking at the old Abdel Hakim – the quiet, gentle, quite ordinary Egyptian I first met in Rafa many years back.

When I returned home early in the morning, the telephone rang. Nasser was at the other end, wanting to know what had happened. I told him what I had seen. I said that I would change to leave for Astal, Amer's home town, so as to take part in the funeral which would take place immediately the body was out of the morgue. But Nasser didn't approve of this. He was afraid Amer's children might make a scene if they knew of their father's fate – and that, he said, wasn't at all desirable. It was absolutely necessary at that critical time to maintain the ruler's dignity.

Before he rang off Nasser said in sorrowful tones: 'Could you believe it, Anwar! Abdel Hakim, you, and I, such good friends ... Who would've thought that Abdel Hakim would die and nobody, I am sure, take part in his funeral. Has it come to this? For even we cannot take part in the funeral.'

Certainly, I would not have believed it possible that anything of the kind could happen, or that the struggle for survival should land friends in such tragedy. But that, it seems, is life.

VI

Amer's assistants had to be tried. In fact, a trial was inevitable insofar as the people, having gone through the emotional upheaval of 9 and 10 June, were beginning to wake up to the reality and examine the defeat – Why had it happened? Who was responsible for it? They began to realize, too, that the Amer-Nasser conflict had played a major role in bringing about the terrible disaster that had befallen Egypt.

El-Shafei presided over the tribunal. To save their necks the defendants endeavoured to change the character of the case by concentrating on the 'flaws' of the 23 July Revolution, as though the revolution itself was on trial. As a result, the positive achievements of the revolution – its brighter side – were dimmed, while its negative aspects – corruption, the proliferating emergency measures, and the suppression of freedoms (everything, in fact, that made people resent the revolution) – were revealed.

People looked at that ugly side of the revolution and believed it had no other. Their dissatisfaction deepened. As they were still broken-hearted, even emotionally devastated as a result of the defeat, an outburst was inevitable. Sparked off by student demonstrations in February 1968, after light sentences had been passed on the air force commanders, who were regarded as the main culprits behind the June defeat, an eruption of popular fury spread far and wide on all levels. The people found out too that the so-called National Charter had never been applied, but had only been introduced to 'absorb' their wrath after the setback when the union with Syria broke up. We tried to contain these uprisings, and it fell to me, at the National Assembly, to put an end to it all. I sent for the student leaders, who had staged a protest sit-in at Cairo University, and talked with them for five hours, after which they all went home.

To defuse the situation, Nasser resorted to his usual tactic of diverting people's attention to something else. He broadcast a statement on 30 March – commonly referred to as the 30 March Statement – which was a kind of programme for future action and therefore designed to neutralize the people's dissatisfaction. Now that the trial had revealed the ugly side of the revolution, Nasser proposed to deal with the root causes of their dissatisfaction. He proceeded to ask the Egyptian people to approve or disapprove of the 30 March Statement in a referendum. Surprisingly for foreign correspondents, who had thought that while still suffering from the aftermath of the defeat people would hardly bother to turn up at the ballot box, the statement was almost unanimously approved and the turnout was practically 100 per cent. But the people soon found out that the 30 March Statement simply tightened the regime's dictatorial grip. It upheld the right of arrest without preferring charges, and promised a permanent Constitution only when the consequences of the Israeli aggression had been removed. It was a disappointment – the people had expected the statement to usher in an era of democracy, but found that it was once again designed simply to 'absorb' the anger that had erupted after the June defeat.

Another feature of this transitional period was the war of attrition which we started in September 1968 when Major-General Ahmed Ismail had completed the building up of our Egyptian line of defence and we had made significant progress in consolidating our armed forces. We started by using artillery. Israel retaliated by air raids on the power transformers at Naj' Hammadi, the Naj' Hammadi barrages, and the Qina Bridge in Upper Egypt. We had to stop until March 1969, when we had completed a network of internal defences around all vital civilian targets. The war of attrition was resumed in 1969, though it never made good our loss in ammunition. No compensation for the lost ammunition arrived, in fact, until the Soviet airlift of the October 1973 War. It was in a way a punishment to Nasser for starting and continuing the war of attrition against the wishes of the Soviet Union.

One of the events of that period had far-reaching effects. One day – on 19 December 1969, to be precise – in a good mood and a moment of inspiration, Nasser turned to me and said: 'I am leaving for Morocco, Anwar, in two days' time, to attend the Arab Summit Conference. As you can see, intrigues are being perpetually hatched against me. It is quite likely that they will "get" me in one of these, and I don't want the country to be at a loss after me – I don't

want to leave behind a vacuum. I have therefore decided
to appoint you Vice-President. You will be sworn in before
I leave.'

I was aware that Soviet agents had started their intrigues
when one Soviet physician (Shazurov) visited Egypt, saw
Nasser, and no doubt intimated to certain people that the
heart attack Nasser had had was serious and that he hadn't
long to live. I thought over what Nasser had said carefully,
then answered: 'Gamal, is this your considered opinion?
Gamal! I don't want to be Vice-President. I shall carry on,
and work side by side with you. If I must have a title,
"Presidential Adviser" will be quite adequate.'

'Oh, no!' he said. 'You must call tomorrow to be sworn
in.'

The next day I called on him, accompanied by Hussein
el-Shafei, to take him to the airport as we always did. At
home, and in the presence of el-Shafei, he asked me to be
sworn in. I agreed. When we were at the airport to see
him off, Nasser announced the news to everybody.

VII

Two clear instances of the struggle for survival during that
period concern a clash between two opposed forces, for
while Nasser's clash with the Soviet Union was a struggle
for the survival of Egypt, the Soviet clash with Nasser was
in effect a struggle for Soviet survival in our region.

When Israel bombed a civilian factory in Abu-Zabal
(on the outskirts of Cairo) early in January 1970, killing
more than seventy innocent workers, Nasser summoned
the Soviet ambassador and the chief Soviet (military) expert and told them that he couldn't now wait until June,
when Soviet SAM-3 missile batteries were due to be delivered. He said that the missiles were needed now, particularly as Israeli aircraft had raided inland and bombed
residential and industrial areas. The Soviet leaders were
informed of this; they invited Nasser to see them in Mos-

cow on 22 January. He did pay a secret four-day visit to Moscow, and when he came back, he looked very happy indeed.

'Well, Gamal,' I asked. 'Any luck?'

'They will apparently keep their word this time. When I told them that it was urgent and asked them to send us SAM-3 missiles, operated by Soviet crews, temporarily, of course, until the Egyptian crews have been trained to operate them by, say, August, a meeting of the political leadership was held and the decision taken to send us the missiles as from March 1970.'

We had repeatedly asked the Soviet Union to help us with our air defence, since the 1967 defeat, so much so, in fact, that Nasser even asked for a Soviet air commander to take over our defence. Air defence was our big weakness, as we saw when Israel bombed the Abu-Zabal factory and the Bahr al-Baqar primary school. So the introduction of the Soviet-manned SAM–3 batteries marked a turning point in our relations with the Soviet Union. We were also promised aircraft of the TU-16 type by April 1970.

No aircraft had come by April, however, and our repeated enquiries were simply disregarded. It was a case of the old methods once again, when we thought the Soviet Union had changed. Nasser was exasperated. 'Listen, Anwar,' he said, 'whether we like it or not, all the cards of this game are in America's hands. It's high time we talked and allowed the USA to take part in this.' Until then we had authorized the Soviet Union to talk on our behalf to the United States, with a view to removing the serious doubts bedevilling our relations with the Americans.

That was why Nasser devoted the bulk of his May Day speech in 1970 to an 'address' to Nixon. The question Nasser put to him was: Are you unable or unwilling to solve the problem? The address was mild in tone; it was, to say the least of it, free of the old 'aggressiveness'. The diplomatic technique used implied a desire on Nasser's part to start a dialogue with the United States.

The dialogue was actually initiated by America in June

1970. The opening chapter was the Rogers Plan, which provided for an Israeli withdrawal and a ninety-day cease-fire period during which a UN mediator would conduct negotiations with the parties concerned for a settlement of the Middle East problem. The mediator appointed was the Swedish diplomat Dr Gunnar Jarring, following the Security Council Resolution 242 of November 1967. But we knew that Dr Jarring's mission was doomed to failure as a result of Israel's intransigence. He couldn't in fact achieve anything and his mission was later terminated, in 1971.

A month after the Rogers Plan had been announced Nasser paid a visit to Moscow (for which the Soviet ambassador Venogradov and I made full preparations) to persuade the Soviet leaders to send us a 'deterrent' weapon. In spite of all the efforts made to this end, the Soviet leaders refused to grant Nasser's request. Nasser was therefore forced to declare – even as he sat for talks with the Soviet leaders in the Kremlin – that he had accepted the Rogers Plan. Brezhnev was beside himself with rage. He asked Nasser how he could accept an 'American solution' and Nasser said he was willing to accept anyone's solution – 'even if it came from the Devil himself'.

Nasser's Moscow trip took twenty days as he was given a special medical treatment, being treated in the astronauts' Oxygen Room for the rejuvenation of all his body's cells. It apparently worked, for when I saw him at Cairo airport on arrival he looked at least twenty years younger. I still remember my words to him: 'I say, I say, boss! What youthful looks!' I can still see him walking vigorously down the tarmac with a healthy ruddy colour on his face and chest thrust forward like a man of thirty. But there could be little joy in the Oxygen Room, I thought, for a man who knew that his hands were tied as a result of the Soviet attitude.

During his absence in Moscow I had convened the Arab Socialist Union political committee for a special meeting to discuss the Rogers Plan. We recommended that it be rejected. However, when Nasser came back, explained what had happened at the Kremlin, and told me that he had accepted it, I said: 'You've done the right thing, for the Soviet Union would have landed us in disaster.' He gave me a long look and said, 'Anwar! The Soviet Union is a hopeless case.'

This was Nasser's last visit to the Soviet leaders. As I said earlier, it had a very bad effect on his health. For the first time, he felt that he had no room at all to manoeuvre. And Nasser was an expert at manoeuvring. But deprived of elbow-room he was reduced to nothing – and he didn't like it. His relations with the United States, western Europe and the Arab countries were either completely broken off or dismally tenuous; he was left with the unreliable Soviet Union – which gave him no room to turn and, consequently, no room for the struggle for survival.

VIII

From the 1967 defeat to the end of his days Nasser was continually in the grip of illness. On 5 June itself his diabetes ran rampant and couldn't be checked for five months, until November 1967. That period was very damaging to his body, for from that time on he began to fall prey to one illness after another. The first was a strange ailment he had in December 1967. Pimples appeared on certain parts of his body which grew so sore that if touched by anything, even his own clothes, they caused tremendous pain. We sent for doctors from all over the world. At length a British physician succeeded in diagnosing the case and advised treatment with female hormones. Nasser was compelled to take the treatment, which gave rise to severe fits of nervous tension for two months. He recovered from this illness only to fall victim to another – he began to feel excruciating pains in his legs. The pain increased daily until it became literally intolerable, indescribable. It was made even worse by

Nasser's need to suppress and hide it so as to appear in public with the full dignity and awe he had created for himself. Once on his own he locked the door of his bedroom (although I was with him constantly) and took to screaming at the top of his voice – like a helpless, wounded lion. He did not improve for many months on end and then left for the Soviet Union to receive mineral water treatment at Skhaltubo in 1969.

In September 1969 he had a heart attack. The news was hushed and we announced that he had influenza, but the Egyptian physicians who examined him confided to me that it was a heart attack. Nasser asked to see me. 'Anwar,' he said, 'you know what to do; I want you to do what you think is right.' 'I am going to send for Dr Shazuf,' I said.

Shazuf was the private physician of the Soviet leaders who had previously treated Nasser in Moscow. He came immediately and his diagnosis confirmed the conclusions of the Egyptian doctors. He advised that Nasser should have complete rest because the heart attack had been very serious indeed. Any physical or mental exertion could prove fatal. And that was what happened to Nasser exactly one year after.

During that year many things proved too exhausting for Nasser, health-wise at least. The first was his acceptance of the Rogers Plan for, the moment he announced it, the Palestinians were all out against him. They launched a fierce, reckless campaign against him, without even bothering to ask why he had acted as he did. They should at least have recognized his stand in support of the Palestinian cause. No other Arab ruler had supported it more vigorously. It is no exaggeration to say that it was Nasser's adoption of that cause that gave it its full political dimension; otherwise it would have remained merely a refugee problem. It was Nasser who filled the Arab world, and the world at large, with the name of Palestine. He violently attacked any Arab ruler who didn't support the Palestinian cause; he devoted all his efforts, and even the Egyptian Revolution itself, to defend the Palestinians' right to their

I.S.I.–K

homeland. It was therefore natural that Nasser should be hurt by the Palestinian attitude towards him. He was deeply and severely hurt, in fact, to see those people in whose defence he had sacrificed his health turn so ungratefully against him. They fought him with inane slogans, reckless emotional outbursts, regular exercises in verbal oneupmanship, and childish tricks.

How could a sick man, one afflicted with the worst possible illness, bear to have his pride hurt in this way – and not only by strangers (as had happened on his last visit to Moscow) but also, which was strange, by friends and brothers whose interests were often put before his own?

It was only natural that all this should affect Nasser's health so much as to precipitate his death. And other events were to exacerbate the situation even further.

In September 1970 Nasser convened an Arab Summit Conference in Cairo to put an end to the September 1970 massacre – the showdown between King Hussein of Jordan and the Palestinian resistance forces. King Hussein had decided to liquidate those forces and so fought them ruthlessly. A massacre, in the full sense of the term, took place. Nasser could not, of course, sit idly by. He convened that conference in Cairo, in spite of all that had been done to him, and it was attended by all the Arab kings and presidents, with the exception of King Hussein himself. I myself had just recovered from my second heart attack and so went to Cairo to take part in the conference.

Muammar al-Qaddafi was there. He was an eye-catching character, with a revolver that never left his belt. He attacked King Hussein constantly, describing him as a madman who should be confined to a lunatic asylum; until then I had put his attacks down to overenthusiasm and youthful impetuosity. The conference members were divided on the question of whether they should still invite King Hussein to take part, but they finally accepted Nasser's proposal that the king should come. He did, in fact, arrive and the conference got off the ground. It was, however, very nerve-racking, not because of King Hussein's participation but because of the off-stage conduct of both Qaddafi and Yasir Arafat.

One example I can recall clearly concerns Arafat's conduct during a morning session in Nasser's private suite. Nasser was eager to find a formula for ending the dispute that involved a few concessions by both sides as, he believed, both had made mistakes. All at once Arafat flew into a temper, which naturally infuriated Nasser. 'I haven't,' Nasser said, 'done all this for you – wrecked my nerves in this way simply for your sake – to be rewarded by this attitude.' Whereupon Nasser left the suite and wanted to go home, being quite resolved to boycott the conference. We caught up with him just before he took the elevator down and persuaded him to come back. But a good deal of arm-twisting was needed before Arafat actually showed any response.

The conference constituted a terrible burden for Nasser's nervous system. He was exhausted by having to deal with the conduct of al-Qaddafi and Arafat – the latter being the man who had asked Nasser to help solve his problem in the first place. The conference ended, its conclusions were declared, and Nasser went to the airport to see off every Arab king or president. The last to leave were King Faisal of Saudi Arabia and the amir of Kuwait. When he saw off King Faisal, the chief aide-de-camp pointed out to me that Nasser was so exhausted he couldn't walk straight. I asked Nasser to go home to rest while I deputized for him in seeing off the amir of Kuwait, but he wouldn't agree.

It was obvious that Nasser forced himself to make the effort. When the amir of Kuwait boarded his plane, Nasser couldn't move at all but simply stood stock still in front of the aircraft, perspiring heavily and looking very pale indeed. He asked for his car to be driven right up to where he stood and take him home, which we did. I said goodbye to him on the understanding that we would leave for Alexandria the next day for a rest. I went home but before I could get any rest myself Nasser's private secretary rang me up to tell me that Nasser would call to have supper with me. I tried to get some sleep. But I was woken up at 6.00 p.m. and told that I had been asked to go to President Gamal's home for a very important reason.

I changed quickly and went to Manshiat al-Bakri. I was immediately shown into Nasser's bedroom. He was lying in bed surrounded by doctors. They told me he had died an hour before. I lifted the bed-cover to see his face – it looked very much alive, as though he were simply fast asleep. I put my cheek against his but did not feel the chill of death. I turned to the doctors and said: 'It's not true ... What you're saying is wrong ... It can't be right!' They said they had done everything possible, and even used an electric cardiac restorer, to no avail. 'But try again ... Surely you can try again,' I said, at which they burst into tears. It was explained to me that they had been working very hard for two hours, but the will of God could not be reversed.

I ordered that the body be taken to the al-Qubbah Palace. It was Monday. I convened the Council of Ministers and the Supreme Committee of the Arab Socialist Union. We decided that the funeral would take place on Thursday, so as to enable the kings and presidents who wished to take part in it. I asked the physicians to make sure the body was properly preserved until Thursday. I myself stayed at al-Qubbah Palace, where Nasser's body was kept, until it was time for the funeral to start. I then went out to supervise the preparations and make sure that all went well. But the funeral cortège had barely started to move from the old Revolutionary Command Council building when I suddenly collapsed. I was carried back to the RCC building and given five injections which put me to sleep for a long time. When I woke up, at 1.30 p.m., my first question was: 'Has Nasser been buried?' I was afraid that the crowds, the millions on the streets, might snatch the coffin and take it away, God knows where ...

Nasser's death was a tragedy that shook the Arab world.

8

The Second Revolution
(15 May 1971)

When Nasser died, I was reluctant to be elected President. In the speech he made on reassuming the presidency on 10 June 1967, Nasser had declared that presidential elections would be held only after the 'consequences of Israeli aggression had been removed'. So, I said that I would carry on as Vice-President until I had removed the 'consequences of aggression', and then allow elections to be held.

I soon began to have second thoughts about this, however, in view of the number of rivalries and manoeuvres going on in the political leadership, particularly on the part of the chief power bloc and most members of the Supreme Executive Committee of the Arab Socialist Union – that is, the Politbureau left me by Nasser. I felt that the country, plunged as it was in grief, was in a state of tense expectation. The people wanted to know which way they were going, having unanimously resolved to heal their wounds and pull themselves together as fast as possible to resume their reconstruction effort. For that is characteristic of the Egyptian people; with cultural roots that date back to the fifth millennium BC, they never lose their sense of identity however hard the circumstances may be.

There was another factor which helped me to change my mind. Just before the funeral took place, President Houari Boumedienne of Algeria arrived in Cairo and saw me. He objected strongly to my staying on as Vice-President because, he said, the image of Egypt should never be allowed to be denigrated in the eyes of the world. The people should elect a President immediately so as to maintain Egypt's position and fulfil her responsibilities both in the Israeli conflict and in her dealings with the Arab world at large.

But the decisive factor was perhaps a note sent to me by the armed forces. It said that Egypt was passing through a difficult and very critical period, that the armed forces had a mission to accomplish, and that they therefore needed a supreme commander under whom they could achieve their objective.

At the top level domestic intrigues had started to have an effect. Certain strong men (alternatively referred to as the 'central power bloc'), who relied on Soviet support, wanted to exploit the situation. There were others, of course, but this bloc, which included actual Soviet agents in Egypt, began to organize effectively. These men made a secret pact to take over power on the pretext that they were the legitimate heirs of Nasser and were therefore responsible for maintaining his political line. So, immediately the funeral was over, I summoned top officials and told them I had changed my mind about staying on as Vice-President, and that presidential elections had to be held. I asked for a meeting of the Supreme Executive Committee of the Arab Socialist Union to endorse my decision. We had to act in accordance with constitutional procedure.

At the meeting, of course, conflicts ensued amid the struggle for power. One person, for instance, asked for the situation to remain unchanged. He said to me, 'I fear that if we nominate you, your pride will be hurt because the country doesn't want you. If the people reject you, it will mean they are rejecting the 23 July Revolution.' To which I replied: 'I have enough courage to convene this Committee once again, if the people do reject me, and to nominate another candidate. If the alternative candidate is rejected in his turn, we shall try again and nominate a third. I will hand over power only to an elected President, regardless of the battles I may have to fight.'

The Committee concluded its deliberations by nominating me as a presidential candidate. The Central Committee, in a plenary session held later, endorsed the nomination, and the People's Assembly followed suit. Elections were held. On 15 October 1970, I was elected President.

Two days after I was elected I appointed Dr Mahmoud Fawzi prime minister, and Abdel Muhsin Abu el-Nour secretary-general of the Arab Socialist Union. I believe that a one-man rule is fraught with dangers. Because no one man can really know everything, some of his assistants will concentrate power in their hands and, so to speak, run amok – creating power blocs, just as had happened in Nasser's case.

II

The leaders of the central power bloc, posing as the guardians of the Nasser line, were now keen to have a showdown with me. I explained that I couldn't possibly do things the way Nasser did, simply because we were different men. True, we never differed on general principles but we did differ, completely, on the means of reaching our goals. I had daily meetings with Nasser in his last year, alternately in his home and mine, and spoke to him incessantly about the need to change the method of government and to put an end to arbitrary measures that had come to be the rule rather than the exception. The people, I said, having gone through the traumatic experience of military defeat and shown such steadfastness in the effort to achieve their objectives, badly needed a change.

On my very first day in office as President – 16 October – I remember, Sami Sharaf called. He had been Nasser's confidant and Minister for Presidential Affairs. He had a heap of papers to submit to me. 'What is this?' I asked.

'The text of tapped telephone conversations between certain people being watched.'

'Sorry,' I said, 'I don't like to read such rubbish. If it contains any information regarding state security I'll look at it and give you a decision. If, however, this is a record – which I assume it is – of telephone conversations between ordinary citizens, I'll have nothing to do with it. And, anyway, who gave you the right to have the telephones of these people tapped? Take this file away.' I swept it off my desk. He collected the papers and went away, but not before I had ordered all telephone tapping to be stopped. In future no tapping would be done except through a court order. My order was carried out immediately.

From the first day I assumed power, I felt my willingness to accept the challenge posed by existing, apparently insuperable difficulties had acquired extraordinary intensity. Although the spirit of challenge in me had always been alive (as a basic constituent of my very character), it had never been so vigorous and intensive as when I took over power. I believed it was my responsibility, when I came to hand over power eventually, to see that we had overcome all our difficulties and hardships – those of a full-blooded military defeat, a collapsing economic situation, and a stifling political isolation. Our relations with Arab and West European countries, as well as the United States, were in shreds. We had what one could call relations only with the Soviet Union – a country that never made us feel there were advantages in having relations with it, since the Russians had practically no relations with anybody. Added to this were some facts I had found out for myself – facts which confirmed that none of the officials in Nasser's entourage ever paid any regard to the interests of Egypt and wanted nothing but to remain in power, seeking their own interests and motivated by hatred and jealousy. So it was only natural that my spirit of challenge should be even further strengthened. It has never weakened or lost its momentum from the day I took office.

I told my former colleagues, members of the old Revolutionary Command Council, and those who had held influence early in my presidential career, that I was accepting that burden – that nightmare with all its vast dimensions – because I believed that I could do something about it, using the power of love, without having to sacrifice, or even hurt, any individual.

I knew that this also meant I should have to challenge many conditions and ethical codes in existence at the time; but I believed I had the capacity for this. Indeed, due to the inner power I always felt, I had never been afraid to challenge existing conditions. And now that I was President, I felt I wielded a tremendous *real* power, which had to be used in doing good. This was my forte, and I proceeded from the ideals I had always adopted, inspired by my love of Egypt and my desire to make the country a happy one. Never had I had a better chance of putting my principles into practice than when the people elected me President.

Looking back at the work done at that early stage in my first term of office, I find it significant that the decree lifting all state custodianship of private property was issued in December 1970 – two months after my assumption of the presidency. This was one of the things our people had hoped to see happen but had almost lost heart over. So I was not surprised to learn that the decree was greatly welcomed, not only by those whose property had been put under state custodianship but by the masses at large – even ordinary people who couldn't possibly benefit by it, such as taxi drivers, for instance.

In the sphere of foreign policy, my 'Peace Initiative' of 4 February 1971, was submitted less than four months after I had taken office. It had a tremendous impact both inside and outside Egypt. I believed that as military action was ruled out at the time, a diplomatic offensive had to be launched: the broad masses wanted to see action being taken all the time.

III

When I took over power, Nasser's legacy was, to put it mildly, unclear to me. I accepted the challenge, I have said, out of a desire to put right many of the conditions which, I was convinced, had for so long been wrong. I knew that human values had been violated, if not shattered altogether; but I also knew that I could redress the situation by instituting and vindicating my own ideals and principles, and not by oppression. The powerholders daily used, or rather abused, their power before my very eyes, and I warned them that although I was tolerant in the extreme I could not allow their disgraceful behaviour to continue.

What they did not realize was that I was against judging people and determining their future careers in the light of reports submitted by agencies I knew to be false, motivated as they were either by vindictiveness or the desire to intimidate the people. Nor did they realize that I wasn't interested in building a self-image abroad; anybody's real image should reflect a genuinely Egyptian reality. They might have been ignorant, too, of the fact that the worst and ugliest feature of Nasser's legacy was what I have called a 'mountain of hatred' – the spirit of hate which was emanated in every direction and at every level, to the smallest family unit. Instances were rife of men working for the regime who spied on their own kin just like the Fascist regimes. Can anyone sink lower than this?

The Constituent Council of the Free Officers' Organization was established before the revolution on the firm basis of the highest ethics and ideals. When renamed the

Revolutionary Command Council, it was still governed by the same ethics and principles. In practice, however, our revolutionary action was unsuccessful. Instead of having confidence in people, allowing them to work, and not harming them until they had shown themselves unworthy of the trust reposed in them (just as I believe and have always done), the revolution began by suspecting everybody until the contrary was proven – which could, in fact, very rarely be done. People began, in turn, to be suspicious of that revolution.

In the first four years of revolutionary rule, when the Revolutionary Command Council wielded all power, there were mistakes and violations of human rights but these were rather limited in scope. It was after 1956 that they began to acquire huge dimensions. After the 1956 War, Nasser should have consolidated his victory by restoring the basic freedoms of the Egyptian people. He didn't. And the result was a passive attitude by the people to whatever the political leadership did. Nasser's victories were accepted only superficially by the people who, deep down, knew that they never participated in whatever was being done, were never even consulted. When the people felt a little uneasy about one thing or another, their uneasiness was regarded as counterrevolutionary; their private property was put under state custodianship and mass arrests were made. This was how human dignity was shattered in practice.

I have had the opportunity to observe that the gravest injustice done to the Egyptian people was the 'cultivation of fear', that is, rather than trying to build up the inner man we did all we could to make him feel frightened. Fear is, I believe, a most effective tool in destroying the soul of an individual – and the soul of a people. The livelihoods of all the people were in the hands of the ruler; it was up to him to give or deny, although in the latter case a man wouldn't be merely denied a livelihood – he would be arrested and thrown into a detention centre, while the members of his family would lose their jobs and be subjected to persecution.

People thus turned into dummies. They became puppets in the hands of rulers, who did what they liked with them. Travel abroad was forbidden. No one could say anything that appeared to contradict the official line of thinking (the penalty being arrest and loss of livelihood). People's passivity increased daily until one day no man felt he could be secure unless he had completely kept to himself, cut himself off entirely, both from public events and from the very stream of life around him, as though he wanted to see nothing, hear nothing, and say nothing.

It is this that makes me say that just as the 23 July Revolution was colossal in its achievements, so it was equally colossal in its mistakes. In time, however, the achievements fizzled out. They either vanished altogether or turned into cold reality, deprived of all glory. The revolution was reduced to a huge, dark, and terrible pit, inspiring fear and hatred but allowing no escape.

It would be a mistake, all this notwithstanding, to think that the spirit of the Egyptian people could ever be stifled. It is a great spirit, capable of enduring all hardships, and is never subdued by adversity. Our people have withstood the worst types of oppression, both domestic and foreign, and emerged unharmed. It was the great fortitude and self-confidence of that people that enabled them to endure the pain: the bleeding, they knew, would stop and the wounds would heal.

Such is the real spirit of the Egyptian people, in whom I have always had total confidence. I hope I shall be able to remove the present obstacles on their road to progress and so enable them to be in complete control of their destiny. They will then, I am sure, work miracles.

IV

The legacy Nasser left me was in a pitiable condition. In the sphere of foreign policy I found that we had no relations, as I have said, with any country except the Soviet Union. The distinction between what Nasser saw as 'progressive' and what he held to be 'reactionary' prevailed in the Arab world, and on the basis of this arbitrary distinction Nasser would maintain or sever his relations with individual Arab states. He was in fact taught a lesson in 1967 when he realized that the only Arab countries that helped him after the defeat belonged to his arbitrary reactionary category – Saudi Arabia, Kuwait, and King al-Sinusi of Libya. He received no financial aid from anybody else.

Nasser's policies were much influenced by his own emotional reactions. Realizing this, his men could make him do exactly what they wanted. They would provide him with a certain piece of information at a time calculated to produce in him a strong reaction designed to have vast international repercussions.

Once in 1964, I recall, Nasser was about to make a speech on Victory Day, 23 December, in Port Said (our usual practice since the 1956 aggression) when Ali Sabri, then prime minister, whispered some sort of report to him. It said that the US ambassador, in answer to a query by the Minister of Supply about the date of shipping US wheat aid to Egypt, had made offensive remarks about Egypt and said that the US Congress hadn't as yet approved the shipment. Ali Sabri's whispered report was transmitted five minutes before the speech was due to be made. Nasser's reaction was a direct attack, fierce and offensive, in that very speech, on the United States. When the US ambassador heard Nasser's accusations, he immediately got in touch with Egyptian government officials to deny the malicious report. The ambassador's version was supported by the Egyptian Minister of Supply himself, who, immediately the speech ended, got in touch with Nasser's press adviser and also denied the report.

When Nasser heard of this he was at a loss what to do. He knew that the destiny of an entire people can never be determined by the emotions of one man. So he was forced to ask me and Amer to redress the mistake. We met with the US ambassador over dinner in the house of Nasser's press adviser and did our best to redress the situation.

The same thing happened earlier in 1964 in connection with the shah of Iran. Nasser's men reported that the shah had said something – which he, in fact, hadn't – a few minutes before Nasser made his usual 26 July speech in Alexandria (again an established practice since King Farouk's departure), and so Nasser declared in that speech that Egypt had severed her relations with Iran. It transpired that the statement attributed to the shah was wrongly reported by news agencies. Once again, Nasser asked me to redress the matter with the shah of Iran when I saw him at the Islamic Congress held in Rabat in September 1969 (I was deputizing for Nasser because he had had a heart attack at the time). Nasser also asked me to let King Hussein mediate in the conciliation effort. I did so – but no reconciliation ever took place.

Such was the political situation I inherited. There was no real Foreign Ministry, no studied or properly planned policy; only the President himself.

I find my position in this connection diametrically opposed to Nasser's. When I wanted to abrogate the Soviet-Egyptian Treaty of Friendship, because the Soviet Union had let me down and denied me the weapons I needed to make 1971 truly a year of decision (apart from its endless evasive tactics), I sought the assistance of a third party, India, which is a non-aligned country. I approached India for certain Soviet military items manufactured under licence in India. When asked for permission to send me such necessary equipment, the Soviet Union would not allow India to do so. The Soviets hoped that by denying me spare parts my weapons would turn into masses of scrap iron, fit only to be fed into the smelting furnaces of our iron and steel complex.

But a third party was my witness to the entire case – India herself. I decided that this was a good opportunity to rid my country of its last foreign commitment – the Soviet treaty. There was the behaviour of the Soviet Union to be considered, of course, but I also wanted to leave no commitment behind that my successor might wrongly exploit. And I was aware, too, that when I signed the treaty the people didn't accept it wholeheartedly; they accepted it only because they had confidence in me.

I believe that no man should act according to his own emotions when it comes to a country's destiny. It is my duty, as I see it, to try to tap all those resources which promise to enhance my people's welfare and happiness. Whatever the effort involved, I have to open all the doors that had been shut in Egypt's face.

Today, having corrected all these mistakes, I am proud to state that Egypt's relations both with Iran and with the whole world are based on mutual respect and trust. I shall never forget the day when the Egyptian petroleum reserves fell to a dangerously low level, after the October 1973 War (due to the closure of our oilfields). I sent word to the shah of Iran and he immediately supplied us with more than 500,000 tons. He actually ordered Iranian oil tankers that were at sea to change course and go directly to Egypt to offer help. He said: 'El-Sadat is a brother to me; I shall respond to his request on the spot.'

V

The economic legacy Nasser left me was in even poorer shape than the political. A free country's real independence is more a matter of economic independence than political slogans. What sort of economic situation was Egypt in, in 1970?

We had, with crass stupidity, copied the Soviet pattern of socialism, although we lacked the necessary resources, technical capabilities, and capital. From £200 million in 1952, the country's budget grew to £E2000 million on

Nasser's death. But it was not real growth at all, in fact, for with the Egyptianization of foreign business concerns in Egypt after the tripartite aggression of 1956 and the release by Britain of £400 million (the reserve deposits since World War II which Eden had frozen after the nationalization of the Suez Canal Company), our budget was flush.

On the first day of January 1957 – when our London reserves were released and all foreign concerns nationalized – our economy was at its best. Hence the public sector came into being with assets of not less than £1000 million. If we had started off properly, we could by now have been a great power. In 1961 the nationalization measures were taken and an economic takeoff could have taken place, based on the public sector as well as a healthily promoted private sector; we could have proceeded to vast economic achievements. However, our socialism began to be tinged in practice with Marxism. Any free enterprise system came to be regarded as odious capitalism and the private sector as synonymous with exploitation and robbery. Individual effort came to a standstill, and from this stemmed the terrible passivity of the people that I still suffer from to this day. A point was reached where the state was expected not only to undertake economic planning (apart from running foreign and domestic policies), but actually to provide eggs and chickens and dozens of other things that individual free enterprise could and should have easily provided. As a result, and according to that 'new' theory, the people came to rely on the state in everything. They expected the state to provide them with food, work, housing, and education. Indeed, having professed to be socialist, the state was expected to provide citizens with everything they needed without their having to make any positive effort at all. It was that shrinking back from active individual enterprise that marked the beginning of our abysmal economic collapse.

In 1970 I read a report issued in the United States which analysed the economic situation in Egypt and said: 'Let Nasser shout as loud as he likes. He will soon be down on his knees, economically.' At the time we were relying totally on our own resources; there was no foreign aid of any kind – Soviet, American, West European, or Arab. All that we received from the outside world was abuse. Our economy had been destroyed by the Yemeni War, the Marxist application of socialism, and the disgraceful 1967 defeat.

I read that report over and over again. One of its conclusions I found particularly disturbing. It said that the increase in population would lead to an increase in consumption and so, within two years at most from 1970, the Egyptian economy would be reduced to zero. Alarmed as I was I thought it must be a Western propaganda stunt, part of the psychological campaign waged against us with a view to making us give in to Israel's terms.

When I took over power, however, I realized the bitter truth. I summoned Dr Hassan Abbas Zaki, then Minister of Finance and Economy, and asked him about the economic situation. He said simply that the treasury was empty and we were 'almost bankrupt'. 'How did it happen, Hassan? What were you doing? Didn't you tell Nasser about it?' I asked. 'Well,' he answered, 'I have been trying to budget myself out, transferring one item of expenditure from one section to another, but now I can't even do that!'

I managed to borrow £E20 million but Dr Zaki said it wasn't good enough. I was very perturbed to learn that our liquidity problem was such that we might soon find it difficult to pay the salaries of our soldiers on the front and the salaries of civil servants. If it came to that, I thought, and they couldn't be paid – if they came to know that their families back home had no food to eat – wouldn't they desert the front? Wouldn't Egypt collapse?

I worked hard on the problem, of course, making use of every possible available resource. Throughout 1971 and 1972 the real dimensions of our economic predicament were not very clear to me. Only five days before the October War I asked the National Security Council to face the reality and learn that our economy had fallen below zero. This would have frightened anyone in my position, I am sure, but I tried to think about it calmly and took my decision.

I do not believe that most people in my position would have plucked up enough courage to take a decision of any sort, but I was confident that the key to everything – politically, economically, and militarily – was to redress the situation following from the 1967 defeat, so as to regain our self-confidence and the world's confidence in us. The economic situation was merely one of the dimensions of the problem.

The basic task was to wipe out the disgrace and humiliation that followed from the 1967 defeat. I reckoned it would be 1000 times more honourable for us – 40,000 of my sons in the armed forces and myself – to be buried crossing the Canal than to accept such disgrace and humiliation. Posterity would say we had died honourably on the battlefield ... and posterity would carry on the struggle.

VI

When the US envoy Mr Elliot Richardson – one of Nixon's ministers, who had been sent to Egypt to offer condolences on Nasser's death – returned home late in 1970, he submitted a report to the effect that Sadat wouldn't survive in power for more than four or six weeks. At home, Soviet agents in the Egyptian political leadership began their power struggle. This emerged very clearly after I had taken my decision to lift all state custodianship of private property, only two months after the result of the elections came out.

At the time the leaders of Egypt, Sudan, and Libya had begun a series of meetings in search of a formula for unity among the Arab countries. Sudan was not ready at that point for any form of unity with other countries pending the completion of her constitutional bodies. But President al-Qaddafi of Libya tried to appear as though he was an extreme 'unionist', and President al-Assad of Syria showed himself genuinely eager for unity from the very first. We agreed to adopt an initial formula – in the form of a looser union than a merger – by setting up a close community of states which we decided to call the Confederation of Arab Republics. This meant that each republic would maintain its individual character, its existing President, and system of government (which accorded with the particular circumstances of each). This step would be followed by the setting up of a Presidential Council which, comprising all presidents, would be charged with organizing 'unionist' action and specifying the steps ultimately leading to unity. This was the agreed formula in Nasser's lifetime, after we had learned the lesson of the breakup of the union with Syria in 1961 (which had been very short-lived indeed).

The chief power bloc – it included Ali Sabri, Sharawi Gomah, and Sami Sharaf, all Soviet agents – thought this was a chance to initiate a fight against me.

Ali Sabri, then a member of the Egyptian delegation accompanying me, made a statement to the effect that the circumstances of Egypt did not allow her to have any kind of union with any other country. That was the earliest manifestation of my conflict with this group. Ali Sabri, together with the rest of the Egyptian delegation which comprised the political leaders Nasser had left me, deliberately sought to erect obstacles at every turn so as to thwart our unity with Libya and Syria. Al-Qaddafi didn't tell me that they kept in touch with him to frustrate our efforts; but President al-Assad said to me: 'You're in a very peculiar position. You tell us one thing, and your side says a completely different thing behind your back.'

On our last day of meetings in the spring of 1971, Gaafar Muhammad al-Nimeiry, President of the Arab Republic of Sudan, said to me: 'I am not, as I have told you, ready for unity yet. I would, however, fully support any measure taken to achieve unity between you and Syria as it really concerns our Pan-Arab cause.' He was due to leave for the Soviet Union the following morning.

After he left, it was quite obvious that the four-party meeting – between Egypt, Sudan, Syria, and Libya – had failed.

When al-Qaddafi notified me about his departure hour, I said, 'I shall be joining you at the airport for the farewell ceremony, but I'd like you, Muammar, to know that President Assad and I will establish today, before he leaves for Damascus, a united Arab republic. This is our destiny, inasmuch as we are fighting a common battle.'

'I am ready to join you,' he said. He had had a completely different view only twenty-four hours before; he had wanted either a unity based on his own dreams and aspirations or no unity at all.

'It might look odd,' I explained, 'because al-Nimeiry has left for Moscow on the understanding that our quadripartite meeting had failed. So, if you'd really like to join us, let us hold the originally planned Benghazi meeting. You could leave for Benghazi ahead of us; in a few hours, we shall join you there.'

We had agreed to hold a tripartite meeting in Benghazi before President al-Nimeiry approached us, and so the meeting was expanded to include Sudan, and the venue changed to Cairo.

The delegation I wanted to accompany me to Libya consisted of Hussein el-Shafei and Ali Sabri, the two vice-presidents at the time. Ali Sabri went to the airport quite early, accompanied by Sharawi Gomah who, in his capacity as Minister of the Interior, had to be there to see al-Qaddafi off. Ali Sabri and Sharawi Gomah took al-Qaddafi on one side and began to sabotage our plan. Al-Qaddafi actually listened, and responded favourably to them. He said he had been against the project but that he found it 'embarrassing not to respond to President Sadat'. So, when I arrived at the airport, Sharawi Gomah said to me: 'Al-Qaddafi says that Your Excellency had put pressure on him and that he really didn't want unity.' Ali Sabri said the same thing to me. I told them I wouldn't listen to such drivel.

In Benghazi the three countries' delegations – Egypt, Syria, and Libya – led by their presidents, met for talks. All the members of the Libyan Revolutionary Command Council were present. I reported my conversation with al-Qaddafi and mentioned the reference to his being 'embarrassed', stressing that we had no intention in seeking this union of embarrassing anybody. Al-Qaddafi remained silent and Ali Sabri had no comment to make. The deliberations began in earnest, but only two days later, it became quite obvious that we couldn't possibly reach agreement. We decided to break up and go home. A statement was prepared to be given to the press saying we hadn't reached agreement and our baggage was actually sent to the airport, where pressmen were waiting, when the Syrian delegation proposed a last-minute amendment in a formula previously discussed. The amendment was submitted to al-Qaddafi and proved to be a breakthrough, for al-Qaddafi was agreeable to the new formula and so was I, actually. Journalists were called in and the Benghazi Agreement was signed. Minutes later, however, Ali Sabri approached me to voice his objections. 'Let's deal with these objections in Cairo, shall we?' I said.

VI

Back in Cairo I convened the eight-member Supreme Executive Committee of the Arab Socialist Union (the Politbureau) and submitted to them the agreement on unity which I had signed for Egypt in Benghazi. A protracted debate followed, during which it emerged that the majority – the Soviet agents who formed the major power bloc in the leadership – had established a group faction in opposition to the agreement and were ready for their first trial of strength to impose tutelage on my decisions. Then the agreement was put to the vote. The result was that five out of eight – the Soviet agents in the leadership – were against it, and three – Dr Mahmoud Fawzi, the prime minister; Hussein el-Shafei, the Vice-President, and myself – for it. Clearly, this was the climax of the conflict. They wanted to finish me off or, at least, to curtail my power so drastically that I would be incapable of taking any decision without their approval.

They were surprised to hear me ask them that the subject be submitted to the Central Committee. Taken unawares, and decidedly unprepared for this turn of events, they tried to play for time by calling for further studies to be made and for a reconsideration of the result of the voting. I insisted, however, that the entire subject be referred to the Central Committee. They tried desperately to win the Committee over, but to no avail. The agreement was ratified unanimously. So the first trial of strength ended in an absolute victory for me, and they gave in ... temporarily.

In January 1971 I had to take a decision on the Rogers Plan. Again, I convened the Supreme Executive Committee and the meeting was also attended by the Minister of War and the Foreign Minister. The discussion revealed that the majority – that power bloc which constituted the bulk of the political leadership Nasser had left me – supported the view that the war of attrition with Israel should be resumed. And this despite the fact that Upper Egypt (50 per cent of our homeland) was open to Israeli raids, as was demonstrated in 1968 and 1969, and that the Soviet Union was temporizing over shipping the missiles to us that would have enabled us to deal with these raids and protect our civilian establishments in Upper Egypt. (The agreement on those missiles had, in fact, been signed but the Soviet Union simply procrastinated and used all sorts of pretexts for the delay.)

It was obvious, too, throughout the discussion, that the object of the exercise was to put me, as well as Egypt, in a most difficult situation. I therefore concluded by saying that I couldn't resume the war of attrition until I had received the SAM batteries promised and until all vital civilian installations in Upper Egypt were properly defended. I said I would allow an extension of the cease-fire provided for by the Rogers Plan for thirty days only, ending on 7 March 1971, so as to give the world, the United States, and above all Israel a last chance to shoulder their responsibilities.

On 4 February 1971, I announced an entirely new 'Initiative' in Parliament. The drift of it was that if Israel withdrew her forces in Sinai to the Passes, I would be willing to reopen the Suez Canal; to have my forces cross to the East Bank; to extend the Rogers Plan cease-fire by six, rather than three, months; to make a solemn, official declaration of a cease-fire; to restore diplomatic relations with the United States; and to sign a peace agreement with Israel through the efforts of Dr Jarring, the representative of the Secretary General of the UN. It was the first time an Arab leader had the courage to declare this in twenty-two years. None of my opponents had foreknowledge of my Initiative; they were surprised, indeed dumbfounded, to hear me declare it to the world in the course of my People's Assembly speech. The outside world welcomed it, however. It was other people who came to realize that we were being, perhaps for the first time ever, objective and realistic rather than emotional and irrational. With their undiminished political sense and keen natural insight, the Egyptian people themselves grasped the meaning of the Initiative and welcomed it warmly.

In that February I thought of visiting the Soviet Union for the first time since my election as President of Egypt, to demand the fulfilment of the second part of the agreement it had concluded with Nasser – the part concerning supplying us with a deterrent weapon (the SAM batteries) as well as making good our losses in ammunition during the war of attrition. I received word that the Soviet leaders would be willing to see me on 1 and 2 March 1971. I wanted it to be a secret trip, and it was.

At the negotiating table in the Kremlin I explained the troubles we had had since Nasser's day and our vital needs at the time. I started by establishing two basic points I was to emphasize in all subsequent meetings with the Kremlin leaders. The first was that we didn't want Soviet soldiers to fight our battle for us; the second that we never sought to initiate a confrontation between the Soviet Union and the United States. I was worked up and made my case in strong terms. There were sharp exchanges between me and both Kosygin, the Soviet premier, and Marshal Andrei Grechko, the Soviet Defence Minister. But I went on using strong language, and finally Brezhnev felt he had to intervene. He told me that the Soviet government would agree to provide Egypt with several kinds of weapons. They were not the ones we had asked for, but we said we would take them as we badly needed weapons of whatever kind. The Soviet Union never changed its method of dealing with us. At that meeting I said, 'Thank you, but I must put on record in the minutes of this meeting that we have our differences.'

In the course of our heated conversation at that meeting I was told they were prepared to send us missile-equipped aircraft, and to train Egyptian crews for them, on condition that they would be used only when prior Soviet permission had been granted. I was livid with rage at this, I remember. 'Nobody,' I said, 'is allowed to take a decision on Egyptian affairs except the people of Egypt itself – represented by me, the President of Egypt! I don't want the aircraft.' Brezhnev then took me to one side and said to me in private, 'You know the MIG-25 aircraft of which you have four?' 'It's excellent,' I said. 'I'll send you thirty MIG-25s for use as bombers.' 'In that case,' I said, 'I'd take back what I said about our differences, provided, of course,' I added, 'that the pilots received their orders from me.'

Brezhnev never sent us the promised aircraft. I ordered that the four Soviet-manned aircraft be grounded. They were MIG-25s of the type recently flown to Japan by a defecting Soviet pilot. The Soviet Union had to choose between taking them back and selling them to us.

These four MIG-25 aircraft I agreed to have in Egypt to perform certain reconnaissance missions for the Egyptian armed forces, although in fact the Russian pilots did so only once and subsequently refused to carry out our orders. It transpired that the aircraft were there to carry out reconnaissance missions for the Soviet Fifth Fleet – against the US Sixth Fleet – in the Mediterranean. They were later withdrawn as the Soviet Union refused to sell them to us.

I reported all that had happened in Moscow to the Supreme Executive Committee. I said: 'I've turned down these aircraft because of the strings attached – namely, that I should seek Moscow's approval before using them. Let it be clear to you all that only the President of Egypt has the right to take a decision on these matters. On the terms presented, that deterrent weapon is unacceptable to me.'

My political opponents wouldn't open their mouths, but they left in a rage. They resented the fact that I would not agree to ask for permission from the Soviet Union.

The Soviet Union sent me the SAM batteries in April 1971. Part of the ammunition promised was also sent, but the rest was not received until the airlift of the October 1973 War. As for the aircraft and the deterrents Brezhnev had promised me, they proved to be part of the lip service I was paid.

This was how the Soviet Union always dealt with me. It liked to see our hands tied, so that we were unable to take a decision. On 7 March I declared in a public speech that we were no longer bound by the cease-fire and that the Rogers Plan was at an end. I should have and was indeed expected to resume the war of attrition straightaway, but the fact that the Soviet Union failed to honour its word immobilized me.

VIII

My Peace Initiative of 4 February 1971 launched an Egyptian diplomatic offensive – the only alternative to a military one which I was, at the time, unable to undertake. As a result, the United States contacted me and proposed that William Rogers, then Secretary of State, visit us. I welcomed the proposal. It was a shock to the Soviet Union and its agents, particularly those working in Egypt for the Soviet Union.

By then both this Soviet power bloc and the other conspirators had come to realize that I was beginning to gain ground inside and outside Egypt. Their fight against me, though still underground, must now, they felt, be speeded up; the plan to get rid of me had to be carried out quickly.

First, they asked me to appoint the Minister of the Interior Sharawi Gomah (one of the main Soviet agents and chief plotters against me) prime minister. I refused. In fact, I had by then decided to get rid of Ali Sabri, who was the chief Soviet agent in Egypt. I told the Soviet ambassador, 'Although I am eager to maintain my good relations with you, I'd like you to inform the Soviet leadership that I have decided to remove Ali Sabri from the Egyptian political leadership. I have informed you of this, even though it is one of our internal affairs in which I can allow no one to interfere, because, I'm afraid, the Western press will say, when this happens, that I have removed Moscow's number one man in Egypt and so upset you. You should know that Moscow has no man in Egypt – you are dealing with a government, not with individuals. I'm removing Ali Sabri because, although I accept differences of opinion, I cannot tolerate a power struggle.'

But the Soviet power bloc remained very active. Meetings were held and people encouraged to join them. I began to receive letters from individuals who complained of 'orders' and 'instructions' issued to them by the Arab Socialist Union, which was dominated by that power bloc. I always made a point of referring such complaints to the intriguers themselves and warned them not to harm their authors. Towards the end of April they all got quite feverish: they met daily, instigated others to join forces with them, and spread rumours up and down the country. Indeed, they had a mechanism for 'rumour-processing' in which they took great pride. They used to boast that they could launch a rumour in Cairo, get it circulated throughout Egypt, then receive it back in record time! This is a well-known activity in Russia, referred to as the work of 'agitation centres'.

My timing, as the struggle against them intensified, was accurate. Zero Hour was May Day, 1971. They did everything in their power to make our celebration of the occasion a failure, but they were disappointed. The speech I made on May Day aroused people's interest and the celebration was a great success. On 2 May I dismissed Ali Sabri from all the posts he had held. It was a mere one-line report in the national papers. While the people rejoiced, the underground activity redoubled. More meetings were held, more people were incited to join them, more discussions of the proposed plot took place – all in the belief that the President had no knowledge of what was going on. Now I had to bring the struggle to a successful conclusion. So I held several meetings with senior officers of the armed forces. In my last speech to them, I said: 'I won't allow any "spheres of influence" to come into being or any kind of power struggle to continue. Anyone who acts against the interests of Egypt will be made mincemeat of ...' War Minister Fawzi, who had fallen under their influence, was sitting right beside me.

I was supposed to pay a visit to al-Tahrir Province on Thursday 13 May. But I learned that a plan had been laid to ambush and assassinate me there. So I said I was tired and postponed the trip.

By now I was determined to get rid of all these people, yet I lacked concrete incriminating evidence against them. There had been many reasons to get rid of them from the day I took office in October 1970, but I had to have concrete proof. On 11 May a young police officer, a stranger to me, called and asked to see me, carrying a recorded tape. The telephone conversation recorded had taken place between two of the chief instigators and proved clearly that they were plotting to overthrow me and the regime. It also revealed that Broadcasting House had been besieged on the day I met with the Central Committee to discuss the Union Agreement. The idea was that if I had made an attempt to address the people on the radio, I would be trapped and assassinated.

With this evidence in hand I decided there should be no further delay in removing the conspirators. They had, beyond a shadow of doubt, plotted to overthrow the legitimate regime and were thus acting against the interests of Egypt. I began by dismissing Sharawi Gomah, the Minister of the Interior who led the plotters. Later that day – 13 May – at precisely 10.57 p.m. (the time of the last full news bulletin on Cairo Radio's home service), Ashraf Marwan, Nasser's son-in-law, who was director of Sami Sharaf's office, called on me to submit the resignations of the Speaker of the National Assembly, the War Minister, the Information Minister, the Presidential Affairs Minister, some members of the Central Committee, and even a few members of the Supreme Central Committee as well. This gambit was designed, if accepted, to precipitate a constitutional collapse – and I accepted it. I accepted their resignations and ordered the news to be broadcast on the spot, putting them all under house arrest. I proceeded to carry out a government reshuffle without delay – in fact, during the night. So, instead of a constitutional crisis, the people couldn't contain themselves for joy. They took to the streets, not really knowing how to express their feelings.

The nightmare of the central struggle for power that had paralysed Egypt for so long was finally lifted.

It was also necessary, however, to undo the evil work of those who had for years been tampering with people's lives, cultivating fear, obstructing the course of justice, practising truly intolerable forms of oppression and torture, and depriving the people of the most essential constituent of human life – freedom. I ordered that all the recorded tapes of individuals' private conversations filed in the Ministry of the Interior should be burned. The action was symbolic of the restoration to the people of their long-lost freedom. I then ordered that all detention centres were to be closed down, and an end put to all arbitrary arrests. And I called on everybody to do and say what he liked, as long as he broke no laws.

The events of 15 May 1971, and the days following represented a serious effort on my part to correct the course of the 23 July 1952 Revolution. They could be regarded as the first brick laid in the edifice of our present socialist society, which is characterized by genuine social justice rather than inane socialist slogans; by positive work and clear objectives rather than twisted interpretations of certain political concepts and foreign ideologies vastly at variance with our genuine Arab values, our religious faith, and the real traditions of our people – all of which stem from the very nature of the cohesive Egyptian family.

IX

Nikolai Podgorny visited Egypt late in May 1971 after the Western press had reported, just as I had predicted, that Moscow's number one man and, indeed, all Moscow's men in Egypt, had been jailed. A cartoon in some Western paper showed Podgorny meeting Moscow's agents in Egypt – all clad in prison overalls! Podgorny asked for a Soviet-Egyptian Treaty of Friendship to be concluded almost immediately. Although I didn't object, I explained that his timing was wrong. 'Your men,' I said, 'have been arrested, it is true, but they haven't been tried as yet. A treaty concluded now could tarnish their image even further in the eyes of the people because you would then confirm that they were your agents in Egypt.' But Podgorny was too eager for the treaty to be concluded to listen to me. The Politburo had met in Moscow, he said, and insisted such a treaty was essential right now.

I accepted, perhaps mainly to allay the fears of Soviet leaders, as I knew they allowed themselves to be unnecessarily suspicious in their foreign relations. Suspicion is second nature to the Russians, whether under the czars or communism. So the following day, a Treaty of Friendship and Co-operation was concluded. When I took Podgorny to the airport to see him off, I asked him just before he boarded his plane to convey the following message to his colleagues in Moscow: 'Please have confidence in us ... Have confidence ... Confidence!' I felt they had no faith in us, which made me fear for our struggle.

During my meeting with Podgorny I had said that although we were not happy in Egypt with the way they treated us, we were still concluding the treaty with them to prove our good intentions. 'Give me four days,' he said, 'and all the weapons you have asked for will be shipped to you, including the "retaliation weapon".'

That was late in May 1971. I waited throughout June, July, August, and most of September for what Podgorny himself had promised, but to no avail. The Soviet leaders were in the habit of falling silent, as silent as the grave, for long periods of time – which annoyed me, I suppose, more than anything else. I often summoned the Soviet ambassador, I wrote to them frequently, but the answer was invariably silence. It was as though one was communicating with imaginary people.

In July 1971 a Communist *coup d'état* took place in Sudan. My attitude was firm. I said we condemned it

because we would not accept a Communist regime established on our doorstep – in a country sharing our borders.
A few days later, however, the coup was foiled and President al-Nimeiry, having got rid of his enemies, was back
in power.

My attitude to the Sudan coup caused the gap between
me and the Soviet leaders to widen. Throughout July,
August, and September, all I could receive in answer to
my messages was that they were away in their Crimean
summer resort.

Towards the end of September, they sent me a message
saying that they would be willing to see me in Moscow
on 11 October. Although I had had enough (anyone in
my position would have lost his patience as a result of
their deliberate failure to respond for almost half a year),
I didn't show that I was upset in the least and did leave
for Moscow. At the talks I repeated the words I had said
to them in March: 'I don't mind, my friends, if you keep
me one step behind Israel [in armaments] but I find it
a bit too much to be twenty steps behind her!'

As usual, the Soviet leaders would let me say what I
liked, occasionally voicing opposition which developed
at times into sharp exchanges. Except for Brezhnev – he
always appeared to be understanding and never opposed
me. This time, however, they promised to send me the
missile-equipped aircraft, together with experts to train
Egyptian crews to use them. This time, too, they waived
their original condition, namely, that to operate those
aircraft in particular, prior permission had to be granted
by Moscow. At the end of the meeting I said: 'It's 12
October today. I hope these weapons will be sent us as
soon as possible so that we can be in a position, before
the year is out, to break the deadlock of the present situation.' I had, in fact, declared that 1971 would be the year
of decision, that we would have to decide then whether to
have a peaceful solution or go to war.

They agreed. I went back to Egypt, this time fully confident that the promised weapons would soon be on their way to us.

There was no sign of anything throughout October and November. I summoned the Soviet ambassador, sent messages to the Kremlin, and so on, but received no reply whatsoever. On 8 December I was surprised to hear of the Indo-Pakistani War and the Soviet involvement in it. On 12 December I summoned the Soviet ambassador and told him I had so far received no weapons whatsoever; I wanted him therefore to tell the Soviet leaders that I must see them to find a means of dealing with a situation in which I felt exposed for having failed to make 1971 truly a year of decision. It was the end of December when the Soviet ambassador called to tell me that the Soviet leaders were very busy at the moment but that they'd willingly see me in Moscow on 1 and 2 February 1972.

I knew then that as a result of having previously declared that 1971 would be the year of decision, I would now have to face a vicious campaign of denigration. And so it turned out. Perhaps in the hope that Jewish public opinion might forgive his standing by me at one time in the past when Golda Meir had rebuked him publicly (in a famous speech in the Knesset), US Secretary of State William Rogers made a speech on 1 January 1972, in which he said that 1971 had come and gone and no decisive action had been taken by Sadat. He went on to say that the United States would supply Israel with more weapons, military equipment, and everything else she needed. He even declared that the United States and Israel had jointly begun to manufacture arms in Israel since November 1971, and that the United States would maintain Israel's superiority over all the Arab nations combined – not just Egypt.

It was all part of the ferocious psychological campaign being waged against us, exactly as I had expected. The Egyptian people had, as always, enough political discrimination to realize that the Soviet Union was to blame for it

20

all. In 1972 the people's resentment of the Soviet Union reached an unprecedented peak, even though I really didn't give them all the facts; on the contrary, I defended the Soviet Union in every public statement and speech I made.

X

I was in Moscow as requested on 1 and 2 February 1972, and asked the reason for the delay in sending the weapons which the Soviet leaders had promised me. Brezhnev said he was personally to blame. It was due, he said, to the necessary paperwork, the inevitable red tape, and similar things. 'I am not convinced of that,' I said, 'and if this is repeated I will have to act – a decision will have to be taken.' I was beside myself with rage. I reiterated what I had told them on my previous visits, particularly that we didn't want Soviet soldiers to fight our battle for us and that we sought no confrontation between them and the United States. The meeting ended with them reading out a list of weapons which they promised would be shipped 'forthwith'. They were not the essential weapons I wanted but they were better than nothing.

Back in Egypt, I realized my patience had run out.

At that point the first-ever summit between Brezhnev and Nixon had been fixed to take place on 20 May 1972, to promote international détente. The weapons the Soviet Union wanted to sell us began to arrive – not the ones we had asked for. On 15 May Marshal Grechko, accompanied by the commander of the Soviet Air Force, arrived in Egypt. They brought along a new aircraft – a Sukhoy 17. It was put on show and a test flight followed. Grechko had a statement prepared as usual in the CPSU Central Committee which, he said, had to be issued by us, acknowledging the receipt of long-range bombers, which wasn't true. The statement was issued, decorations were conferred on members of the Soviet delegation, and then they left. Although I knew that Grechko's visit to Egypt only five days before Nixon was due to arrive in Moscow was designed to demonstrate Soviet influence in the Middle East, I didn't mind; indeed, I decorated the delegation personally.

I have omitted to mention that the Soviet ambassador suddenly called late in April 1972, to convey an 'urgent' message from the Soviet leaders. They wanted me to pay a visit to Moscow towards the end of April. I realized of course that they simply wanted to prove to the United States that their feet were planted firmly in the Middle East region; but despite being disgusted with the whole gesture, I accepted the invitation.

We – the Soviet leaders and I – agreed at our Moscow talks at the end of April 1972 on the need for them to send us a detailed analysis of the situation after Nixon's visit to Moscow on 20 May, preparatory to the shipment to Egypt (in five months' time, from June to October) of all those weapons included in the old contracts. November 1972, when the US presidential campaign would be held, was the agreed deadline. The idea was that we should be adequately prepared by November, when a new American President would have been elected, to resort to military action if all avenues to peace continued to be blocked. They agreed to this and I returned to Cairo.

Nixon made his first visit to the Soviet Union in May 1972 as planned. The first statement on détente was issued jointly by Moscow and Washington, advocating military relaxation in the Middle East. It was a violent shock to us because, as I have previously explained, we lagged at least twenty steps behind Israel and so 'military relaxation' in this context could mean nothing but giving in to Israel.

The Soviet 'analysis', following from the Moscow Nixon meeting, reached me on 6 July – in other words, more than a month late. This analysis explained that no progress had been achieved on the Middle East question in the Soviet-American talks – just as I had predicted during my Moscow visit late in April – in view of the fact that it was the US election year.

What was even more odd, the Soviet analysis conveyed to me by the Soviet ambassador said nothing at all about the failure to ship the requested weapons. More than two and a half pages long, the analysis did not deal with our battle or the weapons needed for it (as agreed in April 1972), except in the last five lines, which said simply that we were unable to start a battle, that they had experience in this respect, and that they had made an unusual effort to persuade Nixon that Security Council Resolution 242 should be implemented.

I asked the Soviet ambassador: 'Is this *the* message?'

'Yes,' he said.

'You were, weren't you, with us in Moscow last April,' I said, 'and you did hear us agree that the weapons should be sent to us before the US elections took place?'

'Yes,' he replied.

'Well,' I continued, 'this message doesn't mention that.'

'This is the message I have received.'

'Well,' I said, 'I cannot accept it, and indeed reject the Soviet leaders' method in dealing with us. Please convey all I am going to tell you to the Soviet leaders as an official message.

'One. I reject this message you've transmitted to me from the Soviet leaders, both in form and content. It is unacceptable. I reject, too, this method in dealing with us.

'Two. I have decided to dispense with the services of all Soviet military experts (about 15,000) and that they must go back to the Soviet Union within one week from today. I shall convey this order to the War Minister.

'Three. There is Soviet equipment in Egypt – four MIG-25s, and a Soviet-manned station for electronic war fare. You should either sell these to us or take them back to the Soviet Union.

'Four. No Soviet-owned equipment should stay in

Egypt. Either you sell it to us or withdraw it within the fixed date.

'Five. All this should be carried out in a week from now.'

The Soviet ambassador didn't believe it. He thought it was an attempt at blackmail.

I summoned the War Minister the following morning and ordered him to carry out the decisions I had taken By 16 July 1972, all my decisions had been implemented. As the Soviet Union refused to sell us the MIG-25 aircraft and jamming equipment, they were withdrawn along with the experts.

One of the reasons behind my decision was the Soviet attitude to me; but another important reason was that within the strategy I had laid down, no war could be fought while Soviet experts worked in Egypt. The Soviet Union, the West, and Israel misinterpreted my decision to expel the military experts and reached an erroneous conclusion which in fact served my strategy, as I had expected – that it was an indication that I had finally decided not to fight my own battle. That interpretation made me happy; it was precisely what I wanted them to think. A further reason for the expulsion of the Soviet experts was that the Soviet Union had begun to feel that it enjoyed a privileged position in Egypt – so much so that the Soviet ambassador had assumed a position comparable to that of the British High Commissioner in the days of British occupation of Egypt. The army Director of Operations, Major-General Muhammed Abdel Ghany el-Gamasy (now commander-in-chief), had told me that the staff of the jamming centre, the crews of the four aircraft and of all the other Soviet-manned equipment had consistently refused to carry out any orders until permission was granted by Moscow.

Yet another reason for my decision was that I wanted to put the Soviet Union in its place – in its natural position as a friendly country, no more, no less. The Soviets had thought at one time that they had Egypt in their pocket, and the world had come to think that the Soviet Union was our guardian. I wanted to tell the Russians that the will of Egypt was entirely Egyptian; I wanted to tell the whole world that we are always our own masters. Whoever wished to talk to us should come over and do it, rather than approach the Soviet Union.

9
The October War

I

I had stopped going to Alexandria for my summer holiday since our June 1967 defeat. When, however, the decision to expel Soviet experts from Egypt had been taken, I felt a little relieved and so thought of having some rest there. I directed my office staff that if any of the Soviet leaders tried to get in touch with me, they should be told I was in my Alexandrian summer resort – just as we were often told that Soviet leaders were in the Crimea, or in other words, out of touch.

The moment I arrived in Alex I began to prepare for the battle although I knew that the entire world (including Egypt) had interpreted my expulsion of the Soviet military experts as an indication that I wasn't going to fight. I summoned Hafiz Ismail, my National Security Adviser, and told him that the United States would inevitably get in touch with us now and so he had to be ready with the necessary alternatives for a dialogue to be conducted successfully with America. I also summoned War Minister Muhammad Sadek and ordered him to convene the Supreme Council of the armed forces on the following day and tell them that I had decided that the armed forces should be ready for fighting, for launching an attack, as from 15 November 1972. Then I summoned Sayed Marei, secretary-general of the Arab Socialist Union, and asked him to hold a meeting with ASU provincial branch secretaries to inform them that my decision to expel Soviet experts meant we would be going to war, not the other way around. And I asked Mamdouh Salem, then in charge of civil defence, to prepare the domestic front for war and to deal with any gaps.

Before my first week in Alexandria was out, Kissinger contacted us and asked for a meeting between Egyptian and US officials at the highest possible level. It was agreed that Hafiz Ismail should see him either in September or October of the same year. (But the date was repeatedly postponed so that the two men in fact were not able to meet before February 1973.)

Early in August 1972 President al-Qaddafi suddenly began to tell the world that he wanted a so-called merger with Egypt. As I had promised him to visit Libya roundabout that time, I left for Benghazi to find out exactly what he was after. He insisted, I found out, that such a form of union be adopted. He had already made great efforts to mobilize the 'masses' for it through a vast mass media campaign, even without prior consultation with me. On my arrival in Benghazi I was surprised to find that he had already prepared a plan for the union. Though far from enthusiastic about the speed with which al-Qaddafi wanted to carry out the project, I thought it better to cover up his position – at the request of some of his colleagues in the Libyan Revolutionary Council – by agreeing to a meeting between Libyan and Egyptian delegations to discuss the matter. I was surprised to find that in accordance with the project drawn up by al-Qaddafi himself, I was to be President of the new state (comprising Egypt and Libya), while al-Qaddafi would be Vice-President and commander-in-chief of the armed forces. I explained to al-Qaddafi and his colleagues that I didn't approve of that project, particularly of the appointment of al-Qaddafi as commander-in-chief, in view of our previous bitter experience. Politicians had been actual commanders of the armed forces in Egypt with disastrous results for us – in the 1956 War, the Yemeni War, and finally in the 1967 War. The armed forces, I insisted, should be professional and should be kept out of politics. Al-Qaddafi didn't object.

The second reason for my opposition to the project was that a merger at that time would have resulted in unnecessary economic troubles for the Libyan people – for which we would be responsible. The conferees accepted my suggestion, which was that we should proceed gradually towards unity. I then returned to Egypt.

On 29 August I sent a message to the Soviet Union which I regard as a landmark in our history inasmuch as it contained a full and accurate description of our relations at the time. I told the Soviet leaders in that message that I was going to allow them another chance to prove their good intentions and respond to our demands by October 1972. However, if by then there was no response, I would be free, I said, to take the decisions I deemed fit. We were at cross-purposes, actually, for the Soviet Union was preparing to infiltrate and incite students to an uprising when the Egyptian universities reopened in October 1972, in accordance with a plan drawn up by the Arab Communist Parties (though issued, naturally, by Moscow) for Soviet agents within our universities.

War Minister Sadek should have submitted a report to me by then on the War Plan as well as the general framework of the envisaged battle. I had asked him, as I have said, to convene the Supreme Council of the armed forces to convey my message to them. Two days later he reported to me that he had done so. He said that the Egyptian armed forces would indeed be ready – and by 1 November, not 15 November as I had requested.

I should explain at this point why I had chosen that date – 15 November – for the armed forces to be ready. The US presidential elections would be over in the early days of November and I wanted to give the President-elect a chance to try to find a peaceful solution to the problem. So, if nothing was achieved in this direction by then, we would be ready to take military action.

I therefore convened the Supreme Council of the armed

forces on 28 October. I wanted to make sure that the armed forces *were* ready, and so asked each commander to give me a report on their state of readiness, especially as November was drawing near. I reminded them that this was the time the War Minister and I had fixed for completing preparations, and referred to the message I had entrusted the War Minister to convey to them in the summer.

One major-general, Nawal, in charge of administration in the armed forces surprised me by asking: 'I haven't heard of any such message before. May I enquire what exactly was that "message" that you sent us? I had no idea that any message had been sent by your Excellency.'

I turned to Sadek, in front of the whole Council, and said: 'What's the meaning of this? We agreed in the summer, didn't we, that you should convene this Council and tell them that we ought to be ready for battle by 15 November? Didn't you report to me, two days later, that you had convened the Council and that they would be ready by 1 November, two weeks ahead of schedule?'

The War Minister whispered to me: 'I thought it unadvisable, sir, to tell everybody. So I just informed the commanders of the armies, so as to maintain secrecy.'

'What kind of "secrecy" would that be?' I thought to myself. 'Should a war decision be kept secret from the very people who are going to fight?' An odd situation had arisen: Could the commanders of the armies be expected to go to war without the knowledge of the Supreme Council of the armed forces? The major-general who had asked about the war was in fact in charge of administration, which includes logistics – the supply of food, water, ammunition, gas, and so forth, to the armies – without which no unit of the armed forces could accomplish its combat mission.

The doubts I had in the War Minister were thus confirmed. He didn't want to fight because he was afraid of an actual battle taking place. So I began to approach the commanders of our armies themselves, beginning with

Major-General Abdel Munim Wasil, who had commanded the Third Army. I asked him how we stood and his
answer was stunning. 'We're completely exposed, sir,' he
said. 'Any attempted concentration of forces this side of
the Canal would be spotted by the Israelis, so that we'd
be attacked before any crossing is made. The reason, sir,'
he went on to explain, 'is that the Israelis have built a
huge chain of fortifications, an earthworks practically 47
feet high, on the eastern side of the Canal. Ours is much
lower – not more than 10 feet, in fact. This makes our
soldiers suspect that the Israelis have established a tremendous network of electronic equipment behind the line
which our men can't hope to deal with.'

What this meant in effect was that Defence Plan 200,
which Nasser had left me, had now completely collapsed.
One month before he died, Nasser asked me to accompany
him to Army Command Headquarters in Nasr City (a
suburb of Cairo) where all the Egyptian commanders, the
Soviet experts, War Minister Fawzi, and Chief of Staff
Sadek had assembled. There Egyptian experts and commanders undertook a seven-hour-long explanation of
Defence Plan 200, which was finally approved. It was a
perfectly sound defensive plan; but it was all that Nasser
had left me. He had made no plans for an offensive
action of any kind.

The War Minister, Lieutenant-General Fawzi, however,
maintained the viability of Defence Plan 200; when the
Israelis increased the height of their fortifications by 3
feet, ours was heightened by 5. But the new War Minister,
Sadek, had stopped this, so that we had failed to add any
further height, while the Israeli fortifications now rose
to 47 feet.

I put the same questions to General Saad Mamun,
commander of the Second Army (at present the governor
of Cairo), and received an identical answer. 'I'm sorry, but
you must know I am very upset,' I said to the Supreme
Council. 'When I came to see you I expected you to be
ready to carry out any plan we might choose to lay down

and now I find that you haven't even a defensive plan ready. How could we hope to launch an offensive when we're not even prepared for defence? Are we going to have another June 1967 defeat?'

I left the meeting determined to find a replacement for the defeatist Minister of War who had lied to me. I summoned the late Marshal Ahmed Ismail Ali, then major-general and director of Intelligence, who was, incidentally, the architect of the first line of defence to be established in 1967 along the Suez Canal from Port Said to Suez. I told him to take over as c.in-c. and to call on me the next morning to be sworn in as War Minister. Meanwhile I sent my private secretary to Sadek to tell him I had accepted his resignation. I ordered the Chief of Staff of the armed forces to take his place as acting c.-in-c. until Marshal Ali had been sworn in. I couldn't afford to have any gaps in my top armed forces' posts, however temporary.

I asked Marshal Ali, when he had been officially installed as c.-in-c., to put Defence Plan 200 back into shape. If the Israeli fortifications were now 47 feet high, ours should be 65. An immediate allocation of £E20 million was made for that purpose.

I had now taken action to redress the situation, but the sleepless nights I began to have following my meeting with the Supreme Council in October 1972 continued. We couldn't afford to have a repeat of the 1967 tragedy. How could such remissness have been allowed in the armed forces, when our people had pinned all their hopes for the future on them? Indeed, I wondered how we could now repel any Israeli attack. Marshal Ali put an end to my anxiety and serious misgivings when he called on 30 November 1972 (he had been appointed on 30 October) to let me know that our defence preparations had been completed and that he was about to draw up a plan for an offensive.

The basic outline of the plan was completed by January 1973. Marshal Ali had in fact done something unprecedented in military history. He asked every officer in the forces stationed along the Canal to climb the fortifications on our side – which were now 65 feet high – to look away into Sinai, and then define precisely the plan of action he could carry out after crossing the Canal. In this way the officers were given a chance to build their self-confidence and to participate in the plan for action, apart from carrying it out themselves.

I can truly say that the October 1973 War Plan was laid down by the whole of our armed forces.

II

To go back to our story with the Soviet Union. President Hafez al-Assad visited Moscow in October 1972 and stopped over in Cairo on his way home to tell me that the Soviet Union expected an Egyptian delegation led by our prime minister to arrive in Moscow for talks on 16 October, in response to the suggestion I had made in my letter to the Soviet leaders of 29 August. I agreed. Premier Aziz Sidqi, at the head of an Egyptian delegation, left for Moscow and met with Soviet leaders. They were very excited, I was told, at that meeting and showed the deepest possible resentment at the decision I had taken (to expel the 15,000 Soviet military experts from Egypt), saying that it put them in a difficult situation before the world. Dr Sidqi came back with nothing but a bunch of promises that were never kept.

A Soviet-Egyptian agreement was in force at the time concerning maritime facilities which Nasser had granted in 1968, for a period of five years, to the Soviet Mediterranean Fleet. It was due to expire in three months' time, in March 1973. So, in December 1972, I asked Marshal Ali to summon the Soviet ambassador and tell him that Egypt had decided to grant a five-year extension of that agreement, ending in March 1978. My object was to show the Russians that in spite of my decision to expel the Soviet military experts, I did not wish to break with them altogether. Two diplomatic trips were subsequently made by Hafiz Ismail, the Egyptian National Security Adviser, and then by Marshal Ali. Hafiz Ismail was scheduled to have a meeting in Paris with Kissinger in February, which took place as planned. Later in the same month, Marshal Ali left for Moscow. More than eight months had elapsed since the decision to expel the Soviet military experts from Egypt had been taken. The Soviet Union had found out by then that I had not contacted the United States before taking that decision – as I had repeatedly affirmed – and it was proven to them that my dealings with foe and friend alike were governed, as always, by a high ethical code. The biggest arms deal ever to be concluded (either with Nasser or myself) was the result of his visit. For the first time, too, shipments started promptly and in record time, at least of a certain part of the deal. They soon stopped, however, to be resumed only partly much later, in 1975. I would like to state at this point that even without that deal we would have fought our battle. We had taken our decision and laid down a plan based on the weapons already in hand. At the visit of the Egyptian foreign minister in 1976, the Soviet Union cancelled all deals with Egypt and refrained from any discussions of the rescheduling of Egypt's debts.

As for the United States, Hafiz Ismail's meeting with Kissinger in Paris, February 1973, failed to produce any results. It was impossible, as I have always said, for the United States (or, indeed, any other power) to make a move if we ourselves didn't take military action to break the deadlock. The drift of what Kissinger said to Ismail was that the United States regrettably could do nothing to help so long as we were the defeated party and Israel maintained her superiority.

I had also to prepare for the battle on the Arab front. And here I must cite that external power which determines the course of human affairs and directs it in ways beyond our control. It is often absurd to say that one has done this or that when one in fact has done nothing at all – which was true of my preparation for the confrontation with the Arab nations. Everything had been prepared, and the scenario completely set, before I even started.

In Kuwait the House of Al Sabah look on me as a member of the family. I had a close link with Abdullah Mubarak al-Sabah, nourished and governed by loyalty. He was heir apparent, Defence and Interior Minister, at the time. It was the will of God, too, that when Nasser died, Jabir al-Ahmad – a close friend with whom I had regular correspondence – was heir apparent and premier. He is now the ruler of Kuwait after the death of my friend, the late Sabah Salem.

In Saudi Arabia King Faisal had been a personal friend of mine for twenty-one years. We were particularly close in the days of the Islamic Congress in 1955, when he was heir apparent. In spite of the Yemeni War, our relations maintained their original warmth. Friendship meant the same thing to both of us.

In Lebanon, Hamid Franjieh, the full brother of President Suleiman Franjieh, was my personal friend. As for Morocco, my relations with King Hassan II dated back to 1969, when I deputized for Nasser at the first Islamic Conference to be held in Rabat following the al-Aqsa Mosque fire and the ties of fraternity and friendship between me and King Hassan were strengthened. King Faisal, who attended the Rabat Conference, said to King Hassan II of Morocco: 'If it is the will of God that Egypt should thrive, Sadat will be in power.' I was reputed, throughout the conference, to be a frank and unequivocal speaker, and always on the side of justice.

In Algeria President Boumedienne had been 'allergic' to Nasser on account of Nasser's friendship with Ahmed Ben Bella. And in Tunisia, President Habib Bourguiba had often differed with Nasser strongly because Nasser accused him of venality and treason.

Thus it was God's will that I should have close personal relations with the leaders of the Arab world. They all welcomed me as President and showed that they were willing to help. My clear and declared policy was that Egypt could not distinguish one Arab country from another on the basis of so-called progressive and reactionary or republican and monarchical systems. We should be committed to one thing only – our Arab character, pure and simple.

As for the situation in Africa, I attended the summit conference which the Organization of African Unity (OAU) held once a year in Addis Ababa. At that year's summit, held in May 1973, the OAU adopted a clear resolution condemning Israel. It was the first time in the history of the OAU that such a clear and strong resolution was adopted, which augured well for the future. In fact, by the time the war broke out, 80 per cent of all African countries had severed their relations with Israel.

Meanwhile, in the summer of 1973, three Palestinian leaders had been assassinated in the heart of Beirut by the Israelis. I sent a message to President Franjieh of Lebanon asking him to call for a meeting of the UN Security Council to discuss the incident; if he didn't, I said, I would do so. In fact he did, and his request was supported by me. The Security Council met in June and July 1973 and began to discuss the Palestinian leaders' assassination. It came therefore as a surprise to everybody, including Security Council members, when Egypt raised the Middle East question at that very session. The deliberations, which went on for two months, ended with the adoption of a resolution in our favour for the first time ever. The voting was fourteen for and one against – the United States had vetoed the resolution.

This was part of the strategy I had worked out, namely that the situation should be manipulated in our favour alike on the Arab front, on the African front (at the OAU summit in Addis Ababa in 1973), on the international scene (through the Security Council resolution), and in the non-aligned world – at the Non-Aligned Summit Conference to be held in September 1973 in Algiers. (This summit is held once every three years, and the fact that it took place in 1973, the war year, was a godsend.)

In September 1973 I attended the Non-Aligned Summit Conference in Algiers, which was chaired by President Boumedienne. I made a speech in which I said that a battle was inevitable because the Israelis wanted it, and put my cards on the table. I explained that nothing short of complete Arab surrender would satisfy Israel, and in this way established that the non-aligned countries were not unprepared for the battle; most of them supported me, actually.

Three weeks before Zero Hour the support of more than a hundred countries had been secured. It had taken me many months – from January to September – to prepare the world for the war.

III

On the domestic front my efforts were not confined to the creation of the right frame of mind for the battle. More than £E127 million were spent on the preparation of the whole country for war. I had based my plan on the assumption that the entire territory from Alexandria to Aswan would be an actual battlefield. Each factory, each power station, and so forth, had alternative plans for operation during the war. We had to make sure that all services could continue to operate, even if only partially, should they be hit during the fighting.

In April 1973 President Hafez al-Assad paid a secret visit to Egypt. General el-Gamasy, Director of Operations of the armed forces, submitted to us a notebook in which he had entered the dates most appropriate, from the military point of view, for starting a war in 1973. The notes, which were in manuscript – being top secret – specified three sets of days: the first a set of days in May 1973; the second in August and September 1973; and the third in October 1973. The most suitable of these for several reasons was the last. An attack could coincide with Yom Kippur – the Day of Atonement – on 6 October when all public services in Israel would be suspended. After October the Syrian front would not be favourable for military action (from November until early spring) because of the climatic and physical conditions.

Next, I had a private meeting with al-Assad in Burg al-Arab, capital of the Western Desert, in which I told him, 'I have decided to fight my battle this year and have issued the relevant instructions to Marshal Ali. What do you say to this?'

'I'll be with you,' he said; 'we're going to fight and are preparing for it.'

I had no intention of starting a war in May, but as part of my strategic deception plan I launched a mass media campaign then and took various civil defence measures which led the Israelis to believe that war was imminent. On the days when war seemed likely to break out there was a full Israeli mobilization, while we enjoyed perfect military calm. I did the same thing in August – and the Israeli reaction was the same. After the October War, Moshe Dayan was asked why he hadn't mobilized in October. He said that Sadat 'made me do it twice, at a cost of ten million dollars each time. So, when it was the third time round I thought he wasn't serious, but he tricked me!'

Hafez al-Assad and I agreed not to go to war until a Supreme Joint Council, with members representing the Syrian and Egyptian armed forces, had been set up to co-ordinate our action. It was formed an actually met in August in Alexandria to add a few finishing touches to the War Plan.

Late in August 1973 I also made a tour which took me to Saudi Arabia, Qatar, and Syria. I met President al-Assad on the 28th and 29th. We decided then that war would be launched on 6 October – D-Day in military jargon.

Meanwhile I paid regular visits to all the units of our

armed forces to explain the political situation and to tell them that the battle was at hand. I can say that by 5 June, four months from Zero Hour, I had given final orders and created a definite sense of the war soon to be fought (although I didn't, of course, specify the date). Everybody in the armed forces was very keyed up. On 5 June itself I was on a visit to al-Qattamia airfield on the front where I met with the pilots. During our meeting the telephone rang. General Ali took the call while I continued my conversation with the pilots.

When the meeting was over, I proceeded into my aircraft to make further visits to the Second and Third armies, but Marshal Ali whispered to me that the Soviet ambassador had asked for an urgent meeting with me, and that he had an important message which he wanted conveyed to me at once. The gist of it was that the Soviet leadership had decided, following a long period of cool relations, to send Nikolai Podgorny, chairman of the Presidium of the Supreme Soviet, to Egypt for a meeting with me on 11 June. 'I won't see him, I'm afraid,' I told Marshal Ali.

The Soviet leadership knew very well that I didn't like Podgorny, the reason being that while on a visit to Turkey he had made derogatory remarks about Arabs, particularly Arab soldiers, saying that the Soviet Union would never again provide the Arabs with sophisticated weapons because they let them fall in Israeli hands. I did write asking for an explanation for this statement by the Soviet head of state, at the time, but no official denial was ever made. No one hated Egypt more than Podgorny. The comments he made every time I met Soviet leaders at the Kremlin were consistently anti-Egypt. How then could I welcome him in our country?

With that settled, I proceeded with my visits to the Second and Third armies. I inspected certain crossing points on our defence line, which consisted of pyramid-shaped mounds, 33 feet higher than the Israelis', and built at regular intervals along the Canal from Port Said to Suez. From the top I could see Sinai very clearly. At the point facing Al-Qantara East I paused for a while. The commander in charge of recovering Al-Qantara from the Israelis – Major-General Fuad Aziz Ghali (commander-in-chief of the Second Army now) – explained to me how he planned to go about it.

I regarded Al-Qantara East as one of the significant positions, which we ought to recapture in the early hours of the war. Its importance for Israel could not be exaggerated – it was the second most vital Sinai town (after Al-Arish, the capital). Still intoxicated by his 1967 victory, Dayan had made a speech at an Israeli university in which he said: 'We have proved worthy of the responsibility handed to us by the older generation. We have expanded our State so much that its present borders now extend from Egyptian Al-Qantara to Syrian al-Qunaytirah.* It is your duty, as our rising generation, to defend and further extend these borders.'

This was one of the main reasons why I showed such interest in Al-Qantara, for I had always hoped to reply to Dayan by saying: 'Your dream has been shattered for ever.' Before Nasser's death, I remember, I once told Lieutenant-General Abdel Munim Riyad, Chief of Staff of the Egyptian Armed Forces after the defeat of 1967: 'When your plan for an offensive is laid down, remember to give me a place in the forces charged with recapturing Al-Qantara East.'

These images floated in my mind as I stood at one of the springboards prepared for our offensive. I gazed across at Al-Qantara East, but never said a word. I hadn't seen the place for seven years but I knew it very well because I had been posted there after I had been reinstated in the army in 1950. The recollection deepened my silence, and a myriad feelings welled up in my heart.

* In Arabic 'al-Qunaytirah' is the diminutive of 'al-Qantarah'; hence Dayan's pun. Translated, the words mean a 'bridge' and a 'small bridge', respectively.

On the way back to Cairo, Marshal Ali turned to me and said: 'When I saw you, sir, wrapped in that awful silence, I felt as though you were about to give me an order to start an attack at once.'

In drawing up the general strategic plan for the battle, I took many things into account, but primarily the strategic basis from which we ought to proceed. I used to tell Nasser that if we could recapture even 4 inches of Sinai territory (by which I meant a foothold, pure and simple), and establish ourselves there so firmly that no power on earth could dislodge us, then the whole situation would change – east, west, all over. First to go would be the humiliation we had endured since the 1967 defeat; for, to cross into Sinai and hold on to any territory recaptured would restore our self-confidence. It would also mean that we had overcome a water barrier surely unprecedented in military history – first because the banks of the Canal are built of solid rock, and, second, because of the Israeli earthworks which stood 47 feet high, and the Bar-Lev Line.

I had taken all this into account in issuing my strategic directives towards the end of February. We should have the upper hand in the first twenty-four hours of fighting, because, I said, 'He who wins the first twenty-four-hour encounter will surely win the entire war.' Our plan and method of execution should be based on the kind of action designed to tip the balance in our favour within the first twenty-four hours.

In September the foreign minister of a certain European country called to see me. As part of my strategic deception I told him: 'Please convey this message to your President and ask him to keep it a secret, which should not be divulged. I am going to be at the UN headquarters in October 1973, but I don't want to announce this at the moment.' I knew that that report would be transmitted in a matter of minutes to Israel – and Israel came to believe, accordingly, that I wasn't planning to go to war.

IV

On 28 September, the third anniversary of Nasser's death, I made a speech designed to add the finishing touches to the general picture of the situation as it now took shape in people's eyes.

I had, many months before, dismissed a number of journalists, or rather, given them different jobs at the Information Department because they had taken part in a campaign calculated to create a sense of instability and a general mood of uncertainty in the country. Furthermore, some of them had been behind the student disturbances organized by the Communists late in 1972 and early in 1973; they wrote and did things aimed at kindling the fires of a misguided, youthful wrath. So as a last finishing touch I declared in my 28 September 1973, speech that I had granted a general amnesty to all such offenders – that all students and journalists awaiting trial had been pardoned. There would be no trial, I said, of anybody, even the hard-core leftist students.

This move was interpreted by the left as an attempt at domestic reconciliation, that is, an attempt at the consolidation of the internal front. Nobody realized it was part of my War Plan. I did it in exactly the same spirit as I had dealt with the sectarian trouble that had taken place earlier.

On 30 September 1973, I convened the National Security Council and asked them to give me their views of the situation. We had a lengthy discussion; some members called for war, others were hesitant. The Minister of Supply said that available food supplies were insufficient for a long-drawn-out battle. All the members dealt in their critiques with the current position of the country, the need to make a move of some kind, and the chances of success in war. When they had finished, I spoke to them frankly:

Now you've said this, let me tell you that our economy has fallen below zero. We have commitments (to the banks, and so on) which we should but cannot meet by the end of the year. In three months' time, by, say, 1974, we shan't have enough bread in the pantry! I cannot ask the Arabs for a single dollar more; they say they have been paying us the aid in lieu of the lost Canal revenue, although we didn't, or wouldn't, fight.

When I had informed them of the reality of our situation, I concluded the meeting. As top officials, they had to be adequately informed.

The following day, 1 October, I convened the Supreme Council of the armed forces. Each commander came up in turn and stood beside the detailed 'Operations' map to explain his plan and the role assigned to him in the war. At the end of the meeting I said: 'Each one of you should be completely ready for an order I'm going to issue any minute now.'

That same day I signed the 'War Order' addressed to the commander-in-chief, Marshal Ahmed Ismail Ali. I had already in September 1973 signed an order of a different kind – a strategic directive, also addressed to the commander-in-chief, in which I specified the strategic target of the war as I saw it. That was the first of its kind in the history of modern Egypt.

The countdown had started earlier – ten days before Zero Hour. At that point our naval units had sailed out to take their combat positions. Each naval unit was given sealed envelopes containing operation instructions which were not to be opened until a certain code word had been received. Other forces needed the ten-day period for further dress-rehearsal training. War was no longer just a plan to be laid down and orders to be carried out: exercises on every move were needed, and the more exercises, the better the chances of success. A general training countdown was over by 21 September, and the last brigade to take part in this ended training on its specific operations on 23 September 1973.

As agreed by President Hafez al-Assad and myself, I summoned the Soviet ambassador on 7th Ramadan – corresponding to 3 October – and told him: 'I'd like to inform you officially that I and Syria have decided to start military operations against Israel so as to break the present deadlock. I would like the Soviet leaders to give me an urgent answer to this question: What will the Soviet attitude be?'

He asked me when we proposed to take that military action, but I said the date hadn't been fixed as yet. I had agreed with President al-Assad, in fact, that he would summon the Soviet ambassador on the following day, Thursday, the 4th, to tell him personally about the date we'd fixed. That was preferable, we thought, in view of my bad relations with the Soviet Union.

On the Thursday the Soviet ambassador wanted to see me urgently. I thought he would give me a reply to my question but instead, the moment he saw me, he said: 'I have an urgent message from the Soviet leadership. Moscow asks you to allow four big aircraft to arrive in Egypt to fly the Soviet families out of Egypt.' (These were the families of Soviet civilians who had worked in factories and civilian establishments. The Soviet military personnel and their families had left a year earlier when I issued the decision to deport all the Soviet military advisers from Egypt.) 'They want them to land at a military airfield,' the ambassador went on, 'so as not to be seen at the international airport and to maintain secrecy. The four aircraft will be here tomorrow morning, 5 October.'

'What a bad omen,' I thought. They obviously implied that I would lose and that they were afraid for the lives of the Soviet nationals. What about the Egyptians – didn't they know that I cared for my people's lives? Practically dumbfounded, I said to the Soviet ambassador: 'I have no objection. You can tell them I've agreed to this but – where is their reply to my question?' He said that Moscow had given him no other message to convey to me.

Sure enough, four big transport planes arrived the next day, 9th Ramadan (corresponding to 5 October, a Friday), and took the Soviet subjects back home. The Israelis spotted the big aircraft on their radar and believed they were transporting Soviet supplies to Egypt and to Syria – for the same thing happened there, at the same time. With our electronic equipment, we and the Israelis could both observe what took place on either side of the borders.

That episode showed a total lack of confidence in us and our fighting ability. But something even more damning happened. A Soviet ship carrying some supplies for us was bound at the time for Alexandria, and was due to anchor, the Soviet Union had informed us, on 9th Ramadan, 5 October. While still at sea, she received orders from Moscow not to head for Alexandria, but to wander around a little in the Mediterranean. Only when it was confirmed that we were winning did Moscow allow the ship to sail on to Alexandria. When we asked about the delay we were told that the ship had gone astray!

That same Thursday, 4 October 1973, on which I had seen the Soviet ambassador I moved to al-Tahirah Palace, in Cairo, which had been temporarily converted into our War Command Headquarters.

On Friday I went for the Friday prayers to the modest little mosque where I had learned to pray fifty years before. I sat in that quiet mosque, overcome by the feeling that I was close to God, while images of childhood rose to the surface of my consciousness – images of innocence and purity. The Friday prayers performed, I went home quietly and, in the evening, sat on the balcony to look at the beautiful young Ramadan moon.

I have always loved nature unadorned, always shied away from busy city life, from tawdriness and glaring lights. My peace of mind was perfect. Though conscious of the decisiveness of the moments to come, I looked forward to tomorrow, when war would rock the world, just like any other day I'd lived through. I approached the battle without the least agitation or nervousness, though my mind was still at work on some details – further finishing touches, no more.

It may sound strange but I slept better on the eve of the battle than I had on most nights before. When I woke up in the morning of 6 October 1973, I felt fresh enough to do the usual daily exercises and to go through my normal morning routine. I was relaxed, and my mind seemed to acquire an added vigour in anticipation of the responsibilities of my own D-Day.

V

On Saturday 6 October 1973, Marshal Ali called. It was precisely 1.30 p.m., as agreed, and we drove together in an army jeep (I wore my military uniform) to the Ops. Room. We arrived in a few minutes and I sat down, with him as c.-in-c. on my right. Our instructions, based on the expert opinion of Islamic law, were that nobody should be fasting – but I wasn't sure this was the case. 'Why aren't you smoking?' I asked the assembled group. 'Why isn't anybody having a drink of some kind? This operation requires your utmost attention and concentration.' I noticed they were very embarrassed, so I ordered some tea for myself and lit my pipe – whereupon they began to smoke and ordered tea. At 2.00 p.m. sharp, Zero Hour for the air force to cross the Canal, a microphone report came in saying that our aircraft had set off.

A total of 222 supersonic jets took part in this first wave and accomplished their mission in twenty minutes. We lost only five aircraft. In those early minutes of the war I lost my youngest brother – Air-Pilot 'Atif – who was as close to me as my own son, since I was the one who had brought him up. I wasn't told at the time, however, that 'Atif was among our early martyrs.

The air strike, in accordance with the plan laid down, was a complete and stunning success. It surprised us, in the first place, by achieving 90 per cent of its targets; and it was equally surprising to Israel, and the world – both East and West. The Soviet Union had estimated – on the basis of the reports submitted by Soviet agents before they left Egypt – that in any future war the air strike would cost the Egyptian Air Force no less than 40 per cent of its entire strength, and achieve no better results than 30 per cent. This estimate by the Soviet Union was meant to intimidate us and make us feel entirely unequal to the battle. They had no confidence at all in us, just as we had lost confidence in them.

Yet in exactly twenty minutes our aircraft had hit the command posts, all aerial combat headquarters, air defence and jamming centres (the electronic-warfare equipment), all liaison points, missile batteries, and gun emplacements in Sinai. When I was assured that this had been done, I congratulated the air force commander, General Husni Mubarak, who had planned and executed the air strike. Then I congratulated all the commanders in the Ops. Room on the strike, which actually determined the future course of the war – Israel was to lose her balance entirely not only during the first decisive twenty-four hours of fighting but for the first four days. She lost control of her forces in Sinai, and her lines of communications with the forces there were broken off completely.

With this admirable air strike, the Egyptian Air Force recovered all it had lost in the 1956 War and the 1967 defeat, and paved the way for our armed forces subsequently to achieve that victory which restored the self-confidence of our armed forces, our people, and our Arab nation. It also restored the world's confidence in us, and exploded for ever the myth of an invincible Israel.

I later asked General Mubarak to abandon his military uniform, don civilian clothes, and assist me as Vice-President.

The air strike was followed by the roaring of our artillery – more than 3000 field guns began to bombard their targets with the greatest accuracy, and the heaviest fire concentrations, the world had witnessed since the Battle of El Alamein in World War II.

The 6 October epic had begun, marked by the superb performance of Egyptian and Arab soldiers. Our soldiers on the Canal didn't wait for the order to cross. The moment the 222 aircraft passed overhead at zero altitude, crossing simultaneously into Sinai, their pent-up feelings and long-checked ardour were released. They pushed their boats into the Canal from behind the fortifications and crossed the Canal immediately, shouting '*Allahu Akbar!*' (Allah is greater!)

Our plan was carried out in careful stages. For the first time in history the Egyptian military planning was changing certain concepts that had been considered, until the October 1973 War, more or less immutable. The rule was that only armour should deal with enemy armour. We were taught, as every soldier everywhere was taught, that the infantry – whatever their level of training or armaments – should never engage armour, because the infantry are, to use the military jargon, 'soft'. However, in the October War our Special Service forces and highly trained infantry forces did cross into Sinai, anti-tank missiles in hand, to confront the Israeli tanks. They engaged them in bitter fighting and hit large numbers of them before our tanks joined them to engage in the big tank battle.

According to our plan, as I have said, our soldiers should have crossed only after the artillery barrage had started, so that, under cover of the vast bombardment by more than 3000 field guns, the personnel could secure a successful crossing. But the crossing began immediately after the air strike, before the artillery barrage started. When they had crossed, our soldiers had to deal with the Israeli earth mound which was as much as 47 feet high at some points. They climbed it using primitive methods that surprised the whole world. A soldier would go up carrying a rope ladder (like the ones we see in movies about medieval times) which, when he reached the top, was let down to his fellows, who then climbed it carrying their weapons – anti-tank missiles and medium artillery drawn by ropes. They soon captured the strongpoints the Israelis had dug in behind the earthworks, on the East Bank of the Canal, and then lay in wait for the enemy and provided cover for further crossing by their fellows.

The whole thing was overwhelming – truly astounding. I followed up the action from my command headquarters in perfect peace of mind, with complete calm ... and if anybody had penetrated my apparent outward tranquillity they would have found me equally calm within. I had no anxiety of any kind; any worries that might have existed before were now entirely dispelled.

First to cross was our Seventh Brigade – the Egyptian flag flew high on the East Bank of the Canal. Reports came in, at regular intervals, that the strongpoints of the Bar-Lev Line were falling into our hands one after another, and so quickly that, only six hours after the attack started, the Israelis began to lose their balance. Israel had been boasting of the Six-Day War; now we could boast of the Six-Hour War. It was obvious that they lost control, too. In military jargon, loss of control means loss of communication between commanders and their men on the battlefield – which was vital if our surprise attack was to be effective.

When our forces had crossed, engineers began to cut out 'passes' in the earthworks by using high-pressure water pumps. This was a completely Egyptian device, thought out and executed by the Egyptian Engineers Corps. When we asked the Germans, I remember, to manufacture these high-pressure pumps for us, they laughed at us – 'Could any fire in the world require such waterpower?' they said. But the gushing water cut like a knife through the sand, forcing large enough gaps for the bridges to be fixed over which our tanks would roll through.

By nightfall, everything had gone according to plan – and even ahead of schedule.

In the morning of that same day the front had looked very different. The local commanders, intent on keeping the plan secret to the last minute, had resorted to a peculiarly Egyptian trick. They made the soldiers relax on the edge of the Canal, and provided them with sugarcane which they chewed and sucked as happily as though they were on holiday. But the major tactical trick which has since forced Israel to respect the Egyptian Army was that five full armoured divisions successfully stormed the enemy positions along the entire line of confrontation, for almost 110 miles.

VI

I had been in the Ops. Room for five hours, forty minutes, when I was told that the Soviet ambassador wanted to see me. It was 7.40 p.m. on 6 October 1973. I told Marshal Ali that I was going to al-Tahirah Palace – which had been prepared as an ultra-modern communication centre so that I could get in touch with anybody anywhere in Egypt, even if our cities and civilian installations were hit – and asked him to keep me up to date on all developments. As well as congratulating everybody in the Ops. Room on the remarkable performance of our forces I had also sent a message of congratulations to our forces on the front: the outcome of the battle had been finally decided.

I thought the Soviet ambassador wanted to convey to me the Soviet leaders' reply to the question I had transmitted to them: What would the Soviet attitude be now? But I was disappointed. He said he had come to tell me that President Hafez al-Assad of Syria had summoned him to a meeting on 4 October and had told him that war would be launched on the 6th. I said I knew about it, as it was done with our prior agreement. The ambassador went on to say that Syria had asked the Soviet Union, at the same meeting of 4 October, to work for a cease-fire forty-eight hours at most from the start of military operations on the 6th. It was on the basis of this that he now called to inform me of this request, officially, and to demand my approval of it.

'I doubt whether President al-Assad,' I said, 'had really demanded a cease-fire before the war started. I'd like to know, all the same, whether this news you're conveying is an official message or just for information?'

'This is,' he said, 'an official message from the Soviet leaders; if you have any doubts you may get in touch with President al-Assad and talk it over with him.'

'I shall indeed get in touch with President al-Assad,' I said, 'to ascertain whether it is so. However, I'd like you to inform the Soviet leaders that, even if Syria did demand it, I won't have a cease-fire until the main targets of my battle have been achieved.'

And I proceeded to enquire once again about the reply as to the Soviet Union's attitude to the war I'd launched. He said it was still being studied. The minute the Soviet ambassador left, I sent a coded telegram to President al-Assad in which I transmitted the Soviet ambassador's statement to me. It was then about 8.30 p.m. Cairo local time, 6 October 1973, that is, only six and a half hours after the start of the October War. I also told President al-Assad that I had informed the Soviet ambassador that I would not accept a cease-fire until the targets of the battle had been achieved. Serious though the matter was, it wasn't until the afternoon of 7 October that I received a reply: President al-Assad denied that he'd said any of the words attributed to him by the Soviet Union.

I did not visit the command headquarters the following day because everything was going according to plan, and the commanders were fully professional. War was their line of business. I also thought that my presence might create a kind of nervous tension. I stayed away but asked Marshal Ali to keep me constantly informed of all developments.

In the evening, to my surprise, the Soviet ambassador again asked to see me urgently. 'Well,' I said, 'I received President al-Assad's reply only half an hour ago. He denies your story altogether – the official message you conveyed to me from the Soviet leaders, yesterday.' His face went white. 'I've in fact called,' he said, 'to convey another message from the Soviet government, following another request by Syria for a cease-fire.'

'Now listen,' I said, 'this subject is closed; I don't want you to take it up any further with me. You know – and I told you yesterday – that I won't have a cease-fire until the objectives of the battle have been achieved. I'd like you to tell the Moscow leadership to send me some tanks at once. This will be the biggest tank battle in history.' (The fighting on 6 and 7 October was extremely fierce, and the tank battle had actually begun.) The Soviet ambassador informed me at this point of the air-bridge which the Soviet Union intended to establish: our long-overdue ammunition and equipment would be airlifted to Egypt immediately. I was pleased to hear this, and said: 'This is the way our relations ought to be conducted.'

The Soviet ambassador in fact called to see me every day thereafter at al-Tahirah Palace for an exchange of information, still urging me to accept a cease-fire, and was consistently told off about it. Each time I told him that I couldn't do it 'before my objective is achieved, namely, to shatter the Israeli "theory of security"'.

VII

The outside world was very confused. Most countries had automatically adopted the Israeli point of view and therefore derived their information from the Israeli military communiqués (which said that the Israelis would crush us utterly). To cover up her defeat, Israel played the video recordings of the 1967 War, both in Israel and outside. The Israelis thought that a propaganda war could change the facts. In the beginning the world refused to believe our communiqués, although Marshal Ali was very much on the conservative side in estimating the number of enemy tanks lost. He insisted on getting confirmation for a given report from a variety of sources; if two reports didn't tally, he accepted the one giving the lesser number. In fact, when we added up the number of enemy tanks lost according to our communiqués, we found it to be 150 short of the actual figure. I had told both Ali and Dr Abdel Kader Hatem (Deputy Premier and Information Minister), 'In this war we'd like the people to know the truth, good or bad. We'd like them to expect to hear the truth, whatever it may be, at all times.'

Meanwhile Brezhnev got in touch with President Tito and asked him to try to persuade me to accept a cease-fire because – Brezhnev told Tito – Syria had submitted three requests for a cease-fire to the Soviet Union which had been rejected by Egypt. By being so stubborn, he said, President Sadat would precipitate a disaster for the Arab world, progressive regimes everywhere, and the world at large. President Tito handled the situation with great tact. He told Brezhnev that he did not have the right, deep as his personal friendship with Sadat was, to intervene in what the Egyptian President did. Only President Sadat could see the situation in its true perspective and act accordingly. President Tito had, meanwhile, prepared 140 tanks which I had asked him to supply me with as a matter of urgency (in view of my experience with the Soviet Union), and which he sent, loaded with fuel and ammunition, direct to the battlefield. President Tito had acquired vast experience in World War II and is a great fighter. I shall always be grateful for that stand by Tito and his country.

From the third day of the war the reports of our victory were confirmed. The world began to accept our communiqués, to show admiration for our fighting ability, and to rejoice in our victory. In those first three days Israel had lost one-third of her entire air force on the Syrian and Egyptian fronts, as well as the cream of her well-trained and experienced pilots. This explains why our subsonic MIG-17s were able to engage and defeat the Phantoms (the most sophisticated weapons the United States had as yet supplied to Israel) in subsequent dogfights.

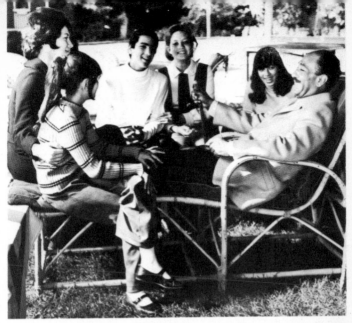

A weekend with the family at the Barage Resthouse, near Cairo.

A family gathering at the residence in Giza, immediately after the author's election as President in 1970.

In the Operations Room, October 1973. With the author is the late Ahmed Ismail Ali.

Addressing the People's Assembly on 16 October 1973.

8 October 1974. The late
Marshall Ahmed Ismail Ali
decorating the author in
honour of his youngest
brother, Air-Pilot 'Atif, who
was killed in the first hour of
the October War.

Reopening the Suez Canal,
6 June 1975.

Planting the first
olive tree, restoring
life and peace to Sinai,
12 December 1975.

The author addressing the Knesset on his historic trip to Jerusalem, 20 November 1977.

The myth of Israel's long arm, of her superior, even invincible, air force, armoury, and soldiers – was finally shattered. On the fourth day of fighting, as though to mark the collapse of Israel's forces on our front, the commander of the Israeli Armoured Corps – a man of world renown, General Abraham Mindler – was killed on the Egyptian front. The telegrams exchanged between Mindler and the Israeli Command do, in fact, throw light on the reality of Israel's defeat on the fourth day of the October War. Kissinger told Mrs Meir: 'You've lost the war – you must be prepared for this.' Kissinger then began to make efforts designed to give the Israelis a breather, as it was obvious that we were simply moving from one victory to another. Most memorable, perhaps, was the destruction on that same day of one of Israel's most important units – Armoured Brigade 190. It was planning to spearhead an advance, right through our forces, to the Canal so as to create a gap for further penetration. Twenty minutes after the engagement, its commander Assaf Yagouri looked around to find all his tanks destroyed; he had a nervous breakdown when he surrendered to the Egyptian forces. He was shocked to realize that the only tank spared out of more than 120 was his own. It was a remarkable feat by one of my young generals – Abu-Sidah.

We had thus broken a record (the new Egyptian military record was the destruction of an enemy armoured brigade in twenty minutes), just as we had put on record six years earlier, on 21 October 1967, that a missile-boat could sink a destroyer. Then, the biggest Israeli naval unit, the destroyer *Eilat*, with her tremendous firepower, rockets, and a crew of over 300, was sunk by a missile-boat with a crew of no more than 17. This marked a stategic change in naval warfare that was thereafter adopted by every country in the world. History has recorded that the first surface-to-surface missile to change world naval strategy was an Egyptian missile, launched from an Egyptian boat, by Egyptian officers and soldiers at a time when the world had thought that Egypt and the Arabs were incapable of assimilating modern technology. This took place in the darkest hours of our defeat in 1967.

In 1973, six years later, Egyptian fighters made history once again by introducing a radical change in old concepts (as I mentioned earlier) regarding the opposition of armour by infantry.

The Egyptian military performance in October 1973 was a landmark in world military history, in more than one way:

1. The first electronic warfare in which missiles were brilliantly used took place in October 1973. The Egyptians and the Arabs are proved to have fought that war and won it. If the United States hadn't intervened in the war and fully supported Israel, the situation could have been far different. Even before the United States intervened, the modern technological devices Israel had previously acquired from America were far ahead of what the Arabs had acquired from the Soviet Union.

2. The tank battles of our era – the age of rockets and electronic warfare – have now come to assume gigantic proportions and involve unprecedentedly large numbers of tanks. Before this the tank battle of Kursk, Russia, in World War II, was the biggest on record, although no more than 500 tanks took part in it. Whereas in the October 1973 battle, which lasted seventeen days (rather than five years), 3000 tanks were lost by the two sides. More than 5000 tanks took part in the fighting.

VIII

At dawn on 13 October 1973, seven days after the war had broken out, I was awakened. The British ambassador, I was told, wanted to see me immediately to deliver an urgent message from Prime Minister Edward Heath of

Britain. I saw him in the living room adjoining my bed-room. He gave me a message from Kissinger, transmitted through Heath of Britain as our relations with the United States were still broken, in which he wanted to make sure I had indeed accepted a cease-fire – as the Soviet Union had told him.

Kissinger was jolted into reality on the fourth day of the war when the distress signal, 'Save Israel,' reached him. For the first three days the Israeli propaganda machine had spoken of 'crushing the bones of the Egyptians' – and the world mass media simply echoed this. Kissinger had no doubt at all that we would be defeated until he was woken up with a start by the 'Save Israel' message – which was an urgent request for 400 tanks to replace those lost on the Egyptian front – and by a Pentagon report to the effect that the war on the Egyptian front was not proceed-ing in favour of Israel. He must have heard too that Dayan had collapsed and wept, in front of all the foreign press correspondents, saying that the Israelis couldn't hope to push the Egyptians back by a single inch, and that the road to Tel-Aviv was now open.

From the moment he knew this, Kissinger worked per-sistently for a cease-fire with the Soviet Union. He began by calling for a cease-fire providing for a return by the belligerents to the lines of 6 October (assuming that the Israelis were 'crushing our bones'); but then he changed his cease-fire terms to save Israel after the famous plea and the Pentagon reports to demand a cease-fire on the existing lines of 13 October. We actually turned down both requests. When, however, the Soviet Union informed him that Egypt would agree to a cease-fire on the existing lines of 13 October, Kissinger was very pleased and con-tacted the US delegation at the UN to prepare for this. He now wanted to make quite sure that it was so. He wanted to hear it from me, and that was the reason why he had sent me this message through Prime Minister Heath. Kis-singer had been told by the Egyptian National Security adviser in Paris early in 1972 that the Soviet Union had no power to speak for Egypt – and this fact was officially transmitted to the United States. Kissinger had therefore been shocked when I conveyed my reply to Mr Heath:

> Please tell Kissinger that this never took place. I haven't agreed to a cease-fire proposed by the Soviet Union or any other party. He should contact Cairo, not Moscow, in respect of anything concerning Egypt. Furthermore, I shall not agree to a cease-fire until the tasks included in the plan have been accomplished.

'Is it true,' the British ambassador now asked, 'that you insist on closing the Red Sea to Israeli navigation?'

'Yes, indeed,' I said.

'Well, what are your terms?'

'I am willing,' I said, 'to have a cease-fire if Israel agrees to withdraw from the occupied Arab territories.'

The British ambassador left to inform Kissinger of these developments and immediately afterwards I received a note from the Soviet Union to the effect that Premier Kosygin would like to come over to see me. I said he would be welcome.

Kosygin arrived swiftly. His main request was that we should have a cessation of hostilities on the existing lines. 'I am not prepared,' I said, 'to have a repeat of the 1948 "truce" which was behind our loss of the war.' 'We'll come in here and guarantee nothing of the sort would happen,' he said. 'With Israel,' I replied, 'you can't guarantee anything! Besides, where are the tanks I asked for on the second day of the war? Your present air-bridge is only providing me with overdue equipment – things you should have sent us much earlier in 1973, long before the war.' (This included, of course, the ammunition which Nasser wanted in replacement for what he had lost in the war of attrition but was denied because he wouldn't grant the Soviet requests.)

Kosygin then resorted to his more vicious side. Kosygin

is aggressive and a bureaucrat. He is noted in the Soviet Union for having served for thirteen years in government posts under Stalin without being liquidated by Beria – the Stalin Minister of the Interior – or sent to Siberia, as was the fate of all those who worked under Stalin. Not one of them except Kosygin was spared – as Khrushchev told us when he visited Egypt in 1964.

'Well,' I said, 'let us go over what you're saying. You sent us bridges to use in crossing the Suez Canal, it is true, but each one takes five hours to build – they are World War II bridges, while you have a different kind – a BMP bridge – that takes not more than half an hour. The equipment you have supplied us with is not up to date; you made us lag behind Israel in armament by a long way, and still I proceeded to fight, and – here we are. I am winning! What sort of friendly relations would you call this? Isn't it high time we buried the past and opened a new chapter?'

'Mr President,' he replied, 'I hadn't thought you'd be so excited.' On this note our first meeting ended. During his four-day visit to Egypt, Kosygin would spend the whole of each day at the Soviet Embassy, then call to see me in the evening. The Israeli counterattack (alternatively referred to as the capturing of the Deversoir Bulge) took place while he was in Egypt. He came to see me, with gloom written all over his face, and said: 'With all this counterattacking you have finally been checked ... A threat is now posed to Cairo.'

'I am sorry to disappoint you,' I replied, 'but no threat will ever be posed to Cairo. However, where are the tanks I asked you for?'

'We've concentrated on Syria because,' he said, 'she took a thrashing and lost 1200 tanks in one day.'

'I've no objection to that; in fact, you should do all in your power to help Syria. But it doesn't mean you should deny me the tanks I asked for. You send the tanks and I'll deal with the counterattacks.'

Four days later he was off to Moscow. I told him on departure: 'I won't have a cease-fire until the final stage of my War Plan has been carried out. I hope this is clear enough for you.'

IX

I later came to know that the US satellite which had begun to transmit information, hour by hour, to the Israelis since they sent out their 'Save Israel' message, now informed them that the Egyptians had taken their Armoured Division 21 across to the East Bank of the Canal in an attempt to relieve the pressure on Syria at President al-Assad's request. I also knew that the Pentagon advised the Israelis to try a counterattack to save the dismal situation of their force in Sinai. In his Memoirs, the Israeli Chief of Staff, during the October War, tried to absolve himself (following the condemnation by the Agranat Report) by reporting that Golda Meir, after receiving the information gathered by the US satellite, had asked the commanders to try to do anything – anything – because the Israelis on the Egyptian front had reached 'the bottom', to quote verbatim.

While the US satellite hourly transmitted information to Israel we received nothing at all from the Soviet satellite which followed up the fighting. I would like to put this on record as a point of historical significance insofar as the Soviet Union claims to champion the Arab cause. Soviet satellites did keep a watch over the battle from the start, for Syria had informed the Soviet Union of Zero Hour. The recordings made were played to the CPSU Central Committee. I asked for a copy of that videotape but have received no reply to this day and won't receive any. Israel, even without demanding it, received hourly information from the Pentagon, provided until this moment by the American satellite. The United States was only too willing to supply her with this because the satellite had shown that the fighting on the Egyptian front was not in Israel's favour, and because Dayan had admitted that the road from Sinai to Tel-Aviv now lay open.

As I followed up the progress of the war from the Operations Room I became conscious of a serious development: the United States was using us for the air-bridge she now established to save Israel. Al-Arish became an airbase where colossal US transport aircraft landed, loaded with tanks and sophisticated weapons. Al-Arish is an Egyptian city; it is the capital of Sinai, and lay directly behind the front.

And I noted, too, another serious development. In the tank battles, which were fierce and which the Egyptians conducted very efficiently, as Israel herself admitted – particularly as we destroyed the tank force led by the renowned Commander Mindler – I noticed that every time I destroyed a dozen tanks, more tanks were to be seen on the battlefield. The United States was taking part in the war to save Israel, following the famous plea sent out on the fourth day. And the Americans were using the Egyptian Al-Arish airfield, immediately behind the front, quite openly, so as to turn Israel's defeat into victory.

I recalled what the United States had done on the German front during World War II, and then on the Japanese front. The US air raids on German military targets and German cities were so intensive that 1000 aircraft took part in each raid, and taught the Germans a lesson never to be forgotten. The atomic bombs dropped on Hiroshima and Nagasaki taught the Japanese an equally unforgettable lesson.

There was a third development, no less serious. Early in the war, the Israeli US Phantoms had fired a dozen rockets at the Egyptian SAM missiles but hit only the aerial of one battery, which was repaired in fifteen minutes. The Egyptian missile batteries never went out of action. Indeed, they managed to shoot down a third of the entire Israeli Air Force in the first three days of fighting – which made the Israeli Command order all Israeli aircraft (on the third day of the October War) to keep away from the Sinai front.

This third serious development was that now two American rockets were fired at two Egyptian missile batteries and put them both out of action completely. I later came to learn that this was a new US rocket called the TV-camera bomb, developed in Japan for the Americans though still being tested in the United States. To save Israel, the USA used them against Egypt.

So, the United States was now taking part in the fighting by supplying Israel with weapons still being tested, with the Maverick bomb, and many other items – to save Israel. I knew my capabilities. I did not intend to fight the entire United States of America.

When I left the Operations Room at 1.30 a.m. on 19 October, I wrote a cable to President al-Assad in his capacity as my partner in the war in which I told him I had decided to accept a cease-fire. I put on record, in that telegram, the substance of my stand on this issue – that I was not afraid of a confrontation with Israel but that I would not confront the United States. I would not allow the Egyptian forces or Egypt's strategical targets to be destroyed once again. And I was willing to be brought to book by my people in Egypt and the Arab world, to answer for this decision.

To go back to my story. On 16 October I ordered Chief of Staff Said Hussein al-Shazli to go to Deversoir to handle the counterattack on the spot. It wouldn't have been difficult on that day to deal with the infiltrating forces; it was a race against time. If he had carried out the orders that both Marshal Ali and I had given him, and at the times fixed by me – to besiege the area around the Bitter Lakes and so stop the advance of the trickle of men that had already crossed and confine them to the narrow strip they had captured – it would have been easy to destroy them. Once there, he could have done it in a matter of hours. But he wasted a whole night marshalling information and establishing a command there for himself so as to compete with Marshal Ali, who was the commander-in-chief. Our stormtroopers had already arrived at Deversoir and actually reached the landing point of the infiltrators. They had been fighting fiercely (both the shock troops and the Special Service forces), as the Israelis themselves admitted, when al-Shazli ordered them to withdraw and wait until he had finished his information-gathering. The result was that the area captured was extended.

On 19 October al-Shazli came back a nervous wreck. He said we ought to withdraw our forces from the East Bank of the Canal because, he claimed, a threat was now posed to our forces on the West Bank (which was precisely what the Israelis had wanted). Marshal Ali asked me to go to the command headquarters. It was midnight on 19/20 October, and he said that I had to take an important decision in my capacity as supreme commander of the armed forces. I went to the command headquarters and studied the situation very carefully. On the East Bank of the Canal we had 5 divisions, complete with 1200 tanks; on the West Bank we had 1 armoured division, facing the infiltrating Israelis. While, in Cairo, we had another division that could be advanced to the Canal (aside from the Republican Guard forces, which actually took part in the war, fought valiantly, and returned without losing a single tank).

Having realized the true dimensions of the situation, I convened a meeting of all commanders. Present too were Marshal Ahmed Ismail Ali, commander-in-chief of the armed forces; General el-Gamasy, Director of Operations; General Muhammad Ali Fahmi, commander of the Rocket Corps (now the Chief of Staff); and General Husni Mubarak, the air force commander (now Vice-President). They were all of my opinion – that there was nothing to worry about. Consequently I issued an order, which I believe was even more important than that of the fighting order of 6 October, that there should be no withdrawal at all (not a soldier, not a rifle, nothing) from the East Bank of the Canal to the West. We had, I directed, to deal with the forces on the West Bank in the light of the actual situation. I then got in touch with our armoured division on the West Bank, commanded by a hero of the October War called Qabil. I told him to restrict the movements of the Israelis, 'confine them to the territory they've seized, prevent them from gaining any more ground, but don't try to engage them until reinforcements have reached you.'

During the night I issued instructions to Marshal Ali that al-Shazli be removed as Chief of Staff, and ordered that that decision be kept secret from the forces so as to avoid all possible reactions in our own or Israeli quarters. Before the night was out I had summoned General el-Gamasy and appointed him Chief of Staff. He is now the commander-in-chief of the Egyptian forces and Minister of Defence.

X

My cease-fire decision was taken during the same night. For the previous ten days I had been fighting – entirely alone – against the Americans with their modern weapons, most of which had not ever been used before. The reality was very different from what the world thought. Everybody believed that the Soviet Union had backed us and established an air-bridge to help us, but that wasn't the situation. I faced the United States and Israel; while the Soviet Union stood behind me, ready to stab me in the back if I lost 85 or 90 per cent of my arms, just as in 1967. It was obvious now that the United States could destroy my entire air defence system with the TV-camera bombs, and thus give the Israelis the 'open skies' of Egypt they had enjoyed in 1967.

Husni Mubarak worked wonders. He used all the aircraft available, even our training aircraft, which he converted into fighters by providing them with cannons and rockets. The MIG-17s, being subsonic, were used very skilfully by our pilots in dogfights with the Phantoms and

Mirages. The Egyptian Air Force achieved an epic feat – heroic and glorious. It was the direct opposite of what the Soviet Union had expected. The Soviets wanted to prove to us that we were not capable of waging any kind of war because I had expelled their experts, and that Egypt should once again resort to reliance on the Soviet Union.

Brezhnev said as much, in fact, to President Boumedienne when he secretly visited Moscow to purchase weapons for us – at the time when our victory was at an unprecedented height. During their conversation Brezhnev lost his temper and told him that Anwar el-Sadat had brought Egypt to ruin – Cairo, Damascus, and all the other progressive capitals – as well as ruining all the Arab nations, and that he was a fool. Boumedienne said: 'I am a customer! I've come to buy weapons. Here is $100 million to pay for the Egyptian arms requests, and another $100 million for the Syrian requests. You will send them what they want, won't you?'

Back in Algiers, President Boumedienne reported what had happened to a specially convened Algerian Revolutionary Council. He said: 'While the Americans and the Israelis *are* eager to defeat President Sadat, the Soviet Union is a hundred times more eager to defeat him.' I wonder if Boumedienne recalls this now (because he did tell me this personally), or would he be denying it as a member of the rejectionist group of my Peace Initiative?

When my 19 October meeting with the commanders had ended, I returned to al-Tahirah Palace and began to put my decision into effect. I asked for the Soviet ambassador to be summoned at once; and while waiting for him, I sent the following cable to President al-Assad:

I have accepted, with a heart that bled, the call for a cease-fire. I am willing to fight Israel no matter how long, but never the USA. Besides, I won't ever again allow my armed forces to be destroyed, or my people and their achievements to suffer another débâcle ...

I told him in conclusion that I was responsible for that decision and would answer for it before our people in Egypt and the Arab nations.

When the Soviet ambassador arrived, I told him I had accepted a cease-fire on the existing lines. Meanwhile Kissinger was on his way to Moscow for talks in connection with the cease-fire. I turned to the Soviet ambassador and said, 'The two superpowers should guarantee the cease-fire and immediate implementation of Security Council Resolution 242.'

The two superpowers did reach agreement on this and the Security Council decided that a cease-fire should come into effect at 19.00 hours on 22 October. I must put on record here, in fulfilment of my historical responsibility, that our forces fought a remarkable battle in the days from 19 to 22 October. *I challenge Israel to declare the real losses she sustained in the Deversoir Bulge, or indeed, in Sinai.* Our Special Service and air forces inflicted great losses on the Israelis in those few days, particularly at Deversoir on the West Bank. The Israelis would not admit this until 1976, when they actually described the Deversoir Bulge on the West Bank as 'the Valley of Death'.

On 22 October, just before the cease-fire came into effect, I went to the Ops. Room and ordered two ground-to-ground rockets fired at Deversoir. I wanted Israel to learn that such a weapon was indeed in our hands and that we could use it at a later stage of the war; even though Israel had in fact realized from the moment the war broke out that we meant and did what we said.

The cease-fire came into effect on the battle lines as of 22 October. The Israelis later came to admit that their position had been more than vulnerable there, since their forces were confined to a very narrow strip by Lake Deversoir, open to attack on all sides. So, as usual, since the 1948 War, they seized the chance of the cease-fire coming into force and, only two hours later, sent a 'flying column' southward to Suez, and another northward to Ismailia.

Our Special Service forces had fought valiantly at Deversoir, mostly at night when darkness struck fear in the hearts of the Israelis. I know the facts, and it is this that makes me challenge the Israelis to declare their real losses at Deversoir. In the first three days of the war we had hit four hundred tanks, which they officially requested the United States to make good. Soon, however, I found that we were facing hundreds of tanks which the United States supplied to the Israelis on the spot.

The attack launched by the Israelis two hours after the cease-fire had come into force was designed to extend the territory seized so that Israeli forces would take up positions behind both the Second and Third Egyptian armies, cut off their supply lines, force our air defences to retreat, deprive the front-line forces of all cover, and so seize both Ismailia and Suez in a last-minute face-saving operation.

What happened was the exact opposite. I ordered the commanders of both armies, particularly the Third, not to allow the Israeli forces to advance to the south. Due to negligence on the part of our Third Army commander, however, the Israeli forces were able to advance and reach the outskirts of Suez. Although they could not enter the city of Suez, they managed to create a gap between the two armies on the East Bank of the Canal, 4 miles wide – a gap between five Egyptian divisions, complete with tanks and other weapons. I had ordered that not a single rifle, not a single soldier in any of these divisions should be withdrawn from the East Bank, whatever the circumstances.

On the West Bank the Israelis tried to seize Ismailia but could not approach even the outskirts of that sprawling city. I had asked Mamdouh Salem, then chairman of the Supreme Council for Civil Defence, to reinforce the city defences. He sent in a 1000-strong contingent from our Central Security Forces, highly trained and fully armed. They joined the army and the population of the city in preparing Ismailia for a potential attack by the Israelis.

When Israel failed to enter either Ismailia or Suez, I

got in touch with the two superpowers, following Israel's unmanly violation of the cease-fire. 'Please come in,' I said. 'I am willing to have your forces land on Egyptian territory to ensure that the Israelis pull back to the 22 October lines – otherwise, let me push them back myself to that line and please don't regard it as a violation of the cease-fire.' I was very eager to prevent the United States from intervening on Israel's side.

The Soviet Union responded by concentrating landing forces in the Mediterranean, while the Americans declared nuclear mobilization – which gave them a lot of trouble as they hadn't consulted their NATO allies. European public opinion in 1973 was anti-Israel and pro-Arab, contrary to what it had been in 1967.

When the Israelis had lost hope of seizing either Ismailia or Suez, they just entrenched themselves at Deversoir, while our forces put pressure on them continuously. The achievement of one officer – Qabil – at that time is simply unforgettable. With a single armoured division he managed to cover the entire area between Ismailia and Suez, performing the task of three divisions. He moved up and down, with consummate tactical skill, until the Israelis were confined to their pocket. The situation would have been very different if we, rather than the Israelis, had meant to violate the cease-fire and allowed the two armies on the East Bank to storm the 4-mile gap from which the Israelis infiltrated to the West Bank and so put an end to it. But we were – and still are – governed in our actions by an ethical code, in war and peace alike.

Israel, on the other hand, has never been committed to any code of ethics since the establishment of the State in 1948. She tried to put psychological pressure on us. Vast forces were concentrated in that tiny strip of land, so as to intimidate us and improve her bargaining position. While the land she seized could barely hold more than 200 tanks, she sent in 400. But my forces surrounded them on all sides: in the east we had five divisions, four in the west, a wall of rockets, and a complete siege by our tanks. The first batch of 150 tank reinforcements that I received came from President Boumedienne. Then came the second batch of 140, sent by President Tito fully loaded with fuel and ammunition so that they were immediately put into action on the battlefield.

As for the Soviet Union, it still had not sent in the tanks I asked for on the second day of fighting. One day the Soviet ambassador called to tell me that the CPSU Central Committee had decided to present Egypt with 250 tanks. I thanked him and asked that they be sent as quickly as possible. My request was not granted until the Israelis had established themselves at Deversoir – although, in fact, the whole counterattack was really an attempt to save Israel's reputation. A French general, M. Bouvre, head of the French Institute for Strategic Studies, came to see me later on and told me that the counterattack was actually insignificant – it was designed, he said, for the television cameras.

XI

Kissinger said he wanted to see me. He arrived in Egypt for the first time in November, and said: 'You've created an international crisis, and that's why I've come to see you. What are your requests?'

'I want a return,' I replied, 'to the cease-fire lines of 22 October. I have 800 tanks, while Israel has only 400; for each Israeli tank I have one and a half rockets; the Israelis are besieged, and the gap they've cut open between our armies – 4 miles wide – could close and so spell the end of them. There can be no question about that.'

We had a three-hour session, during which we agreed on six points, one of which was that Egyptian-Israeli talks for a disengagement of forces and a return to the lines of 22 October would start at Km. 101 on the Cairo-Suez road. The talks were held – under UN supervision. But they were very protracted. I left at the time for Algiers to attend the Arab Summit Conference, and when I came back, the negotiations still hadn't got anywhere. I asked el-Gamasy to suspend them. 'I am not prepared,' I said, 'to engage in this sort of haggling and bickering.'

In December 1973 I was ready to liquidate the Deversoir pocket. Our forces started a war of attrition and consistently put pressure on the infiltrators. We regained a good deal of ground every day – sometimes advancing a few yards, sometimes a few miles, but always advancing. I was really fully prepared to liquidate the Israelis there – especially as we had no water barriers to cross now, no Bar-Lev Line to deal with – but I had to take one risk into consideration, that of possible US intervention. On 11 December 1973, Kissinger came to see me again. I told him, 'I cannot accept this way of conducting the negotiations. I am going to liquidate the Israeli Deversoir pocket. What will be the American attitude?'

'I know you're ready for it; I knew it before I came to see you,' Kissinger answered. 'I asked the Pentagon for a few aerial photographs of the battlefield and received a full report. Your wall of rockets consists of so many batteries [he specified the number], you have 800 tanks surrounding the Israeli Deversoir pocket, the number of your guns is [again he specified it] and you can actually wipe out that pocket. You must know, however, that if you do this the Pentagon will strike at you.'

'Ah!' I said. 'That is the question. What would the US attitude be?'

'The Pentagon will strike at you,' he reiterated. 'The Pentagon will strike you for one reason: Soviet weapons have once before defeated US weapons and, in accordance with our global strategy, we can't allow it to happen again.' And Kissinger went on to say: 'Do you know, when you created an international crisis, when you asked the two superpowers to come in and get the forces back to the cease-fire lines of 22 October, otherwise, you threatened, you'd do it yourself provided the Pentagon didn't stand against you – do you know what sort of plan the

Pentagon laid down at the time? We planned to land in your country, in Sinai, if the Russians landed west of the Canal, to finish you off. Our aim was to show you that the Russians were unreliable, and so we'd have dealt you a blow that actually hit the Russians! We're in the same situation today. If you attempt to liquidate the Israeli pocket, the Pentagon will strike at you because this is US established policy. Besides, the Pentagon wants to avenge the defeat of its weapons in October. But do you insist on a military liquidation of the infiltrating forces?'

'Not at all,' I said swiftly. 'You know I am a man of peace. If you had accepted my 1971 Initiative, no war would have broken out at all. I care very much for human life, and am loath to losing one soldier, not to mention an officer. But you didn't take me seriously – and this is the outcome.'

'Well, just as we embarked on a Peace Process, let us have a forces disengagement which would peacefully put an end to this counterattacking.'

Kissinger asked me on the same day whether I was willing to go to Geneva for talks later in December 1973. I said I was planning to be there.

Kissinger left Egypt on 12 December 1973. But at this point I was in great pain. I was suffering daily, hourly. I could see no way out – everything seemed to have gone wrong, and I wasn't able to put it right because it was no longer up to me. For four days I haemorrhaged. The doctors who examined me, when my urine had turned literally into clots of blood, said it was due to tension but that it wasn't really serious. They gave me some medication which, two days later, stopped it altogether.

On 24 December I convened a meeting of the commanders of all corps, armies, and divisions. The plan laid down to liquidate the Deversoir pocket was discussed for over seven hours, and I endorsed it. A commander was appointed to carry it out – General Saad Mamun, who is governor of Cairo at present.

On 25 December, my birthday, I went to my home village, Mit Abul-Kum. I always spend it there. The next day I left for Aswan. In January 1974 Kissinger arrived and the first disengagement of forces agreement was signed. The United States had played the role of mediator between us and Israel.

In negotiating the Aswan agreement I had only one thing to focus on. I didn't want more than to maintain the real magnitude of my victory *on the ground*. I didn't bother about the Israeli pocket because I knew that they were my prisoners on the West Bank and that their presence there meant their death. On the basis of defining and maintaining the real magnitude of my territorial victory, agreement was reached. Yet I was still in great mental anguish, because all the powers wanted to negate my victory. The United States certainly wanted to discount it, and the Soviet Union to put an end to it because Syria had suffered a setback in spite of the presence of Soviet military experts and I had won a victory in spite of the expulsion of Soviet military experts. And Israel, of course, wanted to undo our victory.

Such attempts did not in themselves worry me. But I wanted my victory to be maintained because I regarded it as the avenue to the just peace for which I had worked unceasingly.

10

The Road to Peace

I

Nowadays I am never happier than when I am on the banks of the Suez Canal. I sit there for hours on end in a small log cabin watching the progress of work on new projects and the ceaseless reconstruction effort.

Every time I visit a Canal town, the memories of 5 June 1975 rise before my eyes. That was the day on which I flew in by helicopter, then took a car and drove to a ceremonial platform where I declared the Suez Canal reopened for international navigation after eight years. I shall never forget that day. The joy that lit up the eyes of men, women, and children was really beautiful. They had been repatriated at last, after long years in exile as homeless and frustrated evacuees.

No one could appreciate the quality of that joy and the way it elevates a human soul better than a man who was himself transplanted into an alien land – forced to leave his own home, street, the familiar faces of daily companions, his city, and his land, the land he knew and loved so well, to which he belonged and without which he could have no life.

Our Egyptian civilization – which dates back over 7000 years and is the earliest in human history – has always been inspired by man's love of, and attachment to, the land. Hence the sparkle of joy on people's faces was different from other, more mundane kinds of joy. Rather than the joy of worldly gain, it was a kind of surprised ecstasy as despair suddenly changed into hope; as the plants, so to speak, that had long been withered and dead suddenly bloomed into life again. Those people had lived as evacuees for eight long years, during which many of them had died and many more were born. An unanswerable question had hung over the years: Could we ever go back? And the hope of discerning any reply seemed to have receded to the furthest horizon.

If we add to this the fact that the 'Canal people' differ from all other Egyptians in having peculiar sea trades that are totally dependent on an operational Canal, it is clear why they felt so happy to be back. For them it was more than a mere repatriation; it was almost like recovering their real identity. They look on the sea and the Canal as practically sacred, as symbols of belonging, much in the same way that we residents of the Nile Valley look on the land. The Canal had determined their way of life and, consequently, their very consciousness, one generation after another – so much so, in fact, that it came to be identified with that consciousness itself.

On that particular day, 5 June 1975, which is ever present in my heart, a certain incident took place that proved almost too moving for words.

My car was slowly advancing to the Canal Authority Building when a man appeared suddenly on the roadway and waved to the driver to stop. He was an old man, tall and lank, his long white hair let down over his shoulders, his features very solemn and his eyes glinting sharply in the morning haze. The guards tried to remove him but I asked them to leave him alone and ordered the driver to stop. The man gave me a long look, then, all of a sudden, went down on his knees to say a prayer – a thanksgiving prayer to God. Then he rose to his feet and signalled to the motorcade to carry on. In a flash, he had disappeared into the vast crowd.

The whole episode lasted hardly a minute, but it seemed as though ages had been compressed into it – years of despair and painful longing. And that minute, short as it was, meant everything to that man. He had survived to see his homeland once again, to know that he had returned. He might not have long to live but he would be buried there, in that very earth. Hence his sense of security, his serenity and peace of mind; he had to kneel down before God, to thank Him for sending that unexpected light to disperse the prolonged darkness he had so painfully survived.

II

I left the solemn old man behind and proceeded to conduct the reopening ceremony. But his image had passed into my soul for ever. It still gripped me as I formally accepted from the armed forces a document transferring the administration of the Canal to the civilian Suez Canal Authority. I signed the document, boarded our destroyer, the *October 6*, and sailed through to reopen the Canal.

The whole world was on my side that day – the same world that only a few months previously had claimed that the Canal had become worthless (while Israel had repeatedly asserted that it was up to her alone whether the Canal would reopen or not).

Deeds speak louder than words, for it is only by actions that one can refute false allegations and change people's attitudes. On 5 June 1975, represented by the many delegations that poured in from all continents, the world celebrated the occasion with me. It was as though the world had declared that 5 June would no longer be a day of sorrow for Egypt and the Arabs but one of rejoicing for both Egypt and the world at large. More than 100 years afterwards, the world seemed to be celebrating another Suez Canal opening.

Two months before, Israel had thwarted the US mediation effort and snubbed the US Secretary of State Kissinger during the negotiations for a second disengagement of forces agreement. Although the United States is Israel's lifeblood, the Israelis believed that President Ford's position was weak, as he was not an 'elected' President. They decided that as the Americans were preoccupied with the 'Watergate Affair', there was an opportunity for Israel to put pressure on the United States – why not seize it, as Israel is wont to do?

My reply to this took the form of action rather than reaction. I reopened the Canal (even though it was within range of the huge guns Israel had been supplied with by the United States) and allowed the evacuees to return to the three Canal towns, Port Said, Suez, and Ismailia. These émigrés, numbering about 700,000, had almost ceased to be human beings, not only because of the difficult living conditions in already overcrowded mainland cities but (far more important) because they had lost hope – that vital human power without which no man can really live.

I knew only too well, as I reopened the Canal, that the entire region – the Canal itself and the three Canal towns – was within range of Israeli American-supplied artillery. And that was why I declared to the entire world that that region was now part of the mainland, and that any Israeli attack on it would be regarded as an attack on the Egyptian inland towns, which would naturally necessitate retaliation by attacking Israeli inland towns.

Undoubtedly that was a gamble on my part. It could have been possible for Israel to prove obstinate enough in the ensuing negotiations (only a few months later) to reject the second agreement on a further disengagement of forces – the agreement that put the Canal Zone out of range for the Israeli artillery. I took that risk, however, for the sake of peace. In the search for peace, everything is permissible.

Two years after the October War, the bodies of thirty-nine Israeli soldiers were unearthed in the Canal Zone. The Israelis began to negotiate the price they expected to pay to recover their dead. 'You won't have to pay anything,' I said. 'This is a humane action for which we accept no payment; just come and collect the bodies.'

Indeed, the thirty-nine bodies were delivered to the Israelis with full military honours and, naturally, nothing was asked for in return. Some of their dead were given official military funerals as they were senior army officers. Again in 1977, nineteen more bodies were unearthed in the course of the digging to deepen the Canal and, again, they were immediately delivered and given all due honours. Why did I do it? For the sake of peace. I believe that for peace a man may, even should, do everything in his power. Nothing in this world could rank higher than peace.

III

The United States played an important role in the reopening of the Canal. Rather than acting as a policeman who throws his weight about, the United States stood by me and showed her real face, scarred though it was by the Vietnam War.

In 1974 when I declared that I would reopen the Canal and clearing operations were already under way, the kind of equipment needed was not to be found outside the United States Navy – not even in the mammoth private American companies with their vast budgets and technical capabilities. I said as much to Kissinger during his visit to Egypt after the first forces disengagement agreement. His response was straightforward. 'Am I to understand that you're asking for assistance?'

'Yes,' I said.

'Well, give me an hour.'

During that hour, I came to know later, Kissinger got in touch with the White House and the Pentagon. Then he returned to me with another question:

'Would you allow the US helicopter-carrier *Iwo Jima*, which belongs to the Sixth Fleet and has on board adequate clearing equipment and helicopters, to anchor in Port Said and start helping you?'

Up to that time, and for eighteen years before, we were supposed to be in confrontation with the United States. But I agreed. Once again Kissinger contacted the White House, and the Pentagon, and came back with the reply: '*Iwo Jima* will be in Port Said after tomorrow. She will co-operate with you and take part in clearing the Canal under the command of the Egyptian Navy.'

Some members of the carrier's crew, and a few diplomats at the US Embassy in Cairo, voiced misgivings at *Iwo Jima*'s sailing to Port Said. They were afraid the Egyptian coast artillery might fire on her. I reassured them that nothing of the sort would happen as I had already given the necessary orders to my navy.

At the appointed hour *Iwo Jima* sailed through, rather slowly, into Port Said Harbour. She was feeling her way, as it were, sheepishly, when the crew became conscious all at once of the unexpectedly warm reception by our navy. They started to work immediately.

The American people may be surprised to learn that no documents were ever exchanged with the United States government regarding its participation in the clearing operations. I would like here to extend our thanks to the American people, for that was a manifestation of American chivalry and an occasion on which the real face of the United States was shown. Although Egyptian, the Canal does not serve Egypt alone but the world at large. And, with her vast capabilities, the United States is bound in duty, even naturally expected, to assist all those striving for a better future alike for themselves and for the whole world.

This has always been the image of the United States in my eyes and in the eyes of our people who, over the entire stretch of human history, have respected human values. The reopened Canal proved to be a lucky strike.

IV

My struggle for peace – a long story – dates back to my election as President of Egypt on 15 October 1970. Although when Nasser died our diplomatic relations with the United States had already been severed, an American delegation led by Ambassador Richardson arrived to offer condolences. Unfortunately our meeting took place in sad circumstances. On the day of the funeral (as I have said) I fainted as a result of great exhaustion and was taken to the nearest place where I could get treatment – the premises of the old Revolutionary Command Council. The first person I saw when I opened my eyes was Mr Richardson. I thanked him, while I still lay in bed, and gave him an appointment for a later meeting. He did come to see me afterwards, accompanied by two Middle East experts, and we had a long talk together.

The cease-fire in the Egyptian-Israeli war of attrition across the Canal – arranged by Secretary of State William Rogers as part of the interim agreement referred to as the Rogers Plan – was still in force. I told my visitors:

'I'd like you to know this, God bless you, and to convey it to the American President: I was against the Rogers Plan and had in fact rejected it. I accepted it only after Abdel Nasser returned from the Soviet Union and explained what took place and the circumstances there. All I want is peace. Let us work together for peace. I'm today committed to the Rogers Plan, but I don't like the USA to support the Israeli claim that Egypt had violated the plan by advancing SAM sites on the West Bank of the Canal. Even so, the West Bank, just like the East Bank, is my land. Once again let me call on you to work for peace. I am prepared to go to any lengths to achieve it.'

Richardson returned to Washington to submit a report to the State Department which said that el-Sadat would not remain in power for more than four or six weeks –

after which no one could tell what might happen in Egypt. The British Intelligence confirmed this report, and, on the strength of it, the Americans and the British decided between themselves to wait and see what would become of me. (I often find it amusing to recall this incident in conversations with US officials.)

In November 1970 when the ninety-day cease-fire provided for by the Rogers Plan came to an end, I convened the National Security Council and told them we needed another ninety-day cease-fire period to keep the Rogers Plan alive; this, however, would be the last possible extension. The plan had in fact provided for an Israeli withdrawal (item II) to be arranged by Dr Gunnar Jarring (as the UN Secretary-General's special emissary to the Middle East) immediately the ninety-day cease-fire period expired; and an agreement on withdrawal from the occupied Arab territories (which Israel was loath to do) was to be reached within the ninety-day period itself.

Our Foreign Minister submitted our proposal to the UN Security Council and the Rogers Plan was renewed. However, again nothing happened in the second ninety-day period – November, December, and January. Israel still claimed that Egypt had violated the terms of the Rogers Plan and the United States, under the influence of a powerful Zionist lobby, supported that claim. It was intended to explode the plan and, as did happen afterwards, to get rid of William Rogers himself.

On 24 December 1970, that is, two months after my election as President, I had a surprise. Dr Mahmoud Fawzi, then prime minister, conveyed a letter to me from President Nixon in which he thanked Egypt for sending a delegation (led by Dr Fawzi) to represent Egypt at President Eisenhower's funeral. I immediately summoned the foreign diplomat looking after United States interests in Egypt and showed him Nixon's letter. 'I have summoned you,' I said, 'to give you my reply to the US President.' The reply read partly as follows:

To begin with, I had sent you a message with Ambassador Richardson who visited Egypt to offer condolences on Nasser's death, but you never replied to it. You have, meanwhile, supported Israel's claim that Egypt violated the terms of the Rogers Plan although you know very well that the territory east and west of the Canal is Egyptian.

Now that you have sent a letter of thanks to our prime minister and wanted it to be conveyed to me, I am writing to you to confirm the contents of the message I sent you with Ambassador Richardson and to add a few things. You would be mistaken to think that we are in the sphere of Soviet influence: we are not within the Soviet sphere of influence nor, for that matter, anybody's sphere of influence. I'd like you to know, furthermore, that nobody could claim to be Egypt's tutelar power. So, if you wish to talk about anything concerning Egypt, the venue will be Cairo and the talks will be with me, not with any other party [by which I clearly meant – as I had explained to the diplomat looking after US interests in Egypt – the Soviet Union, which wanted to act as our master, a 'right' Nasser had granted the Soviets at one time]. I'd like you also to know that we take our own decisions freely and independently, so that if you prove friendly to us, we shall be ten times as friendly; if hostile, we shall be ten times as hostile. As it is the law of nature for each action to have a reaction, a good move by you will be met by a dozen good moves by us, and vice versa.

This was my first direct contact with the United States after my assumption of the presidency (the message conveyed by Richardson failed to produce any response). Nixon's reply was prompt. Indeed, the speed with which it came astonished me. When I wrote to the Soviet Union about anything I would never get a reply in less than four months unless I summoned the Soviet ambassador dozens of times and asked him to speed up things.

The reply, signed by Nixon, reached me in forty-eight

hours. It was a charming letter, in which the US President thanked me and said he did not want our friendship to be at the expense of anybody as in the United States they knew that my will was independent and that no one, apart from Egypt herself, had any right to speak for Egypt.

Nothing happened until the end of January 1971. As the second ninety-day cease-fire period provided for under the Rogers Plan would come to an end on 4 February 1971, I decided to do something before that date. It was obvious that the United States – despite Nixon's letter – was still adopting the Israeli line of thinking, under the influence of Zionist propaganda, and that America gave Israel's interests priority even over her own. After eighteen years of antagonism – and in view of our image in US eyes, which the Soviet Union had greatly influenced – it was not easy for the Americans to extend a friendly hand or to take any measure to restore peace in our region, particularly as US officials firmly believed that I wouldn't remain in power for more than four or five weeks. True, by February 1971, I had been President for more than three months, but they still had their doubts. Would I stay in or go – was I capable of doing anything or not?

In view of all this, the Rogers Plan had to be terminated, though I had, at the same time, to take some constructive action to prove to the United States, to President Nixon, and to the world at large that my intentions were good, that I wanted peace, was ready for it, and that I was capable of taking a decision towards this end. This was how I thought at the time. I didn't reveal my plan to anybody, apart from Dr Mahmoud Fawzi. I summoned him and told him that I had decided to take an Initiative for Peace. My plans were as follows:

1. Israel should withdraw her forces from the East Bank of the Canal to the Sinai Passes within six months, during which time Dr Jarring would revisit the Middle East to arrange the stages of withdrawal, in terms acceptable to both parties. Once the Israeli

forces had withdrawn, the Egyptian forces would cross to the East Bank of the Canal.

2. When the withdrawal to the Passes was complete, Egypt would immediately restore her relations with the United States. As one of the parties directly involved in the crisis, the United States should actively be on the scene for a settlement to be reached.

3. Egypt was willing to conclude a peace agreement with Israel which would end the state of war that had existed to this day, since 1948, between the Arabs and Israel, and to give Israel all the guarantees she had asked for. This would put an end to the most serious problem in today's world – insofar as the interests of the two superpowers were closely related to it.

Dr Fawzi was very happy to learn of that Initiative, and said it would break the deadlock and prove to the whole world that Egypt actually wanted peace.

On 4 February 1971, I made the speech at the People's Assembly in which I propounded my Initiative. As expected, my willingness to conclude a peace treaty with Israel was a stunning surprise to the world at large. No Arab leader in any capacity had plucked up enough courage to say such a thing since Israel was established in 1948. But I meant what I said, because I really wanted peace.

When my speech was finished, I went to the presidential ante-room at the People's Assembly, where government ministers and other leaders – those who made up the political leadership left me by Nasser – were waiting. They looked extraordinarily grim – naturally, I thought, as my Initiative went counter to all their objectives which, as I later came to know, were Soviet inspired.

The popular reception of the Initiative was in sharp contrast to that of the Egyptian political leadership at the time. In less than twenty-four hours the Egyptian people had hailed and welcomed it. Let me put on record here that the Egyptian people are more politically enlightened than all the assistants who have served with me to this minute. It often happens that a subtle political point escapes most of my assistants, only to be immediately grasped and fully assimilated by the people.

In my speech of 4 February in Parliament I had also said that as the second ninety-day cease-fire period came to an end on that day, 4 February, the Rogers Plan was now dead. Another, my own Peace Initiative, was there for the entire world to consider: it was a call for the world, for the Security Council, the Soviet Union, and the United States to shoulder their responsibilities. I gave them all a thirty-day period, ending on 7 March, in which to respond to my Initiative; after that date, however, I would not be bound by anything – not even my own Initiative.

Rogers welcomed the new Initiative. The world was stunned. Israel was in a tight corner, for there she was, confronting an Arab leader declaring for the first time ever that he was willing to conclude a peace agreement – the hardest thing in the world for her to predict or even dream of. In Egypt there were no hostile demonstrations; nobody protested, or voiced the least resentment. On the contrary, people were perfectly happy everywhere, and showed the deepest possible – indeed, most impressive – understanding of what was going on.

If the United States or Israel had shown enough interest in that Initiative, the October War would not have taken place and the process of negotiating peace would have started in February or March 1971.

V

The United States did come to realize that I spoke from a position of strength, that I enjoyed the support of my entire people, and that I was capable of saying and doing things no Arab leader had yet dared to do for the past twenty-two years. For all this, however, the Americans did nothing. Nothing at all happened until May 1971. Then William Rogers got in touch with me, and came to Egypt to see me on 4 May 1971. He personally was very pleased with my Peace Initiative. He asked: 'Do you know you have found a solution to the problem?'

'How?' I asked.

He told me that Golda Meir had summoned the US ambassador in Tel-Aviv and asked him to write to Rogers and Nixon that she, Golda Meir, the prime minister of Israel, challenged any Arab leader to declare that he was prepared to conclude a peace agreement with Israel and that, if this happened, she (and I quote Mrs Meir's words as officially conveyed to the USA) would be '*prepared to put all her cards on the table*'.

Rogers went on to say: 'We received Mrs Meir's message a long time ago. We were surprised to hear you declare to the whole world, on 4 February 1971, that you were prepared to conclude a peace agreement with Israel – *without prior knowledge of what Mrs Meir had said!* We admired that very much, and that was why I asked to see you.

'It was wonderful, too,' Rogers went on, 'to realize how wrong our reports were. For, according to these reports, I quite expected stones to be thrown at me on my arrival in Egypt. Nothing of the sort happened, of course. I did indeed have a walk in Cairo streets – unguarded – and was recognized by some people, was welcomed and greeted.'

I said: 'You are dealing with a people more than 7000 years old. Isn't it about time you knew the Egyptian people? At any rate, what do you want me to do?'

'Nothing at all,' he said. 'You have said in your "Initiative" all that needs to be said, and we stand by you. I shall now proceed to see Mrs Meir in Israel to tell her that el-Sadat had accepted her challenge even before he knew of it. She should, therefore, keep her promise and put her cards on the table so that the USA can come in and solve the problem.'

Rogers left Egypt for Israel. A few days later (as I have said) I got rid of those figures who constituted the majority of our political leadership and who relied on the Soviet

Union and carried out their instructions, whereupon Podgorny arrived in great agitation and trepidation. He wanted a treaty of friendship to be concluded between Egypt and the Soviet Union.

This treaty itself has a story.

After our defeat in June 1967 it emerged very clearly that Johnson as President of the United States had played a definite role in bringing it about. Working for Israel, he had conducted a campaign of deception by suggesting to Nasser that either the late Mr Humphrey, then US Vice-President, would visit Cairo or an Egyptian Vice-President would visit Washington, following the closure of the Aqaba Gulf in May 1967 to Israeli navigation. Nasser said he'd send one of his deputies to Washington to handle the Aqaba Straits affair, which had taken a turn for the worse. Nasser and Johnson officially agreed that an Egyptian Vice-President would see Johnson on Wednesday 7 June, in Washington. Meanwhile Johnson urged the Israelis to attack Sinai, having supplied them with up-to-date satellite photographs of the position and deployment of the Egyptian forces in Sinai. He in fact asked the Israelis to mount an early attack, before the Egyptian Vice-President was due to arrive in Washington, particularly when the Israelis submitted their plan to him at his White House office in the presence of the chief of the CIA and a senior Pentagon official.

Israel carried out Johnson's advice by launching her attack on 5 June, two days before the Egyptian Vice-President was scheduled to arrive in the United States. He never, of course, got there.

This act of deception was not all that Johnson did to help Israel. He used his hot line with the Kremlin to emphasize to the Soviet leaders that Israel would *not* start an attack and asked them to inform Nasser of this. The Soviet leaders responded to this deception – or they might have taken part in it, I cannot state categorically – but they did, at any rate, contact Nasser to convey that message. The Soviet ambassador woke him up at dawn to convey Johnson's message, together with Soviet backing for it.

But to go back to my story. When Johnson's role emerged clearly to us following our defeat in 1967, we had no option but to ask the Soviet Union to sell us arms to make good our losses (more than 85 per cent of our arms). It was also natural that we should try to maintain our friendship with the Soviet Union at any price.

It is well known that suspicion is second nature to the Russians. This tendency to be suspicious has been intensified under Marxism due to the nature of the system itself, to the fact that Russia was literally besieged by the whole world after the 1917 Bolshevik Revolution, and to the civil war which necessitated strict security measures and a policy of trusting no one until proven trustworthy. That is why we were careful to maintain our friendship with the Soviet Union and to remove their grave suspicions first, by asking the Russians to speak to the United States on behalf of Egypt on all matters connected with the Arab-Israeli conflict, having realized that the Soviets were suspicious of any US contact with us. We went so far as to ask the Soviet Union to appoint a Soviet commander for the Egyptian air defence system, and another for the Egyptian Air Force – in view of the unchecked Israeli violations of our air space – but both requests were, fortunately for us, rejected. We couldn't do more in fact than ask them to conclude a treaty with us which might satisfy them and remove their doubts (which we often found incomprehensible), as well as guaranteeing a steady supply of arms to us, which we badly needed even if they were consistently inferior to the arms Israel received from the United States.

Nasser twice proposed that such a treaty be concluded; and I left twice for the Soviet Union, at Nasser's request, and twice asked for the conclusion of such a treaty. But the Soviets consistently refused. Perhaps they didn't and still don't trust us; they might have feared that by such a treaty we could get them involved in a situation they would sooner steer clear of. Just before his death, Nasser went as far as anybody could by asking them to conclude a pact with us if they felt that this could allay their fears. They still rejected us.

I was therefore surprised when Podgorny, the Soviet head of state, arrived in Cairo towards the end of May 1971 to demand, impatiently, the conclusion of a Soviet-Egyptian Treaty immediately. I replied, at once, that I had no objection. I said: 'Nasser asked you for this twice, but you refused; he even proposed a pact during his last visit to you, which you still turned down. I have no objection, but as a friend I must tell you your timing is wrong – very wrong. It will be obvious to all and sundry that you are so eager now to have the treaty concluded, after having rejected it, because some former members of the Egyptian leadership are currently awaiting trial. It will appear, won't it, as though you had relied on those members in your relations with Egypt, which is a grave mistake I've warned you against before.'

Even after the conclusion of the Soviet Treaty of Friendship, my image in the United States had begun to acquire new dimensions, and I came to be better known – my real character better understood. This was not the case with our Soviet friends who, from the very first whatever the circumstances and in spite of the treaty we had concluded, still behaved in their usual crude, even rude, manner, which showed no sign of apprehending reality – or even the slightest attempt at such apprehension.

Barely two months later, another development took place which gave me a headache and caused a further clash with the Soviet Union. In July 1971 the Communist *coup d'état* took place in Sudan. The Soviet ambassador in Cairo called on me to urge a recognition of the new regime. I refused, saying:

'I cannot allow a Communist regime to be established in a country sharing my borders. That's to begin with. Another point you should take into account is that no Communist regime will ever be established in this part of the world because we are religious by nature. It would be much better for you to give up all attempts in this connection. It would be much better all round, in fact!'

The Soviet ambassador was, of course, angry. My attitude once more confirmed the doubts which the Soviet Union had in me.

As for the United States, a period of silence started with Rogers' departure early in May 1971 for Israel to see Golda Meir, and went on for weeks. Throughout June and July I summoned the foreign diplomat looking after US interests in Egypt and asked him to urge Rogers to inform me of the outcome of his talks in Israel, but to no avail. Israel continued to act arrogantly, and the United States continued her inaction. However, on 6 July an official from the US State Department finally arrived from Washington and wanted to see me urgently, 'because it is important'. I saw him in the evening of the same day. He said he carried a message to me from President Nixon and Secretary Rogers but that he had a few questions which he wanted answered first.

The first question was, 'Has the treaty which you concluded with the Soviet Union late in May 1971 changed your position or imposed any commitments that might restrict your freedom in dealing with us for the establishment of peace in your region?'

My answer was, 'Certainly not! I have declared that the treaty had no secret provisions or appendices. You and everybody else must get used to the idea that I won't say anything in private that I can't say in public. My people have the right to know before anybody else of any commitment undertaken by me. I am not prepared to deceive my people at any time, whatever the circumstances. The provisions of the treaty were formally declared in Parliament, before endorsement, and they impose no restrictions of any kind on Egypt. We can never abandon our freedom and independence.'

The second question was, 'Do you still stand by the Initiative which you declared in February 1971 and which you explained to Rogers during his visit to Egypt?'

My answer was, 'But of course! If any changes are necessary I would definitely have to announce them to the people. Let me remind you again that you should talk to me, not to anybody else, about anything concerning Egypt. If you approach anyone else, be sure we won't listen to you.'

He said: 'Fine. According to my instructions, I would like to tell you that now I have received your reply, the US President, as from midnight [6/7 July 1971] will personally intervene to start the ball rolling for a peaceful solution to be reached.'

I said: 'That's perfectly satisfactory. What did Rogers do in Israel?'

'He spoke to them but they still have their doubts and, at any rate, I have no instructions to reveal anything in this connection,' the representative said.

He went, and I waited. Midnight – and many other midnights – came and went, but nothing stirred. On the contrary, Golda Meir made a speech in the Knesset which was tantamount to a lesson – and a hard one at that – for William Rogers. From our study of Mrs Meir's personality we knew that she was fond of dealing with ministers, both in daily life and at cabinet meetings, as though she was still handling students in the Milwaukee classrooms where she worked as a schoolteacher. It appears that all Rogers did was to ask her to put her cards on the table. He should have realized that she conveyed her 'challenge' through the US ambassador only because she was certain no Arab leader could ever call for a peace agreement with Israel. Why did Rogers talk so much? And what would Rogers' naïveté about the Israelis do to both the United States and Israel? Mrs Meir's lesson was a signal to the Zionist lobby in America to assault the Rogers stance.

Indeed, once out of office, Rogers found himself in absolute limbo.

I later came to learn, incidentally, that the US President had no knowledge of the message which a US diplomat –

chief of the Egyptian Section at the State Department – had conveyed to me on 6 July as addressed to me by the US President and Secretary of State. Very odd, to put it mildly.

Well, following Mrs Meir's Knesset speech, my relations with the United States became worse than ever before. The speech influenced US public opinion and terrified Rogers sufficiently to make him take back all he had said. It wasn't only a retreat on Rogers' part; he drastically changed his position by making a statement on 1 January 1972, in which he said that the United States had given Israel fresh assistance, that she was co-operating with Israel in a certain industrialization programme, and that she would not put a stop to her aid until Israel achieved military superiority over all the Arabs put together. Poor man! He wanted to get into Israel's good books again after Mrs Meir's harsh lesson. But it was too late.

In view of Rogers' statement, and particularly as I couldn't keep my promise that 1971 would be the year of decision, I began to suffer from the disillusionment of the outside world and those Soviet agents in Egypt, as well as some others who had been ruled by the US attitude to me. The year was already behind us and no decisive action had been taken. The Soviet Union had deliberately let me down by not sending the equipment I had asked for, as though Moscow wanted to tell me that I couldn't decide on anything without Soviet approval. And indeed two years later, on a reconciliation visit to Moscow in March 1973, Brezhnev admitted to Marshal Ali that he deliberately didn't send any weapons to us.

The Soviet agents inside Egypt made a laughing stock of the year of decision, while I had to suppress my agony and conceal my wounds. I made the speech at the People's Assembly in February 1972 in which I defended the Soviet Union in spite of the stab I had had in the back (for I had visited the Soviet Union four times in less than twelve months to ask for the equipment I wanted, to no avail). And, in the same speech, I deliberately attacked the

United States of America, and William Rogers in particular, in terms as violent as was possible, which, naturally, opened a new chapter of bad relations with the United States – a period of fierce and full-blooded confrontation.

The Americans were naturally stunned to hear of my decision on 16 July 1972, to expel the Soviet military experts from Egypt; but they tried their best to play it down in their media in view of the 'Age of Détente' that had been already ushered in with Nixon's visit to the Soviet Union in May 1972, that is, two months before I took my decision. It looked as though it was a conspiracy of silence.

It would be a mistake, however, to think that I had taken the decision to please the United States or any other power. It was a patriotic decision, in which the people of Egypt rejoiced – my own and my people's decision. My public attack on Rogers and the United States for their attitude to me was no less fierce than my attack on the Soviet Union as I expelled the military experts.

VI

Not long after that Rogers left office and Kissinger took over as Secretary of State. On his appointment, Kissinger wanted to see an Egyptian envoy. However, 1972 being election year, the American government was paralysed (apart from the fact that détente was being already exercised), and so the meeting did not materialize until February 1973 when Hafiz Ismail, my National Security Adviser, was sent to see him in Paris, and again in April 1973.

The drift of Kissinger's argument was that Rogers' efforts had lacked the support of the US President and so nothing, naturally, could be achieved. It was different now as the US President was positively ready to co-operate in the establishment of peace. Hafiz Ismail said that our Egyptian Initiative still stood in spite of the fact that the speech made by Rogers as Secretary of State in January

1972 constituted a challenge to us. Kissinger's reply went as follows:

> Tell President Sadat that, although I don't know him personally, our assessment of him [based on the report submitted by the US envoy at Nasser's funeral] was wrong. Indeed, all the facts indicate the opposite of the report. We have seen him propound a peace initiative and proceed to expel the Soviet experts from Egypt, and these are remarkable actions, there can be no doubt.
>
> I advise Sadat, however, to be realistic. We live in a real world and cannot build anything on fancies and wishful thinking. Now in terms of reality you are the defeated side and shouldn't, therefore, make demands acceptable only from victors. You must make some concessions if the USA is to help you. How can you, in defeat, dictate your conditions to the other side?
>
> You may be capable of changing existing realities – and, consequently, our approach to the 'solution' – or you may not. If not, certain solutions have to be found which *follow from* your position, and these will be different from the solutions you now suggest. I hope my meaning is clear; I am not calling on Sadat to change the military situation for, if he tries to do that, Israel will again defeat you. She will score an even greater victory than she did in 1967, which will make it difficult for us to do anything at all. That would be a great pity and a big loss both for Egypt and Sadat personally – a man I would like to co-operate with one day. I greatly admire his stands and obvious courage. He is a man who, for the first time in your part of the world, applies a sound scientific method and puts things in their right place; besides, he has taken steps never before attempted by any other Arab leader.

This was the gist of what Kissinger said, both in February and in April. We couldn't pin any hopes on the Americans, I thought, as Israel evidently had them completely in her grip. The policy that had been laid down by Johnson and was still being held put Israel's interests before those of the United States herself – or, as the man in the street in Egypt put it, Israel had come to assume the role of the only 'power' guarding US interests in the Middle East. This was a role chosen by Israel herself, or even chosen for her by the United States. In either case, we clearly couldn't hope to achieve peace through US efforts so long as Israel herself didn't want it.

VII

The 6 October 1973 War took the United States totally by surprise. Kissinger was more than surprised; he was very sad and worried about me because, as he later told me, the Israelis had emphasized to the whole world in the first three days of the war that they would 'crush the bones of the Egyptians and the Syrians', and that it would only take a matter of hours, a day or two, for them to destroy the Egyptians and bury them in the Canal. They began to use the war films shot in 1967 both at home and abroad, in the belief that such propaganda would secure their victory.

On the fourth day the US State Department received the message which read simply, 'Save Israel.' The State Department also heard that Israel needed an immediate replacement of the 400 tanks lost on the Egyptian front. Kissinger must have been shocked to receive confirmation for these Israeli reports from US satellite-marshalled information. Once recovered, he began to work for an immediate cease-fire, provided that all forces went back to the positions they had held on 6 October. I naturally refused, as I have explained. We had already crossed the Canal and completely captured the Bar-Lev Line, which meant that the first stage of the war had been completed. We now had to reach the Sinai Passes, the second and last stage.

As Israel's position deteriorated even further, Kissinger came up with a different proposal, that a cease-fire should be enforced on the existing lines. However, as the Syrian forces had actually been pushed back from the lines they had held on 6 October, I had to reject this too. I remembered the situation in 1948 when the Israelis called for a truce and the Arabs responded only to give the Israelis a breather and so helped them eventually to score a complete victory. The second proposal constituted a similar trick and, as the Arabic proverb says, A true believer shouldn't be bitten by the same snake twice.

The Soviet Union asked me three times to accept a cease-fire but I consistently refused. The Soviet premier Aleksei Kosygin arrived in Egypt and stayed with us for four days. On 12 October the Soviet Union informed the United States that el-Sadat had agreed to a cease-fire. Kissinger wanted confirmation of this and so got in touch with British premier Edward Heath, as I have said. I of course denied the report and told the ambassador: 'Please tell Kissinger that I alone am allowed to speak for Egypt.'

Although the United States had supported Israel since the war started (and even before), Israel's deteriorating position now made that support take the form of direct, open, and concrete intervention. American tanks were transported to Sinai, to the Egyptian town of Al-Arish. The United States also supplied Israel with other weapons already referred to.

Suddenly I found myself confronting the United States, and this was what made me announce to the whole world on 19 October 1973, that I wasn't prepared to fight the USA and also what made me subsequently accept a cease-fire. I had four times rejected the request to cease fire over seventeen days when I had been fighting Israel, not the USA.

I would like to put on record once again that the Israeli counterattack often referred to as the Deversoir Bulge was purely America's doing – and the doing of the Pentagon in particular. The aerial photographs, new weapons, and equipment involved had not until then been available to anybody outside the United States.

By concentrating vast forces at Deversoir in an area decidedly too small for them, the Israelis hoped to frighten me into believing that they posed a threat to Cairo! They were, naturally, disappointed. Psychological warfare may get results from certain leaders, but it simply could never work against me: I always know what I'm doing and calculate all the possible consequences of every step I take.

I was fully confident that the counter-crossing was a naïve, though reckless, operation and that it was doomed to failure. If I proceeded with the military plan we had laid down and which I had actually signed, Israel would have lost 400 tanks and suffered 10,000 casualties, killed or wounded. This result wasn't merely possible or probable: it was a definite certainty. In such a battle my forces would have had to cross the Canal and storm the Bar-Lev Line; the enemy was there, stationed on a narrow strip of land with his back to the lake, and behind him, on the East Bank of the Canal, five Egyptian army divisions took their combat positions. The entrance from the East Bank of the Canal to the Deversoir Bulge was a gap merely $3\frac{1}{2}$ miles wide at the junction between the Second and Third armies, which could easily be closed. All military calculations indicated that if such a battle took place it would be a historic bloodbath.

But it never took place. Why? Because it would have meant more bloodshed, more 'bad blood' and hatred. And I would go to the end of the world, as my people and my armed forces know, if it enabled me to spare the wounding, not to say the killing, of one man.

VIII

I met Kissinger for the first time after the cease-fire came into effect at 7.00 p.m. on 22 October, only to be violated by Israel two hours later. As the United States and the

Soviet Union held joint responsibility for the cease-fire, I addressed my appeal to both powers, and held them responsible for Israel's actions. I declared that although I observed a cease-fire I believed I had no commitment to it, so that if they between them failed to make Israel go back to the cease-fire lines of 22 October – verified by the satellites of both superpowers and known to us and the Israelis on the ground – I would have to force her to do so. Thereupon Kissinger sent word that he wanted to come to see me.

Our first session of talks took three hours. The first hour made me feel I was dealing with an entirely new mentality, a new political method. For the first time, I felt as if I was looking at the real face of the United States, the one I had always wanted to see – not the face put on by Dulles, Dean Rusk, and Rogers. Anyone seeing us after that first hour in al-Tahirah Palace would have thought we had been friends for years. There was no difficulty in understanding one another and so we agreed on a six-point programme of action, including a US pledge of return to the 22 October cease-fire line within the framework of the forces' disengagement.

Our agreement on the six-point programme of action marked the beginning of a relationship of mutual understanding with the United States culminating and crystallizing in what we came to describe as a 'Peace Process'. Together we started that process, and the United States still supports our joint efforts to this day.

That beginning was regarded by the Soviet Union as an end to my relationship with them, or so it seemed. The Soviet Union had had to swallow several unpleasant pills: my decision to expel Soviet experts, the liquidation of the 'power blocs', my opposition to the abortive Communist coup in Sudan, and finally my war decision and my victory. This, incidentally, proved them wrong, as they had warned Syria that if I fought Israel I would be drowned in the Canal in less than an hour and leave the Syrians to face Israel alone. (This is what President al-Assad of Syria told me personally.) When the reverse actually happened, that is, when I crossed the Canal, the most serious water barrier in history and stormed the Bar-Lev Line in a matter of six hours and advanced into Sinai, the Soviet Union still went on about it! Even at such an advanced stage, the Soviet Union still demanded a cease-fire; they did it three times, then Premier Kosygin, as I have recounted, came to see me to persuade me for the fourth time to accept a cease-fire, whereupon we had a very heated argument. Now my agreement with Kissinger on the six-point programme was the last straw as far as the Soviet Union was concerned. From that moment to this day, I have been denied everything Russian. The Soviet Union would not sell me weapons to compensate for my war losses as happened in Syria's case, nor supply me with the necessary spare parts or anything else. The Soviet attitude has hardened to the verge of hostility.

On 11 December Kissinger came to see me again, according to plan, to discuss the implementation of the six-point programme. After stressing that all I wanted was a return to the 22 October cease-fire line, Kissinger said he would do his best to arrange a forces disengagement plan.

At the time we had fixed 19 December 1973 for the convention of a Geneva Conference. It was postponed to the 21st. Egypt, Jordan, and Israel had actually gone to Geneva, although Syria did not go. After two or three sessions the conference was adjourned. Kissinger and I then agreed that the disengagement of forces should take place in January 1974 on both the Syrian and Egyptian fronts.

A few months earlier, on 16 October 1973, to be precise, when the war was ten days old and my victory was a fact which stunned the whole world, I made a speech at the People's Assembly in which I declared my willingness to go to Geneva. Let Israel withdraw from the Arab territories occupied in 1967 and let us meet in Geneva to draw up a peace agreement. At the time I could have hit the 'depth' of Israel – and Israel knew I had weapons capable of this. Any man in my position would have done this even if merely in retaliation for three previous Israeli wars; but I didn't, because I am all for peace. Proceeding from the same principle I opted for a peaceful liquidation of the Deversoir pocket.

Kissinger arrived back in January 1974, and kept shuttling between Aswan and Tel-Aviv for a while. But at length he came to me and said: 'It seems, unfortunately, that we have reached a dead end. In Tel-Aviv they are reluctant to reach an understanding.'

'Well,' I replied, 'it is your – the Americans' – turn now. You should come in and iron out a solution yourselves.'

'Would you accept an American proposal?'

'Certainly. I am willing to receive it, study it, and reply to it.'

I did receive the American proposal, which Israel received at the same time. Having agreed on the first disengagement of forces on the Egyptian front, we embarked on a new stage – the second stage in the Peace Process. And here I must reiterate that no one else except the United States can play this role, namely, that of mediator between two sides that harbour intense hate for one another – a gulf of bad blood, violence, and massacres. The United States did not impose the first disengagement agreement: she intervened to achieve a breakthrough and overcome the apparent impasse. The heading of the first disengagement document reads: American Proposal. Hence my assertion that the United States holds 99 per cent of the cards in this game. And I shall go on saying this, even if it angers the others, namely the Soviet agents and the Soviets themselves.

IX

We were supposed to start on the third stage of the Peace Process – the second disengagement of forces – in September 1974. However, certain events took place which de-

cidedly delayed the 'Peace Process'. President Nixon
visited Egypt and when he returned home the Watergate
Affair had come to a head to plunge the United States in
the tremendous political turmoil that went on for years –
from 1974 through to 1976, election year. In March 1975
Kissinger came to see me. President Nixon had resigned
and President Ford had taken over. Now Kissinger began
his Aswan–Tel-Aviv 'shuttle diplomacy' for a second disengagement of forces agreement.

I reckon that the first disengagement of forces agreement
took a week or ten days to negotiate. This time it was
different. Kissinger travelled backwards and forwards for
over two weeks without getting anywhere. No hope at all
was visible, so, ten days before his travels came to an end,
I told him in Aswan: 'Henry, there won't be any disengagement of forces this time. The Israelis won't respond,
either to your current efforts or to the Peace Process. They
know that the US government is weak at the moment, in
view of the Watergate Affair, which is still very much alive,
and because the current President didn't come to power
through a general election.'

'On the contrary,' he said; 'I believe we're doing fine.
We may have to spend a longer time than we spent on the
first disengagement agreement – but that's immaterial.'

'Could you,' I asked, 'submit any American proposals
today?'

'No...'

'See what I mean? You cannot because of your domestic
difficulties; and it is because of this that Israel isn't going
to respond to you.'

Twenty days later he came to me and said: 'You're
right. It's hopeless.'

'Well,' I replied, 'don't announce this in Egypt. Go to
them and announce it there.'

His announcement that the first stage of the second
disengagement of forces had failed was indeed made in
Tel-Aviv. At the same time the Egyptian Foreign Minister
held a press conference in Aswan at which he announced

that Kissinger's efforts had come to grief. The following morning Kissinger left directly for the United States.

What I would like to tell the American people at this point is that although the river of life, so to speak, flows from the United States into Israel carrying everything one can think of – from a loaf of bread to Phantom fighter-bombers to dollars to meet the budget deficit – Israel refused to respond to American peace efforts because she reckoned the US government was at the time weak and therefore not to be trusted. But I too realized the US government's position; and even though I had been in direct, open, and complete confrontation with the United States for eighteen years, I still trusted the Americans to work for the vindication of right and the establishment of peace.

A fact emerges here which, I believe, has not escaped many people. The common notion that Israel 'guards' US interests in our region is fallacious. Did Israel safeguard US interests when the Arab oil embargo posed a serious threat to the US economy and even to Western civilization itself? Israel has no consideration for anything beyond her own immediate interests. But the question is really deeper and more complex than this – it concerns political morality. It is, in other words, a question of whether you want peace or not, regardless of who would pay for the collapse of peace efforts. It was this that made me, in spite of all my previous experiences with the United States, tell Secretary of State Kissinger: 'Whatever the Israeli position may be, let us work together for peace.'

Need we draw any further comparisons between the Israeli and Egyptian stands at that historic stage? Need we dwell any further on the significance of both attitudes – whether or not they imply an eagerness for peace? I don't think so.

X

I have never tried to prove that I am a man of peace only by words. The moment Kissinger's peace efforts failed as a result of Israel's attitude, I made my speech in Parliament explaining all that had happened to my people, then submitted my decision to reopen the Suez Canal for international navigation on 5 June 1975. It was not a nervous decision nor a reaction to anything. It was dictated by the confidence I had in myself and the ultimate triumph of truth. The United States played an admirable role in clearing the Canal, together with Great Britain and France; the Soviet Union cleared only the Gulf of Suez, as it appeared late on the scene. My people and the entire Arab nation heard me say this. The world also heard me announce that the evacuees would go back to the Canal towns, and that I would hand over the thirty-nine bodies of Israeli soldiers killed on the battlefield. Israel was willing to pay any price through Kissinger to get them back, but I handed them over for nothing.

I did all this for peace, although I warned Israel that if she hit any of the Canal towns or the Canal itself I would retaliate by hitting at the Israeli mainland. I had by then met President Ford in Salzburg on 1 and 2 June, after the collapse of the March talks, and agreed with him on a new effort, to be made by him personally.

In August 1975 Kissinger arrived in the Middle East and started his 'shuttle' once again between Egypt and Tel-Aviv. But the man was broken-hearted. The position of the US administration had deteriorated so much since March. New scandals came to light every day, instability continued, and the Israelis seized every opportunity to strike at American interests when in conflict with their own.

I said to Kissinger:

'I told you nothing would come off this time. I have

exposed Israel's real intentions to the world by reopening the Suez Canal, repatriating the evacuees, and the other steps I have taken to restore peace to our region. Now if Israel tries to sabotage the current peace efforts, the reality will emerge clearly. The world will see for itself that Israel alone is responsible for the failure.'

At this point Israel had no option but to say yes, and, sure enough, on 1 September 1975, we signed the second forces disengagement agreement. The third stage of the Peace Process was now completed.

This has obviously put an end to the step-by-step solutions. Today we are working for a comprehensive settlement, that is, a final peace agreement which should end the state of war that has prevailed for thirty years. We should seek to establish permanent and just peace, now that it has been proved that while Egypt, after eighteen years of confrontation with the USA, responded to peace efforts, Israel, who is really America's stepdaughter, was willing to sacrifice US interests when it felt that this might help it achieve some of its ambitions.

XI

When I went to see Mr Carter shortly after his election as President of the United States, I reviewed with him all the stages that had been completed and submitted a definite peace strategy to him. I don't believe Israel is capable of, or willing to, produce a peace strategy similar to, or even faintly resembling, mine.

What exactly was that strategy which I submitted to President Carter and which I today submit to the whole world? Before I go into details, I would like to ask all those who deal with the Middle East question to realize that at the very heart of it lies the Palestinian problem. Let us therefore start by solving that problem. Sinai and the Golan Heights are in effect symptoms of a central malaise which is summed up in the Palestinian problem.

It is ironical that some voices today call on the Palestinians to recognize Israel. How could you call on people who have lost their land, their state, and their very human rights – the homeless Palestinians – to recognize a State – Israel – which is already recognized by 140 UN member countries and enjoys the support of both the United States and the Soviet Union? The Soviet Union never tried, by the way, to conceal its support for Israel's right to existence. Yasir Arafat was recently on a visit to the Soviet Union when Brezhnev asked for the recognition by the PLO of Israel as a basis from which to proceed to a solution of the problem.

Now in my first peace strategy – which I submit to the world today – I do not deny the State of Israel's right to be recognized by all countries of the region, provided that the whole situation is normalized. A peace agreement should provide for the establishment of a Palestinian State on the West Bank of Jordan and the Gaza Strip, and Israel should withdraw from the territories occupied in 1967, so that a formal declaration is made when we meet in Geneva, ending the state of war that has existed since the establishment of Israel.

I told President Carter that Israel should be given all the guarantees she wants. If she wanted to have every Israeli citizen armed with a tank and an aircraft, and got such armaments from the United States, we would not object – provided, of course, that those weapons were used within her own, not other people's territory. We would never object to anything Israel wants, whether from the United States, the Soviet Union, or the UN Security Council, and in any form she wants – whether it is a United Nations force to police the borders; demilitarized zones on a reciprocal basis; or a common defence pact with the United States.

In my peace strategy I declare that I am ready for all this; I have no objection whatsoever to any of it. But I believe it is only right and fair that each guarantee Israel gets, we the Arabs should also get – except one thing. For if Israel chooses to conclude a common defence pact with the United States, I shall not call for a similar one. I shan't call for such a pact to be concluded between me and the United States, the Soviet Union, or any other power. We are a non-aligned country and will continue to be so. Our will is ours, and ours alone.

I put this all to Carter. I spelled it out clearly and emphasized that today, in 1977, we are as willing for peace as we were when in 1971, I first pronounced my Peace Initiative – even more so. I also emphasized that I am willing to comply with all the provisions of Security Council Resolution 242, provided that Israel does the same. We cannot have any bargaining over the rights of the Palestinian people or over one inch of the Arab territories seized in 1967. Only thus can a permanent and just peace be achieved.

XII

What is Israel's reaction to all this?

We are all aware of the Security Theory advocated by Ben-Gurion which constituted a basis for the establishment of the State of Israel. It says openly that peace should be imposed on the Arabs by force of arms. While in the White House I told Carter, 'Peace cannot be imposed. If imposed, it will cease to be peace inasmuch as one party thus dictates its terms to the other. Israel,' I went on, 'has not so far succeeded in dictating her terms in spite of our terrible 1967 defeat. And we, in spite of our victory in 1973, have not been able to dictate our terms to Israel. The idea of imposing peace and secure borders should therefore be discarded.'

This was a myth which the October War exploded, along with the myth of the invincible Israeli soldier. They know this very well in Israel, and that is why they have stopped talking about the theory of Israeli security and started to talk about something different, the 'nature of peace'.

What do they mean by the nature of peace? Do they mean having open borders and the establishment of diplomatic and economic relations between Israel and the Arab countries? They do know only too well that these are new obstacles on the road to peace. Having lived for thirty years in confrontation with Israel, having fought four wars, witnessed massacres and bloodshed, experienced hatred, bitterness, and antagonism, no man in the Arab world today is prepared for a sudden opening of the border overnight, just like that.

Besides, is opening the border the only way to achieve peace? What about those countries which had open borders but still fought one another? The same thing could be said about diplomatic relations: do they really preclude wars? Take the Japanese attack on Pearl Harbor. The Japanese ambassador was visiting the US Secretary of State Cordell Hull even as Japan bombarded Pearl Harbor.

Open borders and diplomatic representation are matters of national sovereignty. Each country has the right to open its borders or to establish diplomatic relations with any other without this preventing a war or helping to establish peace. I asked President Carter to consider the US attitude to the Soviet Union after the 1917 Revolution. It took the United States nineteen years to recognize the Soviet Union, but the lack of recognition never meant, or necessitated, that a war should break out between them. The same thing applies to the People's Republic of China. The level of diplomatic representation between the United States and China, now the Chinese Revolution is nearly thirty years old, is not higher than a consulate or so. Why then ask the Arabs to establish full diplomatic relations with Israel as a peace condition? To ask for this is to posit that peace depends on such relations – which is not true, and has not been true down the centuries.

The nature of the peace which Israel today says she wants to secure is nothing in effect but a new attempt to thwart the establishment of peace – a ruse to help her gain time so as to impose a *fait accompli*, in the short term by having Israeli settlements established on the occupied Arab land (which she does at present) and in the long term by resolving the current conflict between American and Israeli interests when, in the fullness of time, the energy crisis is itself resolved.

Here I would like the reader to compare the Arab and Israeli positions with regard to US interests. I'd say 99 per cent of US interests in the Middle East are in Arab countries. We are friends; and we want to continue to be the friends of the United States. We safeguard her interests, and all we ask is that the United States should not support Israeli expansionism and aggression. We do not call on the United States to throw Israel into the sea or even to break her special relations with the State of Israel. Let America give Israel whatever she wants, provided she remains content with her borders. This will never affect our relationship with the United States in any way. We, as her friends, care about her interests. An example to hand is our decision to lift the oil embargo when we realized it began to affect the interests of the American people.

This is the opposite of what Israel does and has done over the years. Although firm and vital – and described as 'special' – Israel's relationship with the United States never prevented her from sacrificing American interests to serve her own ambitious and expansionist plans. This is a fact that the whole world has recently realized, and I hope America has adequately realized it too. I believe that the United States has a big responsibility, not only as a superpower that should promote the establishment of peace in this region but also towards herself and her interests in this important part of the world. All we ask of the United States is that she should, in drawing up her policy in that respect, think purely in American terms and endeavour to serve the interests of the American people. I do hope American readers will take no offence at this, for the United States has often allowed her policies to be determined by Israel, especially in Johnson's day. We were then told that the United States could not do anything and that it was up to us to seek an understanding, if we wanted, with Israel. As we knew Israel's line of thinking and her arrogance only too well, we realized that such an attitude meant that America shirked her peace responsibility as a superpower, that she shirked, in effect, her responsibility for peace.

I hope this won't be repeated. Now that I have met President Carter, I am very optimistic, and feel confident that he will shoulder his responsibility as the President of the greatest country in the world. I believe that he will continue the Peace Process which we started together and which I hope will be completed in Geneva, in spite of the campaigns Israel will launch to influence American public opinion and the US Congress in an attempt to impose Israel's terms on the Arabs. This we won't accept. We rejected it in defeat. Could we accept it when we have scored the October victory and proved ourselves?

One last thing remains to be said to the American people: We are ready for peace. We want it and welcome it. I have been extending a hand to peace since my 1971 Initiative and up to this very moment. How earnestly I want Israel to do the same was made only too evident to the entire world by the historic trip I took to Jerusalem in November 1977.

XIII

Nearly two months before my Jerusalem trip I received a message from the Egyptian Embassy in Washington to the effect that a 'personal' letter from President Carter (handwritten and sealed with a wax wafer) had been addressed to me but that it wouldn't be conveyed in the diplomatic pouch, which surprised me, but carried by an envoy who would deliver it to me personally. A member of the embassy staff (he was, incidentally, the son of the late Field Marshal Ahmed Ismail Ali) did arrive in Cairo and deliver it to me. I read that personal letter, about which nobody knew anything, and then replied to it. My reply – also handwritten and similarly sealed – went back with the same envoy, who returned to Washington to deliver it directly to President Carter.

Some people might conclude that President Carter in that letter asked me to take my Peace Initiative; but he didn't. We have carried on a regular correspondence, through our respective embassies, since my visit to Washington in April 1977, and have thus consistently exchanged views, reassessed the situation, and agreed on future steps to be taken. I believe that he does this with the other parties as well, particularly Israel (while in Jerusalem I came to know that the US President has a 'hot line' with the Israeli President). I cannot divulge the contents of Carter's letter to me, because of its personal nature, but I can state that it included an up-to-date assessment of the situation, which directed my thinking for the first time towards the Initiative I was to take two months later.

President Carter knew of the tremendous psychological barrier that separated the two sides. He must have realized this himself when I met him in Washington during my April 1977 visit to the United States, and must have concluded then that that barrier prevented him from demanding such an Initiative. As a matter of historical honesty, I must put on record that President Carter is true to himself and true to others. It is because he is so honest with himself that he can be honest with others, and that is why I have no difficulty in dealing with him. I find that I am dealing with a man who understands what I want, a man impelled by the power of religious faith and lofty values – a farmer, like me. His letter included a survey of the situation, as I have said, and my reply to it was similar and was made in the same spirit – *and yet* it indirectly suggested an entirely new course of action to me. Why?

When I had sent him my reply, I began a deep and a completely fresh appraisal of the situation. I realized that we were about to be caught up in a terrible vicious circle precisely like the one we'd lived through over the last thirty years. *And the root cause was none other than that very psychological barrier I have referred to*. It was because of that barrier that Israel was objecting, at a preliminary stage of the Peace Process, to formalities and procedural points – even down to the most insignificant features such as a comma or a period, a word added or deleted here or there in a proposed text – and was very eager to establish that the working paper for the Geneva Conference would be a US-Israeli document. And it was also because of that psychological barrier that we Arabs also objected – automatically – to formalities, declaring that we couldn't accept a US-Israeli working paper. Indeed, even if I for my part accepted a US-Arab working paper, my fellow Arabs would reject the word 'US' (though they know that no solution can be found without US participation). We were thus about to be caught up in the vicious circle of formal procedures and moved away from matters of substance – the core of the entire question.

By a 'psychological barrier' I mean that huge wall of suspicion, fear, hate, and misunderstanding that has for so long existed between Israel and the Arabs. It made each side simply unwilling to believe the other, and quite unprepared psychologically to accept anything transmitted through the USA (if channelled through other parties, a message from one side to the other would be viewed with even greater suspicion). I have therefore tended to compare that barrier to the Australian Great Barrier Reef – which is so dangerous to navigation in the southern hemisphere. And if the apparent barrier goes back only thirty years, it really has far deeper roots in history. For if, as Begin alleges, the question has a religious dimension for the Israelis, it certainly has such a dimension for us. So I decided to look at the situation from a new angle and to embark on a fresh study that took all the dimensions into consideration.

It was then that I drew, almost unconsciously, on the inner strength I had developed in Cell 54 of Cairo Central Prison – a strength, call it a talent or capacity, for change. I found that I faced a highly complex situation, and that I couldn't hope to change it until I had armed myself with the necessary psychological *and* intellectual capacity. My contemplation of life and human nature in that secluded place had taught me that he who cannot change the very fabric of his thought will never be able to change reality, and will never, therefore, make any progress. The fact that change is a prerequisite of progress may be axiomatic; but the fact that change should take place first at a deeper and perhaps subtler level than the conscious level was one I had established as a basis of action ever since I discovered my real self in Cell 54.

What was it, then, that I needed to change? We had been accustomed (and a whole generation had been brought up) to regard Israel as taboo – as an entity whose emotional associations simply prevented anyone from approaching it. The situation went from bad to worse as the cumulative effect of things said and done over the years rendered any change difficult, if it didn't actually preclude that possibility for both the Arabs and the Israelis. So I concluded that any possible change should occur to the *substance* of that attitude itself. If indeed we wanted to get to grips with the substance of the dispute – with the basis of the problem – in order to establish a durable peace, I reasoned, we ought to find a completely new approach that would bypass all formalities and procedural technicalities by pulling down the barrier of mutual mistrust. Only thus, I decided, could we hope to break out of the vicious circle and avert the blind alley of the past.

So much for the position of the two parties immediately involved. But what about the United States? What could the USA do? This was a subject that had to be dealt with, I thought, solely on the basis of the facts, and primarily the fact that President Carter's capacity for movement was governed by the current international situation. Furthermore, the extent of US assistance in this connection was determined by the special relationship between the United States and Israel. It would be unreasonable, I thought, to ask President Carter to do things he obviously couldn't do. I couldn't ask him to suspend that 'special relationship', or to stand on my side in opposition to Israel. I have always known that this wasn't possible, and my knowledge was further corroborated during my Washington talks with President Carter in April of 1977.

In view of these two facts, proceeding from an objective, realistic stand, I found that all I could ask of President Carter was to pursue a line that was genuinely American – that is, a line that *first* served US interests and *second* allowed the United States as a big power to shoulder her responsibility for world peace. This meant an end to the *carte blanche* the USA had given to Israel, in the days of the Johnson administration – an end, in other words, to the unconditional support for Israel's actions, whatever these might be.

More important than all this, perhaps, were the new facts established the world over by the October War. Foremost among these was that the Arab people were no longer a 'lifeless body' but a world power – they could fight, and in fact defeat, Israel. Furthermore, the Arabs were able to use the oil weapon ('energy' being the lifeblood of Western civilization) for the first time – and with remarkable efficiency. I'd like at this point to remind the American people that the moment we felt that the oil embargo had started to hit the American citizen, it was lifted. Our objective was never to penalize the American or Western citizen, but simply to point out that a blind partiality to Israel has a price. The West had its interests and should care about them just as we cared about ours; the West should come to its senses and recognize how the interests of each party could best be served.

These facts, taken together, constituted a focal point for

my thoughts after I received Carter's letter. The Initiative was already taking shape in my mind when I received an envoy sent by President Hafez al-Assad, who still reiterated the same words that had for years dominated the Arab world and that implied the handicaps which bedevilled the two sides' positions. He said Israel didn't want a solution and that she was playing for time (which was true); but he also said that the United States didn't want to solve the problem and that even if she did, she couldn't do it. I didn't subscribe to this view and told the Syrian emissary that President Carter both wanted a solution and was capable of one. I cited the second forces disengagement agreement. Even though the President at the time was not an elected President, the country still in the traumatic grip of the Watergate Affair, and the next presidential elections already rocking the country – even though, in short, the US administration was at its weakest, America succeeded in achieving a second disengagement agreement because President Ford was determined enough. If President Ford could do it under those circumstances, surely we could pin even higher hopes on President Carter.

I was still studying the situation, and my ideas began to look clearer and to take concrete form. A moral stand, stemming from my firm conviction (developed in Cell 54) that no change in the real world could be effected until a genuine change in ideas occurred, had already crystallized. Now I realized that my responsibility towards my people – towards our own and the next generations – made it incumbent on me to do my duty regardless of the office I hold. If I was capable of discharging my duty in sparing the next generations the suffering we had gone through, but shirked that duty, I would have done wrong. I would be sinning both against myself and against my God, who would call me to account for everything I did.

That stage in my thinking was over two months before I took my Initiative – after I received President Carter's letter, but before I made my visits to Rumania, Iran, and

Saudi Arabia. In Rumania I had a long session of talks with President Nicolae Ceausescu, during which he told me of an even longer session he had had with Premier Begin of Israel (it lasted eight hours, six of which were private conversation). I asked Ceausescu about his impressions. He said: 'Begin wants a solution.'

'My main concern in this connection,' I said, 'is whether Israel really and truly wants peace. For my part I do want peace and have proved it beyond a shadow of doubt. But does the Israeli administration today – particularly under Begin, as leader of the fanatical Likud bloc – want peace? Can an extremist like Begin really want peace?'

'Let me state categorically to you,' Ceausescu reiterated, 'that he wants peace.'

Ceausescu sounded very confident, and I trust that man's judgement. Besides, the Rumanian president has maintained a consistent link with the Israelis. His emphasis on Begin's desire for peace, on Begin being a 'strong man', confirmed my conclusion that a change was urgently needed – a change in the positions of both sides. On board the plane that took me to Iran an initiative emerged clearly before my eyes and took definite shape. I was alone with the foreign minister (who, it later transpired, felt that the Initiative was too bold and imaginative for him to handle). I turned to him and said that I was considering inviting the leaders of the Big Five – Carter, Brezhnev, D'Estaing, Callaghan, and Hua Kuo-feng – to a meeting in Jerusalem, at the Knesset.

My reasoning was that you cannot hope to succeed if you proceed from stage A in a given plan to stage C direct; no stages, however brief, can be bypassed. So, if we really wanted the Geneva Conference to be a success, we had to make full preparations for it – at stage B, so to speak. Earlier attempts at such preparations had fallen through; and my proposal that a working committee be set up (which Secretary of State Vance later submitted to the parties concerned) failed to receive any response because of the Arab-Israeli climate of mistrust and suspicion. In short, preparations had to take a different form and proceed along entirely new lines. I therefore thought of inviting the Big Five (the veto-holding Security Council members) to meet with all the Arab parties concerned, that is, the front-line states – Syria, Jordan, Lebanon, the Palestinians, and Egypt – in Jerusalem *to make it absolutely clear to Premier Begin that we were determined to prepare seriously for Geneva*, and that we were now drafting a working paper that included the main guidelines to make a success of the Geneva Conference.

As for the timing, I thought the visit would be a good opportunity for me to perform the Greater Bairam prayers, for instance, or the Friday prayers, at al-Aqsa Mosque and to visit al-Qiyamah Church (the Church of the Ascension) – two houses of God which Moslems and Christians respectively value very highly. In my mind's eye, I could imagine my friends Carter, D'Estaing, and Callaghan visiting these holy places – as well as Hua Kuo-feng.* I wasn't so sure that Brezhnev would accept the invitation, however, although he is the only politically minded member of the Soviet leadership, which was why I never differed with him (I differed a lot with his colleagues and the bureaucrats at the top).

This was the earliest version, even the prototype, of my Peace Initiative. I was sure my friends Carter, D'Estaing, Callaghan, and Hua Kuo-feng would welcome it, and that Brezhnev would have no option, when the others had done so, but to accept it as well. A meeting held with the Middle East parties concerned, in Jerusalem itself, would adequately prepare for the Geneva Conference and drive the point home to Israel that she would have inevitably to fulfil the two prerequisites of a genuine Middle East solution: withdrawal from the Arab territories occupied

---

* Mao Tse-tung, on his deathbed, told Vice-President Husni Mubarak that Hua Kuo-feng was 'an excellent man ... He is quite remarkable and I commend him both to you and the world at large,' was Mao's last recommendation.

after 1967, and the acceptance of a Palestinian state, to be established as a means of resolving the Palestinian problem – the key to the crisis in the Middle East.

The contours, so to speak, of this Initiative were growing increasingly clear in my mind on my itinerary. After Rumania I visited Iran and Saudi Arabia, but decided not to tell anybody about my decision so as to avoid any one of them getting involved: I wanted to take full responsibility for it myself. Back in Cairo I felt that the Greater Bairam prayers would be more impressive than Friday prayers, and that the Bairam would be a good opportunity for me to see our kith and kin in the occupied Arab land. The problem was, of course, one of timing. The Bairam was only a few days away, and it wasn't possible to arrange for a visit to Jerusalem by the Big Five – if indeed they had no prior engagements at the time – within such a limited period.

This earliest version of the Initiative began consequently to give place to another – a visit I would personally pay to Jerusalem to perform the Bairam prayers at al-Aqsa Mosque in fulfilment of my claim that I was ready to go to the end of the world to achieve peace. I had said that I would be willing to go anywhere in search of peace. Could I now exclude Israel? I have always meant what I said and stood responsible for my words. I therefore decided to go right to the Knesset, the political body representing the Israeli people, in order to submit to them the complete facts of the situation, and to confront them with the choice they would have to make if they really wanted to live in peace in this part of the world. I wanted to put the ball in their court.

This modified version of the Initiative soon crystallized and grew quite acceptable to me. I decided to declare it in my speech at the opening of the new session of the People's Assembly. I did so, stressing my willingness to go to the end of the world, not excluding Israel, in order to avoid the unnecessary wounding, not to mention killing, of a single soldier. I stressed that I meant exactly what I said, and that I was willing to go to the Knesset if the trip would help achieve our objectives. Everybody was present – the government ministers and so on, as well as Yasir Arafat. The immediate reaction was quite funny. Some imagined it was a slip of the tongue, or an effusion unbacked by proper thought. Some people still believe that politicians say things they don't mean – which I could never do.

Immediately before I went to the People's Assembly to make my speech, President Hafez al-Assad got in touch with me to remind me of the promise I had made to visit him in the summer for talks in Latakia. Now I said that I would see him soon, and sure enough, I left for Syria shortly after my Assembly speech.

'Do you mean what you said in your speech?' he asked me incredulously. 'Would you really go to Jerusalem?'

'I certainly would,' I replied; 'I never say anything I don't mean.'

'But how? How can it be done?'

I concluded our four-hour meeting by saying: 'Listen, Hafez, if this proves to be the last thing I do as President, I'll still do it and then go back to submit my resignation to our People's Assembly – according to constitutional procedure. Personally, I am absolutely convinced of the need for this Initiative.'

We parted company having mutually failed to shift the positions we held. I said so, in fact, at a press conference unattended by him, then returned directly to Ismailia, where the US ambassador called on me to hand me an official invitation, from Premier Menahem Begin. As it was now Thursday 17 November, I had only two days in which to prepare the speech to be made at the Knesset, for I would have to leave on Saturday if I was to perform the Bairam prayers at al-Aqsa Mosque on Sunday morning.

It was at this point that my foreign minister felt himself unequal to the Initiative. When we were preparing to go to Syria, he had said he couldn't come along because he was unwell. 'All right,' I said to the Vice-President; 'he could come along with me to Israel.' The Vice-President explained that it wasn't like that at all, and that the minister objected to the entire Initiative. 'Fair enough,' I said. 'I can't ask anybody to do something against his wishes.' I subsequently accepted his resignation.

My plane took off from Abu Suwayr airfield in the Canal region and, in less than forty minutes, landed at Lod airport. I was in Israel. Disbelief prevailed and people were practically stunned. The minute I stepped out of the plane, I found myself face to face with Mrs Golda Meir, who had cut short her US visit in order to see me on arrival. We exchanged greetings. I saw Dayan next – recognizing the man against whom I had fought the 1973 battle. Then Abba Eban, and General Ariel Sharon, who had led the famous counterattack. 'If you attempt to cross to the West Bank again,' I told him, 'I'll put you in jail!' 'Oh, no!' he said, 'I'm Minister of Culture now!'

Next I spotted Mordechai Gur, the Israeli Chief of Staff, who had warned that my visit was a trick designed to camouflage an imminent attack. The moment I saw him, I explained that I never practise ethical deception; strategic and tactical deception I can accept, but ethical deception never. After this President Ephraim Katzir (a university professor, an excellent man) and myself were driven to King David Hotel in the Israeli section of Jerusalem.

I left early in the morning, Sunday, for al-Aqsa Mosque to perform the Bairam prayers. I was in Arab Jerusalem for the second time in twenty-two years. (The first time was when I was Minister of State and secretary-general of the Islamic Congress.) I immediately realized that the condition of the mosque had greatly deteriorated. The effects of the 1969 fire were still visible: the Saladin pulpit had been completely burned out, and the process of repairing it was going far too slowly. I ordered that it should be rebuilt. The Egyptian artisans who had originally built the old Saladin pulpit would do so once again. Then I returned to the hotel.

In the afternoon I went to the Knesset. I made my speech, which was followed by speeches from Premier Begin and Opposition leader Peres. The Knesset session was over. In spite of the great emotional and physical fatigue, I felt very happy indeed. And I learned that my daughter had given birth to a girl at eight o'clock that very morning while I had been praying at al-Aqsa Mosque. The fatigue – indeed, the immense exhaustion – wasn't due to overwork or to the hectic time I had spent since I arrived (in meetings, talks, etc.) but to extremely deep mental concentration. It was this that made me feel so tired. My mind was highly alert and my concentration almost unprecedented, for the simple reason that I regarded my mission in Israel as truly sacred. Though confident of my people's support, I was willing, if the least sign of rejection became apparent, to go back and submit my resignation to our People's Assembly.

My confidence was vindicated. On my return nearly 5 million Cairenes were out to welcome me, staging an unprecedented demonstration of support. Everybody was anxious for my safety. Believing that my Initiative had been more risky than brave, their thanksgiving was quite genuine; indeed, they were still stunned and unable to express their joy. I was naturally very happy at this, but felt that it meant I had been entrusted with the binding task of bringing my mission to a successful conclusion. I had been, as it were, ordered to continue to serve my people until the object of the Initiative had been achieved.

Before moving on to talk about the outcome, I must put on record that President Gaafar al-Nimeiry arrived to see me, the moment I was back, to show his full support – just as he had called after the Second Revolution on 14 May 1971. I must express my appreciation for this stand by him personally and by the entire people of Sudan.

But what of the outcome? Did my plan come off?

I had reckoned that my Jerusalem trip would break the vicious circle within which we had been caught up for years. On this my calculations proved accurate enough. For, just as my people's reception was remarkable, even stunning, so too the Israeli people – women, children, and old men – showed a remarkable and equally stunning response. Even the Israeli special forces and paratroopers who were there to guard me actually danced for joy. They saluted me, though I had fought against them in 1973 and inflicted unprecedented losses on them. Why? It was, I believe, because they respect men who fight and, perhaps even more important, because they respect a man who after his victory can stand up and say: 'Right. Let the October War put an end to all wars! And now let us sit down together like civilized men around the negotiating table to discuss what you want – security – instead of resorting to force.'

I returned from Israel having agreed on two basic points: first, that the October War would be our last war; and second, that we should discuss around the negotiating table the question of security both for them and for us. I took this result to our People's Assembly and, having recounted all that had transpired, put it down for their consideration. I was happy to get almost unanimous endorsement (with only 2 or 3 members, out of 360, objecting). As a result my immediate plan, to spend a few days in the Canal region for a rest, was modified. I decided instead to convene the Cairo Conference with a view to maintaining the peace momentum and paving the way for the Geneva Conference.

What the situation will be like when this book is published in a few months' time, I don't know. What I do know is that I will stand by my Peace Initiative, whatever happens; and that I will waste no chance whatsoever of ensuring that the problem of peace in the Middle East receives a radical and civilized solution. Let me reiterate here the point that I made to the Israeli Knesset: that I am not after a bilateral agreement on Sinai (which couldn't solve the problem), but seek a wider peace, based on justice to all concerned. I will work in future – until this book is

THE ROAD TO PEACE

out and after – for the establishment of a just peace in our region, which includes the restoration of the Arab territories occupied in 1967, and the solution of the Palestinian problem through the establishment of a national Palestinian state, or – to use Carter's term – homeland.

My major target is to put an end to the crisis in the Middle East by solving the Palestinian problem and effecting a withdrawal from the Arab land occupied in 1967. I shall always be guided by the principle of just peace and am willing to make any effort, and any sacrifice necessary, however long the process may take. It it turns out to be a question of one side trying to impose its will on the other, let me affirm that, just as I stated my willingness to go to the end of the world to achieve peace, so I would be willing to fight to the end of the world for the same target.

I lost my younger brother, who was like a son to me, five minutes after the start of the October War. I have seen the victims of that war – young people destined to spend the rest of their lives in wheelchairs. I have seen similar cases in Israel and felt equally sad. One cannot help being deeply moved by the sight of war victims, whoever and wherever they may be, and it was this spirit that helped me to achieve the two targets of my visit to Jerusalem.

In conclusion I must put on record that the Egyptian people differ from many other peoples, even within the Arab world. We have recovered our pride and self-confidence after the October 1973 battle, just as our armed forces did. We are no longer motivated by 'complexes' – whether defeatist 'inferiority' ones or those born out of suspicion and hate. And this is why the opposing sides met soon after the battle dust had settled to talk matters over. We did so when the first and second forces disengagement agreements were concluded, and again when I met Mrs Meir in Israel. With the fighting over, we harboured nothing but respect for one another. Our civilized people know this; it is what induced 5 million citizens to come out to greet me on my return, and the armed forces to salute me in an impressive and quite unprecedented manner.

Our cultural depths are there; our cultural roots are alive, as vigorous as ever after more than 7000 years. Those who are surprised by what we do cannot simply understand this fact. They cannot grasp the real nature of a people who are working for a modern civilization comparable to the one they erected thousands of years ago in freedom and peace.

Epilogue

This is not the story of the Arab-Israeli conflict, or of the liberation of Egypt from British occupation, or of the achievements and shortcomings of the 1952 Revolution. It may be all this and more; but it is mainly the story of a search for identity – my own and that of Egypt. They are one and the same thing, because since childhood I have identified myself with my country – the land and the people.

Has the search been successful? Have I been able to realize the image of myself and my country that has been with me since early boyhood? I leave this for the reader to judge. All I can say – and all I know – is this:

I have never been lured by any worldly temptations, nor did I ever try to build my happiness at the expense of others. In every decision I made, in every action I took, I have been directed by my firm belief in the dignity of man and his right to freedom, to peace, and to equality.

I have found myself in friendship, in love, in work that helped those around me to live a better life, in the triumph of truth over falsehood. In short, in everything that made me see my ideals and those of my country being realized.

I have never sought power; for early in my life I discovered that my strength lies within me – in my absolute devotion to what is right, just, and beautiful.

Thank God, I am the same today as I was many years ago when, at sunrise, I went out to the fields to work side by side with others so that the earth might come to life and the trees bear fruit.

So far, the search has not ended – nor do I believe that it will ever end. For with every action we take to realize ourselves, we fulfil the will of God, and His will is everlasting. There is a long way for me and my people to go before we achieve a life where love, peace, prosperity, and the integrity of man prevail. May God guide our steps and those of our fellow men everywhere.

Appendix I

Dear Friend, President Leonid Brezhnev,
    First Secretary of the Soviet Communist Party:

I am writing to you personally because, reposing trust in your friendly feelings, which I have myself come to realize in our numerous meetings, I hope to break the vicious circle in which the relations between our two countries have been caught. Our bilateral relations are today bedevilled by a misunderstanding which I feel will be exacerbated if certain points are not made clear.

I shall therefore be completely frank in this letter, however far this may take me, so that our point of view is fully conveyed to you, free from all tendentious interpretations and the influence of falsehoods.

1. We still bear in mind your own experience in World War II. The Soviet peoples rejected Nazi occupation and would not allow it to continue. They fought valiantly, making all the necessary sacrifices for the liberation of their land, and struggled without stint to secure their dignity. It is hardly surprising, therefore, that the Arab people of Egypt should be equally eager to liberate their land, equally willing to make all the necessary sacrifices, whatever their magnitude may be. This, I believe, should constitute the right point of departure for us.

2. I therefore believe that my eagerness to maintain our friendship requires me to start this message at the point

375

where our dialogue was broken off, since our last meeting in April 1972, and so get to the heart of the matter – the real reason behind the present 'pause'. It is this which I hope will enable us to continue our dialogue and get to the core of the problem. Once we have mutually understood our viewpoints, we shall be able to deal with all other issues.

3. You will perhaps agree, dear friend, that I have shown the utmost eagerness to maintain and consolidate our friendship in all spheres. It was this that made me pay four visits to Moscow – in March and October 1971, then in February and April of the current year. The main topic in our talks at all these meetings was the problem of the Israeli aggression and the steps which need to be taken for the liberation of our land.

Please allow me here to remind you that I have been careful at all the meetings I had with the Soviet leaders under your chairmanship, to emphasize two main principles:

First, that we don't want anybody other than our soldiers to fight our battle for us.

Second, that we don't want, nor do we ever seek, to let our battle spark off a confrontation between the Soviet Union and the United States, insofar as this would be catastrophic to the whole world. I said, literally, that anybody who sought this was undoubtedly a lunatic.

4. The view on which we have concurred at our various meetings, particularly at our last meeting in April 1972, was that Israel and her backer, the United States of America, wouldn't make a move to reach a solution to the problem, peaceful or otherwise, until Israel felt that our military power had grown sufficiently to challenge her military superiority. Only then would Israel, as well as the United States, see that it is in their interests to find a solution to the problem.

I mentioned in our frequent discussions that we needed a retaliation weapon which would deter the enemy from hitting Egyptian targets far inland, as he had done in the past, because of his knowledge that we would then be able to retaliate in kind and attack his inland positions.

It was obvious, and still is, that, deprived of such a retaliation weapon, we would remain incapable of taking any kind of military action and, consequently, Israel would see no need to change her intransigent attitude for a settlement of the problem to be reached.

5. Hence the message I sent you with Marshal Grechko, who visited us in May 1972, a few days before the Moscow meeting. For my part, I was careful to ensure the highest degree of success for his visit, and agreed to issue a statement which he had brought over from Moscow – a statement which claimed that Egyptian pilots had used the Supersonic MIG-25s on three occasions and that new fighter-bombers had been used in Egypt.

It was all untrue.

Still, I agreed to issue that statement to make a success of that visit, as I have said, and because I was conscious of the political objectives of the visit, particularly in view of the fact that it took place a few days before the Moscow meeting, and so wanted, as a friend, to let you conduct your Moscow talks from a position of strength.

However, I gave Marshal Grechko a clear-cut message to convey to you regarding the conduct of our relations after the Moscow meeting. It wasn't difficult to anticipate the conclusions of the Moscow meeting as far as our problem was concerned: there was nothing so mysterious about it, in fact. I specified 31 October as the deadline for what we should achieve during that period – a period just about sufficient for completing our preparations for the post-US elections round. I told Marshal Grechko we needed every minute and could afford to waste no time whatsoever, in order to secure the firm ground needed for the new round by the deadline fixed.

6. When on 6 June your ambassador conveyed your message to me on the outcome of the Moscow meeting – that is, nearly ten days after the meeting ended – I was not surprised: it was no news to us at all. On the same day I

sent you another seven-point message ... specifying the position even further. I earnestly urged that no time should be wasted between then and 31 October: every minute counted.

In that message, you'll find, I officially asked for an immediate resolution of the problem of command and domination: it was unreasonable for Soviet units to be stationed in Egypt without being under our command.

7. A whole month later, and following repeated approaches, both through the Prime Minister and through the Foreign Minister, I received a message from you, on 8 July. It took you a whole month to reply, though I *had* informed you I counted the days, the hours, the minutes.

It was a disappointing message. It completely ignored all that I had conveyed to you first through Marshal Grechko and subsequently on 6 June. It confirmed to me, however, the fact that such a method as you adopted in dealing with us – of ignoring our position and the battle we have ahead – followed from a certain mentality from which we have been suffering year after year since the aggression – for five years, in fact. I have repeatedly tried, over one and a half years, to draw attention to it, to no avail.

That is why I have rejected this message, and rejected this method; and now we have to have a pause – as friends – in order to define our positions frankly.

I would like, my friend, to reveal briefly my impressions of that period, because it is your right as a friend to know the reasons which, I believe, justify my decisions.

The crisis is 'frozen', and no means of breaking the present deadlock are available.

The American claim that the United States, and the United States alone, is capable of finding a solution has been increasingly vindicated, even after the Moscow meeting.

Israel's unbridled actions in our Arab region continue unchecked.

The statement issued by the Moscow meeting calls for

'military relaxation' in the region after the solution of the problem.

Your message of 8 July completely ignores the measures we had agreed upon and which we believe to be absolutely necessary insofar as they would enable us to resort to military action, if need be, after the US elections.

The United States continues to give unlimited amounts of weapons to Israel, and is modernizing the entire Israeli air force, apart from other types of armaments.

Your attitude, following this message, reveals that the partial embargo you have imposed on us for the last five years, in regard to 'retaliation weapons', has been extended at this critical period to cover basic necessities which I had specified in my message to you but which you completely ignored.

In view of all these considerations, my decision to terminate the mission of the advisers has been designed to give us a pause – to mark the inevitable end of a certain era and the beginning of another based on fresh concepts, recalculations and redefinition of our stands.

8. Let me, my friend, cite examples from what happens in the armed forces – and consequently among our people, insofar as the armed forces constitute a part of the Egyptian people. The advisers should have informed you of these before the situation deteriorated so much.

A. *In the Navy:* The commander of our navy has for the last four years been demanding a new submarine-detection device to replace the Soviet one currently in use whose range is a mere 500 metres. Your reply has consistently been that the Soviet Union possessed no other submarine-detection device, while every naval officer in Egypt knows that your warships are equipped with a device which detects submarines as far away as the horizon. The West has it too, and it isn't a secret. We are not a backward country: we read about what both the West and the East have, and follow up advances in all fields throughout the world. What makes it even ironical is that your warships 'live' among us!

The horizon-detection device is on the market in the West; it isn't a secret. Other devices are available that have at least twenty times the range of our device, and they are not secret either.

What would our naval officers say in view of such a state of affairs?

B. *In the Air Force:* All our air force officers – who graduated from your academies – know that you possess superior aircraft such as the M500, such as those we had until recently. But then all that you have is regarded as secret and unapproachable.

The rocket-equipped aircraft which we have fly, loaded with their rockets, at a speed almost half that of the commercial, passenger Ilyushin-62s and Boeings. Their rockets are launched at a subsonic speed and continue to be vulnerable to antiballistic missiles for more than six minutes, while Phantoms, flying at Mach 2.25, are equipped with the US Shrike rockets, which travel at supersonic speeds, naturally. I had drawn your attention to this fact at the time, through your ambassador, even before ten such rockets were fired at us.

What would our air force officers say to this?

C. *In the Army:* You sent us 180-mm guns, in view of the 175-mm guns the United States had supplied Israel with – but the former simply could never compare with the latter.

The American gun is tank-mounted, highly mobile, with a built-in firing mechanism so that it can reach the farthest targets it is designed for. Yours is immobile (it can be moved by no less than twenty men), has no built-in firing mechanism and so falls short of its full range. This was denied us, to ensure that it wouldn't be used offensively – in accordance with the offensive weapons embargo you have imposed on us.

As has been declared, the United States sent unlimited numbers of its offensive guns to Israel, while you sent us no more than four of those guns, to be used on a 160-

kilometre-long front.

Our officers know that you have a more powerful gun than the American one – and mounted too, but it is, as usual, a secret, and your experts deny that you have anything of the sort.

What would our artillery officers say?

In the infantry, each officer and each soldier knows that the weapons used in opening gaps in enemy lines mean simply his life itself – at the start of military operations. All we have in this line is, however, World War II equipment. Our officers who had their military training at Frunz [military academy] know that you and the West possess – which is not a secret – rockets for the opening of gaps. We have been repeatedly demanding such weapons for two years now, and getting the same reply – the Soviet Union hasn't any.

This is just a sample. I could give you hundreds of other examples – all known to every officer and every soldier in the armed forces, and, hence, to the people.

Is this a method of co-operation by a friend?

Our defence system lacks a lot of 'items', though we say the opposite of this to the people and the world at large. And this is where I would like to have a pause, in order to discuss the 'mentality' behind it all.

You look on us as though we were a backward country, while our officers have had education in your academies – just like your own officers. We, furthermore, follow up developments throughout the world – East and West – which are not any longer secret. Armament is dealt with in books which are circulated throughout the world. When the Soviet advisers were asked about a given item, they either fell silent or replied that the Soviet Union didn't have it – while we, and everybody else, knew that the Soviet Union has everything.

9. Let me tell you frankly, my friend, that I feel our future relations to be seriously threatened. And the most serious thing about it is the sense of bitterness our people will be

left with, in regard to the Soviet Union.

You have every right, I believe, in view of my recent decisions, to adopt such a stand as would in your opinion serve your interests. But I do not believe that it is in your interest at all to let our people be so bitter towards the Soviet Union, after such a long period of friendship and constructive work as we have been through together.

Your decision to withdraw the M500 aircraft, especially after a joint Soviet-Egyptian communiqué was issued during Marshal Grechko's visit to the effect that Egyptian pilots had flown them, is, I believe, one of the worst decisions imaginable insofar as it embitters our people and the armed forces.

So was your decision to withdraw the jamming equipment, operated as they were by Soviet personnel, either under the pretext that they were secret, that we couldn't operate them or any other pretext. It was again a most unhappy decision, which dealt a serious blow to Soviet-Egyptian friendship.

Both decisions meant that the Soviet Union was imposing its conditions on us.

We had, together, put an end to armament monopoly in the world since 1955.

There is another, more serious consideration. We are facing, in this battle, an enemy equipped by every possible weapon. What would be the conclusion of the ordinary citizen?

I shall leave it to you to assess the real dimensions of all this, but I would have done violence to our friendship if I didn't tell it all to you as frankly as this.

10. One last thing, which I want you to see very clearly:

The deadline of 31 October had been transmitted to you in the message I already conveyed with Marshal Grechko, the other message sent through your ambassador, and personally through our Premier during his last visit to you.

The air of our Premier's visit was that a joint communiqué be issued to spare us all kinds of malicious reporting and *Schadenfreude*; but you refused to do so.

I would like to tell you, in all honesty and frankness, that I still hold this deadline – 31 October – as the decisive factor in our relationship.

I hope sincerely – and in a spirit of real fraternity – that you will realize that this is not a warning, as some people may tend to interpret it; we never address warnings to anybody because we cannot accept any warnings from anybody.

The deadline is based on two factors: one is political, the other military.

As for the political factor, as we have concurred in our last meeting and in my messages to you – we shall find ourselves, after the US presidential elections, in a situation marked by joint US-Israeli efforts to impose a solution in favour of Israel. Without a solid military base to stand on, we shall simply slip into the vicious circle once again – a Jarring mission, a Security Council resolution, and an Israel that feels too superior militarily to make a move.

As for the second factor, the military, you can ask your military men what kind of military superiority Israel will have by next November and December.

Israel will have fully 'assimilated' all the up-to-date accretions to its air force – the great numbers of Phantoms and Skyhawks – and the gap between us, already so wide, will be even wider.

So you can see very clearly, my friend, that such a deadline is based on political and military considerations already agreed on.

Having said that, let me tell you that we, in Egypt, will continue to show gratitude for your assistance. The evidence of this you will find in the emphasis I consistently laid on the role of Soviet support for us, in all the speeches I addressed to the Arab people in Egypt and the Arab region at large, even when I declared my decision to terminate the mission of Soviet advisers in Egypt.

To be completely honest, however, I have to state that

your very first priority in establishing the co-operation you wish to have with us should be to enable us to liberate our land. We wish to consolidate our co-operation with you to the greatest possible extent – though such an extent will be commensurate with the extent of assistance we shall receive from our friends in the Soviet Union, towards solving our basic and paramount problem, that of liberating our land.

I have written to you, and ask you to intervene personally, because I have complete confidence in your feelings, your understanding of our cause, and your eagerness to solve the problem.

The problem of liberating the land is everything to us – our very life, conduct, relations, and actions. I seriously fear that some people may fail to appreciate this properly and so allow bitterness to take the place of friendship.

Now, if you find that the above clarifications are conducive to a better understanding of our circumstances, Dr Aziz Sidqi, our Prime Minister, will be prepared to pay a private visit to the Soviet Union – at the time you deem appropriate – to pave the way for a meeting between us and for a detailed study of all questions to be made, designed to help our relations to proceed in the future from a firm basis of trust, and co-operation based on mutual frankness to serve our common interests.

Please accept my genuinely amicable sentiments and appreciation. With best wishes to you personally, your colleagues in the Soviet leadership, and the friendly Soviet people.

(signed)
Anwar el-Sadat
President of the Republic

Cairo
30 August 1972

Appendix II

The President

In the Name of God.

Directive issued to the Commander-in-Chief of the Armed Forces, War Minister, Marshal Ahmed Ismail Ali:

I. *The General Situation*

1. The Israeli enemy has been in occupation of parts of Arab land for more than six years.

2. Relying on US assistance, particularly regarding arms supplies, Israel has tried and continues to try to impose her will on us, and to resolve the Middle East crisis in such a manner as to enable her to have almost absolute control of the Arab region, of its security and very destiny.

3. Egypt has tried in every possible way since the Security Council cease-fire decision was issued on 8 June 1967, to find a solution to the crisis. Towards this end Egypt has made a variety of efforts: she accepted the Security Council resolution 242 of 22 November 1967; responded to the mediation efforts of the Big Four, the subsequent efforts of the two superpowers, and the initiative of US Secretary of State William Rogers; then proceeded to propose an Initiative of her own, providing for a solution beginning with the reopening of the Suez Canal. This would have

been the initial step for an Israeli withdrawal, to be completed in stages, in implementation of the Security Council resolution. All these efforts, however, came to grief: they either failed outright, or were suspended; indeed, our enemies even tried to divert them from the goals originally set them.

4. Egypt carried out military operations of a limited nature in 1967, 1969 and 1970. She also gave vast assistance to the Palestinian resistance forces to enable them to carry out guerilla operations both on the firing lines and inside the occupied land. Though they had, on the whole, significant consequences, these operations – for a variety of reasons – failed to put adequate pressure on the enemy.

5. Egypt has always realized that a time would come when she would have to shoulder her responsibilities. What was of paramount importance to us was to be as prepared for this day as best we could, within our potential and in the light of our commitment to defend our land and honour.

6. The people in Egypt have shown more toleration of the behaviour of their foes and friends alike than ever imaginable. The burdens, physical and moral, borne by our people have been heavy indeed: only a people armed with faith in freedom and the willingness to make the necessary sacrifices could have shouldered such burdens.

7. Politically, the Arabs have in general significantly improved their position and so increased the chances of their being an effective force. With the exacerbation of the energy crisis – and the currency crisis – in the world, Arab pressure exerted in propitious circumstances could be a factor to be reckoned with.

8. The potential effectiveness of the Arab position in general may be seen clearly in the level of our armament. Apart from what we have received from the Soviet Union and the Eastern bloc – which is much – we have acquired other kinds of weapons, hitherto unavailable, from other sources.

9. The enemy is practically isolated on the international

plane, following successful Egyptian efforts in the Security
Council, the UN General Assembly, the last OAU Summit
in Addis Ababa, and the subsequent Non-Aligned Countries Conference in Algiers.

10. The international situation is changing, and shows
signs of tending to change even further. We may therefore find ourselves faced with arrangements made for a
long-term international 'balance', which might restrict
our freedom of movement and our right to choose the
most favourable alternatives.

II. *The Enemy Strategy*

The Israeli enemy has opted, as we can see, for a policy
based on intimidation, on claiming a superiority which
the Arabs could never hope to check. This is the basis of
the Israeli Security Theory, which relies on psychological,
political, and military deterrence.

The central point in the Israeli Security Theory is to
convince Egypt and the Arab nation that it is futile to
challenge Israel and that it is therefore inevitable for us
to accept Israel's terms, even if these involved certain
violations of our national sovereignty.

III. *Egypt's Strategy at This Stage*

*The strategic objective I hereby set the Egyptian armed
forces to achieve, and for which I hold full political responsibility*, in the light of all that I have heard and
learned about their preparations, *may be summed up as
follows:*

To challenge the Israeli Security Theory by carrying out
a military action according to the capabilities of the armed
forces *aimed at inflicting the heaviest losses on the enemy*
and convincing him that continued occupation of our land
exacts a price that is too high for him to pay, and that

consequently his theory of security – based as it is on psychological, political, and military intimidation – is not an impregnable shield of steel which could protect him today or in the future.

A successful challenge of the Israeli Security Theory will have definite short-term and long-term consequences. In the short term, a challenge to the Israeli Security Theory could have a certain result, which would make it possible for an honourable solution for the Middle East crisis to be reached. In the long term, a challenge to the Israeli Security Theory can produce changes which will, following on the heels of one another, lead to a basic change in the enemy's thinking, morale, and aggressive tendencies.

IV. *Timing*

The time is now, from the political point of view, perfectly favourable for such an action as I have referred to in Section III of this Directive.

The situation on our domestic front, the Arab front in general – including our accurate co-ordination with the northern front – and the international situation, create, as from now, a favourable opportunity for us to make a start.

The international isolation of the enemy and the atmosphere which dominates at home, due to his party election disputes and clash of personalities, improve the chances of our hitting on the most favourable opportunity.

Cairo   (signed)
5th Ramadan 1393   Anwar el-Sadat
1 October 1973   President of the Republic

Appendix III

THE PRESIDENT

A STRATEGIC DIRECTIVE

From: The President and Supreme Commander of the Armed Forces

To: Marshal Ahmed Ismail Ali, War Minister and Commander-in-Chief of the Armed Forces

1. Pursuant to the politico-military directive issued to you by me on the first day of October 1973, and on the basis of the circumstances of the present political and strategic situation,
I have decided to direct the Armed Forces to accomplish the following strategic missions:

(a) to end the present military deadlock by breaking the cease-fire as from 6 October 1973;
(b) to inflict the greatest possible losses on the enemy, in personnel, arms, and equipment;
(c) to work for the liberation of the occupied land in successive stages in accordance with the growth and development of the potentialities and capabilities of the Armed Forces.

2. These missions shall be accomplished by the Egyptian Armed Forces independently or in co-operation with the Syrian Armed Forces.

(signed)

9th Ramadan 1393 H.   Anwar el-Sadat

5 October 1973   President of the Republic

Appendix IV

The Arab Republic of Egypt
The President's Secretariat for Information

TELEGRAM
No. 20, dated 20 October 1973

To: President Hafez al-Assad

We have been fighting Israel for the fifteenth day running. Israel fought us on its own in the first four days and its real position was exposed on the Egyptian and Syrian fronts: it lost, by its own admission, 800 tanks and more than 200 aircraft on both fronts.

For the last ten days, however, I have been fighting the United States on the Egyptian front, armed as she is with the most sophisticated weapons in her possession. I simply cannot fight the United States or bear the historical responsibility for having our armed forces destroyed once again.

I have therefore informed the Soviet Union that I have agreed to a cease-fire on existing lines on the following conditions:

1. The Soviet Union and the United States shall guarantee an Israeli withdrawal, as proposed by the Soviet Union;

2. A peace conference at the UN shall be held to secure agreement on a comprehensive settlement as proposed by the Soviet Union.

My heart bleeds even as I tell you this, but I feel that I am forced by my sense of responsibility to take this decision. I shall at the right time face our people, our nation, with all this, so that the people may bring me to book for it.

With best wishes,

(signed)
20 October 1973   Anwar el-Sadat

Appendix V

In the name of God, Mr Speaker of the Knesset, ladies and gentlemen, allow me first to thank deeply the Speaker of the Knesset for affording me this opportunity to address you.

As I begin my address I wish to say, peace and the mercy of God Almighty be upon you and may peace be with us all, God willing. Peace for us all, of the Arab lands and in Israel, as well as in every part of this big world, which is so beset by conflicts, perturbed by its deep contradictions, menaced now and then by destructive wars launched by man to annihilate his fellow men.

Finally, amidst the ruins of what man has built among the remains of the victims of mankind there emerges neither victor nor vanquished. The only vanquished remains always a man, God's most sublime creation. Man, whom God has created, as Gandhi, the apostle of peace puts it, to forge ahead, to mould the way of life and to worship God Almighty.

I come to you today on solid ground to shape a new life and to establish peace. We all love this land, the land of

This English translation of President Sadat's speech to the Knesset on 20 November 1977, appeared in the *New York Times* on 21 November 1977, and is reprinted with permission; a few amendments have been made for fuller accuracy. The simultaneous interpretation from the Arabic was done by a parliamentary interpreter.

God, we all, Moslems, Christians and Jews, all worship God.

Under God. God's teachings and commandments are: love, sincerity, security, and peace.

I do not blame all those who received my decision when I announced it to the entire world before the Egyptian People's Assembly. I do not blame all those who received my decision with surprise and even with amazement — some gripped even by violent surprise. Still others interpreted it as political, to camouflage my intentions of launching a new war.

I would go so far as to tell you that one of my aides at the presidential office contacted me at a late hour following my return home from the People's Assembly and sounded worried as he asked me: 'Mr President, what would be our reaction if Israel actually extended an invitation to you?'

I replied calmly: 'I would accept it immediately. I have declared that I would go to the ends of the earth. I would go to Israel, for I want to put before the people of Israel all the facts.'

I can see the faces of all those who were astounded by my decision and had doubts as to the sincerity of the intentions behind the declaration of my decision. No one could have ever conceived that the President of the biggest Arab state, which bears the heaviest burden and the main responsibility pertaining to the cause of war and peace in the Middle East, should declare his readiness to go to the land of the adversary while we were still in a state of war.

We all still bear the consequences of four fierce wars waged within thirty years. All this at the time when the families of the 1973 October war are still mourning under the cruel pain of bereavement of father, son, husband, and brother.

As I have already declared, I have not consulted as far as this decision is concerned with any of my colleagues or brothers, the Arab heads of state or the confrontation states.

Most of those who contacted me following the declaration of this decision expressed their objection because of the feeling of utter suspicion and absolute lack of confidence between the Arab states and the Palestine people on the one hand and Israel on the other that still surges in us all.

Many months in which peace could have been brought about have been wasted over differences and fruitless discussions on the procedure of convening the Geneva conference. All have shared suspicion and absolute lack of confidence.

But to be absolutely frank with you, I took this decision after long thought, knowing that it constitutes a great risk, for God Almighty has made it my fate to assume responsibility on behalf of the Egyptian people, to share in the responsibility of the Arab nation, the main duty of which, dictated by responsibility, is to exploit all and every means in a bid to save my Egyptian Arab people and the pan-Arab nation from the horrors of new suffering and destructive wars, the dimensions of which are foreseen only by God Himself.

After long thinking, I was convinced that the obligation of responsibility before God and before the people make it incumbent upon me that I should go to the far corners of the world – even to Jerusalem to address members of the Knesset and acquaint them with all the facts surging in me, then I would let you decide for yourselves.

Following this, may God Almighty determine our fate.

Ladies and gentlemen, there are moments in the lives of nations and peoples when it is incumbent upon those known for their wisdom and clarity of vision to survey the problem, with all its complexities and vain memories, in a bold drive towards new horizons.

Those who like us are shouldering the same responsibilities entrusted to us are the first who should have the courage to make determining decisions that are consonant with the magnitude of the circumstances. We must all rise above all forms of obsolete theories of superiority, and the most important thing is never to forget that infallibility is the prerogative of God alone.

If I said that I wanted to avert from all the Arab people the horrors of shocking and destructive wars I must sincerely declare before you that I have the same feelings and bear the same responsibility towards all and every man on earth, and certainly towards the Israeli people.

Any life that is lost in war is a human life, be it that of an Arab or an Israeli. A wife who becomes a widow is a human being entitled to a happy family life, whether she be an Arab or an Israeli.

Innocent children who are deprived of the care and compassion of their parents are ours. They are ours, be they living on Arab or Israeli land.

They command our full responsibility to afford them a comfortable life today and tomorrow.

For the sake of them all, for the sake of the lives of all our sons and brothers, for the sake of affording our communities the opportunity to work for the progress and happiness of man, feeling secure and with the right to a dignified life, for the generations to come, for a smile on the face of every child born in our land – for all that I have taken my decision to come to you, despite all the hazards, to deliver my address.

I have shouldered the prerequisites of the historic responsibility and therefore I declared on 4 Feb. 1971, that I was willing to sign a peace agreement with Israel. This was the first declaration made by a responsible Arab official since the outbreak of the Arab-Israeli conflict. Motivated by all these factors dictated by the responsibilities of leadership, on 16 Oct. 1973, before the Egyptian People's Assembly, I then called for an international conference to establish permanent peace based on justice. I was not heard.

I was not in the position of a man pleading for peace or asking for a cease-fire. Motivated by the duties of history and leadership, I later signed the first disengagement agreement, followed by the second disengagement agreement in Sinai.

Then we proceeded, trying both open and closed doors in a bid to find a certain road leading to a durable and just peace.

We opened our heart to the peoples of the entire world to make them understand our motivations and objectives and actually to convince them of the fact that we are advocates of justice and peacemakers. Motivated by all these factors, I also decided to come to you with an open mind and an open heart and with a conscious determination so that we might establish permanent peace based on justice.

It is so fated that my trip to you, which is a journey of peace, coincided with the Islamic feast, the holy Feast of the Sacrifice when Abraham – peace be upon him – forefather of the Arabs and Jews, submitted to God, and, not out of weakness but through a giant spiritual force and by free will, sacrificed his very own son, thus personifying a firm and unshakable belief in ideals that have had for mankind a profound significance.

Ladies and gentlemen, let us be frank with each other. Using straightforward words and a clear conception with no ambiguity, let us be frank with each other today while the entire world, both East and West, follows these unparalleled moments which could prove to be a radical turning point in the history of this part of the world if not in the history of the world as a whole.

Let us be frank with each other, let us be frank with each other as we answer this important question:

How can we achieve permanent peace based on justice? Well, I have come to you carrying my clear and frank answer to this big question, so that the people in Israel as well as the entire world may hear it. All those devoted prayers ring in my ears, pleading to God Almighty that this historic meeting may eventually lead to the result aspired to by millions.

Before I proclaim my answer, I wish to assure you that in my clear and frank answer I am availing myself of a number of facts which no one can deny.

The first fact is that no one can build his happiness at the expense of the misery of others.

The second fact: never have I spoken, nor will I ever speak, with two tongues; never have I adopted, nor will I ever adopt, two policies. I never deal with anyone except in one tongue, one policy, and with one face.

The third fact: direct confrontation is the nearest and most successful method to reach a clear objective.

The fourth fact: the call for permanent and just peace based on respect for United Nations resolutions has now become the call of the entire world. It has become the expression of the will of the international community, whether in official capitals where policies are made and decisions taken, or at the level of world public opinion, which influences policymaking and decision-taking.

The fifth fact, and this is probably the clearest and most prominent, is that the Arab nation, in its drive for permanent peace based on justice, does not proceed from a position of weakness. On the contrary, it has the power and stability for a sincere will for peace.

The Arab declared intention stems from an awareness prompted by a heritage of civilization, that to avoid an inevitable disaster that will befall us, you, and the whole world, there is no alternative to the establishment of permanent peace based on justice, peace that is not swayed by suspicion or jeopardized by ill intentions.

In the light of these facts which I meant to place before you the way I see them, I would also wish to warn you, in all sincerity I warn you, against some thoughts that could cross your minds.

Frankness makes it incumbent upon me to tell you the following:

First, I have not come here for a separate agreement between Egypt and Israel. This is not part of the policy of

Egypt. The problem is not that of Egypt and Israel.

An interim peace between Egypt and Israel, or between any Arab confrontation state and Israel, will not bring permanent peace based on justice in the entire region.

Rather, even if peace between all the confrontation states and Israel were achieved in the absence of a just solution of the Palestinian problem, never will there be that durable and just peace upon which the entire world insists.

Second, I have not come to you to seek a partial peace, namely to terminate the state of belligerency at this stage and put off the entire problem to a subsequent stage. This is not the radical solution that would steer us to permanent peace.

Equally, I have not come to you for a third disengagement agreement in Sinai or in Golan or the West Bank.

For this would mean that we are merely delaying the ignition of the fuse. It would also mean that we are lacking the courage to face peace, that we are too weak to shoulder the burdens and responsibilities of a durable peace based upon justice.

I have come to you so that together we should build a durable peace based on justice to avoid the shedding of one single drop of blood by both sides. It is for this reason that I have proclaimed my readiness to go to the farthest corner of the earth.

Here I would go back to the big question:

How can we achieve a durable peace based on justice? In my opinion, and I declare it to the whole world, from this forum, the answer is neither difficult nor is it impossible despite long years of feuds, blood, faction, strife, hatreds, and deep-rooted animosity.

The answer is not difficult, nor is it impossible, if we sincerely and faithfully follow a straight line.

You want to live with us, part of the world.

In all sincerity I tell you we welcome you among us with full security and safety. This in itself is a tremendous turning point, one of the landmarks of a decisive historical change. We used to reject you. We had our reasons and our fears, yes.

We refused to meet with you, anywhere, yes.

We were together in international conferences and organizations and our representatives did not, and still do not, exchange greetings with you. Yes. This has happened and is still happening.

It is also true that we used to set as a precondition for any negotiations with you a mediator who would meet separately with each party.

Yes. Through this procedure, the talks of the first and second disengagement agreements took place.

Our delegates met in the first Geneva conference without exchanging a direct word, yes, this has happened.

Yet today I tell you, and I declare it to the whole world, that we accept to live with you in permanent peace based on justice. We do not want to encircle you or be encircled ourselves by destructive missiles ready for launching, nor by the shells of grudges and hatreds.

I have announced on more than one occasion that Israel has become a *fait accompli*, recognized by the world, and that the two superpowers have undertaken the responsibility for its security and the defence of its existence. As we really and truly seek peace we really and truly welcome you to live among us in peace and security.

There was a huge wall between us which you tried to build up over a quarter of a century, but it was destroyed in 1973. It was the wall of an implacable and escalating psychological warfare.

It was a wall of the fear of the force that could sweep the entire Arab nation. It was a wall of propaganda that we were a nation reduced to immobility. Some of you had gone as far as to say that even for fifty years to come, the Arabs would not regain their strength. It was a wall that always threatened with a long arm that could reach and strike anywhere. It was a wall that warned us of extermination and annihilation if we tried to use our legitimate

400

rights to liberate the occupied territories.

Together we have to admit that that wall fell and collapsed in 1973. Yet, there remains another wall. This wall constitutes a psychological barrier between us, a barrier of suspicion, a barrier of rejection; a barrier of fear, of deception, a barrier of hallucination without any action, deed or decision.

A barrier of distorted and eroded interpretation of every event and statement. It is this psychological barrier which I described in official statements as constituting 70 per cent of the whole problem.

Today, through my visit to you, I ask you why don't we stretch out our hands with faith and sincerity so that together we might destroy this barrier? Why shouldn't our and your will meet with faith and sincerity so that together we might remove all suspicion of fear, betrayal, and bad intentions?

Why don't we stand together with the courage of men and the boldness of heroes who dedicate themselves to a sublime aim? Why don't we stand together with the same courage and daring to erect a huge edifice of peace?

An edifice that builds and does not destroy. An edifice that serves as a beacon for generations to come with the human message for construction, development, and the dignity of man.

Why should we bequeath to the coming generations the plight of bloodshed, yes, orphans, widowhood, family disintegration, and the wailing of victims?

Why don't we believe in the wisdom of God conveyed to us by the wisdom of the proverbs of Solomon:

'Deceit is in the heart of them that imagine evil: but to the counsellors of peace is joy.

'Better is a dry morsel, and quietness therewith than an house full of sacrifices with strife.'

Why don't we repeat together the Psalms of David the Prophet:

'Unto thee will I cry, O Lord. Hear the voice of my supplications. When I cry unto thee, when I lift up my hands towards thy holy oracle.

'Draw me not away with the wicked, and with the workers of iniquity, which speak peace to their neighbours, but mischief in their hearts.

'Give them according to their deeds and according to the wickedness of their endeavours.'

Ladies and gentlemen, to tell you the truth, peace cannot be worth its name unless it is based on justice and not on the occupation of the land of others. It would not be right for you to demand for yourselves what you deny to others. With all frankness and in the spirit that has prompted me to come to you today, I tell you you have to give up once and for all the dreams of conquest and give up the belief that force is the best method for dealing with the Arabs.

You should clearly understand the lesson of confrontation between you and us. Expansion does not pay. To speak frankly, our land does not yield itself to bargaining, it is not even open to argument. To us, the nation's soil is equal to the holy valley where God Almighty spoke to Moses. Peace be upon him.

We cannot accept any attempt to take away or accept to seek one inch of it nor can we accept the principle of debating or bargaining over it.

I sincerely tell you also that before us today lies the appropriate chance for peace. If we are really serious in our endeavour for peace, it is a chance that may never come again. It is a chance that if lost or wasted, the resulting slaughter would bear the curse of humanity and of history.

What is peace for Israel? It means that Israel lives in the region with her Arab neighbours in security and safety. Is that logical? I say yes. It means that Israel lives within its borders, secure against any aggression. Is that logical? And I say yes. It means that Israel obtains all kinds of guarantees that will ensure these two factors. To this demand, I say yes.

Beyond that we declare that we accept all the international guarantees you envisage and accept. We declare that we accept all the guarantees you want from the two superpowers or from either of them or from the Big Five or from some of them. Once again, I declare clearly and unequivocally that we agree to any guarantees you accept, because in return we shall receive the same guarantees. In short then, when we ask what is peace for Israel, the answer would be that Israel lives within her borders, among her Arab neighbours in safety and security, within the framework of all the guarantees she accepts and which are offered to her.

But, how can this be achieved? How can we reach this conclusion which would lead us to permanent peace based on justice? There are facts that should be faced with courage and clarity. There are Arab territories which Israel has occupied and still occupies by force. We insist on complete withdrawal from these territories, including Arab Jerusalem.

I have come to Jerusalem, the city of peace, which will always remain as a living embodiment of coexistence among believers of the three religions. It is inadmissible that anyone should conceive the special status of the city of Jerusalem within the framework of annexation or expansionism. It should be a free and open city for all believers.

Above all, this city should not be severed from those who have made it their abode for centuries. Instead of reviving the precedent of the Crusades, we should revive the spirit of Omar Ibn Khtab and Saladin, namely the spirit of tolerance and respect for right.

The holy shrines of Islam and Christianity are not only places of worship but a living testimony of our interrupted presence here. Politically, spiritually and intellectually, here let us make no mistake about the importance and reverence we Christians and Moslems attach to Jerusalem.

Let me tell you without the slightest hesitation that I have not come to you under this roof to make a request that your troops evacuate the occupied territories. Complete withdrawal from the Arab territories occupied after 1967 is a logical and undisputed fact. Nobody should plead for that. Any talk about permanent peace based on justice and any move to ensure our coexistence in peace and security in this part of the world would become meaningless while you occupy Arab territories by force of arms.

For there is no peace that could be built on the occupation of the land of others, otherwise it would not be a serious peace. Yet this is a foregone conclusion which is not open to the passion of debate if intentions are sincere or if endeavours to establish a just and durable peace for our and for generations to come are genuine.

As for the Palestine cause – nobody could deny that it is the crux of the entire problem. Nobody in the world could accept today slogans propagated here in Israel, ignoring the existence of a Palestinian people and questioning even their whereabouts. Because the Palestine people and their legitimate rights are no longer denied today by anybody; that is, nobody who has the ability of judgement can deny or ignore it.

It is an acknowledged fact, perceived by the world community, both in the East and in the West, with support and recognition in international documents and official statements. It is of no use to anybody to turn deaf ears to its resounding voice, which is being heard day and night, or to overlook its historical reality.

Even the United States of America, your first ally, which is absolutely committed to safeguard Israel's security and existence and which offered and still offers Israel every moral, material, and military support – I say, even the United States has opted to face up to reality and admit that the Palestinian people are entitled to legitimate rights and that the Palestine problem is the cause and essence of the conflict and that so long as it continues to be unresolved, the conflict will continue to aggravate, reaching new dimension.

In all sincerity I tell you that there can be no peace without the Palestinians. It is a grave error of unpredictable consequences to overlook or brush aside this cause.

I shall not indulge in past events such as the Balfour Declaration sixty years ago. You are well acquainted with the relevant text. If you have found the moral and legal justification to set up a national home on a land that did not all belong to you, it is incumbent upon you to show understanding of the insistence of the people of Palestine for establishment once again of a state on their land. When some extremists ask the Palestinians to give up this sublime objective, this in fact means asking them to renounce their identity and every hope for the future.

I hail the Israeli voices that called for the recognition of the Palestinian people's right to achieve and safeguard peace.

Here I tell you, ladies and gentlemen, that it is no use to refrain from recognizing the Palestinian people and their right to statehood as their right of return. We, the Arabs, have faced this experience before, with you. And with the reality of the Israeli existence, the struggle which took us from war to war, from victims to more victims, until you and we have today reached the edge of a horrible abyss and a terrifying disaster unless, together, we seize this opportunity today of a durable peace based on justice.

You have to face reality bravely, as I have done. There can never be any solution to a problem by evading it or turning a deaf ear to it. Peace cannot last if attempts are made to impose fantasy concepts on which the world has turned its back and announced its unanimous call for the respect of rights and facts.

There is no need to enter a vicious circle as to Palestinian rights. It is useless to create obstacles, otherwise the march of peace will be impeded or peace will be blown up. As I have told you, there is no happiness [based on] the detriment of others.

Direct confrontation and straightforwardness are the shortcuts and the most successful way to reach a clear objective. Direct confrontation concerning the Palestinian problem and tackling it in one single language with a view to achieving a durable and just peace lie in the establishment of that peace. With all the guarantees you demand, there should be no fear of a newly born state that needs the assistance of all countries of the world.

When the bells of peace ring there will be no hands to beat the drums of war. Even if they existed, they would be stilled.

Conceive with me a peace agreement in Geneva that we would herald to a world thirsting for peace. A peace agreement based on the following points:

Ending the occupation of the Arab territory occupied in 1967.

Achievement of the fundamental rights of the Palestinian people and their right to self-determination, including their right to establish their own state.

The right of all states in the area to live in peace within their boundaries, their secure boundaries, which will be secured and guaranteed through procedures to be agreed upon, which will provide appropriate security to international boundaries in addition to appropriate international guarantees.

Commitment of all states in the region to administer the relations among them in accordance with the objectives and principles of the United Nations Charter. Particularly the principles concerning the non-use of force and a solution of differences among them by peaceful means.

Ending the state of belligerence in the region.

Ladies and gentlemen, peace is not a mere endorsement of written lines. Rather it is a rewriting of history. Peace is not a game of calling for peace to defend certain whims or hide certain admissions. Peace in its essence is a dire struggle against all and every ambition and whim.

Perhaps the example taken and experienced, taken from ancient and modern history, teaches that missiles, warships and nuclear weapons cannot establish security. Instead they destroy what peace and security build.

For the sake of our peoples and for the sake of the civilization made by man, we have to defend man everywhere against rule by the force of arms so that we may endow the rule of humanity with all the power of the values and principles that further the sublime position of mankind.

Allow me to address my call from this rostrum to the people of Israel. I pledge myself with true and sincere words to every man, woman, and child in Israel. I tell them, from the Egyptian people who bless this sacred mission of peace, I convey to you the message of peace of the Egyptian people, who do not harbour fanaticism and whose sons, Moslems, Christians, and Jews, live together in a state of cordiality, love and tolerance.

This is Egypt, whose people have entrusted me with their sacred message. A message of security, safety, and peace to every man, woman, and child in Israel, I say, encourage your leadership to struggle for peace. Let all endeavours be channelled towards building a huge stronghold for peace instead of building destructive rockets.

Introduce to the entire world the image of the new man in this area so that he might set an example to the man of our age, the man of peace everywhere. Ring the bells for your sons. Tell them that those wars were the last of wars and the end of sorrows. Tell them that we are entering upon a new beginning, a new life, a life of love, prosperity, freedom, and peace.

You, sorrowing mother, you, widowed wife, you, the son who lost a brother or a father, all the victims of wars, fill the air and space with recitals of peace, fill bosoms and hearts with the aspirations of peace. Make peace a reality that blossoms and lives. Make hope a code of conduct and endeavour.

The will of peoples is part of the will of God. Ladies and gentlemen, before I came to this place, with every beat of my heart and with every sentiment, I prayed to God Almighty. While performing the prayers at the al-Aqsa mosque and while visiting the Holy Sepulchre I asked the Almighty to give me strength and to confirm my belief that this visit may achieve the objective I look forward to for a happy present and a happier future.

I have chosen to set aside all precedents and traditions known by warring countries. In spite of the fact that occupation of Arab territories is still there, the declaration of my readiness to proceed to Israel came as a great surprise that stirred many feelings and confounded many minds. Some of them even doubted its intent.

Despite all that, the decision was inspired by all the clarity and purity of belief and with all the true passions of my people's will and intentions and I have chosen this road, considered by many to be the most difficult road.

I have chosen to come to you with an open heart and an open mind. I have chosen to give this great impetus to all international efforts exerted for peace. I have chosen to present to you in your own home, the realities, devoid of any scheme or whim. Not to manoeuvre, or win a round, but for us to win together, the most dangerous of rounds embattled in modern history, the battle of permanent peace based on justice.

It is not my battle alone. Nor is it the battle of the leadership in Israel alone. It is the battle of all and every citizen in all our territories, whose right it is to live in peace. It is the commitment of conscience and responsibility in the hearts of millions.

When I put forward this initiative, many asked what is it that I conceived as possible to achieve during this visit and what my expectations were. And as I answer the questions, I announce before you that I have not thought of carrying out this initiative from the precepts of what could be achieved during this visit. I have come here to deliver a message. I have delivered the message and may God be my witness.

I repeat with Zacharia: Love, right and justice. From the holy Koran I quote the following verses: 'We believe in God and in what has been revealed to us and what was revealed to Abraham, Ishmael, Isaac, Jacob and the 13 Jewish tribes. And in the books given to Moses and Jesus and the prophets from their Lord, who made no distinction between them.' So we agree, Salam Aleikum – peace be upon you.

Index

411

Fontana Politics

The English Constitution   Walter Bagehot
edited by R. H. S. Crossman

Problems of Knowledge and Freedom   Noam Chomsky

Understanding American Politics   R. V. Denenberg

Marx and Engels: Basic Writings
edited by Lewis S. Feuer

Governing Britain   A. H. Hanson and Malcolm Walles

Edmund Burke on Government, Politics and Society
edited by Brian Hill

Machiavelli: Selections
edited by John Plamenatz

Mao   Ninian Smart

Lenin and the Bolsheviks   Adam B. Ulam

The National Front   Martin Walker

The Commons in the Seventies
edited by S. A. Walkland and Michael Ryle

John Stuart Mill on Politics and Society
Geraint Williams

To the Finland Station   Edmund Wilson

The Anarchist Reader
edited by George Woodcock

Hitler: The Führer and the People

J. P. Stern

His life, his times, his policies, his strategies, his influence have often been analysed. But rarely is the most elementary question of all raised – how could it happen?

How could a predominantly sober, hard-working, and well-educated population have been persuaded to follow Hitler to the awful abyss of destruction? What was the source of his immense popularity? What was the image projected in his speeches, his writings, and his conversation?

Hitler: The Führer and the People is a compelling attempt to reconstruct the nature of Hitler's political ideology, its roots, logic, and function.

'Who really wants or needs another book on Hitler? The short answer is, when the book is as good and original and brief as Professor Stern's, that we all do.'

Donald G. MacRae, *New Statesman*

'Stern's book is, on all counts, a significant achievement.'

Geoffrey Barraclough, *New York Review of Books*

'. . . an excellent book, all the more so because it concerns itself, via Hitler, with the more general problems of the relationship between society and the individual leader, between ideas and action, between myth and reality.'

Douglas Johnson, *New Society*

'His short book is one of the most remarkable studies of Hitler and Nazism to have appeared.'   Christopher Sykes, *Observer*

Understanding American Politics

R. V. Denenberg

In this concise guide to American politics, R. V. Denenberg offers an up-to-the-minute account of the workings, functions and relations of American institutions, from the Constitution and the Presidency, through Congress and the Supreme Court, to the bureaucracy and the mass media.

'Three cheers . . . for this brief, lucid, accurate and exceedingly informative study of a difficult and important subject.'
Hugh Brogan, *New Society*

'. . . a splendid introduction which avoids the patronizing tone that experts often assume when describing an unfamiliar political system, and also succeeds in being humorous without cynicism – not always an easy task.' *Sunday Telegraph*

'. . . a quick, illuminating and often edgy account of some of the things in danger of falling apart.' Martin Hillman, *Tribune*

Fontana History

Fontana History includes the well known series History of Europe, edited by J. H. Plumb, and Economic History of Europe, edited by Carlo Cipolla. Other books available include:

Lectures on Modern History Lord Acton

The English Constitution Walter Bagehot

The Conservative Party from Peel to Churchill Robert Blake

The Mediterranean and the Mediterranean World in the Age of Philip II (2 vols) Fernand Braudel

The English Reformation A. G. Dickens

The Practice of History G. R. Elton

History of Europe (2 vols) H. A. L. Fisher

Debates with Historians Pieter Geyl

A Short History of Socialism George Lichtheim

Ireland Since the Famine F. S. L. Lyons

The Elizabethan House of Commons J. E. Neale

Hitler: the Fuhrer and the People J. P. Stern

The King's Peace C. V. Wedgwood

The King's War C. V. Wedgwood

A selection of Second World War books
in Fontana

Mark Arnold-Forster   *The World at War* (illus)
Douglas Bader   *Fight for the Sky* (illus)
Noel Barber   *Sinister Twilight*
Michael Carver   *El Alamein*
Adolf Galland   *The First and the Last*
Jozef Garlinski   *Fighting Auschwitz* (illus)
Christopher Hibbert   *Arnhem* (illus)
David Howarth   *Escape Alone* (illus)
Ludovic Kennedy   *Pursuit* (illus)
Ian MacHorton   *Safer than a Known Way*
Martin Middlebrook   *The Nuremberg Raid* (illus)
Shankland & Hunter   *Malta Convoy*
Albert Speer   *Spandau: the Secret Diaries* (illus)
J. P. Stern   *Hitler: the Fuhrer and the People*
Desmond Young   *Rommel*